ENTERPRISE JAVA™ SERVLETS

ENTERPRISE JAVA™ SERVLETS

Jeff M. Genender

QA
76
.73
.J38
G45
2002

ADDISON–WESLEY

Boston • San Francisco • New York • Toronto • Montreal
London • Munich • Paris • Madrid
Capetown • Sydney • Tokyo • Singapore • Mexico City

CARROLL COLLEGE LIBRARY
WAUKESHA, WISCONSIN 53186

Many of the designations used by manufacturers and sellers to distinguish their products are claimed as trademarks. Where those designations appear in this book and Addison-Wesley was aware of a trademark claim, the designations have been printed in initial caps or all caps.

The author and publisher have taken care in the preparation of this book, but make no expressed or implied warranty of any kind and assume no responsibility for errors or omissions. No liability is assumed for incidental or consequential damages in connection with or arising out of the use of the information or programs contained herein.

The publisher offers discounts on this book when ordered in quantity for special sales. For more information, please contact:

Pearson Education Corporate Sales Division
One Lake Street
Upper Saddle River, NJ 07458
(800) 382-3419
corpsales@pearsontechgroup.com

Visit AW on the Web: *www.awl.com/cseng/*

Library of Congress Cataloging-in-Publication Data

Genender, Jeff M.
Enterprise Java servlets / Jeff M. Genender.
p. cm.
Includes bibliographical references and index.
ISBN 0-201-70921-X
1. Java (Computer program language) I. Title.
QA76.73.J38 G45 2001
005.2'762--dc21
2001035712

Copyright © 2002 by Addison-Wesley

All rights reserved. No part of this publication may be reproduced, stored in a retrieval system, or transmitted, in any form, or by any means, electronic, mechanical, photocopying, recording, or otherwise, without the prior consent of the publisher. Printed in the United States of America. Published simultaneously in Canada.

ISBN 0-201-70921-X
Text printed on recycled and acid-free paper.

1 2 3 4 5 6 7 8 9 10 –MA– 0504030201

First printing, August 2001

This book is dedicated to my wife Nazarena, my daughter Madisyn, and my dogs, Pancha and Sierra, who have supported me, unconditionally, throughout my career.

CONTENTS

Preface *xiii*

Chapter 1 Introduction to Enterprise Servlets 1

Developing Servlets and Servlet Containers 2
Setting Up and Running Servlets *3*
Registering Servlets with the Servlet Container *4*
What You Need *6*

The Base Enterprise Servlet 7
The Single-Servlet Approach *14*
Base Enterprise Servlet Basics *14*

Implementation of a Base Servlet 18
The Class.forName() Method *24*
The HttpMethod Class *31*
The ConfFile Class *32*
The MethodList Class *34*

Sample Application 35

Summary 37

Chapter 2 AppContext: Managing Applications **39**

The Configuration File Revisited 41

The AppContext Object 42

Restructuring BaseEnterpriseServlet 49

A Two-Application Example 56

Forcing Uniqueness across Applications: AppManager 63

Summary 69

Chapter 3 Forms, State, and Session Management **71**

HTTP Forms: A Review 72

The <FORM> Tag 72

Packaging the Query with GET and POST 75

HTTP Forms and Enterprise Servlets 77

Form and HTML Development in the Enterprise 79

Maintaining State with Sessions in the Enterprise 86

Standard Servlet Architecture and Sessions 90

The Enterprise Session 93

Session and Form Example with Multiple Applications 103

Summary 114

Chapter 4 HTML with Templates **117**

Using Templates 118

JSP as a Template Engine 119

Developing a Template Engine 120

The HTMLTemplate Object 126

Templates with Enterprise Servlets 134

Nesting Templates 136

Making the Template Engine Scream: Caching Templates 143

Building the Template Cache 146

Integrating the Template Objects and Cache into Enterprise Servlets 157

Using the Template Cache in Enterprise Servlets 163

Summary 166

Chapter 5 Logging and Error Handling **169**

Logging in a Servlet Engine 169

Anomalies of a Servlet Engine Log File 171

Components of a Standardized Log File 172

The EnterpriseLog Object 175

Logging in Enterprise Servlets 188

A Logging Example 195

Error Handling 201

The DefaultErrorHandler Object 204

The Logger Application with Error Handling 208

Summary 210

Chapter 6 Security **213**

Types of Security 213

Web Authentication 216

Under the Hood *218*

Customizing Web Authentication *220*

An Example Using Pluggable Security Components *223*

Form-Based Authentication 228

Integrating Form-Based Authentication into Enterprise Servlets *230*

Summary 236

Chapter 7 Pools **239**

What Is a Pool? 240

Using Pools in Web Development 242

The Base Pool Object *244*

Using the Pool Object *253*

Using the Pool: An Example *255*

The Pool Anomaly 259

PoolList and PoolObjectManager *262*

Using PoolList and PoolObjectManager: An Example *269*

Summary 270

Chapter 8 Database Connectivity **273**

JDBC: A Quick Review 273

Loading the Driver and Connecting to the Database *274*

The JDBC Statement and ResultSet Objects *275*

The PreparedStatement and CallableStatement Objects *276*

Transactions *277*

Closing the Connection *278*

Managing the Connection in a Server Environment 278

Understanding Connection Management 281

Building Connection Management 284

The JDBCManager Object *284*

The SQLCursor Object *287*

The DBConnection Object *293*

Using the Connection Management Objects 294

Database Pooling with the Connection Management Objects 297
Using the DBConnectionPool Object 300
Making the DBConnectionPool Object Easier to Create 304
The NameValuePair Object 306
The DBPoolParser Object 307
Using DBPoolParser in Enterprise Servlets 313
Summary 314

Chapter 9 LDAP Connectivity **317**
A Little History of LDAP 318
How LDAP Works 318
Distinguished Names 320
Advantages and Disadvantages of LDAP 320
LDAP with Java: The JNDI 321
Connecting to LDAP 321
Searching LDAP for Values 322
Sorting Results 325
Adding and Removing an Entry 325
Modifying Attributes within an Entry 327
Closing the LdapContext Object 327
LDAP Considerations in a Server Application 327
Building the LDAP Connection Management Objects 329
The LDAPManager Object 330
The LDAPConnection Object 337
Using the LDAP Connection Management Objects 338
The LDAPConnectionPool Object 340
Putting the Connection Management Objects to Use 343
Summary 349

Chapter 10 Dynamic Graphics **351**
How a Browser Requests Images 352
Handling Image Types 354
Dynamic Images 355
Memory Management 360
Creating Objects Is Your Worst Enemy 361
Pooling Memory Buffers 361

Random Pie Chart Example 364
Summary 373

Chapter 11 Using JSP with Enterprise Servlets **375**
Is There a Preference? 375
JSPs with Servlets 376
JSPs and Enterprise Servlets 384
Releasing BaseEnterpriseServlet's Grip on AppContext 385
Tapping into Enterprise Servlets 388
A Quick Look at the Java Tag Library 389
Bridging JSPs to Enterprise Servlets 395
Using the ESBridge Tag Library 404
Accessing the EnterpriseSession Object 408
Using the <ESSession> Tag 413
Handling Errors 415
Summary 417

Chapter 12 Taking Enterprise Servlets Further **419**
Web Server Startup in a Multiapplication Environment 419
Enhancements for the Reader 428
The Template Engine 428
Database and LDAP Pools 428
An Administrative Tool 429
A Pager or E-Mail Monitor 429
Anything You Want 429

Bibliography **431**

Index **433**

PREFACE

This book is intended for intermediate and advanced Java servlet developers. It is not an introductory book about servlets; there are already a number of excellent books on that topic on the market.

If you are only beginning to work with Java servlets, consider purchasing *Inside Servlets: Server-Side Programming for the Java™ Platform, Second Edition* (2001), by Dustin R. Callaway, and/or *Java Servlet Programming, Second Edition* (2001) by Jason Hunter, with William Crawford. *Inside Servlets* is an excellent book about Java servlets and is a good companion for this book. Callaway's book is easy to read, flows well, has basic and advanced sections, and gives an excellent introduction to servlets, teaching you all you need to know to write Java servlet applications. *Java Servlet Programming* covers a broad range of Java servlet topics.

Although it did not seem that way at the time, it was while working for one of my clients that I happened on a most fortunate set of circumstances. In mid-1999, my team of developers inherited a servlet-based Web application from a previous team. The application was a workflow application to automate travel requests and authorizations that had been slammed together in a short period of time and then "thrown over the wall" to the company. The application's documentation was sparse, the code's database was a mess, the functionality was just basic at best, and the structure and flow were barely functional and nonscalable.

To clean it up, my team worked on the application for a considerable period of time, nearly double the time it took the original developers to code it. It was during this process that I began to more fully understand servlet architecture, including the best way to code applications so that it is possible to add functionality more quickly, to make scalability and reliability more certain, and to ensure that future maintenance of code is simpler. After revamping the entire application, my team suddenly realized what we had—the basis for a framework and architecture that others could use to create robust, scalable, extensible, well-documented servlets.

At the client's company, the scripting language of choice was ASP and a smattering of server-side JavaScript. Managers were skeptical about Java; they were convinced that a Java programming language application would take longer to write than an ASP application. We were racing against time to prove that Java servlets could be created just as fast as scripted solutions. We had to beat the ASP guys in terms of time-to-market for applications, as well as make our projects more reliable, scalable, and extensible.

We gave ourselves a target of three weeks—three weeks in which to create an entire expense-reporting application. But instead of diving right into the code, we sat down and planned out a base-servlet architecture, something we could use to create this application, as well as subsequently. We wanted to have something on which to build future applications, all the while improving the base from which we worked.

We came up with a base servlet from which all servlets would be created. So as not to make the same mistakes the consulting company had made, we were always mindful of what we learned while cleaning up the travel application. We wanted to be sure that we would need to code the application only once, and that we could easily add more functionality, as needed, later. The end product was completed in just over a week, and the expense application was completed a week and a half later, just as quickly as an ASP team could have done the work. The application was stable, reliable, and extensible, and it formed a framework for all future projects.

It was at that moment that I started to talk about writing this book, to pass on what we had learned. As my team talked with other developers and mentioned what we had built, invariably they asked for the code. The architecture provided so much functionality right out of the box that it didn't make sense to code servlets from scratch anymore. As we continued to develop applications on top of the base servlet and to augment it with many other useful enterprise-scale enhancements, my interest in writing the book grew.

In the intervening months before this book was done, my team didn't rest on its laurels. We pressed on and built a servlet architecture that surely will be valuable for every corporate Java developer. This is not *the* right way to build servlets, merely *a* right way. While other servlet architectures may work well (a select few may even work better), the ideas in this book certainly will improve any architecture. My hope is simply that I can pass on what my team learned so that your applications will be better, faster, more reliable, and easier to code and maintain.

Enterprise Java™ Servlets is not intended to compete with any other Java-based technology, such as Enterprise JavaBeans (EJBs) and/or JavaServer Pages (JSPs), but to complement them. Because many JSP-based applications delegate the more intensive processing to servlets, the techniques here can be applied and used in this environment. In addition, EJBs are now used to facilitate many aspects of server-side processing. In our world of e-commerce applications, however, we still use servlets as the interface to the Enterprise JavaBeans; thus many of the techniques in this book will be useful. Because servlets are the center of Java-based server technologies, either through the compilation or delegation of a JSP page or as an interface to EJBs, this book shows some effective and efficient techniques for developing servlets in an enterprise environment.

There are many excellent books about JSPs and EJBs, so I do not need to describe how we use these technologies with servlets; other books do a fine job of that. Instead, this book discusses the problems and issues that developers will run into when developing servlets, as well as development methods that can be implemented to streamline how servlets execute. This by no means prevents one from using these techniques when developing servlets with JSPs or EJBs, and I hope you will find them useful when you are writing enterprise applications.

CHAPTER 1

Introduction to Enterprise Servlets

This book is about writing servlets in the enterprise. It has nothing to do with Enterprise JavaBeans or the starship *Enterprise* from *Star Trek,* as its name may suggest. What is the enterprise? The *enterprise* typically is known as a "large organization that uses computers"—a definition that would classify a corporate entity. When we talk about developing enterprise-level applications, we are talking about applications that can sustain a high volume of traffic, are incredibly stable, and have a high degree of reliability and speed.

An enterprise application is a system that is considered mission critical with little tolerance of downtime. The word *enterprise* has a very broad meaning in business, but it has one single foundation: reliability. So what are enterprise servlets? They are a method and a framework for developing Java servlet applications that allow the developer to create enterprise-level Web-based applications.

Any of us who are corporate developers will encounter the various situations that are presented in this book at one time or another when working on servlet applications. Some of the topics covered here include the following:

- Running multiple applications on a single server and how this affects the session component and application variables
- HTML development in servlets
- How templates can ease the burden of content management within the servlet code
- Pool objects that streamline the use of objects and database connections in a Web environment
- Dynamic image generation and pluggable security models for servlets

- How enterprise servlets remove the drudgery and mundane aspects of developing servlets and allow the developer to concentrate on the business rules within the applications

The information here may not offer the "best" way to implement a solution to servlet development in the enterprise, but it represents one of the "right" ways. Because there are always ways to build a better mousetrap, the goal here is to provide developers with a solid base for understanding the pitfalls of developing applications in the enterprise in order to build on this foundation in their own programming endeavors.

Because this book covers advanced topics in servlet development, it is geared toward developers who have a basic understanding of servlet development. The reader should be familiar with creating a servlet and using some of the associated objects (such as `HttpServletRequest`, `HttpServletResponse`, and `HttpSession`), and with JavaServer Pages (JSP).

Developing Servlets and Servlet Containers

When developing any kind of servlet application, you will need a Web server and a servlet container. The *Web server* handles requests for static pages, images, and other documents, while the *servlet container* handles the calls to servlets. Sometimes the Java servlet container is a pluggable component of a Web server built with the Web server's API; this is known as running in-process. Sometimes the container runs as its own process outside of the Web server. Sometimes the Web server has a servlet container as part of its integral code, such as iPlanet Enterprise Server. In addition, some enterprise Java application servers act as both a Web server and a servlet container, while supporting several other Java technologies, such as Enterprise JavaBeans (EJB), Remote Method Invocation (RMI), and Java Message Service (JMS). (WebLogic is a good example.) The bottom line is that to effectively develop and deploy Java servlets, you will need to serve HTML pages and images and be able to execute a Java servlet through a servlet container. In addition, you will need the Java Servlet class libraries, which have become a part of the Java 2 Enterprise Edition (J2EE), to compile and execute your servlets.

In the development of a servlet application, a servlet container is typically used—preferably one that is written in Java so that the servlet may be "stepped" through during debugging. A servlet container is nothing more than a simplified servlet engine. There are a few types of servlet containers on the market, some with more options than others. Two such containers are Tomcat and the ServletExec debugger by New Atlanta; the first is free, the second, commercial.

Tomcat is managed by the Apache project. Although the name *Apache* may make you feel as though you must use the Apache Web server, this is not true. Tomcat is just a Java application that acts as a container for Java servlets, and it comes with plug-ins to allow it to run with Apache, Internet Information Services (IIS), and iPlanet. Because it is a Java application, it is not only a great production-level servlet container, but can also be used to debug servlets in an integrated development environment (IDE). In fact, versions of Borland's JBuilder 4 include Tomcat as part of its servlet development platform for debugging servlet applications.

The ServletExec debugger can be purchased with the ServletExec servlet engine, which allows the developer to debug in an environment that appears like the production engine but run it in an IDE for debugging. The nice thing about this product is that no configuration files need to be edited directly. The entire servlet control interface is done through HTML and a Web browser. This really helps when you're setting up a servlet application.

Pure Java application servers, such as WebLogic, can also be used for debugging servlets. However, the downside of using application servers for development and debugging is that they usually consume a very large amount of memory and take a long time to launch. These requirements could slow down the software development cycle and require more memory to be installed on workstations, but debugging can be done successfully with application servers.

Setting Up and Running Servlets

Most servlet engines provide three ways to execute servlets. One way is by what can be called the servlet "dumping ground," in which all the class files are deposited in a designated `servlet` directory. When we want to run the servlet, we simply call the complete class name as a URL in a Web browser. For example, say we have a servlet called MyServlet that belongs to the `com.mycompany` package. We would place the class structure in the "dumping ground" in the package directory structure, and the browser would execute the servlet with the URL `http://localhost:8080/servlet/com.mycompany.MyServlet`.

This is one way to run servlets and install them as part of an application. However, running servlets in this way could potentially pose a security risk. In addition, it gives away too much information about the application, and it does not give us much control over how we execute servlets. For example, taking this approach might mean that we cannot have the servlets initialize automatically when we start the Web server or set other parameters that tell us how the servlet should execute. In addition, this approach tells the end user the structure of the application, as well as what technology is being used. It is not too difficult to figure out the package structure when servlets are run in this way. This is usually a lot more information than end users need to know. Minimizing the information that users receive about how an application executes dramatically lowers the chances of a security breach.

The second way to run an application is to register the servlet with the servlet container. We usually register the servlet through a configuration file, an HTML interface (which edits a configuration file), or an XML-based configuration file. The type of file we edit (whether XML or regular text)—including its syntax and its interface to edit the file (through HTML)—depends completely on the servlet container. Each engine has its own style, method, and possible interface. Registering servlets is preferred over the "servlet dumping ground" because it gives us much more control over the servlet's execution and security, and it allows us to pass initialization parameters. Some engines allow us to control which user or group can execute the servlet through its configuration files.

The third way to run servlets is through a Web Archive (WAR) file (Servlet 2.2 and later specifications). A WAR file allows us to package servlets, JSPs, HTML, and images all in one file package. This provides for a very simple means to deploy applications to production servers. Not all servlet engines support WAR files yet, but WAR files will become the de facto standard in time. Using WAR files is a great way to deploy applications when you are ready to install the final product. For development, this approach can be a bit cumbersome because we typically need to package all of the files into the WAR file each time a change is made. With a small application this may not be so bad. But with a very large application with hundreds of classes, this could take some time and could slow down the development process. WAR files still require that the servlets be registered within an internal configuration file, just as registering the servlet with the servlet container does.

Registering Servlets with the Servlet Container

In this book nearly all of the examples are based on the assumption that you are familiar with your servlet container and that you know how to register servlets. As mentioned already, different servlet containers may register servlets a little differently, so it is important to understand how your engine does it. The most important aspects of registering a servlet are the URL of the servlet, the servlet class, and any initialization arguments that you want passed to the servlet when it is executed the first time. The text contains frequent references to `initArgs` and registering the servlet. By registering a servlet, we are editing a configuration file to tell the servlet engine about the servlet. The designation *initArgs* in this book represents the initialization parameters that are passed to and can be accessed by the servlets.

Listings 1.1, 1.2, and 1.3 are snippets from the configuration files of three separate servlet engines. Each listing shows what the file needs to contain to register a servlet that has two initialization parameters and automatically loads upon startup. Listing 1.1 is what we would find in the Web Application Deployment Descriptor file, `web.xml`, that is a part of the Tomcat servlet engine, or any Servlet 2.2–compliant container, such as WebLogic 6.x. Listing 1.2 is the snippet that would be a portion of the `weblogic.properties` file for a WebLogic 5.1 server, which complies with Servlet 2.1 or earlier versions. Listing 1.3 is an iPlanet Enterprise Server's `servlet.properties` file snippet, also a Servlet 2.1 container. Notice the differences in how each engine registers its servlet.

Listing 1.1 Tomcat- and Servlet 2.2–compliant servlet registration of `TestServlet`

```
<servlet>
        <servlet-name>
            TestServlet
        </servlet-name>
        <servlet-class>
            com.myservletpackage.TestServlet
        </servlet-class>
        <init-param>
            <param-name>ConfFile</param-name>
            <param-value>C:\Projects\test.conf</param-value>
        </init-param>
        <init-param>
            <param-name>myparam</param-name>
            <param-value>My params value</param-value>
        </init-param>
        <load-on-startup>
            1
        </load-on-startup>
</servlet>
```

Listing 1.2 WebLogic 5.1 servlet registration of `TestServlet`

```
weblogic.httpd.register.TestServlet=com.myservletpackage.TestServlet
weblogic.httpd.initArgs.TestServlet=\
    ConfFile=C:\Projects\test.conf,
    Myparam=My params value
weblogic.system.startupClass.TestServlet=\
    weblogic.servlet.utils.ServletStartup
weblogic.system.startupArgs.TestServlet=servlet=TestServlet
```

Listing 1.3 iPlanet Enterprise Server servlet registration of `TestServlet`

```
servlet.TestServlet.classpath=C:\projects\classes
servlet.TestServlet.code=com.myservletpackage.TestServlet
servlet.TestServlet.initArgs=ConfFile C:\Projects\test.conf,
    Myparam=My params value
    servlet.TestServlet.startup=true
```

Look very carefully at how the initialization parameters are configured. The Tomcat version (Listing 1.1) separates the parameter name from its value via XML, and each initialization parameter is also delimited by its own `<init-param>` group. In the other versions (Listings 1.2 and 1.3), the parameter name and the value are delimited by an equal sign (=). A comma delimits each parameter set. As these listings show, each servlet engine may have its own way of doing things.

It is important that you understand how the initialization parameters work with your particular servlet engine so that you can properly set up and try the examples in this book. All references to `initArgs` have to do with setting up the initialization arguments in the servlet container's configuration file.

What You Need

To run the examples in this book, you need version 1.3 (or later) of the Java SDK (JSDK) or a similar Java development kit, as well as the Java 2 Enterprise Edition (J2EE), which contains the necessary servlet libraries to compile and run the code. In addition, if you want to run the examples in Chapter 9, you will need the Lightweight Data Access Protocol (LDAP) provider library from Sun. You can obtain these libraries and the JSDK from Sun's Java Web site at `www.javasoft.com`. The examples in Chapter 8 will interact with Oracle, so you need to download the Java Database Connectivity (JDBC) thin driver from Oracle's Web site (`technet.oracle.com`). You will also need to have access to an Oracle database with the scott/tiger schema that comes with Oracle.

The database and LDAP servers that are used in the examples in this book are the ones most often found in the enterprise. I chose Oracle for the database and the Netscape/iPlanet Directory Server for the LDAP server. If you do not have access to an Oracle database, you may sign up for a free developer's license at Oracle's Web site and either order the free CD or download the product for your particular platform. You can use any database you wish, as long as the tables and fields in that database match those in the sample code and you have the proper JDBC driver to connect to your database.

The LDAP server can be downloaded from `iPlanet.com` and comes with a trial license. The code in Chapter 9 relies on the `airius.ldif` file loaded into the server, which is included with the Netscape/iPlanet Directory Server installation. However, the techniques and code will work with other LDAP implementations, such as OpenLDAP, as long as the `airius.ldif` file is obtained and loaded to these other servers.

The Base Enterprise Servlet

One of the main advantages of Java is the "write once, run anywhere" (WORA) concept. We can create applications on Windows NT using any of the robust IDEs and then move them over to a production UNIX machine without ever having to recompile or alter any of the source code. There are huge advantages to this approach—primarily the time we gain by not having to deal with platform issues. We can focus on the functionality of the application, rather than the subtleties of different platforms. The language itself avoids many of the pitfalls of other languages (like pointers in C) but implements a robust object-oriented framework, so creating applications is more straightforward.

Another advantage of Java is the concept of "write once, *use* anywhere." With Java you can create classes that you use over and over again in your code. Because the classes are loaded at runtime, you don't even have to recompile the entire application; you just recompile (and test) each class as it changes. In fact, one of the cool things about Java servlets is that you can create a servlet called a *base servlet* that serves as the basis for a host of other servlets. This means that we can write the functionality once and then use it in every servlet application.

The most commonly used servlet (`HttpServlet`) is derived from the abstract base class `GenericServlet` and implements the `Servlet` interface. The `Servlet` interface class defines the methods that all servlets must implement. Because the enterprise servlets in this book will use HTTP exclusively, we will use `HttpServlet` as a base. However, because we don't want to rewrite functionality in every servlet we create, we will extend `HttpServlet` to add functionality. That's what a base servlet is all about and what we'll be covering in this chapter—the idea that we can extend `HttpServlet` to speed up the development cycle for an application, ensure consistency between applications, and make maintenance easier.

The base-servlet architecture is packaged together in a library of class files (`enterprise.*`). The base library helps us keep all classes organized in a logical manner and makes it easier for us to distribute the library to others. The easier it is for people to distribute and use the libraries, the more likely it is that they will be used. The benefits of reusability can be realized only if the code is distributed and implemented.

We will extend `HttpServlet` to create the `BaseEnterpriseServlet` base servlet (which we will store in the package `enterprise.servlet`), and then all of our servlet applications will extend `BaseEnterpriseServlet`. That way we can add more functionality and/or fix bugs in the base servlet, and all of the existing applications will inherit that functionality. This means that if we find a more efficient way of doing something, we simply recode the relevant part of the base servlet instead of rewriting every servlet. The base servlet can be extended to automatically handle several important tasks:

- **Method dispatch.** Applications are written as a collection of extended `HTTPMethod` classes that are invoked by a corresponding name (`http://server.domain.com/servlet/ApplicationBaseServlet?method=nameOfMethod&var1=val1&var2=val2`).
- **Context management.** This ensures that variables in one application don't interfere with those of another application.
- **Template processing.** This cleanly separates the presentation layer (coded in HTML) from the business logic (coded in Java).
- **Database pooling.** The application maintains a shared pool of database connections.
- **Logging.** The application implements a consistent logging and error-handling scheme that makes maintenance easier. If the functionality is easy to implement, it is more likely that it will be included in every application.
- **User authentication.** This ensures that the user authentication method is consistent between applications, so users can be identified and tracked throughout their current sessions.

To understand the real advantage of having a base servlet, let's look at a concrete example. Say we write ten servlets. Then we decide we need some logging and error handling in these servlets. We must now go back and modify the ten servlets to import and implement the solution. The next ten servlets we create can use the same solution (if it's packaged in its own class), but we must remember to include it in the servlet.

Wouldn't it be nice if, after creating the solution just once, all current and subsequent applications automatically had it? Developers wouldn't have to hunt for the right classes to import because they would already be included by default. That's what a base servlet is for—to ensure that we can add functionality to a servlet and have it easily reflected in all other servlets. As we add more features, each servlet gains instant access to those features without our having to modify each servlet to explicitly import the required class files. It also ensures that applications are more consistent, which makes maintenance easier.

Every Java servlet is implemented from the Java `Servlet` class, which provides the core functionality. `HttpServlet` extends the `Servlet` interface class and implements features that are specific to HTTP. The Java `Servlet` interface allows for the possibility that a future protocol may be ideal for servlet implementations. The base enterprise servlet will extend `HttpServlet` to provide the same kind of extensibility for our applications.

Table 1.1 shows the interface methods defined by `Servlet` and `HttpServlet`. To create a base servlet we simply extend the `HttpServlet` class.

Table 1.1 Methods Defined by `Servlet` and `HttpServlet`

`Servlet` Interface	`HttpServlet` Class
`destroy``()`. This method cleans up resources used by the servlet. **`getServletConfig`**`()`. This method returns the `ServletConfig` object stored by the `init()` method. The `ServletConfig` object contains initialization parameters for the current servlet. **`getServletInfo`**`()`. This method returns a string object that contains information about the servlet (author, version, copyright, and so forth). **`init`**`(ServletConfig)`. This method initializes a servlet. The servlet engine calls this method automatically when it loads the servlet. It also creates a reference to the `ServletConfig` object so that the `getServletConfig()` method can return it. **`service`**`(ServletRequest, ServletResponse)`. This method handles a single request from a client and returns an HTTP response.	**`doDelete`**`(HttpServletRequest, HttpServletResponse)`. This method handles HTTP `DELETE` requests (called by `HttpServlet`'s `service()` method). This method is not commonly used. **`doGet`**`(HttpServletRequest, HttpServletResponse)`. This method handles HTTP `GET` requests (called by `HttpServlet`'s `service()` method). **`doHead`**`(HttpServletRequest, HttpServletResponse)`. This method handles HTTP `HEAD` requests (called by `HttpServlet`'s `service()` method). This method is not commonly used. **`doOptions`**`(HttpServletRequest, HttpServletResponse)`. This method handles HTTP `OPTIONS` requests (called by `HttpServlet`'s `service()` method). This method is not commonly used. **`doPost`**`(HttpServletRequest, HttpServletResponse)`. This method handles HTTP `POST` requests (called by `HttpServlet`'s `service()` method). **`doPut`**`(HttpServletRequest, HttpServletResponse)`. This method handles HTTP `PUT` requests (called by `HttpServlet`'s `service()` method). This method is not commonly used. **`doTrace`**`(HttpServletRequest, HttpServletResponse)`. This method handles HTTP `TRACE` requests (called by `HttpServlet`'s `service()` method). This method is not commonly used. **`getLastModified`**`(HttpServletRequest)`. This method returns the time at which the requested entity was last modified. **`service`**`(HttpServletRequest, HttpServletResponse)`. This is an HTTP-specific implementation of the `Servlet.service` method.

That way we still have access to all of the methods and properties of the `HttpServlet` class, but we can add methods and properties that all of our enterprise applications will use. Normally we would construct a servlet like so:

```
public class HelloWorld extends HttpServlet
{
  // Implementation goes here
}
```

When we create a base servlet (`BaseEnterpriseServlet`), however, we start by creating an abstract class like so:

```
public abstract class BaseEnterpriseServlet extends HttpServlet
{
    // Implementation goes here
}
```

Then each enterprise application extends `BaseEnterpriseServlet`—the abstract base servlet—rather than extending `HttpServlet`, like so:

```
public class TestServlet extends BaseEnterpriseServlet
{
    // Implementation can go here
}
```

Whatever functionality we implement in the base servlet will be passed on to each subsequent servlet. We could create an error-handling and logging solution in the base servlet that every application we created could then use. Because we don't have to write the logging solution again, it's consistent across all applications, and a change made to the code for one application is useful for all of them. Figure 1.1 shows how `HttpServlet` inherits from `Servlet` and how `BaseEnterpriseServlet` then inherits from `HttpServlet`.

In traditional servlet programming we create a separate servlet for each functional part of an application. Each servlet is specific to a given task. This is very much like Active Server Pages (ASP) or Common Gateway Interface (CGI) application programming, in which each part of an application is a separate ASP or CGI. (Server-Side JavaScript [SSJS] is different because it provides a tool for compiling all pages into a single application or *.web* file.) So for a simple database-driven application you might have the following servlets:

- `Add.class`, to add information to the database
- `Modify.class`, to modify the information in the database
- `Delete.class`, to delete information from the database
- `View.class`, to view the information in HTML format
- `Report.class`, to view a report with totals that is formatted for printing

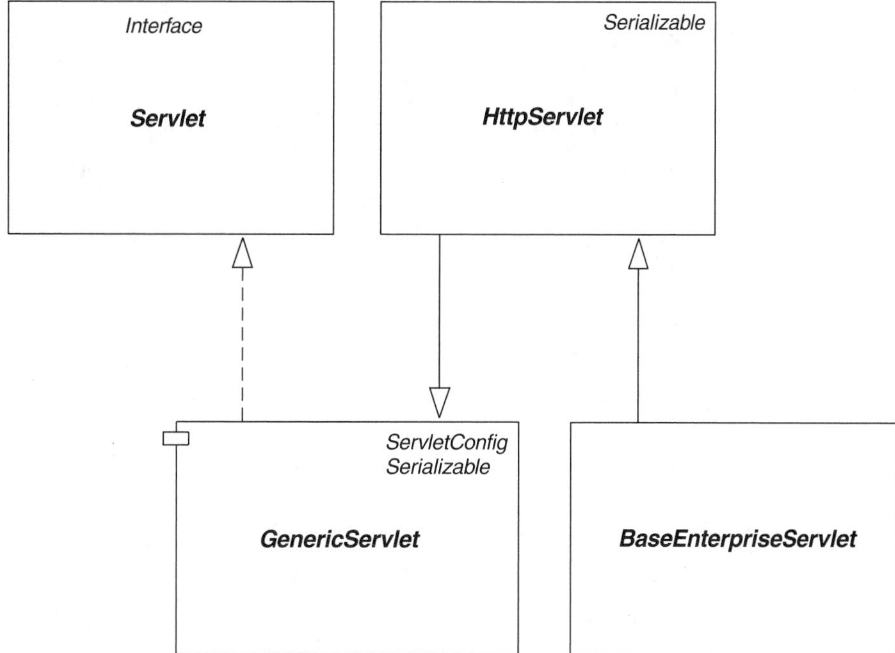

Figure 1.1 The family tree of `BaseEnterpriseServlet`

You can see how quickly an application can get out of hand. To make this work, we would put all the servlets in a directory on the server and then register each servlet with the servlet engine. Migrating them all from the testing server to the staging and/or production server would be quite a task and would inevitably be error prone. We must migrate to the server not only all of the servlet files, but also any supporting class files that have changed.

Generally the best approach is to bundle all of the files into a Java Archive file and move them to the server or use a tool like SourceSafe or CVS (Concurrent Versions System) to update all of the files. This approach will eliminate some migration headaches. However, using multiple servlets for an application can become unwieldy. A better way to create servlet applications is to use one servlet per application. We'll say more about this in a moment, but first it might help to demonstrate the advantages of a single-servlet approach. Consider the example in the case study that starts on the next page.

At company A, the first servlet application for the intranet team was a Travel application—so that employees could make their travel requests online. The developers of the application were former ASP programmers, and they created a separate servlet for every major piece of functionality—add a request, update a request, cancel a request, authenticate the user, print a report, and so

Case Study

Company A's first Java Servlet application was called Travel. This application automated the approval cycle for travel requests (all travel had to be approved by a vice president or more senior executive). Until this time, Company A had used ASP technology for all of its applications—a solution that enabled the fast creation of Web applications but was problematic in terms of scalability and reliability.

Company A farmed out the programming of its first Java servlet to an outside contractor that slammed together an application in a couple of months. The resulting application was barely functional and extraordinarily difficult to maintain. It consisted of multiple servlets, hard-coded variables, no database pooling, extremely poor error handling (e.g., it displayed stack traces to the user), and so forth.

The Java team decided to reorganize the entire application from the ground up. They started by creating a base servlet. That way, all servlets would be derived from the same base code, and therefore would all work in the same way, look the same, and be much easier to maintain. And they could be created in half the time. After working with ServletExec, a servlet engine plug-in for Web servers, the team found that having multiple servlets created deployment problems. Setting up each servlet correctly on the development, staging, and production servers was sometimes problematic.

The Travel application had over 70 servlets, and nobody knew exactly what each servlet did or what parameters were required for setting it up on the servlet engine. Deploying the application was therefore difficult and problematic. In addition, the servlet engine sometimes deleted its own configuration files, so the servlets had to be reregistered with all their initialization parameters. It was a mess.

With a single servlet for each application, the applications were easier to test, deploy, and maintain. Each servlet had only one parameter: the location of its configuration file. When the servlet was initialized by ServletExec, it's `init()` method read in the configuration file and set all the necessary parameters. Migrating applications suddenly became much easier. We'll show you shortly how a single-servlet solution is employed, and you'll begin to see why it makes sense.

Because every application was derived from a base servlet, as features were added to the base servlet they were immediately available to all subsequent servlets. Thus the time-to-market for each application went down over time. The Java team added functionality to the base servlet, which was then used by each application. If the team had had to create the functionality from scratch for each application, or even figure out how to implement the classes in each different application, the time-to-market would have been much greater. However, because the functionality was available as soon as the new servlet was created, the time-to-market was greatly reduced.

The end result of these efforts by the servlet team was that they suddenly had a robust base architecture from which to create servlet applications. Now servlet applications could be created as fast as ASP applications, and given the better scalability and reliability of Java-based solutions, servlets were an easier sell in the enterprise. This design proved to be invaluable as the team moved beyond the initial basic applications into more innovative solutions.

In this case, Company A benefited almost immediately from a base-servlet architecture. Applications were easier to set up on the server and easier to maintain. Another benefit was that code reuse became a necessity for every application; a new Java application could not be created without including a huge chunk of reusable code. Development time went down, application quality went up, and maintenance became easier. Understanding how one application worked meant understanding how they all worked.

forth—over 70 different servlets for a single application. Each servlet had to be registered with the servlet engine, and several had configuration parameters. It was frightening. Migration to production was extremely tedious and error prone. It just wasn't the best way to create servlet applications.

To avoid the mess caused by having multiple servlets for each application, it's best to create a single servlet. This means that we have only one servlet to keep track of for each application, keeping the applications very simple and making it easy to migrate them to production. We'll explain in a moment how to do this. But first, the preceding case study helps illustrate the advantage of a single-servlet architecture.

The Single-Servlet Approach

To create a base-servlet architecture in your company, you must first decide whether to use a single-servlet approach. This book is based on this approach, but many of the concepts discussed here can be used in a multiple-servlet environment as well. The advantage to a single servlet is that only one servlet must be set up on the server, and all application functionality is stored in Java class files. Set up the one servlet, copy the class files to the server, and your application is up and running.

With a single servlet we use what's called a *dispatch service* to load and execute the class file that contains the code we wish to run. For example, let's assume we have an application with the following features: add, modify, delete, view, and report. In a multiple-servlet architecture we would have five separate servlets, each performing a given task. In a single-servlet architecture, however, we would have a single servlet that would dispatch an HTTP request to the appropriate class file.

So given the URL `http://machine.company.com/servlets/MySingleServlet?method=add`, the servlet `MySingleServlet` would look for a requested method in the query string (`method=add`) and then dispatch the request to the corresponding class file (`add.class`). (The optional query string in a URL is the text following the question mark.) With this approach we need to set up only a single servlet. All of the associated classes can be packaged together and distributed via a JAR file. That makes deployment and management of the servlets easier. The applications are no longer a collection of servlet files, but rather a collection of Java class files and a single-servlet file. The differences between a multiple-servlet application and a single-servlet solution are depicted in Figure 1.2.

Base Enterprise Servlet Basics

In the following section we will walk through a large amount of code to demonstrate how to design and build a base enterprise servlet. The lines are numbered so that you can reassemble the code if you wish. However, I felt it was best to step through it section by section to help you better understand how the base servlet is constructed and the purpose for each part of the servlet.

The following three essential ideas are demonstrated in the code:

1. The base-servlet architecture
2. The use of a configuration file
3. The use of a dispatch service

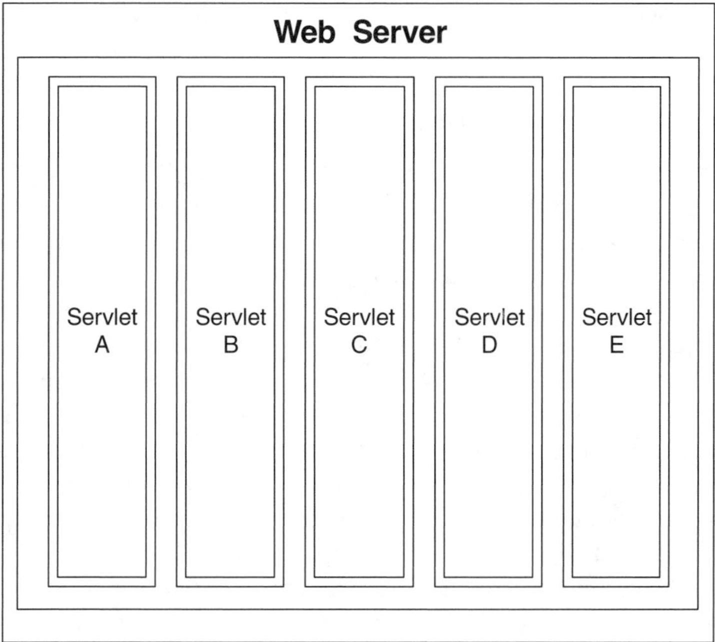

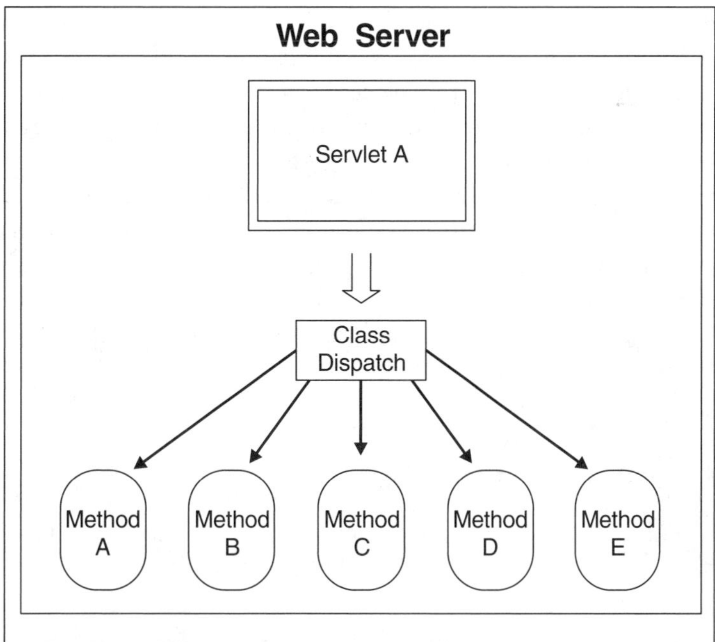

Figure 1.2 A comparison of multiple-servlet (*top*) and single-servlet (*bottom*) architectures

We've spent some time talking about the base-servlet architecture. Now we'll talk more about the use of configuration files and the dispatch service.

The Configuration File

Most servlet containers (like ServletExec and JRun) allow us to specify initial values for servlet variables. We generally specify things like database connection strings, log file location, initial variable values, and the like. We wouldn't specify them in the actual code of the application because then we would have to recompile the servlet every time the database name, location, or username and password information changed. So normally we specify this information when setting up the servlet for the servlet engine. However, as applications grow in complexity, the information required to properly initialize the servlet generally increases. If we need to specify many initialization parameters for the servlet engine, moving an application from one server to another can become confusing and prone to error. Therefore, we need another mechanism to control servlets.

The *configuration file* is a simple text file that has entries consisting of a key name and a value in the format *key=value*. The configuration file is read into a Java `Properties` object so that we can easily retrieve a value for a given name. This gives us far more flexibility in the way we design servlets and makes deployment easier. The use of a configuration file makes moving applications from one server to another a relatively trivial matter. All parameters for a given servlet are stored within the configuration file. The only thing we tell the servlet engine is where to find the configuration file (e.g., `ConfFile=/opt/netscape/suitespot/workflowapps/myTestApp/myTestApp.conf`).

Again, a configuration file is a text file containing several entries that control how a servlet application is initialized. All comments begin with the pound character (#), and all entries have a name and value pair separated by an equal sign (=). The following example is from the configuration file `test.config` for the sample servlet in this chapter:

```
# Config file
Default.Method=hello
Method.hello=TestMethod
```

Notice that there is a single comment—`# Config file`—and two name/value pairs: `Default.Method=hello` and `Method.hello=TestMethod`. When the base servlet is set up on the servlet engine, we give it one parameter: the name and location of the configuration file. When the servlet is instantiated by the servlet engine, the `init()` method is executed and the configuration file is loaded into a `Properties` object. Thereafter, we can get to any of the values in the configuration file by calling the `Properties` object and giving it the key that is associated with the value we want to retrieve. We can have as many values in the configuration file as we desire.

As we'll see in later chapters, we can also use this mechanism to control debugging, to specify the location of resources, and to set initial values for the servlet application.

The Dispatch Service

A dispatch service enables the creation of applications that employ a single-servlet architecture. That means there is one servlet for each application on the server, rather than hundreds of servlets that constitute a handful of applications. This smaller number of servlets makes it easier to control, maintain, and administer servlet applications. The dispatch service is quite simple: In the URL for a given request we simply add a query string parameter specifying which servlet method to run.

In a traditional multiservlet application we would call the specific servlet we want to run. If the application were called Employee and we wanted to add a new employee, we would probably call the `AddNewEmployee` servlet like so:

*http://machine.company.com/servlets/**AddNewEmployee**?name1=value1*

Each servlet would have a different name (`DeleteEmployee`, `UpdateEmployee`, and so on).

With a single-servlet architecture we have only one servlet, so if our application were called Employee, we would call that one servlet and pass in the key for the Java class we wanted to run. The servlet would then use a dispatch service to pass control to the Java class file we requested, as shown here:

*http://machine.company.com/servlets/**Employee?method=add**&name1=value1*

The base servlet (Employee) would receive the request, parse out the query string *method=add,* and then check a list of method keys to find the name *add.* It would find that `add` matched with `com.mycompany.employee.AddNewEmployee.class` in the `com.mycompany.employee` package, so the base servlet would create an instance of `AddNewEmployee.class` and then pass the request and response objects to it. `AddNewEmployee.class` would handle the request just as a servlet would, and it would return the results to the client browser.

We create the list of key/value pairs in Employee when the servlet is loaded. We parse the configuration file for Employee, remove the "*Method.*" prefix from any lines that contain it, and then associate the name that follows "*Method.*" with the value that follows the equal sign (=). So the key used in the URL does not have to match the Java class file.

Implementation of a Base Servlet

In this section we will step through the code for the base servlet. We've numbered each line to make it easier for you to follow the code and implement it in your own base servlet. To start, we package all of the code for the base servlet in the enterprise package, as shown on line 1.

```
1.   package enterprise.servlet;
```

This will help us organize all the code and make it easier to reuse. The entire base servlet and all associated code will be physically organized in the enterprise directory and logically organized within the enterprise package.

Next we import all of the libraries that we'll need for the base servlet. The javax.servlet.http library contains the HttpServlet class that we extend in the base servlet. HttpServlet is a subclass of the GenericServlet class, which implements the Servlet interface class in the javax.servlet library. By extending HttpServlet, we have a base implementation of the GenericServlet class and inherit the base HTTP-handling methods and code. The two HttpServlet methods we will override in this example are the init() and service() methods. We will accept the default behavior of the other methods.

```
2.
3.   import javax.servlet.*;
4.   import javax.servlet.http.*;
5.   import java.io.*;
6.   import java.net.*;
7.   import java.util.*;
8.
9.   import enterprise.common.*;
10.  import enterprise.io.*;
11.
12.
```

The first five libraries are all standard Java libraries for implementing servlets, handling input/output, and so on. The last two libraries, however, are part of the enterprise package. The enterprise.common library contains the MethodList class, which creates the list of key/value pairs used by the dispatch service to identify the Java class file associated with a given method. The URL for a request will contain the name of a key (method=<key_name>) and the dispatch service will query the MethodList class to get the Java class associated with the key. Then the base servlet will create an instance of that Java class and pass the request to that instance. The enterprise.io library contains the ConfFile class, which reads in the configuration file associated with the servlet application and creates a Properties object that we can query to get properties that we need when initializing a servlet.

```
13.    /**
14.  * The base enterprise servlet from which all enterprise servlet
15.  * applications derive
16.      * @author Jeff Genender
17.      * @version $Revision: 1.41 $
18.     */
19.
20.    public abstract class BaseEnterpriseServlet extends HttpServlet
21.  {
```

Note that because we are extending `HttpServlet`, we will have access to all methods and properties of the `HttpServlet` class, in addition to any new properties or methods that we add for the enterprise servlet. When Sun extended `GenericServlet` to create the `HttpServlet` class, they created something narrower in scope than `GenericServlet`. The `HttpServlet` class is specific to HTTP, so it's used specifically for handling HTTP requests. If we want to create a servlet that handles File Transfer Protocol (FTP) requests, we must extend `GenericServlet` rather than `HttpServlet` and then add FTP-specific code to handle such requests.

In the same way we extend `HttpServlet` to create `BaseEnterpriseServlet`. When we create an application, we will extend `BaseEnterpriseServlet` to gain access to all the methods and properties in `GenericServlet`, `HttpServlet`, *and* `BaseEnterpriseServlet`. `BaseEnterpriseServlet` is narrower in scope: It is specific to servlets created in a given enterprise in which each application has specific procedures or requirements (database connection pooling, logging, error handling, and so on).

```
22.       // Servlet constants
23.       private final String METHOD_PREFIX   = "Method.";
24.       private final String DEFAULT_PREFIX  = "Default.Method";
25.
```

In lines 23 and 24 we create two new properties that will be available to every `BaseEnterpriseServlet`: `METHOD_PREFIX` and `DEFAULT_PREFIX`. The value specified for `METHOD_PREFIX` (“`Method.`”) is the text that precedes the name of a Java class in the configuration file. So in the configuration file we would have an entry like this:

```
Method.hello=TestMethod
```

where the prefix “*Method.*” indicates that a key name and its associated value will follow. When the configuration file is read and converted into a `Properties` object, `hello` is associated with `TestMethod`.

When `BaseEnterpriseServlet` receives a request from the client like so:

http://machine.company.com/servlets/TestServlet?method=hello

the query string is parsed, *method=hello* is extracted, and the `Properties` object is queried with the string `hello` and returns `TestMethod`. Then the base servlet creates an instance of `TestMethod.class` and passes the request to the new `TestMethod` object. The `TestMethod` object then processes the client request and returns the results just as a traditional servlet would. (You can think of the method as a component, class, or function. It's all the same thing really—we're just telling the servlet which chunk of code to execute when it's called.)

The servlet is like a police dispatcher: Calls come in to a central dispatch service and then are relayed out to the appropriate place to be handled. The servlet is a central place where we can easily control all client requests for a given application.

```
26.        // Servlet globals
27.        private MethodList m_methodList = null;
28.        public  String     m_default    = null;
29.
```

The global variables created in lines 27 and 28 are used by the dispatch service in the following way.

- `m_methodList` keeps a list of all methods associated with this servlet.
- `m_default` keeps track of the default method for an application. If a method is not specified in the query string of the URL that calls this servlet, the request is dispatched to the default method.

```
30.  /**
31.   * Runs initialization code the first time the servlet is
32.   * instantiated
33.   *
34.   * @param config the ServletConfig to work from
35.   */
36.     public final void init(ServletConfig config)
37.     throws ServletException
38.  {
39.      super.init(config);
40.
41.      // Check for ConfFile parameter on the initialization string
42.      String        sConf = config.getInitParameter("ConfFile");
43.
44.      if(sConf == null)
45.      {
46.        throw new ServletException("ERROR - " +
            "BaseEnterpriseServlet "+
```

```
47.               "needs a ConfFile param.\n");
48.       }
49.       try
50.       {
51.         // Parse the configuration file
52.         parseConfigFile(sConf);
53.
54.       }
55.       catch(Exception e)
56.       {
57.         e.printStackTrace();
58.         throw new ServletException(e.getMessage());
59.       }
60.   }
```

In lines 30 through 60 we implement the `Servlet init()` method that is executed when this servlet is first instantiated on the server. All we are checking for right now is the existence of a configuration file (which we'll discuss later in this chapter). In later chapters we'll add more code in this section to set up database connection pooling and other useful features. For now, however, we are simply checking for the existence of a `ConfFile` parameter that specifies where the configuration file is located on the server. If no configuration file is specified, an exception is thrown.

The configuration file parameter is `ConfFile`, and the value is a fully qualified path and filename on the server. We have to give the server only a single parameter—the location of the configuration file—for each servlet. `ConfFile` contains all of the parameters for a given application (database connection information, initial values for variables, and so on). A configuration file allows us to pass in as much information to the servlet as we wish. If the configuration file for your servlet is under the `/www/servlets/test/test.config` directory (UNIX in this example), when you set up the servlet for your servlet engine, `ConfFile=/www/servlets/test/test.config` is the only initialization parameter you'll include.

```
61.   /**
62.    * Processes the GET and POST method requestS to this servlet
63.    * @param req the HttpServletRequest to work from
64.    * @param res the HttpServletResponse to write back on
65.    */
66.   public void service(HttpServletRequest req,
67.                       HttpServletResponse res)
68.       throws ServletException, IOException
69.   {
70.     PrintWriter   out        = null;
71.
72.     // Caching dynamic content is very bad;
73.     // set the default response header to not cache
74.     res.setContentType("text/html");
```

```
75.    res.setHeader("Pragma", "No-cache");
76.    res.setHeader("Cache-Control", "no-cache");
77.    res.setDateHeader("Expires", 0);
78.
```

Next we implement `Servlet`'s `service()` method. The `service()` method, as described earlier, is one of the key servlet methods. If we implement the `service()` method, then we don't need to implement the `doGet()` or `doPost()` method. By implementing the `service()` method in the base servlet, we will make our servlet applications behave more consistently: They'll handle `GET` requests (which are necessary because we specify the requested method in the query string) and `POST` requests (which we'll need when submitting forms to the servlet application).

On line 70 we create a new `PrintWriter` object (the general method for sending data back to the client who made the request; we'll assign something to `PrintWriter` later). In lines 74 through 77 we tell the base servlet always to set the content type to `text/html`. In an enterprise setting, it is reasonable to assume that we will almost always respond to client requests with an HTML or text response. Therefore, we set `text/html` as the default in the base servlet. In addition, we tell the browser never to cache pages. This stipulation ensures that the client will make a fresh request every time it calls one of the methods in our applications. As you can see, we don't have to add this code to every servlet we write; we just add it one time in the base servlet, and then every application we create that extends the base servlet will instruct the client browser not to cache pages in the application.

```
79.        try
80.        {
81.            // Check whether we have a "method" parameter
82.            // in the query string
83.            String method = req.getParameter("method");
84.
85.            // If we don't, then let's use the default parameter
86.            if (method == null)
87.            {
88.              method = m_default;
89.            }
90.
91.            HTTPMethod methodInstance = null;
92.
```

On line 83 we check for the requested method in the URL. If no method was requested, then lines 86 through 88 will help us use the default method for this application. So every request to this servlet will be dispatched—either to the requested method or to the default method. The default method generally is found on the home page of the application or possibly on an error page indicating that a method must be specified in the URL. The default method is specified in the configuration file with an entry similar to this:

```
Default.Method=hello
```

If no method is specified in the URL when the base servlet is called, the request is dispatched to the default method.

`Hello` is the requested method in the URL `http://machine.company.com/servlets/TestServlet?method=hello&data1=value1`. So the client request will be dispatched to the Java class specified by `Method.hello=TestMethod.class` in the configuration file. The key `hello` is associated with `TestMethod.class` in the configuration file, so the request will be dispatched to an instance of `TestMethod`. Again, the dispatch service is there simply to route client requests to the correct Java class file for handling.

```
93.       // Let's dynamically load the class through a lookup
94.       // in our method list. Take the method name and look up
95.       // the cross-reference for the full class name.  If we
96.       // Find it, then load it
97.       Class c = Class.forName( m_methodList.get(method) );
98.
99.       // Manually create the instance of the class
100.      methodInstance = (HTTPMethod)c.newInstance();
101.
102.      // Set request and response parameters in our subclassed
103.          // HTTPMethod, so it has access to these parameters
104.          methodInstance.registerMethod(req, res);
105.
106.          // Dispatch the request
107.          // This is where BaseEnterpriseServlet dispatched the
108.          // control to subclassed HTTPMethod through the execute
109.          // call.
110.          methodInstance.execute();
111.
112. }
```

Now that we've determined what the requested method is (we either got it from the query string `[?method=hello&data1=value1]`, or we used the default method specified in the configuration file), we'll dispatch the client request to that class.

Line 97 calls `m_methodList.get()` with the `String` variable `method` (which contains the value "`hello`") and does a lookup in `m_methodList` to get the name of the Java class associated with the key `hello`. The Java class that is associated with the key `hello` is `TestMethod.class`. The `Class.forName()` method is thus called with the parameter "`TestMethod.class`". `Class.forName()` loads

TestMethod.class (if it is not already loaded into memory), creates an instance of it, and returns the new TestMethod object as type Object. (Class.forName() doesn't know in advance the Java class for which an instance will be created, so it returns a generic Object type. It's up to you to cast this generic object as the Java type that you need. In this example we cast the object returned by Class.forName() as type HTTPMethod.) So we can break down line 97 like this:

```
Class c = Class.forName( m_methodList.get(method) );
```

which really is

```
Class c = Class.forName( m_methodList.get("hello") );
```

which really is

```
Class c = Class.forName( "TestMethod.class" );
```

The Class.forName() Method

The Class.forName() method is used by Java to dynamically load class files at runtime. When we enter "java myFile" on the command line, Class.forName("myFile.class") is called behind the scenes. Class.forName() loads myFile.class and returns the generic object to the Java runtime engine. Then Java casts the object as type <WHAT TYPE IS IT?> and executes the main() method if one is found.

When you call the servlet with http://machine.domain.com/servlet/MyServlet, Class.forName("<servlet_path>/MyServlet.class") is called and creates a generic object. The returned object is then cast as type HttpServlet and the init() method is executed. Future calls to http://machine.domain.com/servlet/MyServlet do not require that the class file be loaded again from the disk. Instead, if another instance of MyServlet needs to be created, Class.forName() simply reads MyServlet.class from memory and creates a new instance. If enough instances of MyServlet are running to handle incoming requests, one of them is called rather than a new instance being created.

On line 100 we construct a new instance of the TestMethod class and we cast it as an HTTPMethod class. We'll cover the HTTPMethod class later, but here we'll provide a brief explanation of what it does.

HTTPMethod is a Java class with three members (m_request, m_response, and m_object) and two methods (registerMethod() and execute()), as shown in Table 1.2. The registerMethod() method is concrete; it takes two arguments: an HttpServletRequest object and an HttpServletResponse object. It then assigns m_request a reference to HttpServletRequest and m_response a reference to HttpServletResponse so that those objects can be easily referenced from within HTTPMethod.

Table 1.2 The `HttpMethod` Class

Members	Methods
`m_request`	`registerMethod(HttpServletRequest, HttpServletResponse)`
`m_response`	`execute()`
`m_object`	

The `execute()` method of `HTTPMethod` is abstract, so when we create a class of type `HTTPMethod` we *must* implement the `execute()` method. (We'll go into more detail on this point later in this chapter, but for now simply realize that anytime you create a class that extends `HTTPMethod` you must implement the `execute()` method.)

Line 104 calls `registerMethod()` so that the `HttpServletRequest` and `HttpServletResponse` objects will be available to `HTTPMethod`. Line 110 calls the `execute()` method of the `HTTPMethod` object to run the Java code.

Now we have an object that we can use to process the client's request. We've taken the client request, parsed out the method the client wishes to run, and created a new object; now we're ready to pass control from the dispatch service to the Java class that will process the client request. The last thing we do in the `service()` method is handle any errors. Lines 113 through 128 catch any exceptions and return a generic message to the user. We'll improve this error handling later in the book, but this basic error handling will work for now.

```
113.            catch (IllegalArgumentException ex)
114.            {
115.              // If we got here, the method name was not found in
116.              // the method list
117.                out = getPrintWriter(res);
118.                out.println("<HTML>");
119.                out.println("Invalid method");
120.                out.println("</HTML>");
121.                out.flush();
122.            }
123.            catch (Exception ex)
124.            {
125.                 ex.printStackTrace();
126.                 return;
127.            }
128.
129.        }
130.
131.
```

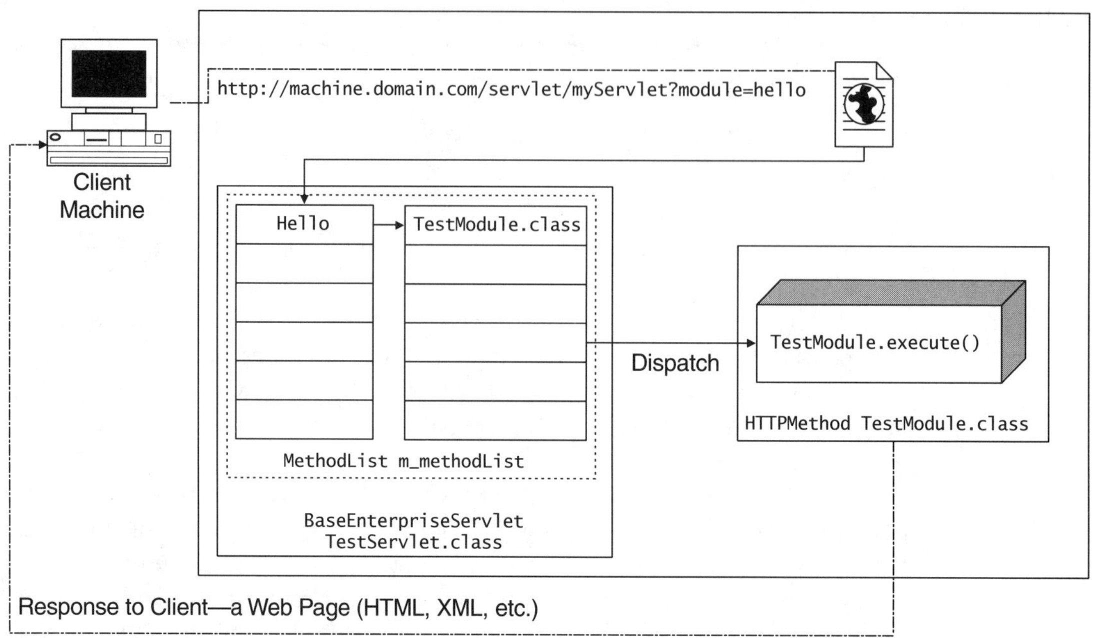

Figure 1.3 Flow of a dispatched servlet request

Figure 1.3 shows the flow of a servlet request. The client calls the base servlet and includes *?method=hello* in the URL. The base enterprise servlet `TestServlet` receives the request, parses out *method=hello,* and then checks the method list `m_methodList` to find the Java class file with which `hello` is associated. It finds that `hello` matches with `TestMethod.class` and uses `Class.forName()` to load `TestMethod.class`. After `TestMethod.class` is loaded, we use reflection and call the `newInstance()` method on the class to create a new instance. The `newInstance()` method returns an instance of type `Object`, which we cast as type `HttpMethod` (remember, `newInstance()` will create an object but won't know what type it is, so it returns a generic object; we must therefore cast it to the proper object type so that we can use it).

After we create an instance of `TestMethod`, `TestServlet` calls `registerMethod()` (a method of `TestMethod`) to pass in the `HttpServletRequest` and `HttpServletResponse` objects. Then it calls the `execute()` method of `TestMethod` to run the Java code. All results are passed back to the client through the `HttpServletResponse` object.

```
/**
 * Parses a configuration file
 *
 * @param fileName The full path name of the configuration file.
```

```
136.    */
137.
138.    public synchronized void parseConfigFile(String fileName)
139.          throws ServletException, IOException
140.    {
141.
142.         ConfFile cf = new ConfFile(fileName);
143.
144.          try
145.          {
146.             cf.load();
147.          }
148.          catch (IOException ioe)
149.          {
150.              ioe.printStackTrace();
151.              throw new ServletException(ioe.getMessage());
152.          }
153.
154.          // Build our list of methods
155.         buildMethodList(fileName);
156.
157.    }
158.
```

Lines 138 through 157 take the name of a configuration file, create a `ConfFile` object, and pass the object to the `buildMethodList()` method. The `init()` method of `BaseEnterpriseServlet` calls `parseConfigFile()` to create the list of methods for the given application. The `parseConfigFile()` method then calls `buildMethodList()` to create the `Properties` object to which `m_methodList` will point. Recall that `m_methodList` is used to match a key in the URL with the Java class file that needs to be loaded and run. Given the URL `method=hello`, `hello` is matched with `TestMethod` in `m_methodList`, and then an instance of `TestMethod` is created and run.

```
159.   /**
160.    * Build the list of methods
161.    *
162.    * @param cf The configuration file.
163.    */
164.
165.     public void buildMethodList(String confFile)
166.       throws ServletException, IOException
167.     {
168.          String defaultMethod = null;
169.
170.          // Get the list of methods
171.          ConfFile cf = new ConfFile(confFile);
172.          cf.load();
173.
174.          MethodList ml = new MethodList();
175.
```

Lines 165 and 166 define `buildMethodList()`, which takes one argument: a `String` object that contains the fully qualified name of a file on the server. Line 171 creates a new `ConfFile` object (`cf`) using the string passed into this method. Table 1.3 lists the methods and properties in the `ConfFile` class.

The `ConfFile` object's `load()` method reads in the configuration file on the server and builds a Java `Properties` object (a key/value pair is created for every *key=value* line found in the file). However, the `Properties` object contains more values than we need; we want only the list of methods and their associated Java class files. At the heart of the `MethodList` object is another Java `Properties` object, but that `Properties` object is more specific; it will be populated with the key/value pairs for the list of methods in the application. So `MethodList` is essentially a subset of `ConfFile`'s list of properties or key/value pairs. The purpose of the `MethodList` object is to match the key passed in each URL (`http://machine.domain.com/servlet/MyServlet?method=key`) with the Java class file to execute.

```
176.        Enumeration x = cf.getKeys();
177.        boolean y = x.hasMoreElements();
178.
```

On line 176 we create an enumeration of the keys in the `ConfFile` object (`cf`). In lines 179 through 229 we loop through each key, searching for `METHOD_PREFIX`, which we defined in `BaseEnterpriseServlet`. In the sample application we define `METHOD_PREFIX` as "`Method.`", so we check each key in `cf`

Table 1.3 The `ConfFile` Class

Members	Methods
`pProps`, a `Properties` object containing the key/value pairs from the configuration file.	**`getKeys`**`()`. This method returns an enumeration of all property names (or keys) in `pProps`.
`sFName`, a `String` object containing a fully qualified filename on the server that contains the configuration parameters for this application.	**`getValue`**`(String key)`. This method gets the value corresponding to `key` in `pProps`.
	`load``()`. This method creates an instance of `FileInputStream` using `sFName` to identify the configuration file and then populates the `Properties` object `pProps`.
	`putValue``(String key, String value)`. This method adds a key/value pair to `pProps`.
	`save``()`. This method saves the properties in `pProps` to the file identified by `sFName`.

to see if it starts with "*Method.*". If it does, we know it is part of our method list. Basically, then, we are looking for a property in `cf` that looks like this:

```
Method.hello
```

If we find anything starting with the prefix defined in `METHOD_PREFIX` (i.e., "*Method.*"), we remove the prefix and use the remaining string (`hello`) as the key in `m_methodList` and grab the associated value: `TestMethod`. Now we have a list of methods and their associated Java class files in `m_methodList`.

```
      for (Enumeration m = cf.getKeys(); m.hasMoreElements();)
      {
          String key = (String) m.nextElement();

          // If it starts with the method prefix, it is a
          // method setup parameter, so use it.
          if (key.startsWith(METHOD_PREFIX))
          {
            // Get the method's name
            String method = key.substring
                                (METHOD_PREFIX.length());

            if (method.length() > 0)
            {
              // Get the cross-referenced class name
              String classpath = cf.getValue(key);

              // Add it to the method list
              ml.add(method.trim(),classpath.trim());
            }
          }

          // If the parameter is the Default.Method
          // parameter, then set this up
          if (key.equals(DEFAULT_PREFIX))
          {
            // Get the method that it references
            defaultMethod = cf.getValue(key);
          }
      }

      // Verify that we indeed have a DefaultMethod parameter
      if (defaultMethod == null)
      {
        throw new ServletException("Default method " +
              "defaultMethod + " not found in ConfFile.");
      }

```

```
            // Verify that Default.Method parameter is valid method
            try
            {
              ml.get(defaultMethod);
            } catch (IllegalArgumentException iae)
            {
              throw new ServletException("Default method " +
                    "defaultMethod + " is not a valid method.");
            }

            // Set the global default value
            m_default = defaultMethod;

            // Set the global MethodList
            m_methodList = ml;
      }

```

We also check to see if any keys start with the prefix defined in DEFAULT_PREFIX (i.e., "*Default.*"). If so, we remove the prefix and add the method to m_methodList. Finally, we assign the name of the Java class for the default method to m_default. We check for a default so that if the servlet is called without a method—by http://machine.domain.com/servlet/MyServlet, for example—we can still return something to the user other than an error message. Generally, the default method specified in a servlet is a splash page or initial page of some kind.

```
        /**
         *
         * Ensures that a print writer is returned, even if
                  an OutputStream object has been created
         *
         * @returns a PrintWriter for HTTP output
         **/
        private PrintWriter getPrintWriter
                (HttpServletResponse res)
            throws IOException
        {
            PrintWriter pw = null;

            try
            {
                pw = res.getWriter();
            }
            catch(IllegalStateException ise)
            {
                pw = new PrintWriter(res.getOutputStream());
            }

```

```
            return pw;
        }

    }
```

The last method in BaseEnterpriseServlet is getPrintWriter(), which returns a PrintWriter object. We use this method to trap for errors when trying to get a PrintWriter object that we will use to return results from the servlet to the requesting client.

Now let's look at the additional classes in BaseEnterpriseServlet: HttpMethod, MethodList, and ConfFile. Because we covered what these methods do while stepping through BaseEnterpriseServlet, we'll give just a brief overview.

The HttpMethod Class

BaseEnterpriseServlet controls the entire application, including the dispatch service. Method requests are dispatched from BaseEnterpriseServlet to a given HttpMethod object. Instead of creating separate servlets for each bit of application functionality, we'll create a Java class file that extends HttpMethod. The only method we need to implement is HttpMethod's execute() method, which is where all of the application code for a given component will go. So we'll have one class that extends BaseEnterpriseServlet and up to *n* classes that extend HttpMethod.

BaseEnterpriseServlet instantiates HttpMethod, calls registerMethod() to pass in the HttpServletRequest and HttpServletResponse objects to this class, and then calls the execute() method where the custom code resides.

```
package enterprise.servlet;
import enterprise.common.*;
import javax.servlet.http.*;
import javax.servlet.*;

/**
 * Base abstract class of all dynamically loaded classes from a
 * servlet. This is where the actual work of an application takes
 * place.
 */
public abstract class HTTPMethod
{
    // HttpServletRequest object
    protected HttpServletRequest m_request;

    // HttpServletResponse object
    protected HttpServletResponse m_response;
```

```
    // User-defined parameter object
    protected Object m_object;

    // Sets the basic required parameters. This is not called
    // directly. The BaseEnterpriseServlet class calls this
    // before invoking execute() below.
    public void registerMethod(HttpServletRequest  req,
            HttpServletResponse res)
    {
        m_request     = req;
        m_response    = res;
    }

    // Processes the request and outputs HTML; must be declared
    // by all inherited classes
    public abstract void execute();
}
```

The ConfFile Class

This class is used to control the configuration file where the initialization parameters for the application are located. The value `fName` passed to the constructor is the fully qualified filename on the server for the configuration file that's associated with the current application. This class will take care of loading the configuration file into a `Properties` object (`pProps`), saving the `Properties` object back to disk, getting property values, setting property values, and getting a list of all the keys.

```
package enterprise.io;

// Class to allow developer to manage a configuration file with
// key=value properties
import java.io.*;
import java.util.*;

public class ConfFile
{
   private Properties pProps;
   private String sFName;

   // Constructor
   public ConfFile(String fName)
   {
      pProps = new Properties();
      sFName = fName;
   }

   // Loads the key/value pairs into the object
   public void load()
      throws IOException
```

```
{
   FileInputStream fis;

   try
   {
      fis = new FileInputStream(sFName);
   } catch(FileNotFoundException e)
   {
      throw new IOException("Cannot open file:" + sFName);
   }

   pProps.load(fis);

   fis.close();
}

/**
 * Saves the key/value pairs to a configuration file
 */
public void save()
   throws IOException
{
   FileOutputStream fos;

   try
   {
      fos = new FileOutputStream(sFName);
   } catch(FileNotFoundException e)
   {
      throw new IOException("Cannot create file:" + sFName);
   }

   pProps.save( fos, "");

   fos.close();
}

/**
 * Gets a value from a key
 *
 * @param sKey    A string containing name of key to query.
 * @return        Value that corresponds to the key.
 */
public String getValue(String sKey)
{
   return pProps.getProperty(sKey);
}

/**
 * Sets or replaces a key/value pair for the configuration file
 *
```

```
     * @param sKey   A string containing name of key to store.
     * @param sValue A string containing the value to store.
     * @return
     */
    public void putValue(String sKey, String sValue)
    {
       pProps.put(sKey, sValue);
    }

    /**
     * Gets all key values in the configuration file
     *
     * @return Enumeration of keys.
     */
    public Enumeration getKeys()
    {
       return pProps.propertyNames();
    }

}
```

The MethodList Class

A subset of ConfFile, this object contains only the key/value pairs to identify the HttpMethod objects used in the application.

```
package enterprise.common;
import java.util.*;

// Maintains the key/value pairs for the method names used by the
// BaseEnterpriseServlet class as part of a servlet application
// method dispatch mechanism
public class MethodList
{
    // User-defined parameter object
    private Properties m_list;

    // Default constructor
    public MethodList()
    {
        m_list = new Properties();
    }

    // Adds a method key/value pair to the list
    public void add(String methodName, String methodClass)
    {
        m_list.put(methodName, methodClass);
    }
```

```
    // Removes a method key/value pair from the list
    public void delete(String methodName)
    {
        m_list.remove(methodName);
    }

    // Retrieves a class name from a passed-in method name
    public String get(String methodName) throws
            IllegalArgumentException
    {
        String sRet = (String)m_list.get(methodName);
        if (sRet == null)
            throw new IllegalArgumentException("Method not" +
                    "found in list.");

        return sRet;
    }

    // Retrieves the number of methods in the list
    public int getCount()
    {
        return m_list.size();
    }
}
```

Sample Application

The sample application is included in the text of this chapter to help you understand the components you must create for every application after you have developed `BaseEnterpriseServlet`. Every application must have the following components:

- A configuration file
- One servlet
- One or more methods

Here are the sample files for the sample application:

- **Configuration file: `test.config`**

  ```
  # Config file
  Default.Method=hello
  Method.hello=TestMethod
  ```

- **Servlet: `TestServlet` class**
  For this example there will be no need to put any code in this servlet. Although it may appear that this inherited servlet is not needed, in Chapter 2 we will show you the code that goes here. For now, no

code is required in this part, but the servlet itself is needed because we inherit the `init()` and `service()` methods in `BaseEnterpriseServlet`.

```
import enterprise.servlet.*;
import enterprise.common.*;

import java.io.*;

public class TestServlet extends BaseEnterpriseServlet
{

}
```

- **Method: `TestMethod` class**
  This is the most important section of code—the actual implementation that will be executed when the application runs. It's a simple "Hello World" application. In the configuration file we indicated that `method=hello` would be associated with `TestMethod.class`. So this method will be executed when you request the sample application with the URL `http://machine.domain.com/servlet/TestServlet?method=hello`.

```
import enterprise.servlet.*;
import enterprise.common.*;
import java.io.*;

public class TestMethod extends HTTPMethod
{
  public void execute()
  {
    try
    {
      PrintWriter out = m_response.getWriter();

      out.println("<HTML>");
      out.println("<H1>Hello World!</H1>");
      out.println("</HTML>");
    } catch(Exception e)
    {
      e.printStackTrace();
    }
  }
}
```

The sample application, in response to the URL given previously, will produce the following response:

```
<HTML>
<H1>Hello World!</H1>
</HTML>
```

To set up and run this application, we need to set the initialization arguments in the servlet container. At this point we should be familiar with setting up and registering a servlet in the servlet container. This application will require that the initalization arguments contain a line that points to the configuration file. In a Servlet 2.2–compliant servlet container, this servlet would be set up in the following way:

```
<servlet>
        <servlet-name>
            TestServlet
        </servlet-name>
        <servlet-class>
            TestServlet
        </servlet-class>
        <init-param>
            <param-name>ConfFile</param-name>
            <param-value>C:\Projects\test.config</param-value>
        </init-param>
        <load-on-startup>
            1
        </load-on-startup>
</servlet>
```

Notice that we set the `ConfFile` parameter to point to the configuration file. In addition, it is convenient to have the servlets automatically launch when the container starts. It's a good idea to have the servlets initialize themselves at startup instead of when a client attempts to request a servlet. This is especially true for an application that may have an extended initialization sequence (processing templates, connecting to databases, and so on).

That was a lot of work for just a "Hello World" style example. A standard servlet would probably work well in this scenario. In the chapters that follow, however, we will begin seeing the fruits of our labors and how this work makes application development much easier. The point here was to explain the single-servlet dispatching mechanism and provide a basis of understanding for the rest of the book.

Summary

This chapter has shown you the mechanics of `BaseEnterpriseServlet` so that you could better understand how it works. In subsequent chapters we will begin to build on these concepts, and you'll start to see the value of having a base-servlet architecture. Remember that one of the biggest advantages to this complex structure is that you code it only once. Thereafter, you can focus on creating your applications.

With this approach the time-to-market for your applications will quickly decrease because instead of reimplementing a solution, you'll simply extend the base servlet and immediately start writing your application. All of the conveniences that we'll cover in later chapters will be available to every application immediately upon creation.

CHAPTER 2

AppContext: Managing Applications

Almost any employee who works for a corporation has come up against scarcity of resources at one time or another and lived under the confines of a budget. Whether the issue is office supplies, computer equipment, software, or additional labor, we have all heard the boss say something like, "I would love to get you some new paper clips, but we just don't have the budget."

Resources can be hard to come by in the corporate world, especially for IT folks! When we develop a new Web application, we are always faced with where to deploy the application, which server has the room, which server has disk space, and which server has the memory capacity. The IT manager usually suggests placing the application on a server that other departments are already using. Who cares if it's already hosting eight other applications, right? In other words, in the corporate world budget constraints may very well demand that multiple applications be hosted on a single server.

Once we have decided that we will share a server with another application, we are faced with several application management issues, especially when dealing with a servlet architecture: How can we manage the application's configuration? How do we ensure that the application contains its own set of objects and is not accessible from another application? And so on.

The best way to handle these issues is with an *application context*—that is, an object whose only purpose is to encapsulate data and objects that are specific to a particular application. An application context understands which application it belongs to and manages its major components. It provides access to global application resources, yet encapsulates and protects these objects from other applications on the server.

Huh? Say that again? In lay terms, an application context is an object that administers its data and configuration, verifies this data, and prevents other applications or servlets from using this data. How is the application context idea applied to the real world? Let's assume we have four departments sharing a Web server. Each department has its own application running on this server. Let's also assume that each department's application was developed by a different group of developers or by developers who were trying to develop their application with reusable code.

Typically, servlets use static variables for global information that needs to be accessible throughout an application. If groups of developers do not communicate when developing their applications and they reuse static code and do not standardize naming conventions across the enterprise, the static variables may conflict with each other and confuse the applications. By applying an application context to the applications on this Web server, we can be assured that each application will use its own data and not clash with the other applications.

Case Study

At a major company, the e-Business Department had just deployed a mission-critical application for Human Resources. Part of the initialization in the application was to set up database connections and load default information into variables such as user IDs, passwords, and logging information. To allow other classes that were developed in the application to access some these variables, the developers made the variables static.

The application ran beautifully, and the e-Business group received praise for their hard work and efforts. Good news traveled fast, and the Accounting Department requested a similar application. Two months later the accounting application was developed and ready for deployment.

Because the company was in merger talks, the executives mandated cost-cutting initiatives, and the company was faced with a budget cut in hardware. The Accounting Department would have to share the Human Resources Web server. This actually seemed like a great idea because the two applications were so similar that the developers could copy the initialization code from the HR application and reuse it in the accounting application. When the Web servers were started, however, the developers noticed that database connections were getting mixed up, and user IDs weren't working. Closer examination revealed that the static variables and code duplication were causing the applications to clash.

To combat the problem, the developers designed an object that encapsulated the configuration file and setup information specific to the context of each application. The object needed to be reusable because many of the configuration file parameters and much of the initialization code were very similar across applications. This new object was called `AppContext` and was responsible for buffering the application variables from other applications and initializing these variables from the configuration file. The object was implemented into the HR and accounting applications, and the software ran as originally intended.

As a result of this experience, the manager of the development team came up with a warning using the word *STATIC* as an acronym: "Before declaring something *static*, **ST**op **A**nd **T**hink, **I**t's **C**hancy."

In this chapter we will explain why an `AppContext` object is needed and demonstrate how to manage each application's data. We will restructure and enhance the design of `BaseEnterpriseServlet` by using an instance of `AppContext` that will provide the enterprise architecture basis for the rest of the concepts in this book.

The Configuration File Revisited

Chapter 1 described the concept of single-servlet dispatch for an application. This architecture easily lends itself to a multiapplication environment on a single server, as Figure 2.1 shows. The idea is that each servlet is responsible for its own application. If you have seven applications on a server, then you have seven servlets, as well as seven configuration files. Each configuration file likely contains data that is specific to the corresponding application, but it also has data that is required in all applications.

For example, in Chapter 1 we emphasized the `Method` parameters that exist in a configuration file. Almost every application will have its own set of `Method` parameters to enable dispatch. Of course, nearly every application will require many more parameters, such as template pointers, database and LDAP connection specifications, database and LDAP pool configurations, and many other configuration items. In fact, throughout this book we will be adding new parameters to the configuration file to give our enterprise architecture more functionality. As you begin writing your own applications, you will probably add customized parameters to the configuration file that hold special meaning for your application.

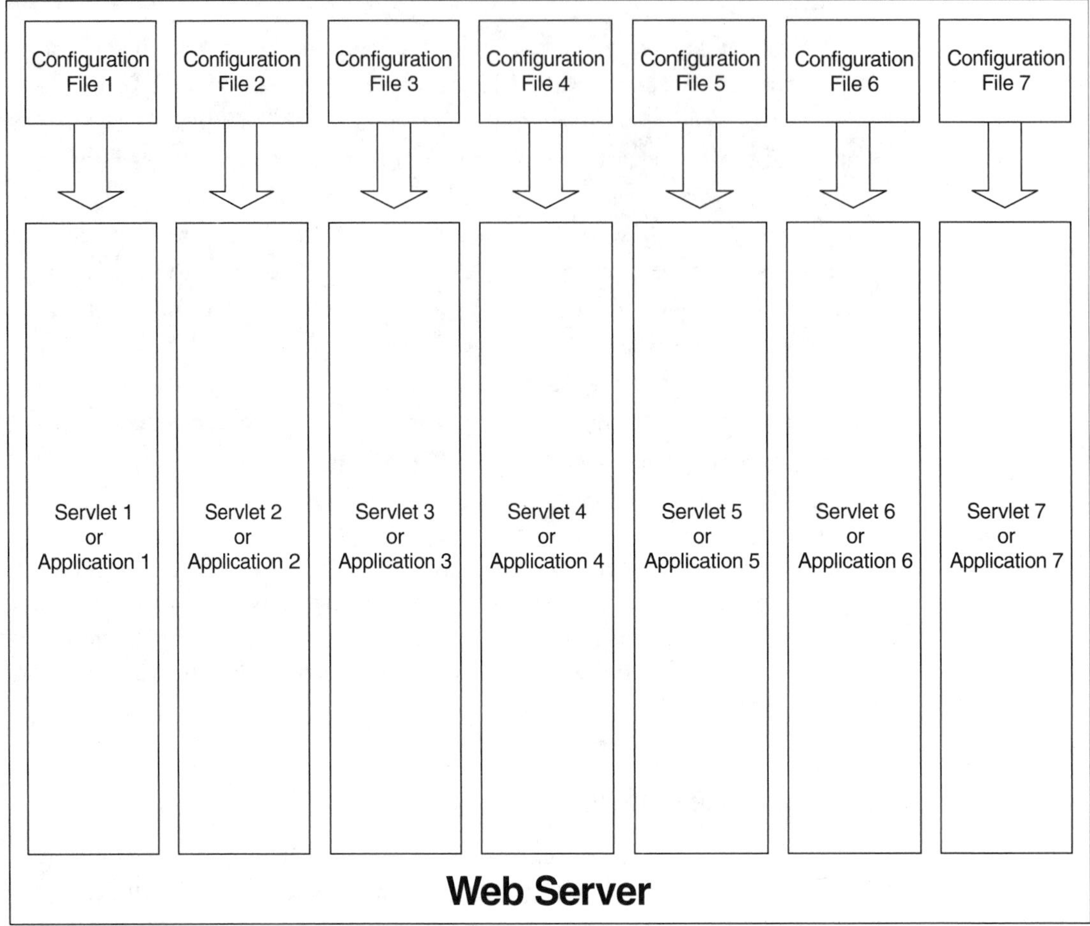

Figure 2.1 Multiple-servlet architecture for enterprise dispatch applications

You may wish to add parameters with certain user IDs considered by your application to represent "super users," or you may wish to include your company's stock symbol so that you can deliver real-time stock quotes to the staff. The combinations and additions are endless. With the many combinations and customized additions to a configuration file, we should build an object that contains and manages the most frequent parameters, yet is flexible enough to let us use customized parameters. `AppContext` is such an object.

The AppContext Object

Throughout this book we will be adding parameters to the configuration file to alter and specify the way an application works. Do we want database pools?

How many connections should we have? Where do we store templates and the like? We need to be able to manage the configuration file parameters and make them accessible to the other classes in the application. In other words, we should develop an object that exposes the setup of an application to the other parts of the application but prevents access by other applications.

Here we will introduce the `AppContext` object. We call it `AppContext` because it is an object that manages data only for the *context* of the *application.* As of Servlet API 2.2, an application's resources are encapsulated by the servlet context, and therefore kept separate from other servlet contexts running on the same servlet container. Therefore, as long as each application is run in its own servlet context, its resources will not clash with those of another application. In some circumstances, however, we may run multiple subapplications in a single-servlet context. For example, we may have an accounting application and an administrative application that are part of one grand system but are two distinct applications. Although these applications have no need to share resources, because they are part of the bigger system we may choose to run them within the same servlet context.

So `AppContext` not only protects its application-specific data, but more importantly, it is a central repository of application resources. Because `AppContext` will consist of objects that are read and initialized from the configuration file, we should begin designing the `AppContext` object by adding the configuration file parameters to it. In essence we should create variables inside `AppContext` for the most common configuration file parameters, such as the list of methods we use for dispatch and the default method.

The objective with `AppContext` is to provide a home for the most common parameters in a configuration file that are a part of most applications. For now we will create the object and work with only a few important, familiar parameters, such as the configuration file, the application name, the method list that was originally defined in `BaseEnterpriseServlet`, and of course, the default method for the application. Later in the book we will add other common parameters, such as database pools and template caches, but for now we will keep it simple and deal with just the parameters listed here.

Let's begin developing the `AppContext` object by defining the configuration file parameters as variables within the object. We will also define constants to represent some of the parameter names found in the configuration file.

```
package enterprise.servlet;

import enterprise.common.*;
import enterprise.io.*;

import javax.servlet.*;
import java.io.*;
import java.util.*;
```

```
public class AppContext
{

  // The items used by an enterprise application
  public static final String METHOD_PREFIX   = "Method.";
  public static final String DEFAULT_METHOD  = "Default.Method";

  private ConfFile           oConf           = null;
  private String             sAppName        = null;
  private MethodList         oMethods        = null;
  private String             sDefaultMethod  = null;
```

The AppContext object eventually will be the primary means for classes to access the configuration file parameters. Because we have created these private parameters, we should also build getters and setters for these members, so let's "partially beanify" them. The phrase *partially beanify* means that for the defined parameters we create public getters, but protected setters. Because AppContext will be a shared object within the context of the application, allowing public setters would force us to synchronize methods (which can slow down a high-capacity Web site because it allows only a single thread at one time to execute the code and ultimately causes bottlenecks) and would open up too many potential problems by permitting developers to change application parameters at their leisure. Normally, we would not even allow setters in this object, but we don't wish to restrict AppContext for future inheritance or allow users access to the package to set these values. So we will stick to public getters and protected setters at this point.

```
  public String getAppName()
  {
    return sAppName;
  }

  protected boolean setAppName(String appName)
  {
    sAppName = new String(appName);

    return true;
  }

  protected boolean setConfigFile(ConfFile confFile)
  {
    oConf = confFile;
    return true;
  }

  public ConfFile getConfigFile()
  {
    return oConf;
  }
```

In Chapter 1, `BaseEnterpriseServlet` used its own `MethodList` object for dynamic dispatch. Because the methods that we define in a configuration file are parameters, to be consistent we will place the method list in the `AppContext` object. We will show the new version of `BaseEnterpriseServlet` later in the chapter to illustrate these changes. For now we provide the getters and setters for this list (see Listing 2.1), as well as for the default method parameter, which we use if a method name is not specified in the URL or query string (see Chapter 1 for more about this parameter).

Listing 2.1 Getters and setters for `MethodList`

```
protected boolean setMethodList(MethodList methods)
{
  oMethods = methods;

  return true;
}

protected MethodList getMethodList()
    throws ResourceNotConfiguredException
{

  if (oMethods == null)
  {
    throw new ResourceNotConfiguredException(
      "No methods are configured.");
  }

  return oMethods;
}

protected boolean setDefaultMethod(String methodName)
{
  sDefaultMethod = new String(methodName);

  return true;
}

public String getDefaultMethod()
  throws ResourceNotConfiguredException
{

  if (sDefaultMethod == null)
  {
    throw new ResourceNotConfiguredException(
         "The default method is not configured.");
  }

  return sDefaultMethod;
}
```

Now that we have a list of the most common properties that we would include in a configuration file, we also need a way to expose customized values or not-so-common configuration file parameters. We will create a `getValue()` method that gives us access to any parameter in the configuration file. Because the `ConfFile` object is nothing more than a glorified `Properties` object, we will build a wrapper for `ConfFile`'s `getValue()` method (see Listing 2.2). This wrapper allows us to expose the functionality for getting a value from `ConfFile`, yet also detects that `ConfFile` is a valid object.

Listing 2.2 Wrapper for the `getValue()` method

```
public String getValue(String key)
   throws ResourceNotConfiguredException
{

  if (oConf == null)
  {
    throw new ResourceNotConfiguredException(
        "The application name is not configured.");
  }

  return oConf.getValue(key);
}
```

We have created getters and setters for the most common configuration file parameters and provided a function to access the less common parameters. For common parameters, we need a way to load the configuration file values into the member variables of the `AppContext` object. Because `AppContext` will hold the configuration file values, parsing of these values should probably be the responsibility of `AppContext`. Therefore, we will move `parseConfigFile()` from `BaseEnterpriseServlet` to `AppContext`. We will also alter this method slightly so that it fits the `AppContext` object and sets its internal variables.

Because we also need a way to get the application name, we will pass the name as a parameter to the parser method. The application name's use within the servlet will be important for identifying the application, especially when we discuss session concepts. For now we will pass it as a required parameter. Listing 2.3 shows the code for `parseConfigFile()`, with the changes made for `AppContext`.

Listing 2.3 The `parseConfFile()` method within `AppContext`

```
public void parseConfigFile(String appName,String fileName)
       throws ServletException
 {
  ConfFile cf = new ConfFile(fileName);

  try
  {
```

```
    cf.load();
  }
  catch (IOException ioe)
  {
    ioe.printStackTrace();
    throw new ServletException(ioe.getMessage());
  }

  setConfigFile(cf);

  // Get the required application name

  if (appName == null || appName.length() == 0)
  {
    throw new ServletException("Application Name Not Supplied.");
  }

  setAppName(appName);

  buildMethodList();

}
```

Because the method list builder in `BaseEnterpriseServlet` is part of the parsed configuration file, the `buildMethodList()` method should be moved to `AppContext` as well. `AppContext` is a more appropriate place for it. The code for `buildMethodList()` (see Listing 2.4) is the same as the code for the method list builder in `BaseEnterpriseServlet`, as shown in Chapter 1, except that it is slightly altered to use `AppContext`'s variables.

Listing 2.4 The `buildMethodList()` method

```
public void buildMethodList()
  throws ServletException
{
  // Get the list of methods

  ConfFile cf = getConfigFile();

  MethodList ml = new MethodList();

  for (Enumeration m = cf.getKeys() ; m.hasMoreElements() ;)
  {
    String key = (String) m.nextElement();

    if (key.startsWith(METHOD_PREFIX))
    {
       String method = key.substring(METHOD_PREFIX.length());

       if (method.length() > 0)
       {
```

```
                String classpath = cf.getValue(key);
                ml.add(method.trim(),classpath.trim());
            }
        }
    }

    setMethodList(ml);

     // Get the default method name
    String defaultMethod = cf.getValue(DEFAULT_METHOD);

    if (defaultMethod != null)
    {
      try
      {
        ml.get(defaultMethod);
      } catch (IllegalArgumentException iae)
      {
        throw new ServletException("Default method " + defaultMethod
            + " is not a valid method.");
      }

      setDefaultMethod(defaultMethod.trim());
    }
  }

}
```

You should note that in the AppContext object we are using the exception ResourceNotConfiguredException (see, for example, Listing 2.4). This exception is customized for exactly what the name implies: to indicate that a resource (or parameter) is not configured when we request it. When we request a parameter's information, this exception helps us determine whether the parameter exists in the configuration file. ResourceNotConfiguredException is a basic extension of the Java Exception class (see Listing 2.5).

Listing 2.5 The ResourceNotConfiguredException class

```
package enterprise.common;
public class ResourceNotConfiguredException extends Exception
{

  public ResourceNotConfiguredException()
  {
    super();
  }

  public ResourceNotConfiguredException(String msg)
  {
    super(msg);
  }
}
```

This is the basic AppContext object. It contains convenience methods to access the general parameters of the application. It takes the responsibility of parsing the configuration file to verify and load the object with the parameters. It also provides a getValue method to allow access to parameters that are not parsed into the internal variables of AppContext.

Now we need to know how to use AppContext. So let's take a new look at BaseEnterpriseServlet, which was introduced in Chapter 1, and restructure it to use AppContext and to allow accessibility to AppContext from the derived HTTPMethod objects.

Restructuring BaseEnterpriseServlet

Chapter 1 introduced BaseEnterpriseServlet, the primary mechanism for the dynamic single-servlet dispatch architecture. There we kept our concepts and code relatively simple to demonstrate how the configuration file, the HTTPMethod class, and BaseEnterpriseServlet's dynamic dispatch operate. We kept the configuration file parsing and parameters local to BaseEnterpriseServlet. This arrangement did not allow HTTPMethod-inherited classes access to the configuration file parameters, nor did it provide for customized values. The architecture shown in Chapter 1 would have provided for many changes to BaseEnterpriseServlet and HTTPMethod for any additional parameters that we wished to add and use. Because we have created the AppContext object that encapsulates most of the access to the configuration file parameters, we need a way to create the object in BaseEnterpriseServlet and pass it to any derived HTTPMethod classes. Figure 2.2 illustrates the restructured BaseEnterpriseServlet dispatching AppContext to HTTPMethod.

Let's start by changing the HTTPMethod class. BaseEnterpriseServlet sends the HttpServletRequest and HttpServletResponse objects to HTTPMethod by calling registerMethod() and passing these objects as parameters. We should expand this method to allow the AppContext object to be passed as a parameter, and to set a private member variable, just as we did with the request and response objects. Listing 2.6 shows this change.

Listing 2.6 Changes to HTTPMethod to support AppContext

```
public abstract class HTTPMethod
{
        .
        .
        .
    protected AppContext m_context;
```

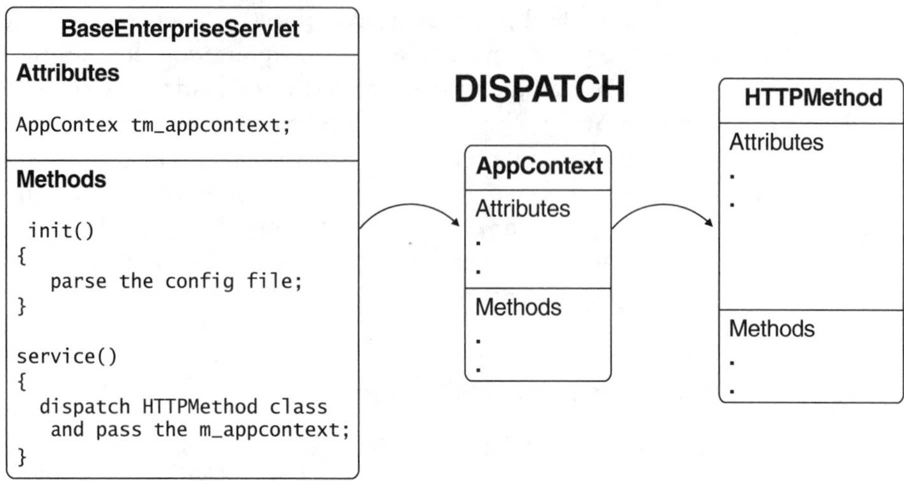

Figure 2.2 Restructured BaseEnterpriseServlet and dispatch mechanism

```
    public void registerMethod(HttpServletRequest  req,
                               HttpServletResponse res,
                               AppContext ac)
    {
        m_request     = req;
        m_response    = res;
        m_context     = ac;
    }
        .
        .
        .
}
```

Now we have a means of accessing AppContext through HTTPMethod, but we need to get AppContext to HTTPMethod from BaseEnterpriseServlet. Before we update BaseEnterpriseServlet, let's examine some of its new requirements and what will be needed to implement the AppContext object for a more robust architecture.

- BaseEnterpriseServlet must contain and create a single AppContext object. Upon creating the object, it must parse the configuration file in the initialization of BaseEnterpriseServlet.
- Instead of managing its own method list, BaseEnterpriseServlet must use the method list contained within AppContext for class dispatch. Method lists are configuration file parameters and should be managed through the AppContext object.

- `BaseEnterpriseServlet` must pass the `AppContext` object to the `HTTPMethod`-derived class upon dispatch through the `HTTPMethod.registerMethod()` function call.

This looks simple enough: We need to create an `AppContext` object, parse the configuration file in the `init()` method of `BaseEnterpriseServlet`, and dispatch the object to `HTTPMethod`. But something isn't quite right. One of the reasons we created `AppContext` was to allow access to customized parameters. What if we want to verify some custom parameters? Say, for example, that we have a parameter called `BackgroundColor` and we must use the value of this parameter to provide a background color for Web pages. In addition, we want this parameter to be required in our application, and we want it to take one of three values: `red`, `green`, or `blue`. Since `BaseEnterpriseServlet` is using the `init()` call, how do we check the parameters in the initialization of the servlet?

Each servlet has a member function called `init()` that is passed a `ServletConfig` object. The `ServletConfig` object is typically used to extract the initialization string that was used during setup of the servlet in the servlet container. Normally we pass startup or configuration information to a servlet through the `ServletConfig` object.

The `init()` method is run only once, when the servlet is first launched or executed. Because the `init()` method is encapsulated in `BaseEnterpriseServlet`, we need a way to enable the servlet or application to verify and do its own initialization. We could override the `init()` method and call the `super.init()` method to run `BaseEnterpriseServlet`'s version first, but this leaves too much margin for error for the programmer. Can you imagine what would happen if we accidentally did not call `super.init()`? `AppContext` wouldn't be loaded, and consequently the servlet would not be able to run. Even if we did call `super.init()`, we would need access to `AppContext`'s data because we are more interested in the configuration file parameters than the `ServletConfig` parameters.

What we need to do is force the programmer to create an initialization function in the inherited class, even if it is not used. We do this by creating an abstract method in `BaseEnterpriseServlet` called `initializeApp()`, and we pass `AppContext` as a parameter. Creating an abstract method forces the developer to implement the method in the inherited servlet. We can thus be sure that both `BaseEnterpriseServlet`'s initialization function and the initialization function of the derived class will be called without worrying about forgetting to call the function of the superclass. We then make a call to the abstract function in `BaseEnterpriseServlet` after processing `AppContext`. We will show this call when we get into code for `BaseEnterpriseServlet`.

Having identified some more needs of BaseEnterpriseServlet, let's add the following to our requirements:

- BaseEnterpriseServlet must provide for a customized initialization in the derived class. Because the init() method has been contained in BaseEnterpriseServlet, we need a way to give the programmer access to an initialization function. This function should operate as if the servlet were a standard implementation running the function once, upon startup of the servlet.
- BaseEnterpriseServlet must ensure that an application name is obtained from its derived class, so that we can include the name in AppContext. For several reasons we want each application to uniquely identify itself. Most importantly, having each application create its own identity ensures a session that is unique across applications—a topic that will be covered in Chapter 3.

We are now ready to restructure BaseEnterpriseServlet with these requirements. Let's start as we did in Chapter 1, but this time we'll add AppContext as a member variable.

```
package enterprise.servlet;

import javax.servlet.*;
import javax.servlet.http.*;
import java.io.*;
import java.net.*;
import java.util.*;
import java.sql.*;

import enterprise.common.*;

public abstract class BaseEnterpriseServlet extends HttpServlet
{
  private AppContext m_ac = new AppContext();
```

Now we'll create an abstract method that forces any derived classes to have a method named getAppName() that returns the name of the application. The derived implementation should be a unique name that identifies the application, such as *StockQuote, ExpenseApp,* or *TravelApp*. Making this method an abstract member means that the derived class must include its implementation or it will not compile.

```
  public abstract String getAppName();
```

We'll do the same thing to initialize and destroy an application. We'll create two abstract functions—initializeApp() and destroyApp()—that will allow users to customize initialization and destruction for the servlet in any way they like. In a "regular" servlet, the programmer would normally use the `init()` function for initialization, which receives a `ServletConfig` type of parameter. This parameter is the initialization object that is used when we set up the servlet in a servlet container. We want to mimic this capability in `BaseEnterpriseServlet` through the `initializeApp()` function. Instead of passing the `ServletConfig` object, however, we will pass the `AppContext` object because `AppContext` is used for initialization parameters through the configuration file. In addition, when the container is about to remove an instance of the servlet, it calls the `destroy()` method. We will do the same and create a `destroyApp()` method.

```
public abstract void initializeApp(AppContext appContext)
    throws Exception;

public abstract void destroyApp(AppContext appContext);
```

As for the servlet's initialization call, it isn't too different from the initialization described in Chapter 1, except that we removed the `parseConfigFile()` method from `BaseEnterpriseServlet` and are using `AppContext`'s method instead.

```
public final void init(ServletConfig config) throws
        ServletException
{
  super.init(config);
  String  sConf = config.getInitParameter("ConfFile");

  if(sConf == null)
  {
    throw new ServletException("ERROR - BaseEnterpriseServlet " +
        "needs a ConfFile param.\n");
  }

  try
  {
    m_ac.parseConfigFile(getAppName(),sConf);
```

Here's where we run the derived servlet's initialization. This is the reason we declared the `initializeApp()` method as an abstract member: to ensure that the derived class can have an initialization function and is indeed run. We place the `initializeApp()` call at the end of `init()` to ensure that `AppContext` has fully parsed the configuration file and verified the major parameters before passing it on for use in initialization of the derived class.

```
    initializeApp(m_ac);
  }
  catch(Exception e)
  {
```

```
        e.printStackTrace();
        throw new ServletException(e);
    }
  }
```

The destroy() method is not too different. It calls the destroyApp() method. Just as we did with initializeApp(), we will call destroyApp() with AppContext as a parameter.

```
public final void destroy()
{
  destroyApp(m_ac);
}
```

For the service method, most of the code is the same. Again, however, we will use AppContext for the method list instead of the built-in calls to BaseEnterpriseServlet's members because AppContext will be the primary container for the method list and its supporting methods.

```
public void service(HttpServletRequest req,
                    HttpServletResponse res)
    throws ServletException, IOException
{
  PrintWriter   out         = null;
  res.setContentType("text/html");
  res.setHeader("Pragma", "No-cache");
  res.setHeader("Cache-Control", "no-cache");
  res.setDateHeader("Expires", 0);

  // Then write the data of the response

  try
  {

    String method = req.getParameter("method");

    if (method == null)
    {
      try
      {
        method = m_ac.getDefaultMethod();
      }
      catch (ResourceNotConfiguredException rnce)
      {
        out = getPrintWriter(res);
        out.println("<HTML>");
        out.println("Invalid method");
        out.println("</HTML>");
        out.flush();
        return;
      }
    }
```

```
    HTTPMethod methodInstance = null;

    MethodList methods = m_ac.getMethodList();
    Class c = Class.forName( methods.get(method) );

    methodInstance = (HTTPMethod)c.newInstance();
```

Here's where we will pass the AppContext object down to HTTPMethod. Recall that we updated HTTPMethod.registerMethod() to accept an AppContext object. The passing of this object is what will give all of our derived classes of HTTPMethod access to AppContext.

```
    methodInstance.registerMethod(req, res, m_ac);

    methodInstance.execute();

  }
  catch (IllegalArgumentException ex)
  {
    // If we got here, then the method name was not found in
    // the method list
      out = getPrintWriter(res);
      out.println("<HTML>");
      out.println("Invalid method");
      out.println("</HTML>");
      out.flush();
  }
  catch (Exception ex)
  {
       ex.printStackTrace();
       return;
  }
}
```

Finally, we want to create a method that allows us to get the PrintWriter object without any worry that it will throw an IllegalStateException because we use PrintWriter to output error information in this class. Why would we worry about getting an IllegalStateException in this class by just calling the getWriter() method? If at any point we call the getOutputStream() method from the HttpServletResponse object, we cannot call getWriter() within that request.

Why would we call getOutputStream() instead of getWriter(), and where would we call it? We would potentially use getOutputStream() when sending out type content that is not necessarily text/html. For example, we would use the getOutputStream() method when sending binary data such as an image or an Excel spreadsheet. Typically, this method would be called in one of the HTTPMethod objects. The problem is that when getOutputStream() is called, getWriter() cannot be called, and vice versa. Only *one* of these output methods can be used per servlet request.

This constraint is set by Java Servlet API. However, the constraint is not acceptable when we're trying to output an error message and need to use `PrintWriter`. If `getOutputStream()` has already been called, we will have difficulty obtaining a `PrintWriter` object from the `getWriter()` method because it will throw an `IllegalStateException`. Therefore, we will create a wrapper method that attempts to get the `PrintWriter` object from the `getWriter()` method. If it throws an `IllegalStateException`, we will call `getOutputStream()` and create a `PrintWriter` object from an `OutputStream` object. This guarantees that we will have access to a `PrintWriter` object, regardless of the API's constraints.

```
  private PrintWriter getPrintWriter(HttpServletResponse res)
      throws IOException
  {
    PrintWriter pw = null;

    try
    {
      pw = res.getWriter();
    }
    catch(IllegalStateException ise)
    {
      pw = new PrintWriter(res.getOutputStream());
    }

    return pw;
  }
}
```

Whew! Including the `AppContext` object, that was a lot of code! Unfortunately, we needed to redesign `BaseEnterpriseServlet` to make it more useful and easier to use for developing applications. Although most of the major enhancements we have made to `BaseEnterpriseServlet` have had to do with its basic architecture, we will be adding a few snippets of code (and we do mean a *few!*) to `AppContext`, `HTTPMethod`, and `BaseEnterpriseServlet` throughout the book as we present some of the major topics. But for now, let's get to the fun part. Let's look at `AppContext` and the newly restructured `BaseEnterpriseServlet` in a real example and see how easy it is to develop an enterprise servlet.

A Two-Application Example

In the beginning of this chapter we explained how a lack of resources can lead to multiple applications sharing a single server. We described the necessity for each application to have its own configuration file that contains general parameters and quite possibly custom parameters specific to that application. One of the major constraints for each application or servlet was that only the relevant application should be able to see its own parameters—that is, the parameters should not be shared by other applications on the server. We emphasized the importance of isolating an application's configuration file parameters through `AppContext`, allowing access to `AppContext` from `HTTPMethod` objects, and providing a way to let developers initialize their applications.

In this example we want to emphasize these points by creating two applications that run on the same server. The goal is to demonstrate the creation, parsing, and encapsulation of configuration file parameters within an `AppContext` object and to show that the `HTTPMethod` subclasses have access to this object. In essence, we want to show how simple it is to write and use a basic enterprise servlet. Each application will display its application name and some of the parameters defined in its configuration file, and attempt to access a parameter that was defined in the other application's configuration file.

The setup will consist of two servlets or applications, and we will call them App1 and App2. If you haven't already guessed, we like to use the terms *servlet* and *application* synonymously. The reason is that under an enterprise servlet architecture, each application consists of only one servlet. Each of the servlets will have one method and its own configuration file. Each servlet will parse the configuration file and validate that it contains custom parameters when it is being initialized. The custom parameters will be stored in the servlet's own `AppContext` object, which will be passed to the `HTTPMethod` object when the servlet dispatches the request.

Let's begin by defining the configuration files. We want each application to set up its own method, a default method, and one custom value. Listing 2.7 shows the code for App1. Listing 2.8 shows a similar type of configuration file for App2.

Listing 2.7 Configuration file for App1

```
# Configuration file
Default.Method=app1
Method.app1=App1Method

# Customized parameters
App1.custom.value=This is a custom value for App1
```

Listing 2.8 Configuration file for App2

```
# Configuration file
Default.Method=app2
Method.app2=App2Method

# Customized parameters
App2.custom.value=This is a custom value for App2
```

Note the parameters for both applications and their differences. Pay particular attention to the custom values. Notice that the names and values are unique. We named each custom value with its application name to demonstrate the encapsulation and custom-value accessibility of the applications.

Now that we have our configuration files, let's build the servlet for the first application. We will derive this servlet from `BaseEnterpriseServlet`.

```
import enterprise.servlet.*;
import enterprise.common.*;

import java.io.*;

public class App1Servlet extends BaseEnterpriseServlet
{
```

We need to include `initializeApp()`, `destroyApp()`, and `getAppName()` methods in the servlet because of `BaseEnterpriseServlet`'s abstract declarations. If we don't declare these members, we will get compilation errors. This is how `BaseEnterpriseServlet` forces us to create an application name and define an initialization function, as described in the previous section. To show how one would use the servlet's initialization, we will make the application's configuration file custom parameter a requirement. By *requirement,* we mean that the parameter must exist in the configuration file or an error will result. We enforce this requirement by checking for the existence of the parameter through the `getValue()` function of the `AppContext` object.

```
  public void initializeApp(AppContext appContext) throws Exception
  {
    String customValue = appContext.getValue("App1.custom.value");

    if (customValue == null)
      throw new Exception("App1.custom.value has not been " +
                          "defined.");

    System.out.println("Resource App1.custom.value = " +
                       "customValue);
  }

  public void destroyApp(AppContext appContext)
  {
    System.out.println("Shutting down App 1");
  }

  public String getAppName()
  {
    return "App1";
  }
}
```

Let's build the same structure for the App2 servlet. We will do the same as we did for App1, but instead we will look for App2's custom parameter and set a different name in the `getAppName()` method for the servlet (see Listing 2.9).

Listing 2.9 The App2 servlet

```
import enterprise.servlet.*;
import enterprise.common.*;

import java.io.*;

public class App2Servlet extends BaseEnterpriseServlet
{
  public void initializeApp(AppContext appContext) throws Exception
  {
    String customValue = appContext.getValue("App2.custom.value");

    if (customValue == null)
      throw new Exception("App2.custom.value has not been " +
                          "defined.");

    System.out.println("Resource App2.custom.value = " +
                       "customValue);
  }

  public void destroyApp(AppContext appContext)
  {
    System.out.println("Shutting down App 2");
  }

  public String getAppName()
  {
    return "App2";
  }
}
```

Now that the servlets are ready, we need to create the `HTTPMethod`-derived dispatch classes. We want each class to display some HTML text and list the application's name, its default method, and the custom parameter that was defined for that particular application. To demonstrate encapsulation we also want to try to access the custom parameter that was defined in the other application's configuration file. Let's define App1's class. This class will extend `HTTPMethod`, thereby forcing us (through abstraction) to create an execute member. The execute member is the function that is run by `BaseEnterpriseServlet` when it dispatches the call.

```
import enterprise.servlet.*;
import enterprise.common.*;

import java.io.*;
```

```
public class App1Method extends HTTPMethod
{

  public void execute()
  {
    try
    {
      PrintWriter out = m_response.getWriter();

      out.println("<HTML>");
```

When BaseEnterpriseServlet called registerMethod() before dispatching the servlet, it passed in AppContext as one of its parameters, and HTTPMethod set AppContext as a member variable. The fact that AppContext seems to be magically available for use is pretty cool. Here we will use AppContext's get functions to retrieve and display some of the configuration file parameters:

```
      out.println("<H1>My AppContext for "
      + m_context.getAppName() +
                  " has access to the following...</H1>");

      out.println("Default.method = " +
      m_context.getDefaultMethod() +
                  "<br>");

      out.println("Application Name = " + m_context.getAppName() +
                  "<br>");

      out.println("App1.custom.value = " +
                  m_context.getValue("App1.custom.value") +
                  "<br>");
```

App1 attempts to access App2's custom value. If this attempt fails, we will generate a message stating that we do not have access to the parameter.

```
      if (m_context.getValue("App2.custom.value") == null)
        out.println("We do not have access to App2.custom.value <br>");
      else
        out.println("App2.custom.value = " +
                  m_context.getValue("App2.custom.value") +
                  "<br>");

      out.println("</HTML>");

    } catch(Exception e)
    {
      e.printStackTrace();
    }
  }
}
```

Let's write the same class for App2. In fact, we will follow our paradigm and call it `App2Method` (see Listing 2.10). The main difference is that we will attempt to access App1's custom parameter.

Listing 2.10 The `App2Method` class

```
import enterprise.servlet.*;
import enterprise.common.*;

import java.io.*;

public class App2Method extends HTTPMethod
{

  public void execute()
  {
    try
    {
      PrintWriter out = m_response.getWriter();

      out.println("<HTML>");

      out.println("<H1>My AppContext for " +
      m_context.getAppName() +
                  " has access to the following...</H1>");

      out.println("Default.method = " +
      m_context.getDefaultMethod() +
                  "<br>");

      out.println("Application Name = " + m_context.getAppName() +
                  "<br>");

      out.println("App2.custom.value = " +
                  m_context.getValue("App2.custom.value") +
                  "<br>");

      if (m_context.getValue("App1.custom.value") == null)
        out.println("We do not have access to App1.custom.value <br>");
      else
        out.println("App1.custom.value = " +
                  m_context.getValue("App1.custom.value") +
                  "<br>");

      out.println("</HTML>");

    } catch(Exception e)
    {
      e.printStackTrace();
    }
  }
}
```

Once we have completed the code and successfully compiled it, we are ready to set up the servlets with the servlet container. Depending on the servlet container used, the configuration will differ. In all cases, however, each servlet container will allow the developer to set up initialization arguments. Be sure to set each of the initialization arguments to contain a *ConfFile=<configuration file path>* statement identifying the path to each application's configuration file. For example, if we created configuration files on the C: drive in the `\projects\example` directory, the initialization arguments for App1 would be `ConfFile=C:\projects\example\App1.config`, and the arguments for App2 would be `ConfFile=C:\projects\example\App2.config`. With a Servlet 2.2 API, the servlet setup for both servlets (App1 and App2) would include the following configuration in the `web.xml` file:

```
<servlet>
        <servlet-name>
         App1
        </servlet-name>
        <servlet-class>
         App1
        </servlet-class>
        <init-param>
            <param-name>ConfFile</param-name>
            <param-value> C:\projects\example\App1.config
            </param-value>
        </init-param>
        <load-on-startup>
            1
        </load-on-startup>
</servlet>
<servlet>
        <servlet-name>
         App2
        </servlet-name>
        <servlet-class>
         App2
        </servlet-class>
        <init-param>
            <param-name>ConfFile</param-name>
            <param-value> C:\projects\example\App2.config
            </param-value>
        </init-param>
        <load-on-startup>
            2
        </load-on-startup>
</servlet>
```

Having configured the servlet container, we're now ready to run the example.

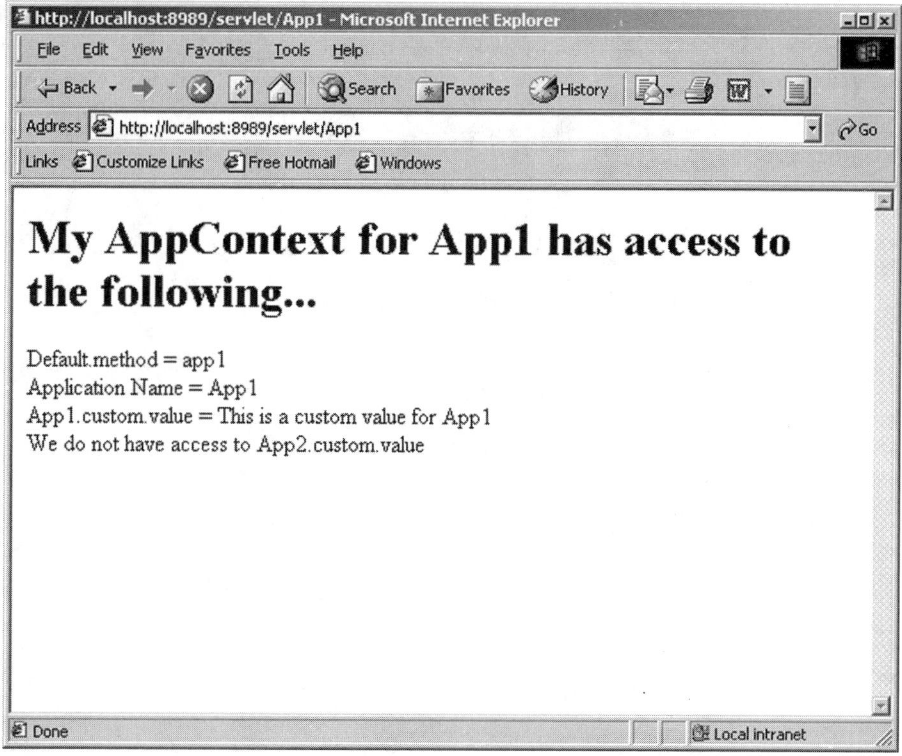

Figure 2.3 Output from the App1 servlet

Figures 2.3 and 2.4 show the HTML output of the two applications. Notice that each application displays its own configuration file parameters. Also notice that when each application tries to read the other application's custom parameter, the second application reports that the first one does not have access.

That's it. All the code in `AppContext` and the restructuring of `BaseEnterpriseServlet` made it very easy to build an enterprise servlet that isolates itself from other servlets.

Forcing Uniqueness across Applications: AppManager

In this chapter we added the application name in the `AppContext` object and noted that this name is a mandatory item in the base servlet. We didn't really explain the reasoning behind this requirement. It may have appeared to be a way to show how to place the application's name in a dispatch servlet and how `AppContext` manages it. You may have also wondered why we have this

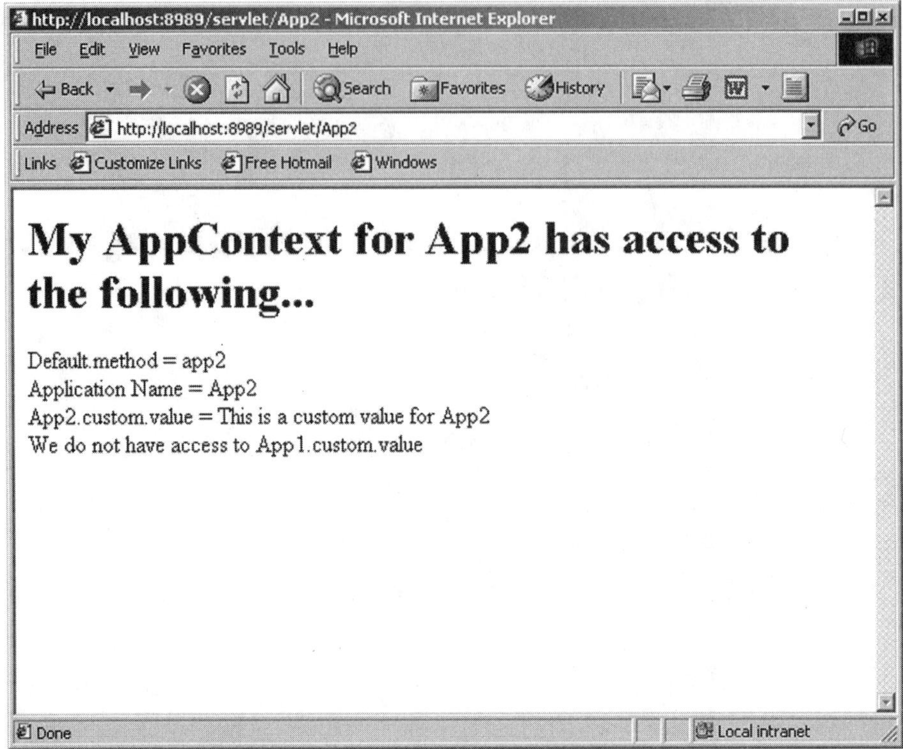

Figure 2.4 Output from the App2 servlet

parameter as an `AppContext` member, since the point of `AppContext` is that it is an extension of the configuration file's parameters.

Well, `AppContext` really is an extension of the application and anything that needs to be accessed by the `HTTPMethod` objects. So what is the point of having the application name? Who cares what an application is called internally? Every person has a name, and it is the name that identifies each person. In a perfect world, a person's first and last name would be unique (we know this isn't true, but for the sake of this example we will make this assumption). This unique name would identify a person as a separate entity from others. We want our applications to be able to identify themselves uniquely as well.

There are many reasons for wanting an application to identify itself uniquely. Here we will touch on some examples that will be covered in more detail later in the book. The most important reason is to be able to uniquely identify information coming from and going to this application when we're running multiple applications on the same server. If we write information to the Web server log with the `System.out` object and are running several servers, it may be helpful to send the application name to the log so that we can better identify which application created the entry.

Before calling `printStackTrace()` on an exception, we may wish to add the application name to the system error message so that we know which application caused the exception. If we don't do this on a server with seven or eight applications, it may become very difficult to identify which application caused the error and where the error occurred. Another reason is to create session objects uniquely. We will save the details for Chapter 3, but we can use the application name to help separate session variable objects, which is a critical function for running multiple applications on the same server.

So it stands that we want our applications to have a unique name. We have demonstrated this in the code throughout this chapter, but we have not created a means to prevent two applications from having the same name. With the code we have developed so far, we potentially could code the same name in the `getAppName()` method and the servlets would run fine. But we don't want this to happen because we don't want two applications to be able to run with the same name.

We need to build an object that will manage application names and not allow duplicates. `BaseEnterpriseServlet` will register the application's name to the manager upon successful initialization and will remove itself when the container (servlet container) decides to remove the instance of the servlet (destroy). The manager is really nothing more than a list that allows you to add and remove names. The main objective is that if an application attempts to add a name that already exists, the manager needs to throw an exception stating that the application already exists on the server. This object is like a traffic cop. When the application launches, the cop "checks the application's license" (its name), and "decides" whether to allow it to continue executing. The code for this object, which we will call `AppManager`, is displayed in Listing 2.11.

Listing 2.11 The `AppManager` class

```
package enterprise.servlet;

import java.util.*;
import java.io.IOException;
import javax.servlet.*;

import enterprise.common.*;
import enterprise.io.*;

public class AppManager
{

  private Set m_appList = null;
```

```
/**
 * Constructor
 */
public AppManager()
{
  m_appList = Collections.synchronizedSet(new HashSet());
}

public synchronized void addApp(String appName)
    throws Exception
{

  synchronized(m_appList)
  {
    if (m_appList.contains(appName))
    {
      throw new Exception("Application " + appName +
                          " already exists on this Web Server");
    }

    m_appList.add(appName);
  }

}

public synchronized void removeApp(String appName)
{

  synchronized(m_appList)
  {
    m_appList.remove(appName);
  }

}

public String[] getAppNames()
{
  synchronized(m_appList)
  {
    Iterator i = m_appList.iterator();

    if (m_appList.size() == 0)
    {
      return new String[0];
    }

    String names[] = new String[m_appList.size()];

    int x = 0;
    while(i.hasNext())
    {
```

```
            names[x] = (String) i.next();
            x++;

        }

        return names;
    }
  }
}
```

AppManager's easy-to-use methods, such as addApp() and removeApp(), pass a string that represents the application name to the object. We will also have an information helper method called getAppNames() that returns a String array of all the applications. Other than that, the object is just an intelligent wrapper for a HashSet object. The objective now is to integrate AppManager into BaseEnterpriseServlet—a task that entails creating a static AppManager member of BaseEnterpriseServlet and ensuring that AppManager.addApp() is then called in the init() method and that AppManager.removeApp() is called in the destroy() method.

Let's begin by adding AppManager as a static member in BaseEnterpriseServlet. We want this object to be static so that all applications have access to it because they all need to add and remove themselves from the list.

```
public abstract class BaseEnterpriseServlet extends HttpServlet
{
.
.
.
 private static AppManager  m_appManager       = new AppManager();
.
.
.
```

Now let's allow the application to register itself with AppManager. We want to place this code at the bottom of the init() method because when init() throws a ServletException, the entire instance of the servlet is removed from the container. The servlet fails, so it would never have the opportunity to register itself. If we placed the code at the beginning of the init() method, it would register itself first and fail, and the destroy() method would never be executed. Hence the application would never remove its name from the manager, and we would never be able to load the servlet without restarting the container. Therefore, we do not want to register the application with the manager until *all* initialization has successfully completed.

We ensure that application registration follows initialization by positioning its code last in the init() method. The call to addApp(), with the application name passed in, will trap for an exception. Any exception will be wrapped in a

ServletException object, so the exception can be thrown in the init() method. Throwing a ServletException forces the container to remove the servlet from the container, which is the primary goal when another application with the same name is running on the same machine.

```
  public final void init(ServletConfig config) throws
  ServletException
  {
.
.
.
    try
    {
      m_appManager.addApp(getAppName());
    } catch (Exception e)
    {
      throw new ServletException(e.getMessage());
    }
  }
.
.
.
```

Of course, we want the application to remove itself from the list when the servlet is being shut down. We may shut it down manually through the servlet container, or the container may decide to remove the instance for other reasons. In either case, if the servlet doesn't need to run anymore, it should be removed from the list. We want AppManager to have only running and fully initialized applications in its list. This code should go in the destroy() method. However, we will make this code the first code that is executed. If the destroy() method is being called by the framework, this servlet is going to crash! So let's just remove the application from AppManager first, and then worry about customized destruction afterward.

```
  public final void destroy()
  {
    if (getAppName() != null)
    {
      m_appManager.removeApp(getAppName());
    }
.
.
.
  }
.
.
.
}
```

Integrating `AppManager` into `BaseEnterpriseServlet` should prevent duplicate application names from being added to the list. To see how this works, let's take our sample application and use `AppManager` and the newly updated `BaseEnterpriseServlet`. Try running the application and each of the servlets; it should execute just fine and look the same as before. Now to experiment, edit the App2 servlet and change its name to *App1,* thereby creating a duplicate name. Run the servlet container and go to each servlet with your browser. You should see that one of the servlets, most likely the second servlet you go to (unless you are preloading the servlets), has an exception thrown stating that the application name is a duplicate.

Summary

This chapter presented some of the realities of sharing resources in a corporate environment, which lead to a need to separate and manage multiple applications on a single Web server. We presented the `AppContext` object, which manages all aspects of the configuration file and is the primary vehicle for accessing configuration file parameter values for the rest of the application. `AppContext` helps to clarify the separation between applications on a single Web server and to simplify the development of enterprise servlets. We also redeveloped the `BaseEnterpriseServlet` architecture to use `AppContext`, as well as to supply a more robust base for designing enterprise applications.

To summarize, the new design, along with `AppContext`, ensures that the application's data is protected and won't be accessed or set by other applications. The design also provides a strong initialization and configuration file management architecture. In addition, we learned that an application's name can play an important role in determining uniqueness in applications. This uniqueness needs a "traffic cop" that gives the application a license to run and does not allow applications with the same name to execute on the same server. We developed `AppManager` to take this responsibility and ensure that each application has its own unique name. In Chapter 3 we will take application separation a step further and examine the critical role of session management.

CHAPTER 3

Forms, State, and Session Management

Nearly every application needs some type of interaction from the end user. When we use the Web, we are always interacting with an application in one way or another. When we use search engines, we type in a query or words that we want to see in our results. When we shop online, we need to tell the company what we want to buy and where to ship the product. Many of us have access to financial sites or are members of a group whose Web site requires us to log in by submitting a user ID and password, and thus the site appears to be personalized for us. Forms are what make all this personalization possible. Because practically all users have interacted with the Web through forms, this topic is probably one of the more important ones in Web development.

Often when we submit forms, we are submitting information based on previous entries. The Web was originally meant to be *stateless;* that is, each form submission was supposed to have no knowledge of previous submissions or of information entered by the user. Thus it is interesting that when we shop online, we can add items to the shopping cart, and when we check out, the items we chose and their prices are listed and ready for payment. Sometimes such information is preserved even if we leave the Web store, go to another site (perhaps to check the news or weather), and return to our shopping cart. The Web site appears to be maintaining state, remembering our choices and preferences between the different submissions and calls. Our friends at Sun Microsystems were kind enough to provide state and give the developer an opportunity to manage a user's *session.*

It is obvious that processing forms, maintaining state, and managing sessions go hand in hand. You usually don't have a session without processing a form. In this chapter we will examine forms and how they fit within the enterprise servlet architecture. We'll discuss techniques for using forms and the role that maintaining state plays in the enterprise servlet paradigm. We'll describe some of the pitfalls of maintaining state with the `HttpSession` object in a single-server environment, and we'll introduce the `EnterpriseSession` object and explain how it fixes some of the anomalies of `HttpSession`.

HTTP Forms: A Review

Because this book is geared toward developers who have a basic knowledge of Web software design and development, we will only very briefly review forms and how they work. Let's start by examining HTTP and its history. In 1989 Tim Berners-Lee invented the World Wide Web, and he developed the World Wide Web server and client (browser-editor) in 1990. These developments were intended to allow hyperlink-based text and graphics over the Internet, thereby allowing users to view documents and select links referencing and displaying other documents. One of the more important design points was the provision of a platform-independent way to view a document. Within the next three years, the Web's popularity exploded as users and developers from all over the world began designing and publishing their own Web pages. The popularity of the Web made standards necessary, and the World Wide Web Consortium (W3C) became a major player in defining these standards.

Part of the original HTML specification was to support the ability of the Web developer to solicit information from the user. The user would enter his/her information and have that data packaged as a payload to be sent back to the server through HTTP. When received by the server, the payload would be broken down into its original data components, and the data would then be processed. In a nutshell, the concept of forms is simple. A form that requests information is displayed on a Web page to the end user. The user enters the information and submits it to the Web server for processing, and the Web server sends back a response.

Today, forms are used in many creative ways and request all kinds of information. Some of the more common forms that we see on the Web are search engines, login screens, shopping carts, and name/address requests. In fact, many of us use HTML forms as our main e-mail client through free e-mail services such as Hotmail.com and Yahoo! Mail. The uses for forms are endless in our day-to-day interaction with the Web.

The <FORM> Tag

All forms have one common component that is required to solicit information from a user: the `<FORM>` tag. Basically, a form consists of a set of `<FORM>` tags,

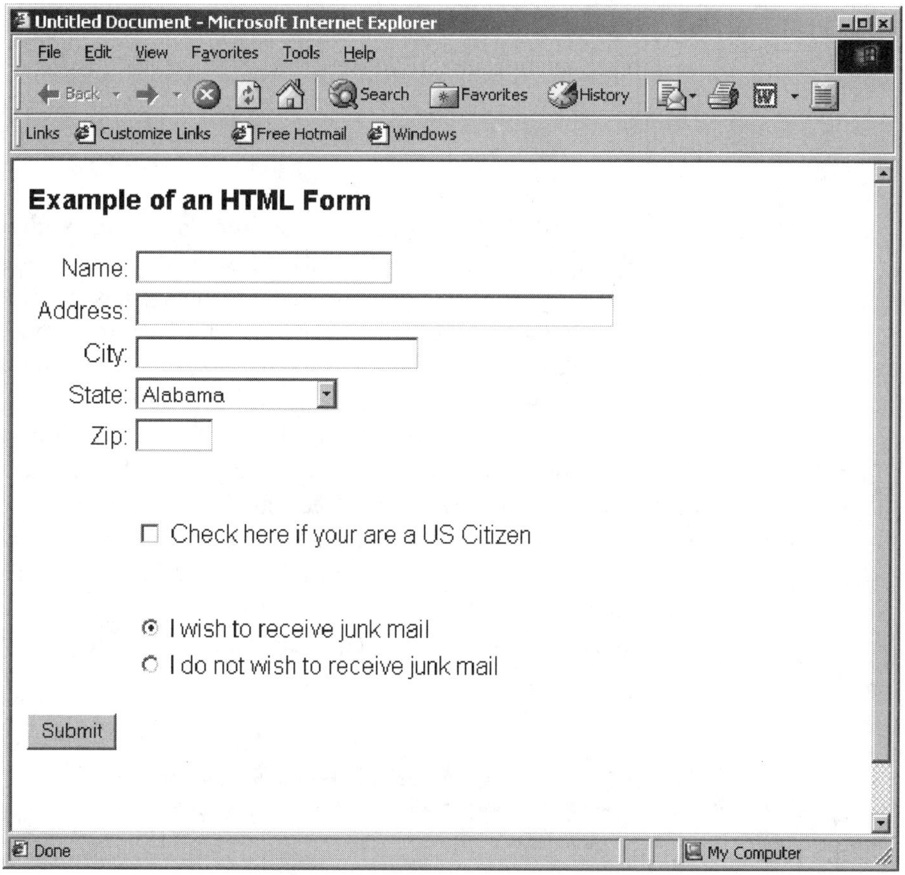

Figure 3.1 A typical HTML form

and <INPUT> control tags in between, that provide the end user the ability to submit and format information entered into fields or controls on a page. The <FORM> tag tells the browser where to look for input controls. The typical controls for storing data are text boxes, list menus, radio buttons, option buttons, hidden fields, and plain old pushbuttons. Creating a form on a page is very easy. At first it might seem complex to create a form such as the one in Figure 3.1, but really this form requires no more than a few lines of HTML. Listing 3.1 shows the code for a very simple form.

Listing 3.1 HTML for a simple form

```
<html>
<body>
<form method="get" action="http://localhost/servlet/ColorServlet">
  <p>What is your favorite color?
    <input type="text" name="color">
```

```
  </p>
  <p>
    <input type="submit" name="MySubmitButton" value="Submit">
  </p>
</form>
</body>
</html>
```

Notice that all of the input controls and data reside within the <FORM> tag. In this example we have two controls: a text field and a submit button. Each of the <INPUT> tags has a `type` parameter, which specifies the kind of control that will be shown; a `name` parameter, which identifies the name with which the value will be associated when sent to the server; and possibly a `value` parameter, which may seed the control with a value or label.

As the user submits the form, each <INPUT> tag—including the one for the submit button—is sent with a name/value pair to the server. Let's assume that in this example the user inputs "red" as the color. The server will receive the name/value pairs `color=red` and `MySubmitButton=submit`. Each input control should have a name, such as *color* or *MySubmitButton* in this example, and the value will come from the user's input to the control. Table 3.1 lists all input controls and each of their HTML equivalents.

Table 3.1 Form Control Types and Their Associated HTML Equivalents

Control Type	HTML Equivalent
Text	`<input type="text" name="???">`
Text area	`<textarea name="???">Your text goes here</textarea>`

Combo box	`<select name="???">`
	`<option value="option value"> [selected] Text for Option </option>`
	`. . .`
	`</select>`

Password	`<input type="password" name="???">`
File	`<input type="file" name="???">`
Check box	`<input type="checkbox" name="???">`
Radio button	`<input type="radio" name="???">`
Submit button	`<input type="submit" name="???"> or` `<input type="image" name="???">`
Reset button	`<input type="reset" name="???">`

Now that we have shown how the server translates the data, we need to describe how the form packages the data so that the server can receive the name/value pairs. How does the form know where to send the data and how to send it? In our example, the `<FORM>` tag contains three parameters: `name`, `method`, and `action`. The `name` parameter is self-explanatory: It names the form. The `method` parameter tells the form how to package the data, and the `action` parameter tells it where to send the data.

The `method` parameter usually contains one of two types of values—`GET` and `POST`—which package the data in different ways. The `action` parameter tells the form the URL (typically some form of a CGI) that will receive the data.

Packaging the Query with GET and POST

The two methods of sending the data to the server—`GET` and `POST`—package the data in very different ways. Each method has its advantages and disadvantages. Let's examine each type and see how the server receives the information. The `GET` method packages the information as a one-line URL. It takes the `action` parameter as defined in the `<FORM>` tag and appends a question mark ("?") as a delimiter between the URL and the name/value pairs. Then it takes all the name/value pairs and concatenates them on a line, delimiting each pair with an ampersand ("&"). In our simple form example, the resulting `GET` URL would be `http://localhost/servlet/ColorServlet?color=ired&MySubmitButton=submit`.

As this example shows, the name/value pairs become part of the URL. The data is combined as though the client browser were requesting or getting a single URL. Now let's see how this method gets the name `GET`. When the browser submits the information in this sample URL, it packages the data in what in HTTP is called a `GET` method. What the server receives is the HTTP request shown in Listing 3.2.

Listing 3.2 An HTTP `GET` example

```
GET /servlet/ColorServlet?color=red&MySubmitButton=Submit HTTP/1.0
Connection: Keep-Alive
User-Agent: Mozilla/3.72 [en] (Windows NT 5.0; U)
Host: localhost
Accept: image/gif, image/x-xbitmap, image/jpeg, image/pjpeg,
        image/png, */*
Accept-Encoding: gzip
Accept-Language: en
Accept-Charset: iso-8859-1,*,utf-8
```

Notice that the request begins with a `GET` call. This really isn't any different from submitting a request for a basic HTML page, image, or any other type of document. The server looks at the URL and parses the name/value pairs directly from the actual URL. Because this is a GET request, the browser also believes the submission to be a link to a URL and typically displays the entire URL in the address or location area on the browser.

The advantages of a GET submission are that the user can bookmark the link in a browser and can submit the browser as if it were a link. The main disadvantage of a GET submission is that many browsers limit the amount of data that can be submitted as a URL. Some browsers limit the length to 1,024 characters, others to more or fewer characters. In addition, the server application may limit the amount of data that is parsed from the GET line. This constraint would prevent developers from allowing text controls for long comments or information from the user. It would also prevent the developer from having too many input controls on a single form.

Now let's look at the POST request type. HTTP communicates with two basic blocks of information: a header and a message or content block. In GET requests, only the header portion of an HTTP request is used. In a POST request, however, both the header and the content block are used. In our example, the POST method looks as if it is calling just the action parameter as defined in the <FORM> tag, without any parameters:

http://localhost/servlet/ColorServlet

This is what the browser may show in the address or location area because the browser is not packaging the information in the same way as a GET method does, and the form data is not part of the URL. The browser essentially issues a POST request type in the header with only the call to the <FORM> tag action parameter. The rest of the header is similar to that of a GET request, except it also defines a content type and content length of the message area. A blank line after the content lines defines the end of the header and the beginning of the message or content block, as shown in Listing 3.3.

Listing 3.3 An HTTP POST example

```
POST /servlet/ColorServlet?module=test HTTP/1.0
Connection: Keep-Alive
User-Agent: Mozilla/3.72 [en] (Windows NT 5.0; U)
Host: localhost
Accept: image/gif, image/x-xbitmap, image/jpeg, image/pjpeg,
        image/png, */*
Accept-Encoding: gzip
Accept-Language: en
Accept-Charset: iso-8859-1,*,utf-8
Content-type: application/x-www-form-urlencoded
Content-length: 31

color=red&MySubmitButton=Submit
```

The message block contains the name/value pairs delimited by an ampersand ("&"). Pay particular attention to the `Content-length` parameter, the value of which matches the size of the message block. This parameter defines the maximum size of the content. The `POST` request hypothetically could allow for a submission of any size. I say *hypothetically* because some Web servers may limit the maximum size they will accept. However, the limit is usually reasonably large.

The advantage of a `POST` request is that it allows for a much larger submission than a `GET` request does. It also does not produce a cryptic URL on the address line and divulge all of the name/value pairs to the end user. Its main disadvantage is that it does not allow the user to bookmark the form's submission in his/her browser.

Is there a preference for the type of form submission? The answer depends on the particular circumstances. If you're writing a short form that checks the status of a few financial stocks and you want a user to be able to bookmark the results, a `GET` method is probably preferable. However, if you have a form with many fields, especially text controls, a `POST` method is probably better. For form submissions in the real world, the `POST` method is typically the most commonly used.

HTTP Forms and Enterprise Servlets

We have reviewed forms and the methods for submitting them. But how do forms fit into the enterprise servlet architecture? Remember that the basic strategy for the enterprise servlet architecture is a single servlet with dynamic dispatch. Dynamic dispatch requires that we send a `method` parameter along with requests. Somehow we need to send the `method` parameter along with the form's `action` parameter, so that `BaseEnterpriseServlet` knows how to dispatch the request within the application.

Let's take the simple example given earlier and assume that we have developed it with the enterprise servlet architecture and created a class called `ProcessColor`. Let's also assume that in the configuration file we defined the method as follows: `Method.process_color=ProcessColor`. The goal would be to have the form call `http://localhost/servlet/ColorServlet?method=process_color`.

As a simple test, we can try to change the `action` parameter in the `<FORM>` tag to look something like

```
action="http://localhost/servlet/ColorServlet?method=process_color"
```

Let's try this with `GET` as the value of the `method` parameter in the `<FORM>` tag. We find that this just doesn't work. The browser appears to completely ignore the *method=process_color* part of the action. So how can we get the method parameter to the servlet through the form? We will use a special input control of type hidden. This control allows us to pass a hidden name/value pair to the servlet without presenting data or the ability to input data from the end user. Its syntax allows us to set a name and a value. Let's look at the simple form that we introduced in Listing 3.1 again, but this time let's add the hidden input control with the method name (see Listing 3.4).

Listing 3.4 A simple form for enterprise servlets with the hidden input control

```
<html>
<body>
<form method="GET" action="http://localhost/servlet/ColorServlet">
  <input type="hidden" name="method" value="process_color">
  <p>What is your favorite color?
    <input type="text" name="color">
  </p>
  <p>
    <input type="submit" name="MySubmitButton" value="Submit">
  </p>
</form>
</body>
</html>
```

Now let's try submitting the form in a browser. Note that we now have *method=process_color* in the query string. The hidden control allowed us to add a name/value pair to be passed to the server that could not be altered by the end user.

Let's try this experiment again from the beginning, this time making POST the value of the method parameter in the <FORM> tag. Voilà! The action works with *method=process_color* in the URL. We don't need to implement a hidden input control when we do a POST operation, and we can code the necessary dispatch name/value pair right on the URL. This works because of how the browser handles the packaging of the GET and POST operations. Let's try this again with the hidden input control and just the servlet in the action parameter of the <FORM> tag. This approach also works.

Is there a preferable implementation here? In my opinion, if you use the hidden input control method, you can't go wrong. You are guaranteed that this will work with enterprise servlets every time without having to worry about the submission type. So as a rule, when we're using enterprise servlets, all forms should have a hidden input control that is named *method*, and this parameter should identify the method that will be dynamically dispatched. As long as we follow this rule, all the forms will interact very nicely with enterprise servlets, whether the submission type is GET or POST.

Now that we have a good understanding of how a form can work with dynamic dispatch and enterprise servlets, we should look at how developing a form and HTML fits in an enterprise environment.

Form and HTML Development in the Enterprise

In most software development efforts, especially in the enterprise, software is executed in three environments: development, testing, and production. These three environments could look very different. Typically they are on three different machines, with three different URLs. The enterprise usually stipulates which tools should be used for development and which tools for production. For example, a company may purchase the license to run a WebLogic server in its production environment but not wish to pay for the license for each of its seven developers who are programming the Web site. Instead the company has its development team use the free Tomcat servlet development environment for licensing costs. These are two distinct products that run servlets differently.

In addition, there are many different kinds of servlet containers on the market today that run in many different types of environments. Some are add-ons or plug-ins to existing Web servers such as ServletExec, JRun, or the Apache JServ. Some are built into the Web servers themselves, such as the iPlanet Web server, and some are Web servers in their own right, such as BEA WebLogic.

Each servlet container handles servlet URLs a little differently and has its own idiosyncrasies. The point is that we want to focus on how each container handles the servlet URL, and that the URL may change when we switch environments. For example, many servlet containers access Java servlets through a *servlet* type of URL, such as *http://machine1.foobar.com/servlet/xyz.* Others create or let the user create an alias to the servlet and/or do not contain the word *servlet* in the URL. When we move the URL from environment to environment, the machine and URL may change from `http://localhost/servlet/RunMe` to `http://test.foobar.com/servlet/RunMe` to `http://www.foobar.com/RunMe`. These changes in machines and servlet environments may have a large impact on our forms and HTML.

Going back to our simple example, in the `<FORM> action` tag we have `http://localhost/servlet/ColorServlet` as the URL. The designation *localhost* works great when we're developing on one of our own machines. However when we move this piece of code to another box and it is called from a remote client, this code will not work because we are not calling the local host. Our initial thought would be to make this a relative URL, such as `/servlet/ColorServlet`. This would work fine, but sometimes using the full URL is desirable. In addition, assuming that we're developing in a generic servlet container and wish to deploy to a WebLogic server, we may omit the */servlet* portion of the URL. This also would render the form useless.

Case Study

A development team was writing an employment verification system that allowed managers to review and update their direct reports. This servlet-based application was to be accessed by the rest of the company after each pay period. Because its budget was limited, the e-Business Department had the developers write the application using one of the free development platforms. The testing and production environments were using the latest WebLogic server. Most of the servlet HTML coding was done inline and with templates, and the application's code spanned about 50 HTML pages.

After the development was completed, the team placed the system in the testing queue and deployed it to one of the WebLogic test machines. In a primary test, the servlets did not run properly and the forms appeared to be "broken." Closer examination revealed that the `action` parameters of the `<FORM>` tags had *localhost* coded as part of the HTML and that WebLogic didn't require */servlet* in the call to the servlet.

The system was sent back to the development team to review the issues, and the team went back to the whiteboard to figure out the best way to handle the situation. After a few discussions, the concept of the *base URL* was born, in which a configuration file parameter that contains the base of all URLs for the application is configured and accessed from one place. The team stipulated that no base-URL addresses should be hard-coded, and that the base URL should be used in all HTML produced by a servlet.

A few days later the system was tested again, and it passed with flying colors. When the team deployed the system to production, it was a simple matter of changing the configuration file parameter, and the system was up and running in production in just a few minutes.

Because a lot of the HTML and form development is written as part of a servlet, the concept of a *base URL* is important. `BaseURL` is a central `String` object that is accessible to the entire application and contains the base call to the servlet. Because the enterprise servlet architecture is based on use of a single servlet, the base URL always remains the same for an application. It is then used inline and affixed or inserted into forms or standard HTML that is produced by a servlet. This approach allows us to declare the base URL as `http://localhost/servlet/MyServlet` in one location and, when we move to production, as `http://prodserv.foobar.com/MyServlet`. This simple change requires a single update, yet affects all forms and HTML in the application.

Let's take an example of what we have learned about enterprise servlets and forms thus far, and implement the base-URL concept. First we can identify the fact that base URL is probably specific to an application, yet the concept is common to all applications. This makes the `BaseURL` object an excellent candidate for a required configuration file parameter, and it should be a component of `AppContext`. Let's start by adding the type of configuration file parameter that the `AppContext` object will look for, a string to hold the base URL, the getters and setters that affect the string, and the code that parses this data in the configuration file. We'll call the new configuration file parameter *Application.Base.URL*. Listing 3.5 shows these changes to the `AppContext` object.

Listing 3.5 Changes to `AppContext` to support `BaseURL`

```
.
.
.
public class AppContext
{
.
.
.
  public static final String APP_BASE_URL     =
          "Application.Base.URL";
.
.
.
  private String             sAppBaseURL      = null;
.
.
.
  public String getAppBaseURL()
  {
    return sAppBaseURL;
  }

  protected boolean setAppBaseURL(String baseURL)
  {
    sAppBaseURL = baseURL;

    return true;
  }
.
.
.
```

```
  public void parseConfigFile(String appName,String fileName)
       throws ServletException
  {
.
.
.
    String baseURL = cf.getAttribute(APP_BASE_URL);
    if (baseURL == null || baseURL.length() == 0)
    {
       throw new ServletException(APP_BASE_URL + " not Supplied.");
    }
.
.
.
  }
}
```

After altering the AppContext object, we are ready to begin the example. We'll create a small application, called Accounting, that displays a form requesting the user's name, and then displays a page repeating the name with a simple greeting. The goal of this application is to show a working example of how forms are used with enterprise servlets, and how BaseURL is used with the generated HTML.

Let's begin with the configuration file. The application has two methods: one that displays the original form and one that displays the results. We will call these Java classes AccountingForm and AccountingResult, respectively. We will place corresponding methods in the configuration file and call them *form* and *result* for their dispatch names. Because the default method will be the one that initially displays the form, we will make AccountingForm, or *form,* the default dispatch method. Finally, we need to support the newly required parameter for BaseURL. Because we are running the servlet container on the development machine and the main servlet call will be to /servlet/Accounting, we will use http://localhost/servlet/Accounting as the base URL. Listing 3.6 shows the configuration file.

Listing 3.6 Configuration file for the simple Accounting application

```
# Configuration file
Default.Method=form
Method.form=AccountingForm
Method.result=AccountingResult
# Change the following value to reflect the servlet
# that is executed in your servlet engine.
Application.Base.URL=http://localhost/servlet/Accounting
```

We can begin the coding by developing the base servlet, which we will call AccountingServlet. We will name the application *Accounting* and place the name in the getAppName() method. In this application we have no special initialization or destruction, so we will leave the `initializeApp()` and `destroyApp()` methods empty. Listing 3.7 shows the code for `AccountingServlet`.

Listing 3.7 The main base servlet: `AccountingServlet`

```
import enterprise.servlet.*;
import enterprise.common.*;

import java.io.*;

public class AccountingServlet extends BaseEnterpriseServlet
{
  public void initializeApp(AppContext appContext) throws Exception
  {
  }

  public void destroyApp(AppContext appContext)
  {
  }

  public String getAppName()
  {
    return "Accounting";
  }
}
```

The main form, as explained earlier, will be `AccountingForm`. The only responsibility of this class will be to create an HTML form and display it to the user. As usual with enterprise servlet architecture, because `AccountingForm` is an inherited `HTTPMethod` class, we will create an `execute()` method and code the HTML at this location. We will write out the HTML with `out.println()` calls. When we write the `<FORM>` tag, notice what happens when we get to the `action` parameter. We do not hard-code *http://localhost/servlet* in the `action` tag. Instead we use the `m_context.getAppBaseURL()` call to substitute the URL value. This is the value that we defined in the configuration file as `Application.Base.URL`, and the `AppContext` object conveniently parsed and provided access to this value.

We also need to provide for the dispatch mechanism of the enterprise servlet architecture within this form. Remember that the form must contain a hidden control type that is named *method* so that the base servlet knows how to dispatch the form's submission. Because we are going to dispatch this form to the `AccountingResult` class through the `result()` method, which we named in the configuration file, the `value` parameter of the `hidden` control must contain `result`. Listing 3.8 shows the code for `AccountingForm`.

Listing 3.8 The `AccountingForm` class

```
import enterprise.servlet.*;
import enterprise.common.*;

import java.io.*;

public class AccountingForm extends HTTPMethod
{

  public void execute()
  {
    try
    {
      PrintWriter out = m_response.getWriter();

      out.println("<HTML>");

      out.println("<BODY>");

      out.println("<H1>Forms Example for the Accounting " +
                  "Application</H1>");

      out.println("<FORM method=\"get\" action=\"" +
          m_context.getAppBaseURL() + "\">");

      out.println("<input type=\"hidden\" name=\"method\" " +
                  " value=\"result\">");

      out.println("Please enter your name:");
      out.println("<input type=\"text\" name=\"myname\" " +
                  "value=\"\">");

      out.println("<input type=\"submit\" name=\"submit\" " +
                  "value=\"Submit\">");

      out.println("</FORM>");

      out.println("</BODY>");

      out.println("</HTML>");

    } catch(Exception e)
    {
      e.printStackTrace();
    }
  }
}
```

The `AccountingResult` class will be the ultimate receiver of the form's data input by the end user. In Chapter 1 the `HTTPMethod` class was shown to contain two member variables that allow access to the standard servlet objects,

HttpServletRequest and HttpServletResponse. These objects are called m_request and m_response, respectively, in HTTPMethod. BaseEnterpriseServlet set these variables just before dispatch so that all classes inherited from HTTPMethod would have access to them.

Although both objects are used in the AccountingResult class, we have seen only the use of m_response up to this point, so now we want to emphasize the m_request variable. The m_request object is no different from the HttpServletRequest object passed in directly from a standard servlet's doGet() or doPost() method. It is used exactly the same as if it were in any of a standard servlet's service methods. Therefore, in the AccountingResult class we want to look for the existence of a query parameter called *myname.*

As anyone who has been introduced to the basics of servlets knows, we call HttpServletRequest.getParameter() to retrieve the value of an HTTP query string parameter. This situation is no different; in AccountingResult we call m_request.getParameter("myname") to retrieve the value of myname and display it in a friendly message. Later in the HTML generation, we will again use the getAppBaseURL() method to get the BaseURL object and use BaseURL to display a link back to the original form. Listing 3.9 shows the code for AccountingResult.

Listing 3.9 The AccountingResult class

```
import enterprise.servlet.*;
import enterprise.common.*;

import java.io.*;

public class AccountingResult extends HTTPMethod
{

  public void execute()
  {
    try
    {
      PrintWriter out = m_response.getWriter();

      String myname = m_request.getParameter("myname");

      if ((myname == null) || (myname.trim().length() == 0))
      {
        myname = "N/A";
      }

      out.println("<HTML>");

      out.println("<BODY>");
```

```
            out.println("<H1>Forms Example for the Accounting " +
                        "Application</H1><br>");

            out.println("<h3>Hello " + myname + "!</h3>");

            out.println("<A HREF=\"" + m_context.getAppBaseURL() + "\">");
            out.println("Click here to return to main page");
            out.println("</A>");

            out.println("</BODY>");

            out.println("</HTML>");

          } catch(Exception e)
          {
            e.printStackTrace();
          }
        }
      }
```

Before running the application, remember to set up the servlet in the servlet container and pass `ConfFile=<path to the config file and config file name>` as an initialization argument so that the servlet can find and process the configuration file. Keep in mind that this application will work only if the browser and the servlet engine are running on the same machine because we coded `localhost` into the configuration file as the base URL. After running this application as `localhost`, try changing `Application.Base.URL` to the DNS (domain name service) name of the machine, restart the servlet, and run the browser from a remote computer. Note how easy it would be to move this application to another machine or to another servlet engine. If we change the `Application.Base.URL` parameter in the configuration file, the HTML pages that are generated by the servlets appear to magically change the base URL.

We have shown how forms fit in the enterprise servlet architecture and how changing an application's base URL through the configuration file can easily change the generated forms and HTML. We are now ready to discuss the next topic associated with forms: maintaining state.

Maintaining State with Sessions in the Enterprise

Generating forms and maintaining state seem to go hand in hand. When we need to maintain state, we typically require input from the user, so we use forms to get this input. Why do we need to maintain state? What is maintaining state? We usually maintain state when users log into a system, or when the application includes shopping carts, so that we can preserve static information about the user between requests. Maintaining state allows us to save the condition and position of a user within the confines of an application, thereby obviating the need to continually resubmit the same information to server.

As mentioned earlier when the Web was first invented, it was meant to be stateless. Each request depended on no other request. As the Web proliferated to the masses, having requests depend on previous requests became more and more of a requirement. In early attempts to maintain state, hidden input controls were continually supplied to forms that held information such as login details or items in a shopping cart. This approach placed the burden of maintaining state on the client and was found to be a security risk.

Because copying and altering HTML pages allowed users to bypass some of the security mechanisms of a site and client-side state, this approach quickly became unpopular. Many software vendors listened to developers and began allowing servers to maintain state. One of these vendors was Sun Microsystems. When developing the Java Servlet Development Kit API (the JSDK), Sun created an interface called `HttpSession`. In its Javadoc (`http://java.sun.com/j2ee/tutorial/api/javax/servlet/http/HttpSession.html`), Sun gives the best definition of `HttpSession`:

> [`HttpSession`] provides a way to identify a user across more than one page request or visit to a Web site and to store information about that user. The servlet container uses this interface to create a session between an HTTP client and an HTTP server. The session persists for a specified time period, across more than one connection or page request from the user. A session usually corresponds to one user, who may visit a site many times. The server can maintain a session in many ways such as using cookies or rewriting URLs.

The *session* concept is an integral part of many Web sites; sessions are used in most shopping-cart and financial Web sites. In the enterprise, sessions are used in executive information systems, procurement systems, and online employee information systems. As Java servlet developers, we will probably come into contact with sessions and the `HttpSession` interface at some point in our development endeavors.

Let's take a quick look at the `HttpSession` object and how we apply it in a standard servlet application. `HttpSession` has a predefined life span that is managed by the servlet engine. Most engines allow `HttpSession` to live for a default of 30 minutes of no activity from the client (i.e., no requests to the Web server from a particular client). This time is usually configurable either programmatically or through the servlet engine. The `HttpSession` object has a multitude of management methods that allow the developer to control and manage the session. Table 3.2 lists and describes these methods.

How is `HttpSession` used? In a nutshell, `HttpSession` is received by a call to the `HttpServletRequest.getSession()` method. If a session already exists, `getSession()` passes the session ID to the user, and if a session ID doesn't exist, it creates one. Many other methods control how and when a session is created. After receiving the session object, the `setAttribute()` method may be called to set session variables and `getAttribute()` to retrieve them.

Because this section is meant primarily as a review, we will not get into too much detail about the `HttpSession` object. A more in-depth look at the `HttpSession` object can be found in servlet books that cover the basics, such as *Inside Servlets* by Callaway (2001). Listing 3.10 shows two simple servlets in a standard servlet architecture. One servlet creates and sets a session variable *my_session_var;* the other retrieves the variable and value from the session. This is a good example of how sessions are handled in a classic servlet architecture.

Listing 3.10 Standard servlets using the `HttpSession` object

```
public SetSessionServlet extends HttpServlet
{

  public void doGet(HttpServletRequest req, HttpServletResponse res)
    throws ServletException, IOException
  {
    HttpSession session = req.getSession();
    session.setAttribute("my_session_var", "This is my session var!");

    PrintWriter out = res.getWriter();
    out.println("<HTML> my_session_var has been set!</HTML>");
  }
}

public GetSessionServlet extends HttpServlet
{

  public void doGet(HttpServletRequest req, HttpServletResponse res)
    throws ServletException, IOException
  {
    HttpSession session = req.getSession();

    String myVar = (String)session.getAttribute("my_session_var");
    if (myVar == null)
    {
      myVar = "myVar has not been created. Please go to Servlet1.";
    }

    PrintWriter out = res.getWriter();
    out.println("<HTML> my_session_var = " + myVar + "</HTML>");
  }
}
```

Table 3.2 HttpSession Methods

Method	Description
`getAttribute(String name)`	Returns the object bound with the specified name in this session, or `null` if no object is bound under the name.
`getAttributeNames()`	Returns an `Enumeration` of `String` object containing the names of all the objects bound to this session.
`getCreationTime()`	Returns the time when this session was created, measured in milliseconds since midnight January 1, 1970 GMT.
`getId()`	Returns a string containing the unique identifier assigned to this session.
`getLastAccessedTime()`	Returns the last time the client sent a request associated with this session, as the number of milliseconds since midnight January 1, 1970 GMT, and marked by the time the container received the request.
`getMaxInactiveInterval()`	Returns the maximum time interval, in seconds, that the servlet container will keep this session open between client accesses.
`getSessionContext()`	Deprecated. As of Version 2.1, this method is deprecated and has no replacement. It will be removed in a future version of the Java Servlet API.
`getValue(String name)`	Deprecated. As of Version 2.2, this method is replaced by `getAttribute(String)`.
`getValueNames()`	Deprecated. As of Version 2.2, this method is replaced by `getAttributeNames()`.
`invalidate()`	Invalidates this session, then unbinds any objects bound to it.
`isNew()`	Returns `true` if the client does not yet know about the session or if the client chooses not to join the session.
`putValue(String name, Object value)`	Deprecated. As of Version 2.2, this method is replaced by `setAttribute(String, Object)`.
`removeAttribute(String name)`	Removes the object bound with the specified name from this session.
`removeValue(String name)`	Deprecated. As of Version 2.2, this method is replaced by `removeAttribute(String, Object)`.
`setAttribute(String name, Object value)`	Binds an object to this session, using the name specified.
`setMaxInactiveInterval (int interval)`	Specifies the time, in seconds, between client requests before the servlet container will invalidate this session.

Source: Adapted from Sun's Javadoc (`http://java.sun.com/j2ee/tutorial/api/javax/servlet/http/HttpSession.html`).

The creation and use of the HttpSession object, then, is quite simple. By using this object along with the setAttribute() and getAttribute() methods, we can set and get values between separate requests to the Web server. In the example in Listing 3.10, we set the value of my_session_var in the request to SetSessionServlet, and this variable is retrieved in the request to GetSessionServlet.

How does the session know that the variable that is set is specific to a particular user and not anyone else? Behind the scenes, the Java Servlet engine sends a token to the client. This token is a unique ID that is specific to that session and is generated when the servlet decides a session is required. It is passed in one of two ways.

The first and most common method is through the use of *cookies*. Cookies are small files that are stored on the system by the browser and are requested by a Web server. When you return to the Web server, the browser "stuffs" the cookies that are pertinent for that Web site in the header of all requests, and the Web server looks for the cookie information in this header. With sessions, the token is placed in the HTTP header request, and this is how the Web server uniquely identifies the user. However, if cookies are shut off on a browser, or if the programmer wishes to develop an application for browsers that don't support cookies, this type of session token passing will not work.

This leads us to the second way in which session tokens are passed between the user and the Web server: *URL rewriting*. This method is much less common and much more program intensive. In URL rewriting, the burden of ensuring that the session ID is part of every URL call that accesses a session falls onto the developer. Even URLs to links and forms must include the session ID, and this requirement may prevent the developer from using static HTML in an application. It is much easier to use the cookie method for session tracking.

We have seen how the HttpSession object is used and how it tracks sessions. The next step is to understand how HttpSession fits into an enterprise environment and look at some of the pitfalls of this object. In the discussion that follows we will examine how running multiple applications on a single server affects HttpSession.

Standard Servlet Architecture and Sessions

Let's first examine how the servlet architecture affects a multiapplication environment. Servlets were designed so that they could be called as separate URLs and could share information and objects between each call.

For example, let's assume we have an application that has two servlets: servlet_A and servlet_B (see Figure 3.2). The purpose of servlet_A is to validate a user ID and password. Upon successful validation, `servlet_A` sets a `boolean HttpSession` variable named *validated* with the `setAttribute()` method. Then `servlet_B` checks the status of `validated` with the `getAttribute()` method and decides whether to display an error message (*not validated*) or information that is only for users who have properly passed the security (*validated*).

This is a perfectly reasonable implementation for a single application. Now let's take this example a step further to see the implications of multiple applications on a single server. Let's add a second application on the same server that also contains two servlets, named *servlet_C* and *servlet_D* (see Figure 3.3). These servlets were written by another department in IT and have a similar layout as the servlets in the first application had. The security servlet, `servlet_C`, is the precursor to its system and also loads an `HttpSession` variable named *validated* before allowing the user to access `servlet_D`.

We now have four servlets on the server, and they are split between two applications. Remember that, as defined by the original design, each servlet can be called as a different URL and thus can share objects and data between different requests to the Web server with `HttpSession`. Notice that under this

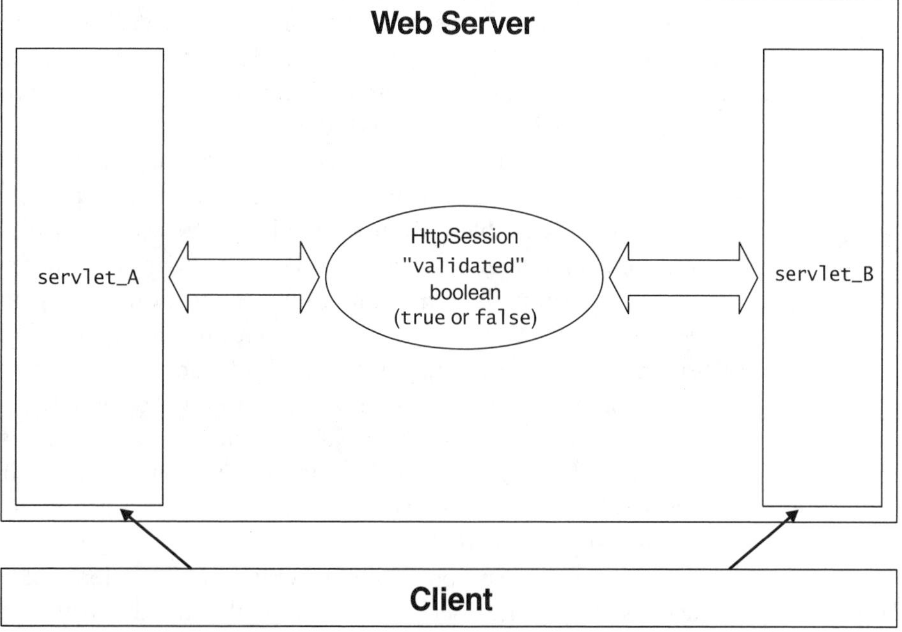

Figure 3.2 A single application with multiple servlets

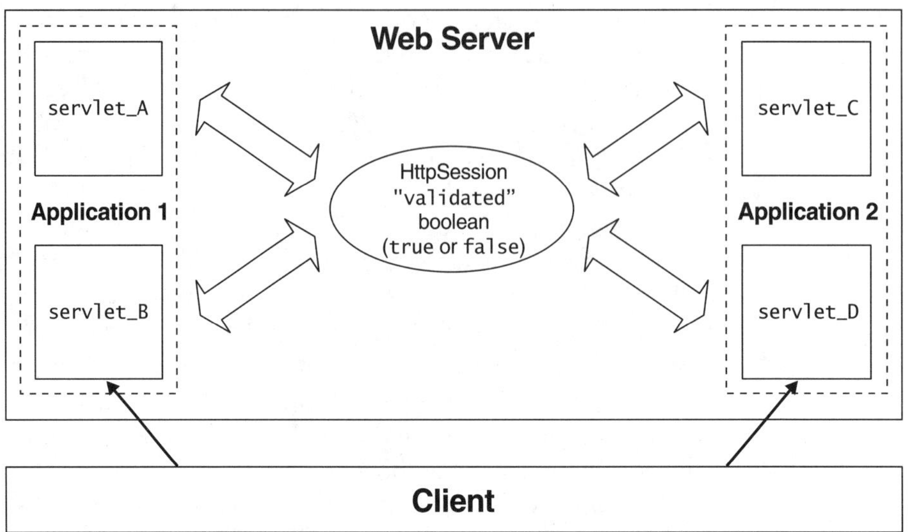

Figure 3.3 Multiple applications with multiple servlets

paradigm, all servlets can share resources, and therefore share the `validated` variable. Such a scenario has potential for disaster because both applications have access to the `validated` session variable and may overwrite each other.

Assume, for example, that application 1 is an accounting system and application 2 is a human resources system. Users of each system probably do not need to access both applications. Therefore, if a user has access to application 1 and has been validated automatically, he/she will automatically have access to application 2 because the `validated` session variable looks the same to both applications. This is a very large security hole. Imagine the implications of seven or eight applications on a single server, each one overwriting the other applications' session variables. We need a solution to seamlessly divide each application's session data and prevent the clashing of data from different applications.

Does session data from multiple applications always clash? No. With the new WAR (Web Archive) file format and multiple servlet contexts in the Servlet 2.2 specification, sessions really do not clash in this way. The servlet engine or application server that supports WAR files is pretty good about separating sessions with similar variable names. But not all servlet engines support WAR files. In fact, one of the fastest servlet engines, iPlanet Enterprise Server 4.1, has a very powerful servlet engine included with the server, but it does not support WAR files.

Note that when you deploy several subapplications under one WAR file, such as in an end-user application with an administrative/monitoring application, you will still potentially run into this problem between these subapplications.

The Enterprise Session

Because we may share Web servers and run multiple applications on a single server, and because many programming efforts probably develop from a common code base, it is very likely that you will run into the situation described in the previous section. Application session data would clash in this scenario, and debugging applications would be difficult at best. Our goal is to have a session containing variables that are unique and cannot clash with other applications on the server. We need to develop a session object wrapper that helps us separate applications in the enterprise. We'll call this object `EnterpriseSession`.

The requirements of this object are that it uniquely identify a variable from other applications, while at the same time allowing us to use simple variable names, such as *userid* and *password.* This object also must support all of the `HttpSession` member functions (see Table 3.2). These requirements allow any developer who has worked with `HttpSession` to use `EnterpriseSession` nearly interchangeably. With these requirements in mind, we can begin our design.

Let's look at enforcing uniqueness across different applications. We need a way to take a simple variable, such as `userid`, and have it uniquely identified so that it is distinguished from the `userid` variables of other applications. The only way to do this is to change the name of the variable somehow. At the same time, however, the developer should be able to use the variable exactly as it was declared, as `userid`.

To uniquely identify this variable, we should prefix the variable's name with a string. We could create a random string, but then there is a chance (albeit remote) that two strings will be the same. But in Chapter 2 we learned that the application name that is stored in `AppContext` is guaranteed to be unique by the `AppManager` object. If `AppManager` finds another application with the same name running on the server, it throws an exception and aborts the execution. So the application name is probably a good string to add as a prefix to `userid` to give it a unique name. For example, if we wrote an accounting application named *Accounting,* the `userid` variable would be `Accounting.userid`.

Now that we know how to make a variable's name unique, we need to support all of the `HttpSession` methods in the same way. However, we want the user to be able to use the simple method name and not be bothered with the prefix; that is, we want the name modification to be transparent to the end user. Remember that the end user will still want to use *userid* as a variable name and not have to worry about prefixing application names. The goal is to make `EnterpriseSession` as similar to `HttpSession` as possible. This means that for each method in `HttpSession`, we will have to create a wrapper method in `EnterpriseSession` that will prefix the name with the application name, and then pass the call to `HttpSession`.

Now that we have designed EnterpriseSession, we can begin developing the object. Let's start with the definition of EnterpriseSession, the member variables, and the constructor. Because this will be a wrapper for HttpSession, we will need an HttpSession member variable, as well as a member variable that defines the application name prefix.

```
package enterprise.servlet;

import javax.servlet.*;
import javax.servlet.http.*;
import java.util.*;

public class EnterpriseSession
{
  private HttpSession m_sess    = null;
  private String      m_prefix  = null;
```

We can define the constructor as passing in an application name string and an HttpSession object, allowing us to set the member variables. We will declare the constructor as protected because we do not want the developer to create the session object directly. We will write a method within the HttpMethod object that will manage the creation of EnterpriseSession.

```
  protected EnterpriseSession(String appName, HttpSession sess)
  {
    m_prefix  = appName + ".";
    m_sess    = sess;
  }
```

We now need to create the same methods as in the HttpSession object. EnterpriseSession's methods will be wrappers for the HttpSession methods, and will therefore pass the calls to the HttpSession methods. For methods that require the variable's name, the prefix will be attched before the method is passed to the HttpSession call.

```
  public long getCreationTime() throws IllegalStateException
  {
    return m_sess.getCreationTime();
  }

  public String getId()
  {
    return m_sess.getId();
  }

  public long getLastAccessedTime()
  {
    return m_sess.getLastAccessedTime();
  }
```

```
public int getMaxInactiveInterval()
{
  return m_sess.getMaxInactiveInterval();
}


public boolean isNew()
  throws IllegalStateException
{
  return m_sess.isNew();
}

public void setMaxInactiveInterval(int interval)
  throws IllegalStateException
{
  m_sess.setMaxInactiveInterval(interval);
}

public Object getAttribute(String name)
  throws IllegalStateException
{
  String uName = m_prefix + name;

  return m_sess.getAttribute(uName);
}

public void setAttribute(String name, Object value)
  throws IllegalStateException
{
  String uName = m_prefix + name;

  m_sess.setAttribute(uName, value);
}

public void removeAttribute(String name)
  throws IllegalStateException
{
  String uName = m_prefix + name;

  m_sess.removeAttribute(uName);
}
```

In the `getAttributeNames()` method, we need to handle the prefix a little differently. This method is supposed to return a listing of all the session's variable names. This one is a little tricky. Although several applications may be running on a server, still only one `HttpSession` object will be shared among all the applications. As we return the variables, each application is interested in only those variables that are specific to itself. We need to get a list of all the variables that have a prefix of a particular application's name and then strip this value away so that the original name of each variable is returned.

We will do this by spinning through all variables in HttpSession, looking for names that begin with the application's prefix, stripping the prefix, and adding the remaining string to a Vector object containing variable names. Because HttpSession.getAttributeNames() returns an Enumeration object containing the names, we will match this call and will convert the Vector object into an Enumeration object and return this object to the user.

```
public Enumeration getAttributeNames()
    throws IllegalStateException
  {
    Enumeration valueNames = m_sess.getAttributeNames();
    Vector appValues = new Vector();

    if (valueNames != null)
    {
      while (valueNames.hasMoreElements())
      {
        String name = (String) valueNames.nextElement();
        if (name.startsWith(m_prefix))
        {
            appValues.addElement(name.substring(m_prefix.length()));
        }
      }
    }

    return appValues.elements();
  }
```

For the sake of compatibility with any servlets that have been written before, we will include the *value* functions that are now deprecated in the current version of the Java Servlet Development Kit.

```
  public void removeValue(String name)
    throws IllegalStateException
  {
    String uName = m_prefix + name;

    m_sess.removeValue(uName);
  }

  public Object getValue(String name)
    throws IllegalStateException
  {
    String uName = m_prefix + name;

    return m_sess.getValue(uName);
  }

  public void putValue(String  name, Object value)
    throws IllegalStateException
  {
```

```
    String uName = m_prefix + name;

    m_sess.putValue(uName,value);
  }

  public String[] getValueNames()
    throws IllegalStateException
  {
    String[] valueNames = m_sess.getValueNames();
    String[] returnValues = new String[0];
    Vector appValues = new Vector();

    if (valueNames != null)
    {
      for (int v = 0; v < valueNames.length; v++)
      {
        if (valueNames[v].startsWith(m_prefix))
        {
          appValues.addElement(valueNames[v].substring(
              m_prefix.length()));
        }
      }
    }

    returnValues = new String[appValues.size()];

    appValues.copyInto(returnValues);

    return returnValues;

  }
```

As we come down to the final `HttpSession` method that we have not discussed—`invalidate()`—we need to think about the ramifications of this method—that is, how it may affect all of the applications on a server. This method invalidates the session for an application. Executing a call to `invalidate()` directly with `HttpSession` would effectively invalidate the session for *all* applications on the server. This is probably not a good idea because one application's session should not be affected by another application's action. To invalidate the session for a particular application, we will remove all the variables associated with that application. We will spin through the variable names and remove those with the relevant prefix as we did for the `getAttributeNames()` method earlier. We will then call the `removeAttribute()` method to remove each of the session variables for this application.

```
  public void invalidate() throws IllegalStateException
  {
    Enumeration e = m_sess.getAttributeNames();
```

```
    while(e.hasMoreElements())
    {
      String name = (String)e.nextElement();

      if (name.startsWith(m_prefix))
      {
        m_sess.removeAttribute(name);
      }
    }
  }

}
```

And that, then, is the EnterpriseSession object. We can now make calls, such as setAttribute("userid", "JeffG"), and EnterpriseSession will store the variables with the application name prefixed to them (in this case <NameOfMyApp>.userid and <NameOfMyApp>.JeffG). This process is completely transparent to the end developer.

The next question is, How do we create this object? Well, we don't. We don't really create an HttpSession object either. When we want an HttpSession object, we call the HttpServletRequest.getSession() method, or one of its several varieties, to retrieve the session. For EnterpriseSession, we will build a similar method for retrieving a session. The most appropriate place for such a method is probably the HttpMethod class.

Before we build retrieval methods for EnterpriseSession, let's talk a little more about EnterpriseSession itself. Remember that EnterpriseSession is no more than a wrapper class for HttpSession and that a single HttpSession object is shared among all applications on a Web server for one user. You may have noticed that when we built the EnterpriseSession.invalidate() method, we cleared the variables instead of invalidating the entire session.

This may have led you to ask, "If the application's session is based on the existence of variables, how do we know whether or not a session has been created already by another application?" This is a good question because knowing whether a session has been created is a good way to detect a *timeout condition.* A timeout condition is a way to determine if the user's session has timed out or if the session is new. This distinction is important because most applications that use sessions have a "doorway"—that is, only one or two pages that allow a user into a system without having a session. This doorway typically is the login page or information page. All other pages usually want to detect that a valid session has been created, and if not, generate the message *Your session has timed out or you have not logged in* and redirect the user to the login page.

We will use a special variable, *ENTERPRISESESSION*, to detect whether a session has been created. When this variable is set, we have created a session, and if it does not exist, then we know the session has not been created. When we call the `EnterpriseSession.invalidate()` method, it clears all of the variables for the application and thus removes the `*ENTERPRISESESSION*` variable. How does this variable get set? The `HTTPMethod` class is a great place for managing an `EnterpriseSession` object and setting the session state or the `*ENTERPRISESESSION*` variable. `HTTPMethod` should be in charge of retrieving and managing the session, as well as detecting a timeout condition, and it should be the only way the developer can access a session.

Let's examine how `HTTPMethod` should manage `EnterpriseSession`. We want `HTTPMethod` to be able to detect a timeout or invalid session. However, we also want it to allow the developer to specify either that he/she is interested in receiving the timeout condition or that `HTTPMethod` should go ahead and create the session object if it doesn't already exist.

For example, let's assume we have decided to create a login servlet that will be one of the doorways. We don't care about detecting a timeout condition, so we want to create a call that gets the session without any question. If a session exists, the engine hands it off; if no session exists, the engine creates one. But for other servlets we may wish to detect a timeout condition, so we could pass a `boolean` value to a method that notifies us that we do want to detect a timeout condition. Because `HTTPMethod` is part of the same package as `EnterpriseSession`, it has the ability to create the object (because the constructor of `EnterpriseSession` is protected). And because it will manage timeout conditions and invalid sessions (which look the same), `HTTPMethod` should also be responsible for setting and detecting the `*ENTERPRISESESSION*` variable.

Let's take a look at `HttpSession`, then, and see how it will manage `EnterpriseSession`. First, and most importantly, we will want a member variable of type `EnterpriseSession`. This allows us to get an `EnterpriseSession` object when we first request it, and then return it in subsequent requests for a session throughout the servlet's execution. In other words, the member variable allows us to go through the long process of creating the `EnterpriseSession` object the first time we request a session, and then just pass the object back when we request it again during the life of the servlet.

We also need a couple of ways of getting a session. One way should allow us to get a session without any question. The other way should allow us to detect a session timeout condition. We will then create a method called `getEnterpriseSession(boolean testTimeOut)` that, if a timeout condition is detected, will throw an `InvalidSessionException`. We will detect a timeout condition only if it is requested, so we can pass `true` if we wish to detect the condition, or `false` if we wish to create the session without any question if a session does not exist or is invalid. We will also create a convenience method called `getEnterpriseSession()` that does not throw any exception. Instead it creates the try/catch loop for the developer and passes true to the getEnterpriseSession(boolean testTimeOut) method. This allows the developer to create the session without having to instantiate a try/catch loop for the call to getEnterpriseSession(). Listing 3.11 shows the updated code for HTTPSession.

Listing 3.11 HttpSession updated to manage EnterpriseSession

```
.
.
.
public abstract class HTTPMethod
{
.
.
.
  private EnterpriseSession m_session = null;

  public EnterpriseSession getEnterpriseSession()
  {
    EnterpriseSession es = null;

    try
    {
      es = getEnterpriseSession(false);
    } catch (InvalidSessionException te)
    {
      // This should never happen
    }

    return es;
  }

  public EnterpriseSession getEnterpriseSession(boolean testTimeOut)
      throws InvalidSessionException
  {
    if (m_session == null)
    {

      if (testTimeOut)
      {
        if (!m_request.isRequestedSessionIdValid())
        {
          throw new InvalidSessionException();
        }
      }

      HttpSession sess = m_request.getSession(false);

      if(sess == null)
      {
```

```
          sess = m_request.getSession(true);
        }

        EnterpriseSession eSession =
               new EnterpriseSession(m_context.getAppName(), sess);

        if (eSession.getAttribute("*ENTERPRISESESSION*") == null)
        {
          if (testTimeOut)
          {
            throw new InvalidSessionException();
          }

          eSession.setAttribute("*ENTERPRISESESSION*", new Date());
        }

        m_session = eSession;

      }

      return m_session;

    }

  .
  .
  .

  }
```

Let's take a more in-depth look at how the session is created. When the developer requests a session, `getEnterpriseSession()` checks to see if the member variable `m_session` exists. If it does, the session has already been created, so the `EnterpriseSession` object is passed back. If it does not, we need to build the `EnterpriseSession` object from an `HttpSession` object.

First we check to see if we need to test for a timeout condition, by testing if the requested session is a valid session—that is, whether the cookie session that is passed in is a current session ID or does not exist. If we are testing for a timeout condition and the session is not valid, an `InvalidSessionException` will be thrown. Otherwise we will create the `EnterpriseSession` object. We create the session by retrieving the application name from the `AppContext` object and passing the `HttpSession` object, which is created by a call to the Java Servlet API's `getSession(true)` method.

Here's where the interesting part begins. If the basic session has been created, either by another application or by the current application in a previous request, once again we must check if a session exists for this particular application. This is where the `*ENTERPRISESESSION*` variable comes into play.

The getSession(true) method will check for the existence of this session variable. Once again, we need to test if we want notification of a timeout condition. If the *ENTERPRISESESSION* does not exist, an InvalidSessionException will be thrown. If we are requesting that we create the session if it does not exist, we will create the session variable *ENTERPRISESESSION* and store its value with a Date value that gives us the creation date and time. At this point we return the EnterpriseSession object. When we want to detect a timeout condition and such a condition occurs, an InvalidSessionException is thrown, as Listing 3.12 illustrates.

Listing 3.12 InvalidSessionException

```
package enterprise.servlet;

public class InvalidSessionException extends Exception
{

  public InvalidSessionException()
  {
    super();
  }

  public InvalidSessionException(String msg)
  {
   super(msg);
  }

}
```

Now that we have developed EnterpriseSession and updated HTTPMethod to manage this object, we need to see how to use it. It's very simple. When we're coding the methods, we either call getEnterpriseSession() to request a session or we call getEnterpriseSession(boolean testTimeOut) with a parameter value of true to detect a timeout condition. We will need to implement a try/catch block when we use the getEnterpriseSession(boolean testTimeOut) method to catch an InvalidSessionException if we need to trap for the timeout condition. By trapping for the timeout condition, we can return HTML that notifies the user of this condition, as shown here:

```
EnterpriseSession es = null;
try
{
  es = getEnterpriseSession(true);
} catch (InvalidSessionException ise)
{
  out.println("<HTML><BODY>");
  out.println("Your Session has timed out or you have not ");
  out.println("entered the application through the login page.");
```

```
    out.println("</BODY></HTML>");
    return;
}
```

If we do not need to trap a timeout or invalid session condition, getting a session is as simple as implementing the following line of code:

```
EnterpriseSession es = getEnterpriseSession();
```

From this point, when you have the `EnterpriseSession` object, using the session is the same as using an `HttpSession` object. Because we have implemented all the methods that are in an `HttpSession` object, using `EnterpriseSession` should not be any different. The example in the next section will demonstrate all of what we have learned in this chapter, including `EnterpriseSession`.

Session and Form Example with Multiple Applications

In this example we want to demonstrate how we use forms with the hidden input control, as well as how we use the base URL. We will also demonstrate how we use `EnterpriseSession`. Most importantly, we want to show how `EnterpriseSession` can take variables with the same name from two different applications and still know that the variables belong to different applications.

The example will consist of two applications, and thus two servlets: an accounting servlet and a human resources servlet. The goal of each application is to display a form that sets session variables and requests information from the user. When the form is submitted, the screen shows a greeting based on the information provided by the user, a session variable identifying the number of times the user has visited the page during the current session, and the contents of the other session variables (see Figure 3.4).

Both applications have essentially the same code to show that they use the same variable names. The accounting application's main and default servlet will be `AccountingServlet`, and it will contain two classes: `AccountingForm` and `AccountingResult`. We will name the `AccountingForm` and `AccountingResult` classes as our dispatch methods with `Method.form=AccountingForm` and `Method.result=AccountingResult` in the configuration file. In the accounting example, the base URL, which we will also set in the configuration file, will be `/servlet/Accounting`. The `AccountingServlet` configuration file will look like this:

```
# Configuration file for the accounting application
Default.Method=form
Method.form=AccountingForm
```

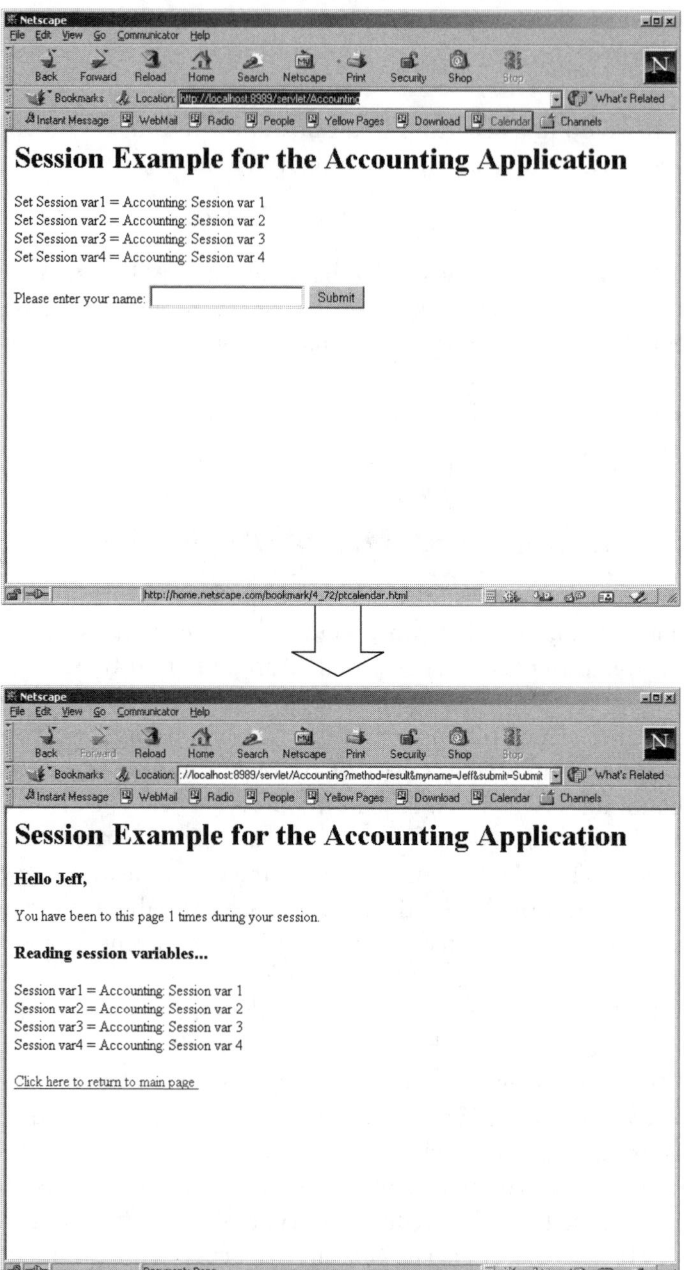

Figure 3.4 Flow of the sample application

```
Method.result= AccountingResult
# Change the following value to reflect the servlet
# that is executed in your servlet engine.
Application.Base.URL=/servlet/Accounting
```

The human resources application will look essentially the same. However, instead of using the name *Accounting* in the classes and configuration file, we will use *HR*. The configuration file for the human resources application will look like this:

```
# Configuration file for the HR application
Default.Method=form
Method.form=HRForm
Method.result=HRResult
# Change the following value to reflect the servlet
# that is executed in your servlet engine.
Application.Base.URL=/servlet/HR
```

Let's begin building the applications. We will start by creating the main servlet for the accounting application: `AccountingServlet`. This servlet will have no special configuration or destruction; therefore, the `initializeApp()` and `destroyApp()` methods will be blank. Listing 3.13 shows the code for `AccountingServlet`.

Listing 3.13 The accounting application's main servlet: `AccountingServlet`

```
import enterprise.servlet.*;
import enterprise.common.*;

import java.io.*;

public class AccountingServlet extends BaseEnterpriseServlet
{
  public void initializeApp(AppContext appContext) throws Exception
  {
  }

  public void destroyApp(AppContext appContext)
  {
  }

  public String getAppName()
  {
    return "Accounting";
  }
}
```

We will do the same for the HR application, except that in this case the main servlet will be called *HRServlet* (see Listing 3.14).

Listing 3.14 The HR application's main servlet: `HRServlet`

```
import enterprise.servlet.*;
import enterprise.common.*;

import java.io.*;

public class HRServlet extends BaseEnterpriseServlet
{
  public void initializeApp(AppContext appContext) throws Exception
  {
  }

  public void destroyApp(AppContext appContext)
  {
  }

  public String getAppName()
  {
    return "HR";
  }
}
```

In the main form of the accounting application, the class we wish to execute is `AccountingForm`. We set the corresponding method as the default method in the configuration file, and this is what will be executed when we go to the main page. We want to set four session variables—`sessionVar1`, `sessionVar2`, `sessionVar3`, and `sessionVar4`—to values that are specific to the accounting application. So we will include the *Accounting* name in the variable values. But before doing this, we need to get an `EnterpriseSession` object.

We will call `getEnterpriseSession()` to get the session, and we do not need to test for a timeout condition because this is the "doorway" to the application. In HTML, we will print out the session variable values to show that they have been set. We will also create a form requesting the user's name. We want this form to go to the `AccountingResult` class, which we defined as `result` for dispatch in the configuration file. Therefore, we will add a hidden input control named *method* and set the value to `result`. Listing 3.15 shows the code for `AccountingForm`.

Listing 3.15 The accounting application's main form class: `AccountingForm`

```
import enterprise.servlet.*;
import enterprise.common.*;

import java.io.*;

public class AccountingForm extends HTTPMethod
{

  public void execute()
  {
```

```
    try
    {
      PrintWriter out = m_response.getWriter();

      EnterpriseSession es = getEnterpriseSession();

      String sessionVar1 = "Accounting: Session var 1";
      String sessionVar2 = "Accounting: Session var 2";
      String sessionVar3 = "Accounting: Session var 3";
      String sessionVar4 = "Accounting: Session var 4";

      out.println("<HTML>");

      out.println("<BODY>");

      out.println("<H1>Session Example for the Accounting " +
                  "Application</H1>");

      out.println("<FORM method=\"get\" action=\"" +
          m_context.getAppBaseURL() + "\">");

      es.setAttribute("var1", sessionVar1);
      out.println("Set Session var1 = " + sessionVar1 + "<br>");
      es. setAttribute ("var2", sessionVar2);
      out.println("Set Session var2 = " + sessionVar2 + "<br>");
      es. setAttribute ("var3", sessionVar3);
      out.println("Set Session var3 = " + sessionVar3 + "<br>");
      es. setAttribute ("var4", sessionVar4);
      out.println("Set Session var4 = " + sessionVar4 + "<br>");
      out.println("<br>");

      out.println("Please enter your name:");
      out.println("<input type=\"hidden\" name=\"method\" " +
                  "value=\"result\">");

      out.println("<input type=\"text\" name=\"myname\" " +
                  "value=\"\">");

      out.println("<input type=\"submit\" name=\"submit\" " +
                  "value=\"Submit\">");

      out.println("</FORM>");

      out.println("</BODY>");

      out.println("</HTML>");

    } catch(Exception e)
    {
      e.printStackTrace();
    }
  }
}
```

We also need to build a main form for the human resources application, and the code should be identical to that for `AccountingForm`. The difference is that we will place the HR values inside the session variables to make these specific to the HR application. In addition, the title of the application will state that the application is the HR application. Listing 3.16 shows the code for this new class: `HRForm`.

Listing 3.16 The HR application's main form class: `HRForm`

```
import enterprise.servlet.*;
import enterprise.common.*;

import java.io.*;

public class HRForm extends HTTPMethod
{

  public void execute()
  {
    try
    {
      PrintWriter out = m_response.getWriter();

      EnterpriseSession es = getEnterpriseSession();

      String sessionVar1 = "HR: Session var 1";
      String sessionVar2 = "HR: Session var 2";
      String sessionVar3 = "HR: Session var 3";
      String sessionVar4 = "HR: Session var 4";

      out.println("<HTML>");

      out.println("<BODY>");

      out.println("<H1>Session Example for the HR" " +
                  "Application</H1>");

      out.println("<FORM method=\"get\" action=\"" +
          m_context.getAppBaseURL() + "\">");

      es.setAttribute ("var1", sessionVar1);
      out.println("Set Session var1 = " + sessionVar1 + "<br>");
      es.setAttribute ("var2", sessionVar2);
      out.println("Set Session var2 = " + sessionVar2 + "<br>");
      es.setAttribute ("var3", sessionVar3);
      out.println("Set Session var3 = " + sessionVar3 + "<br>");
      es.setAttribute ("var4", sessionVar4);
      out.println("Set Session var4 = " + sessionVar4 + "<br>");
      out.println("<br>");
```

```
        out.println("Please enter your name:");
        out.println("<input type=\"hidden\" name=\"method\" " +
                    "value=\"result\">");

        out.println("<input type=\"text\" name=\"myname\" " +
                    "value=\"\">");

        out.println("<input type=\"submit\" name=\"submit\" " +
                    "value=\"Submit\">");

        out.println("</FORM>");

        out.println("</BODY>");

        out.println("</HTML>");

      } catch(Exception e)
      {
        e.printStackTrace();
      }
    }
}
```

Now we need to code the result class. As defined in the configuration file, the results will be shown in the `AccountingResult` class. The objective of this class is to test for a timeout condition when we get the `EnterpriseSession` object, to display session variables, and to display a counter session variable that shows the number of times we have submitted the form.

We will start by retrieving the `EnterpriseSession` object. We want to detect a timeout condition here because this form depends on the four session variables that were to have been set in `AccountingForm`. We ask the API to detect a timeout condition by using the `getEnterpriseSession(true)` method call. A timeout condition will throw an `InvalidSessionException`, so when we request a session, we must wrap the call in a `try/catch` block. If this exception is thrown, we will display a message to the user stating that the session has timed out and that the user has not entered the application through the main page. If a timeout has not occurred, we will print out a greeting along with the four session variables we set in `AccountingForm`. We will also set a counter session variable to increment by one and display the result as the number of times we have been to this page in this session. Listing 3.17 shows the code for `AccountingResult`.

Listing 3.17 The accounting application's result class: `AccountingResult`

```
import enterprise.servlet.*;
import enterprise.common.*;

import java.io.*;
```

```
public class AccountingResult extends HTTPMethod
{

  public void execute()
  {
    try
    {
      PrintWriter out = m_response.getWriter();

      EnterpriseSession es = null;
      try
      {
        es = getEnterpriseSession(true);
      } catch (InvalidSessionException ise)
      {
        out.println("<HTML><BODY>");
        out.println("Your Session has timed out or you have not ");
        out.println("entered the Accounting application through " +
                    "the main page.");
        out.println("<A HREF=\"" + m_context.getAppBaseURL() + "\">");
        out.println("Click here to return to main page");
        out.println("</A>");
        out.println("</BODY></HTML>");
        return;
      }

      String myname = m_request.getParameter("myname");

      if ((myname == null) || (myname.trim().length() == 0))
      {
        myname = "N/A";
      }

      out.println("<HTML>");

      out.println("<BODY>");

      out.println("<H1>Session Example for the Accounting " +
                  "Application</H1>");

      out.println("<h3>Hello " + myname + ",</h3>");

      Integer counter = (Integer) es.getValue("count");
      if (counter == null)
      {
        counter = new Integer(0);
      }

      counter = new Integer(counter.intValue() + 1);
      es.setAttribute ("count", counter);
```

```
        out.println("You have been to this page " + counter +
                    " times during your session.<br>");

        out.println("<h3>Reading session variables...</h3>");
        out.println("Session var1 = " + es.getValue("var1") + "<br>");
        out.println("Session var2 = " + es.getValue("var2") + "<br>");
        out.println("Session var3 = " + es.getValue("var3") + "<br>");
        out.println("Session var4 = " + es.getValue("var4") + "<br>");
        out.println("<br>");

        out.println("<A HREF=\"" + m_context.getAppBaseURL() + "\">");
        out.println("Click here to return to main page");
        out.println("</A>");

        out.println("</BODY>");

        out.println("<HEAD>");
        out.println("<META HTTP-EQUIV=\"PRAGMA\" CONTENT=\ " +
                    "NO-CACHE\">");
        out.println("</HEAD>");

        out.println("</HTML>");

      } catch(Exception e)
      {
        e.printStackTrace();
      }
    }
}
```

Once again, we'll do the same for the HR application. We'll create a class called `HRResult` that duplicates the `AccountingResult` class. The main difference is the name of the class and the title of the page. Listing 3.18 shows the relevant code.

Listing 3.18 The HR application's result class: `HRResult`

```
import enterprise.servlet.*;
import enterprise.common.*;

import java.io.*;

public class HRResult extends HTTPMethod
{

  public void execute()
  {
    try
    {
      PrintWriter out = m_response.getWriter();
```

```
EnterpriseSession es = null;
try
{
  es = getEnterpriseSession(true);
} catch (InvalidSessionException ise)
{
  out.println("<HTML><BODY>");
  out.println("Your Session has timed out or you have not ");
  out.println("entered the HR application through the main ");
  out.println("page.");
  out.println("<A HREF=\"" + m_context.getAppBaseURL() + "\">");
  out.println("Click here to return to main page");
  out.println("</A>");
  out.println("</BODY></HTML>");
  return;
}

String myname = m_request.getParameter("myname");

if ((myname == null) || (myname.trim().length() == 0))
{
  myname = "N/A";
}

out.println("<HTML>");

out.println("<BODY>");

out.println("<H1>Session Example for the HR" +
            "Application</H1>");

out.println("<h3>Hello " + myname + ",</h3>");

Integer counter = (Integer) es.getValue("count");
if (counter == null)
{
  counter = new Integer(0);
}

counter = new Integer(counter.intValue() + 1);
es.setAttribute("count", counter);

out.println("You have been to this page " + counter +
            " times during your session.<br>");


out.println("<h3>Reading session variables...</h3>");
out.println("Session var1 = " + es.getValue("var1") + "<br>");
out.println("Session var2 = " + es.getValue("var2") + "<br>");
out.println("Session var3 = " + es.getValue("var3") + "<br>");
out.println("Session var4 = " + es.getValue("var4") + "<br>");
out.println("<br>");
```

```
        out.println("<A HREF=\"" + m_context.getAppBaseURL() + "\">");
        out.println("Click here to return to main page");
        out.println("</A>");

        out.println("</BODY>");

        out.println("<HEAD>");
        out.println("<META HTTP-EQUIV=\"PRAGMA\" CONTENT=\ " +
                    "NO-CACHE\">");
        out.println("</HEAD>");

        out.println("</HTML>");

      } catch(Exception e)
      {
        e.printStackTrace();
      }
    }
  }
```

To set up the applications, we register `AccountingServlet` and `HRServlet`—the two servlets—with the servlet container. We also have each of the servlet's initialization arguments contain a `ConfFile` parameter that points to the appropriate configuration file. In each configuration file, we also want to be sure that the base URL specified in `Application.Base.URL` is the one that will respond to a servlet call. ServletExec requires that */servlet* be part of the URL. In WebLogic or its aliases, registering the servlet may negate the requirement of having the */servlet* in the URL. For example, in a configuration file with some servlet containers, the base-URL statement in the accounting configuration file would look like this:

```
Application.Base.URL=/servlet/AccountingServlet
```

With other servlet containers, or if we used an alias name in the servlet container (aliasing allows us to create an alias to a servlet so that we do not need to include */servlet* in the URL), the base-URL statement would look like this instead:

```
Application.Base.URL=/AccountingServlet
```

We would set up `HRServlet`'s configuration file in the same way.

When you're ready to try the example, go to each application and see how the enterprise servlet architecture panned out. You will notice that it appears you are given two separate sessions—one for the HR application and one for the accounting application. The session variables do not clash with each other, even though it appears that they are named the same.

In the form classes (AccountingForm and HRForm), we used a GET method for submitting the form so that you can test the timeout features of the applications. You do this by going to one of the applications and submitting the form. The results page will show the entire URL in the address field of your browser. Copy this line and shut down your browser. Start a new instance of your browser and paste in the URL that you copied. The server should return with the timeout HTML that we defined in the result classes we developed.

Another way to try the timeout is to wait the default amount of time that the server times out a session, or set this value to a lower value in your servlet engine. Keep in mind, however, that the main forms of these applications will create a new session because these are the doorways to our applications. By going to the main forms first, you will never receive a timeout condition.

Summary

In this chapter we learned about the different form submission types. We discussed the differences in how GET and POST package submissions and described the advantages and disadvantages of these two methods. There are essentially two techniques for submitting forms within the enterprise servlet architecture. One is to code method=<method dispatch name> into the action parameter of the <FORM> tag. Although this technique is straightforward and clean, it does not work well with GET submissions. The other technique is to use a hidden input control in the form that is named *method* and the method dispatch name as the value. This technique works for both GET and POST submissions.

We also learned that applications may move through different environments from development to testing to production. These environments may contain different URLs and different servlet engines. Changing environments and servers can affect the HTML generated in the servlets. The base-URL concept allows us to configure the base server and servlet call into applications through a configuration file parameter. This makes it easy to make changes to the server and servlet container environments. By changing the Application.Base.URL configuration file parameter, we are able to dynamically change the generated HTML to fit the servlet environment.

Because forms typically go with sessions, we learned about the pitfalls of using a shared session in a multiapplication environment and about the potential of session variables to clash. In viewing the anomalies of implementing sessions with multiple applications on a single server, we were able to design the EnterpriseSession object. This object allows us to encapsulate session variables and uniquely identify variables across applications, even though they appear to have the same name. Using `EnterpriseSession` is nearly the same as using `HttpSession`, and the variable encapsulation is transparent to the end user. Integrating the management of `EnterpriseSession` into the `HTTPMethod` class allowed us to develop a couple of ways of retrieving an `EnterpriseSession` object and gave us a choice of detecting a timeout condition or simply creating a session object without issue.

CHAPTER 4

HTML with Templates

What exactly are *templates?* We hear about them in many facets of life. When we were kids, we used templates to help us draw a perfect circle or square. When we use a word processor, we sometimes use a template to put together a document or a fax cover page. The U.S. government uses templates to print money, and Visa uses templates to press credit cards. We use templates often in our everyday lives. Templates help us build, make, or do something that is normally complex. Imagine if the U.S. government didn't use templates to print money; it would take forever to draw each dollar bill individually! Templates simplify some of our tasks and allow us to concentrate on completing the product.

It should be no surprise that in software development we also have a fairly large need for templates. Developers who have programmed in C++ may have used templates as part of their code. The C++ Standard Template Library contains templates of code that allow the developer to avoid "reinventing the wheel" when using linked lists, arrays, and other common objects of programming. A template allows the user to declare types within its declaration, and the template appears to contain customized code according to the declaration. For Web developers, however, the need for templates lies in manufacturing HTML. Often we reuse the same set of HTML in servlets, particularly with headers and footers. Given the complexities of today's HTML, the result can be a lot of code.

This chapter will demonstrate the use of templates in the enterprise servlet architecture, showing how they can considerably decrease the amount of code that is needed to develop HTML in servlets. We will look at nesting templates (i.e., building templates within templates) to help reproduce complex HTML with only a few lines of the Java programming language code. Finally, we will examine ways to tune the Web server's use of templates through cacheable template objects that are stored in memory for rapid retrieval.

Using Templates

In today's Internet environment, Web pages are becoming more and more complex. As competition heats up among companies vying for attention, they are coming up with more and more creative ways to dazzle us in our Web experience. Encountering these rich-looking Web pages as we surf the Internet has raised our expectations, and these high expectations have extended to the corporation. Gone are the days when a drab and average Web page that just listed data was considered acceptable in the workplace. When we present a time-and-expense Web application to the vice president of finance, she wants it to have the same dazzle as we get when we shop at Amazon.com. However, this rich content comes at a price: very large and complex HTML pages. With Dynamic HTML (DHTML), JavaScript, and multinested tables, it is not uncommon for an HTML page to be several thousand lines long.

What does this mean for servlet developers? Under a standard servlet paradigm—which is taught through the multitude of "how to be a servlet developer in three hours" books—we would need to code all HTML in the servlet. This approach is fine for simple HTML, but not for a 4,000-line, spectacular-looking HTML page. Could you imagine coding 4,000 `println` statements to get a single page of HTML to the end user? In addition, just after this monster was coded, what if marketing came down to the development team and said, "Hey, we just changed the layout and the look and feel of our site. Can you guys implement these changes?" No doubt a few of the developers' resumes would be floating around.

With templates, we take a complex HTML page, reuse the HTML, substitute data as appropriate, and send the result to the end user. The template itself is an HTML page. Usually placeholders in the HTML tell the developer where to substitute the real data. The developer reads in the template, searches for the data placeholders, and replaces them with the real data.

Anyone who has used Active Server Pages (ASP) or JavaServer Pages (JSP) has used the most advanced template engines there are. In addition to having HTML pages with placeholders that are substituted by the engine, ASP and JSP usually are backed up by some kind of language. The HTML can have loops, `where` clauses, and all sorts of other neat code. In addition to JSP and ASP, a few sophisticated template engines that can be downloaded for free on the Internet have their own customized "template language."

JSP and ASP are excellent technologies, but it is easy to mix too much code with the content. There are two reasons for avoiding too much content and code in the same file. First, as the HTML becomes more complex and the code that generates the HTML becomes more intricate, it becomes very difficult to read and maintain the file. Second, and more importantly, developers don't always write the bulk of the HTML anymore. In many corporate environments a marketing department is in charge of HTML layout and graphic design, and the IT group develops applications with the HTML that was created by Marketing according to Marketing's specifications. In other words, Marketing manages content, and IT is in charge of development.

With one of the scripting languages, such as ASP or JSP, parts of the program become an integral part of the HTML, and changing or rearranging HTML can become a difficult process. In addition, Marketing seldom has the knowledge or skill to understand the code that has become part of the HTML. For this reason, I am strongly opposed to mixing heavy amounts of code and content. A content manager should be responsible for changes to the look and feel of an application. Technologies such as JSP are a major breakthrough for the Web development community, but they can easily be abused if too much code is mixed with HTML. Maintaining the code can quickly become a nightmare in this scenario.

JSP as a Template Engine

Am I discouraging the use of JSP? Absolutely not. JSP is a very viable technology. It allows for a simple way to implement some fantastic and powerful dynamic pages very quickly. In many production sites, JSP has been used to create dynamic HTML for information and lightweight processing purposes, and the heavy processing load has been delegated to servlets. When a Web server compiles a JSP, it is creating the source code for a servlet, compiling that code into its byte code, and running it as a Java servlet behind the scenes. So a JSP is nothing more than a servlet in disguise. I like this technology! JSP and servlets are cousins that work together to bring us a robust Web site.

We write servlets for the more intense processing because servlets allow for finer-grained control over applications. JSP and servlets are excellent complements in a Java-based Web system. JSPs can handle lightweight user interaction—login, information pages, feedback forms, and so on—which does not require heavy coding. Servlets handle heavy database processing, customer processing, order control, and so on. On many sites the two technologies are used in exactly this fashion.

JSP is very powerful when used with JavaBeans and tag library objects, and quite a lot can be completed with JSP. Is it better to use JSP than to use servlets—or vice versa—in some circumstances? This is a tough question; the answer depends on the application and design. JSP can do a lot with the tag library and JavaBeans, but will some pages have a lot of scriptlet code and be code intensive? In this situation a servlet may be more appropriate so that those who edit content don't become confused or need to learn any Java. Servlets also should be used when frequent modification and processing of intensive code may not be necessary.

Deciding whether to code an application in JSP or servlets is easy. The answer is both. But the question of which functions of an application should be handled by JSP and which by a servlet does not necessarily have a correct answer. It depends on the design and the intended function of the JSP or servlet.

Why do we need to have templates in our servlets when we can just have JSP do all of the template work? The reason is that the use of JSP involves an extra step. Often JSPs delegate control, pass parameters, and forward information to a servlet for finer-grained processing. It is much simpler to have the servlet produce the HTML itself in this circumstance, rather than having the servlet send the HTML back to a JSP. Because typically we write servlets so that they output *something* to the user, we might as well have them create the HTML when they are called. Therefore, a good approach is to use JSP to output most of the lightweight workload and content that is not code intensive but, when using servlets to handle the heavy stuff, to let the servlet be responsible for its own HTML.

Placing HTML in servlets inline and scattered throughout the code—that is, mixing HTML and code in servlets—should be taboo. It is even messier to write HTML in a servlet than in a JSP, and the maintainability of the HTML is horrible. So just as with JSP, when creating HTML for servlets we should separate the code and the HTML content.

Developing a Template Engine

If we are separating content from code, it makes sense to make each template all HTML, with placeholders for dynamic content. By using templates, we can allow the content manager to build the HTML in any fashion, place the proper placeholders in the HTML, and submit this HTML to IT to use in a system. How should we do this? Let's start by looking at some HTML and defining what a template may look like and what a placeholder is. Figure 4.1 shows an HTML page containing personalized data. The personalized content is easily identifiable. The name, Jeff, that is used a couple of times on the page, and the Place, City, and State values would probably be easily substitutable. The rest is pure HTML. How do we know where to substitute data? We use placeholders.

Let's examine what a placeholder does and what it should look like. A *placeholder* is a piece of text that tells the template engine to substitute a value in that location. It should be text that is not common in ordinary language or

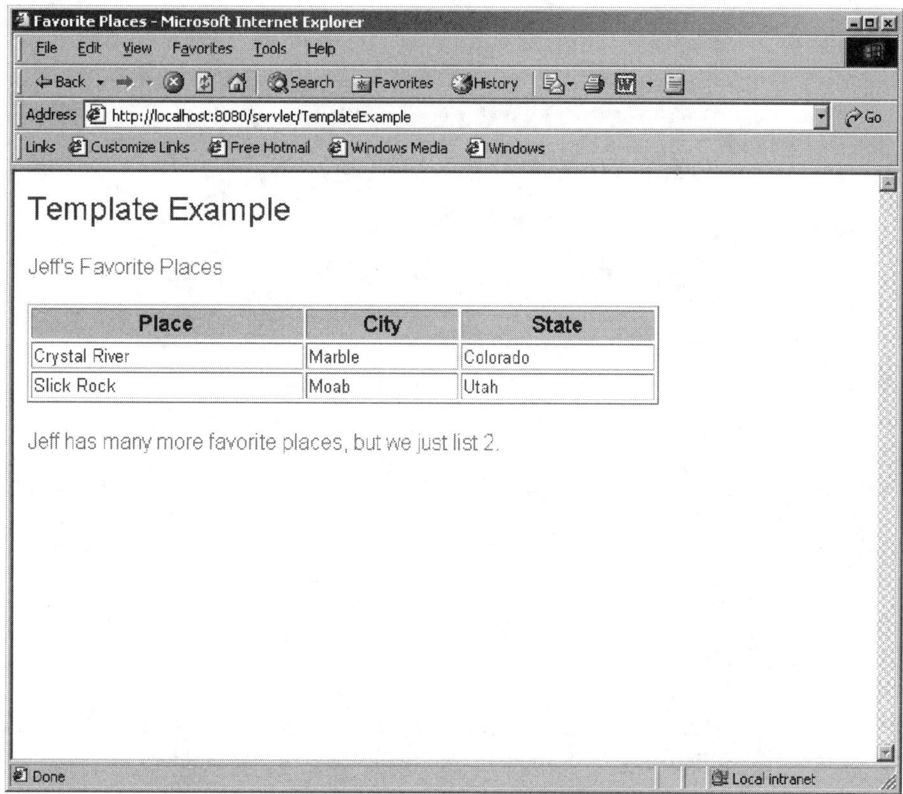

Figure 4.1 Sample browser view of complex HTML

in HTML. For example, neither *<HTML>* nor the word *the* would make a good placeholder because one is commonly used in HTML and the other is used in ordinary language. In addition, choices such as these would not help us differentiate among different placeholders on an HTML page.

An alternative is to have a syntax that allows inclusion of a variable or name as part of the placeholder itself. We also need to tell the engine that this is a placeholder, so we need a flag that passes this information to the engine. We can enclose a name with *${}*. For example, we could name the placeholder for a city *${CITY}*. Why did we choose *${}*? It is highly unlikely that any text in HTML will match *${*. HTML does not have reserved words that match *${*, and very few contexts in ordinary language use this combination.

In any context in which this combination is possible (e.g., accounting or other financial scenarios), another combination can be used—for example, **{* or *^&*. In most cases, however, the *${* combination should be safe—a fact borne out by extensive experience. Figure 4.2 shows the page from Figure 4.1 with placeholders instead of the dynamic content.

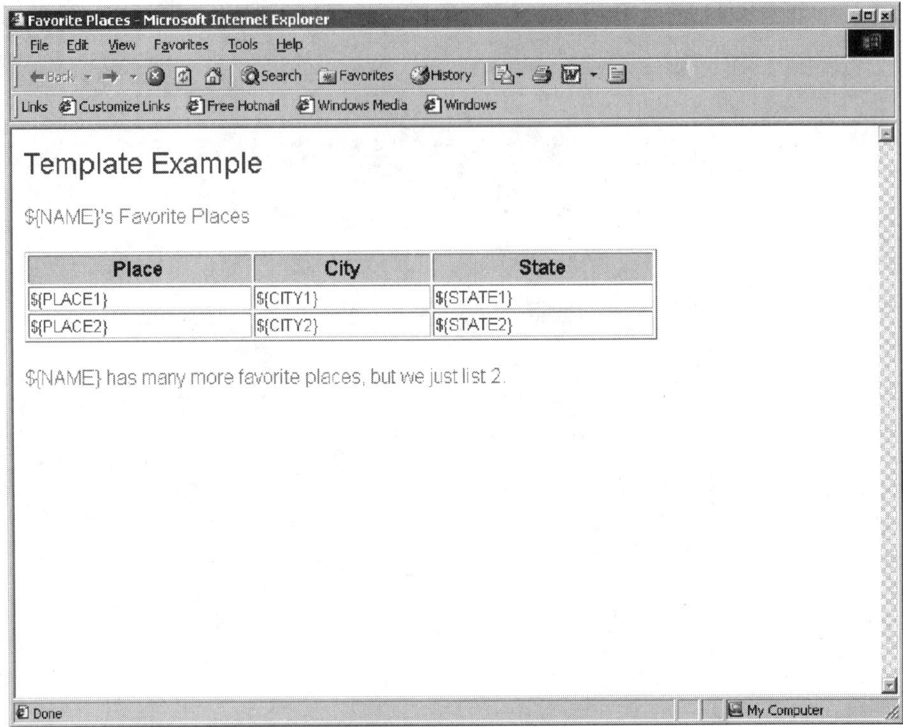

Figure 4.2 Sample HTML template with placeholders

Notice that the HTML now contains *${}* variable placeholders where the data should go. This is exactly what a content designer such as a graphic artist or marketing department could create for IT. There is no need for code, and the *${}* variables would tell the IT department where to place the data. The HTML that is created for Figure 4.2 (see Listing 4.1) shows what would be created by a content organization, along with the HTML placeholders (set in boldface).

Listing 4.1 An HTML template with placeholders

```
<html>
<head>
<title>Favorite Places</title>
</head>

<body bgcolor="#FFFFFF">
<p><font face="Arial, Helvetica, sans-serif" size="5"
color="#0000FF">
Template Example</font></p>
<p><font face="Arial, Helvetica, sans-serif"
color="#FF0000">${NAME}'s Favorite Places</font></p>
```

```
<table width="75%" border="1">
  <tr>
    <th bgcolor="#CCCCCC">
      <div align="center"><font face="Arial, Helvetica,
      sans-serif">Place</font></div>
    </th>
    <th bgcolor="#CCCCCC">
      <div align="center"><font face="Arial, Helvetica,
      sans-serif">City</font></div>
    </th>
    <th bgcolor="#CCCCCC">
      <div align="center"><font face="Arial, Helvetica,
      sans-serif">State</font></div>
    </th>
  </tr>
  <tr>
    <td><font color="#0000FF" face="Arial, Helvetica, sans-serif"
    size="2">${PLACE1}</font></td>
    <td><font color="#0000FF" face="Arial, Helvetica, sans-serif"
    size="2">${CITY1}</font></td>
    <td><font color="#0000FF" face="Arial, Helvetica, sans-serif"
    size="2">${STATE1}</font></td>
  </tr>
  <tr>
    <td><font color="#0000FF" face="Arial, Helvetica, sans-serif"
    size="2">${PLACE2}</font></td>
    <td><font color="#0000FF" face="Arial, Helvetica, sans-serif"
    size="2">${CITY2}</font></td>
    <td><font color="#0000FF" face="Arial, Helvetica, sans-serif"
    size="2">${STATE2}</font></td>
  </tr>
</table>
<p><font color="#FF0000" face="Arial, Helvetica, sans-serif">${NAME}
has many more favorite places, but we just list
  2.</font></p>
</body>
</html>
```

Notice that Listing 4.1 contains a lot of HTML. Could you imagine hard-coding this as a part of the code in a servlet—that is, creating a `println` statement for each line of HTML? As developers, we should be concerned with only the placeholders and substituting the values. We do this by building a template engine. How do we know where to place the data? That is, how does the template engine know where to substitute the values? We'll go through this process step by step. We need to build a template engine that will allow us to set the placeholder value names, read a template, parse the HTML into its two subcomponents (clear-text HTML and substitutable values), and then output this HTML to the user.

Let's look at how the engine will find the placeholders. We need to build a parser that identifies four types of objects in a template: clear text, *${* (which

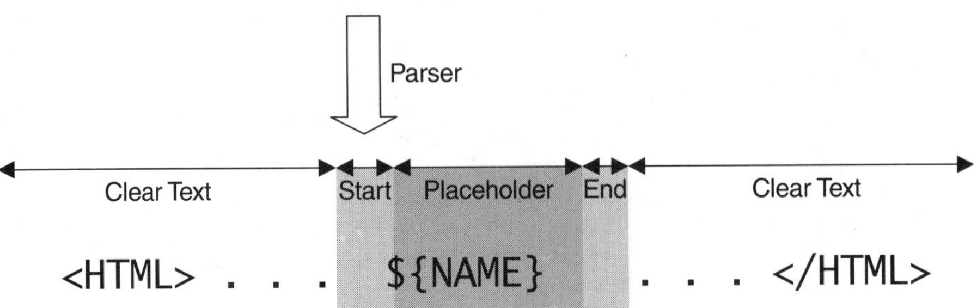

Figure 4.3 The different parts of a template identified by a parser

identifies the start of a placeholder name), the placeholder variable name, and *}* (which signifies the end of a placeholder name). We must have the parser identify each of these sections by placing itself into different *states*. Figure 4.3 depicts how the parser will identify the different parts of the template.

The parser will begin by taking the template and reading each character. We start the template in `TEXT` (clear text) mode because this is the default state. We append each character we find to a clear-text buffer. The parser is looking for a dollar sign (*$*), which is a signal to change state. When we find one, we go into `DOLLAR` state. This is a temporary state in that the next character that is read will determine whether we go back to the `TEXT` state or into a different state. Our placeholders always begin with *${*. Therefore, if we are in `DOLLAR` state (i.e., we found a dollar sign) and the next character is not *{*, then we have not found a placeholder, so we go back to the `TEXT` state and append the *$* and the current character to the clear-text buffer. If the next character is *{*, then we have found a placeholder and we go into `FIELDNAME` state. From here we begin appending characters into a field name buffer. We are now looking for *}* to end the field name. The character *}* also tells us to switch the state back to `TEXT`. The process continues until the entire template has been processed. This is essentially how the template parser works.

When we run the parser, we need to look at each placeholder and see if we want to replace it with data. So we need to create a list of values and placeholders that we wish to replace when the parser finds them in the HTML. We create this list before running the parser, probably in some form of a `Properties` object. When we find a field name while parsing the data, we look up the field name or placeholder in the `Properties` object, and if we find it, we append this value to the output buffer. Because this process is a bit complicated, let's look at some pseudocode of the parser.

First we need to write a `substitute()` method that allows us to create a list of placeholders and values.

```
Declare the Properties pList as a member variable of the class.

Public void substitute(name_of_placeholder, value_to_substitute)
{
   Add or replace the value of the placeholder in the pList.
}
```

This method allows the developer to create a list of placeholder names and their associated values. Now let's look at the parser's pseudocode.

```
Public StringBuffer parse()
{
  Create a StringBuffer object named output.
  Create a StringBuffer object named fieldname.

  Place ourselves in TEXT mode as a default and begin reading the
  template file.

For each character in the file
  Look at each character
     If it is a "$"
    {
        Are we currently in a DOLLAR state?
        {
          No - Then put us in the DOLLAR state.
          Yes - Then this is not the start of a placeholder, so
          append the "$" to the output buffer
                    and return us to TEXT state.
        }
    }
     If it is a "{"
    {
        Are we currently in a DOLLAR state?
        {
          No - Then just append the "{" to the output buffer.
          Yes - Then put us in the FIELDNAME state.
        }
    }
     If it is a "}"
    {
       Are we currently in a FIELDNAME state?
       {
        Yes - Then end the field name buffer and replace the value,
        and place us in TEXT mode.
         {
           Look up the field name in the pList. Did we find a
           value?
           {
             Yes - Then append the value to the output buffer.
             No - Then don't do anything.
           }
         }
```

```
        No - Then are we currently in a DOLLAR state?
         {
           Yes - Then the "$" was not the beginning of a
           placeholder,
                      so append the "$" and the "}" to the output
                      buffer, and return us to
                      TEXT state.
           No - Then just append the "{" to the output buffer.
         }
      }
   }
   For all other characters
   {
      Are we currently in a FIELDNAME state?
      {
        Yes - Then append the character to the field name buffer.
        No - Then are we currently in a DOLLAR state?
        {
          Yes - Then the "$" was not the beginning of a
          placeholder,
                     so append the "$" and the "}" to the output
                     buffer, and return us to
                     TEXT state.
          No - Then just append the character to the output buffer
        }
   }
   Return the output buffer to the developer.
```

Whew! That's one heck of an algorithm! But actually it's quite simple. It checks each character's type, looks at the current state, and acts on the answer. It's a big algorithm because it needs to account for every case it might encounter.

Now that we have a good understanding of how the template engine works, let's build one.

The HTMLTemplate Object

Let's begin by building a simple template object that allows us to add placeholder/value combinations and parse the template. First let's look at what we require of a template engine. We need a method that allows the developer to add a placeholder and a value. We need a parsing routine that implements the pseudocode shown in the previous section. We should also have helper and convenience methods that (1) send the parsed HTML to the user and (2) return `String` and `StringBuffer` values of the parsed HTML.

Let's call the new object `HTMLTemplate` and have it reside in a new package in the enterprise servlet library named `enterprise.html`. In this package we will place anything that has to do with HTML generation or utilities. Let's begin by declaring the object and some important constants.

```
package enterprise.html;

import java.io.*;
import java.util.*;

public class HTMLTemplate
{
  private static final int TEXT = 0;
  private static final int DOLLAR = 1;
  private static final int FIELDNAME = 2;
```

These constants help us declare states for the parser and make reading the code a little easier. We also need to declare member variables. When we wrote the pseudocode, we knew that we needed a `Properties` object to contain placeholder names and associated `String` values. We also need a variable to hold the path and filename of the template.

```
  private Properties          pList  = null;
  private String              sFName = null;
```

Let's create the constructor. The constructor will take the template filename and path as parameters. It will initialize the `pList` object in preparation to getting the list of placeholders and values and will store the filename in the `sFName` member variable.

```
  public HTMLTemplate(String fName)
     throws IOException
  {
    pList  = new Properties();

    if (fName == null)
    {
      throw new IOException("Filename passed to HTMLTemplate is null");
    }

    sFName = fName;
  }
```

Now we need a method that allows the developer to create the placeholder and value substitution list. We will call this method `substitute()`, and the parameters will be the placeholder name and an associated `String` value. This method will check to see that we have not passed any `null` values because a `Properties` object does not handle `null` values very well. We will then call the `Properties` object's `put()` method to add and replace the placeholder in the list.

As we put the placeholder in the list, we will convert it to uppercase so that when we compare values during parsing, case does not matter.

```
public void substitute(String var, String str)
{
  if (var != null)
  {
    if (str != null)
    {
      pList.put(var.toUpperCase(), str);
    }
    else
    {
      pList.put(var.toUpperCase(), "");
    }
  }
}
```

Now we're ready to develop the parser. The method, which we'll call `parseFile()`, will return a `StringBuffer` object of the fully substituted HTML from the template. However, let's declare this method private because we will develop some accessor methods that are more standardized in Java for creating `String` or `StringBuffer` objects. Methods called `toString()` and `toStringBuffer()` will call the `parseFile()` method. Creating these methods gives us tools that are a little more common and helps developers understand basically how the object works. The `parseFile()` method will be responsible for opening the HTML template and reading it into a memory `StringBuffer` object. After loading the template, `parseFile()` will call a `parse()` method to actually parse the HTML. First let's declare the method and some memory objects.

```
private StringBuffer parseFile() throws IOException
{
  char cBuf[] = new char[4096];
  int  cLen = 0;
  FileReader fr;

  StringBuffer sBuf = new StringBuffer();
```

We have created a character buffer of 4,096 bytes, which speeds things up by allowing the file to be read in 4,096 blocks at a time. We have also declared the `StringBuffer` object into which we will load the memory. The next thing we need to do is begin reading the file. We will read the file in the blocks that we declared; then we'll call the `parse()` method, which we'll develop later in this section.

```
    try
    {
      fr = new FileReader(sFName);
    } catch(FileNotFoundException e)
    {
      throw new IOException("Cannot find file:" + sFName);
    }

    while ((cLen = fr.read(cBuf)) > 0)
    {
      for (int c = 0; c < cLen; c++)
      {
        sBuf.append(cBuf[c]);
      }
    }

    fr.close();

    return parse(sBuf);
  }
```

Now let's make the magic happen. We will turn the pseudocode defined in the previous section into Java code. The `parse()` method will take as a parameter a `StringBuffer` object that contains the entire contents of the HTML template that was read in by the `parseFile()` method. It will return a `StringBuffer` object containing the replaced and final HTML.

NOTE: Why are we using so many `StringBuffer` objects? Why don't we just use `String` objects? In Web development, creating and destroying objects require a lot of overhead. Each time we concatenate a `String` object, a new `String` object is created and the previous one is destroyed. Therefore, when we're concatenating a lot of `String` objects, there will be a large amount of creation and destruction. These processes not only fragment memory, but they make a lot of work for the garbage collector, and they weaken the performance of the application. We are much better off appending to the end of a `StringBuffer` object; then if we need a `String` object, we need to create it only once. This approach streamlines the use of memory and gives the garbage collector a break.

Let's declare the `parse()` method and create some local variables that will be important to running this method. We will declare a `StringBuffer` object called `output` that will contain the final, replaced HTML. We will also create some temporary `StringBuffer` objects that will hold the blocks of clear text and field names.

```
private StringBuffer parse(StringBuffer sBuf) throws IOException
{
  StringBuffer output = new StringBuffer();

  int length = sBuf.length();
  StringBuffer fieldBuf = new StringBuffer();
  StringBuffer clearBuf = new StringBuffer();
  char charRead;
```

Now let's implement the pseudocode and turn it into Java code. We'll start by setting the default state to TEXT.

```
  int state = TEXT;

  for (int i = 0; i < length; i++)
  {
    switch (charRead = sBuf.charAt(i))
    {
      case ('$'):
        if (state == DOLLAR)
        {
          clearBuf.append("$");
        }
        state = DOLLAR;
        break;
      case ('{'):
        if (state == DOLLAR)
        {
          if (clearBuf.length() > 0)
          {
            output.append(clearBuf);
          }
          clearBuf.setLength(0);
          fieldBuf.setLength(0);
          state = FIELDNAME;
        }
        else
        {
          clearBuf.append(charRead);
          state = TEXT;
        }
        break;
      case ('}'):
        if (state == FIELDNAME)
        {
          if (fieldBuf.length() != 0)
          {
            // Compare the placeholder by first making it uppercase
            // so that case will not matter.
            String parm = pList.getProperty(
                             fieldBuf.toString().toUpperCase());
```

```
              if (parm == null)
              {
                parm = "";
              }

              output.append(parm);
            }
            else
            {
              clearBuf.append("${}");
            }
            state = TEXT;
          }
          else
          {
            if (state == DOLLAR)
            {
              clearBuf.append("$");
              state = TEXT;
            }

            clearBuf.append(charRead);
          }
          break;
        default:
          if (state == FIELDNAME)
          {
            fieldBuf.append(charRead);
          }
          else
          {
            if (state == DOLLAR)
            {
              clearBuf.append("$");
              state = TEXT;
            }
            clearBuf.append(charRead);
          }
          break;
      }
    }

    if (clearBuf.length() > 0)
    {
      output.append(clearBuf);
    }
```

Finally, we'll clean up after ourselves, setting the scratch variable to zero and releasing the objects by setting the buffers to `null`. Then we'll take the final HTML that we built in the `output StringBuffer` object and return it to the user.

```
    clearBuf.setLength(0);
    clearBuf = null;
    fieldBuf.setLength(0);
    fieldBuf = null;
    sBuf.setLength(0);
    sBuf = null;

    return output;
  }
```

To finish developing the HTMLTemplate class, let's define the accessor and helper methods. We want the developer to call toStringBuffer() or toString() to return the final, parsed HTML. The toStringBuffer() method will call the private parseFile() method and will return the parsed HTML to the developer. The toString() method is even simpler. When we call toString(), it will call toStringBuffer(), which will return a StringBuffer object. Then we will call toString() on the StringBuffer object to convert the final StringBuffer object into a String object. Finally, we will return this String to the developer.

```
  public StringBuffer toStringBuffer()
      throws IOException
  {
    return parseFile();
  }

  public String toString()
  {
    try
    {
      return toStringBuffer().toString();
    } catch(IOException e)
    {
      e.printStackTrace();
      return null;
    }
  }
```

The helper method doHTML() allows the developer to pass in the servlet's PrintWriter object, and it sends the output to the client. Although this method isn't really necessary, it makes using the PrintWriter object a little easier. We will also flush the PrintWriter object because sometimes the entire contents of the output buffer stay in the buffer, especially with a large amount of data. By calling flush() we guarantee that the full output buffer is sent to the client.

```
  public void doHTML(PrintWriter out)
     throws IOException
  {
```

```
        out.print(this.toString());
        out.flush();
    }
}
```

Now that we have created the HTMLTemplate object, let's look at how we use it. First we construct the HTMLTemplate with a path and a filename. Then we call the substitute() method with the name of the placeholder and the string that will replace the placeholder.

NOTE: Why do we include \\ in our paths? In Java, just as in C, a backslash is considered a flag for a control or special character. For example, when we print a string and we wish to add a new-line character to it, we append *\n*. When the string contains a Microsoft-based directory, we need to use the backslash a lot. But when we do this in Java strings, the virtual machine thinks that we want to use the backslash as a control character in the strings. Therefore, a path such as *C:\nicks project* will look like *C:<NEWLINE>icks project* to the Java Virtual Machine, and an error may occur. To prevent the error, we use \\ in the strings when we truly need a backslash. Thus in our example here the path should be coded as *C:\\nicks project.*

When we're ready to produce the HTML, we pass the response object PrintWriter to the doHTML() method, and voilà! We have sent the template to the user. What follows is a typical example of code that we would use for HTMLTemplate. This code loads a template named template.html and replaces the placeholder NAME with the value George; then it sends the output back to the client.

```
HTMLTemplate ht = new
                    HTMLTemplate("C:\\myTemplates\\template.html"));

ht.substitute("NAME", "George");

PrintWriter out = m_response.getWriter();
ht.doHTML(out);
```

Not bad! A template with substituted values for the placeholders in just a few lines of code. This sure beats coding the entire HTML inline in the servlet. Note also that the HTML templates no longer need to be the responsibility of the developer. A content management group such as a marketing department or a graphic designer can design the HTML layout and the look and feel using a favorite editor (e.g., Macromedia Dreamweaver or Microsoft FrontPage) and put the placeholders where text will appear. This is a simple solution to a classic problem in Web development.

Templates with Enterprise Servlets

Now that we have an understanding of how `HTMLTemplate` is used, let's create an example with enterprise servlets that will produce the HTML output in Figure 4.1 from the template that is defined in Listing 4.1. In this example the template from Listing 4.1 will be read in, and the placeholders will be replaced with real data. The dispatch servlet will be called `TemplateExample`, and we will have one method defined as `show`, which will be a class named `ShowTemplate`.

Let's start with the configuration file and define some of the application's parameters. We'll create a configuration file, `TemplateExample.config`, that will contain the following data:

```
# Configuration file
Default.Method=show
Method.show=ShowTemplate
Application.Base.URL=/servlet/TemplateExample

# Substitute your path to the HTML in the following parameter.
MyTemplate=C:\\Book\\Chapter 04\\Example 1\\templates\\myplaces.html

# Place your name in the following parameter.
MyName=Jeff
```

Note that it is important to place template location information in the configuration file. Just as we learned in Chapter 3 about the base URL, it is important to keep paths and filenames in a configuration file so that we can easily move the application to another machine that may have a different directory structure. In addition, we can change the names of the templates as we update them, so we can make changes without recompiling. Of course, if you are using a PC-based system, remember to include \\ in the path if it contains a backslash.

Now let's create the base dispatch servlet. As usual, this is the main servlet, and it will inherit `BaseEnterpriseServlet`. We have no special initialization or destruction, so these methods will be left empty. The name of the application will be *TemplateExample,* so this is the string we will return from the `getAppName()` method. Listing 4.2 shows the code for the base dispatch servlet, `TemplateExample`.

Listing 4.2 The `TemplateExample` main base servlet

```
import enterprise.servlet.*;
import enterprise.common.*;

import java.io.*;
```

```
public class TemplateExample extends BaseEnterpriseServlet
{
  public void initializeApp(AppContext appContext) throws Exception
  {
  }

  public void destroyApp(AppContext appContext)
  {
  }

  public String getAppName()
  {
    return "TemplateExample1";
  }
}
```

In the configuration file we want the default method to be the `ShowTemplate` class. `ShowTemplate`'s responsibility will be to load the template and substitute the variables. We have eight placeholders and seven substitutions. But how can this be? Look closely at the template in Listing 4.1. In this template, `NAME` appears twice, so one substitution will replace both placeholders. Therefore, we have eight placeholders, six of which are different, and one of which is a duplicate placeholder, so only seven substitutions need to be made.

In the `ShowTemplate` class we will pull the template name from the configuration file. Remember that in the configuration file we created a customized parameter named `MyTemplate` that points to the path and filename of the template. So we will call the `getValue()` method from `AppContext` to retrieve this value. We also created a custom parameter in the configuration file for the name that will be displayed, and we called this parameter `MyName`. We will also retrieve `MyName`'s value from the configuration file. `ShowTemplate` will then make the substitutions and output the HTML to the client. Listing 4.3 shows the code for `ShowTemplate`.

Listing 4.3 The `ShowTemplate` class

```
import enterprise.servlet.*;
import enterprise.common.*;
import enterprise.html.*;

import java.io.*;

public class ShowTemplate extends HTTPMethod
{

  public void execute()
  {
    try
    {
      PrintWriter out = m_response.getWriter();
```

```
            ht.substitute("NAME", m_context.getValue("MyName"));

            ht.substitute("PLACE1", "Crystal River");
            ht.substitute("CITY1", "Marble");
            ht.substitute("STATE1", "Colorado");
            ht.substitute("PLACE2", "Slick Rock");
            ht.substitute("CITY2", "Moab");
            ht.substitute("STATE2", "Utah");

            ht.doHTML(out);

        } catch(Exception e)
        {
            e.printStackTrace();
        }
    }
}
```

Now let's set up the application. In the servlet engine we need to register the servlet and set the initialization arguments to contain the following: *ConfFile=<Place your path to the TemplateExample.config file here>*. Once this is done, launch the browser to execute the servlet; you should see the Web page shown in Figure 4.1. Wasn't that easy? All of that HTML goes to the user in just a few lines of code!

Nesting Templates

As we just saw, creating a template and substituting the values with an `HTMLTemplate` object is incredibly simple. Using a template helps define the line between content and code. However, a good look at the code and the HTML reveals that we are essentially substituting values in a table. This is a good approach for a static table that never changes, but what about a dynamic table? What if we want this table to be able to grow to accommodate more data? What if we're querying a database and want to substitute the database record for each row?

There are basically two ways to create a table dynamically. With both scenarios we need to change the table definition to allow dynamic creation of the content. We do this by removing the part of the table that we need to create dynamically and replacing it with a placeholder. For example, in the template in Listing 4.1, we would remove the `<td>` tags and the `<tr>` tags that enclose them, as well as the HTML between these tags, and replace all this with a `${TABLE_CONTENT}` placeholder. Listing 4.4 shows the code for the new template.

Listing 4.4 An HTML template that allows for dynamic table content

```
<html>
<head>
<title>Favorite Places</title>
</head>

<body bgcolor="#FFFFFF">
<p><font face="Arial, Helvetica, sans-serif" size="5"
color="#0000FF">Nested Template
  Example</font></p>
<p><font face="Arial, Helvetica, sans-serif"
color="#FF0000">${NAME}'s Favorite Places</font></p>
<table width="75%" border="1">
  <tr>
    <th bgcolor="#CCCCCC">
      <div align="center"><font face="Arial, Helvetica,
      sans-serif">Place</font></div>
    </th>
    <th bgcolor="#CCCCCC">
      <div align="center"><font face="Arial, Helvetica,
      sans-serif">City</font></div>
    </th>
    <th bgcolor="#CCCCCC">
      <div align="center"><font face="Arial, Helvetica,
      sans-serif">State</font></div>
    </th>
  </tr>
${TABLE_CONTENT}
</table>
<p><font color="#FF0000" face="Arial, Helvetica, sans-serif">${NAME}
has many more favorite places, but we just list ${COUNT}.</font></p>
</body>
</html>
```

Notice that in the HTML shown in Listing 4.4, the `<th>` and `<tr>` tags that enclose them—which contain the header information—are retained because this information is usually static. Also added is some new HTML that contains a `COUNT` placeholder, which we will use to show how many records are in the table.

In both methods of creating a dynamic table, we need to replace the `TABLE_CONTENT` placeholder with the dynamic table content. In the first method, we can create a `StringBuffer` object by coding the table data in the servlet. The servlet would contain something like the following code:

```
.
.
.
HTMLTemplate ht = new(HTMLTemplate(m_context.getValue("MyTemplate"));
```

```
StringBuffer content = new StringBuffer();
.
.
.
// This is the content block that we will repeat for each table record.
content.append("<tr>\n");
content.append("<td><font color=\"#0000FF\" face="Arial, Helvetica, " +
               "sans-serif\" size=\"2\">");
content.append(place);
content.append("</font></td>\n");
content.append("<td><font color=\"#0000FF\" face="Arial, Helvetica, " +
               "sans-serif\" size=\"2\">");
content.append(city);
content.append("</font></td>");
content.append("<td><font color=\"#0000FF\" face="Arial, Helvetica, " +
               "sans-serif\" size=\"2\">");
content.append(state);
content.append("</font></td>");
.
.
.
ht.substitute("TABLE_CONTENT", content.toString());
ht.doHTML(out);
.
.
.
```

This code builds a content block based on the number of rows in the table. It codes the raw table HTML with the `<tr>` and `<td>` tags directly into the servlet. Instead of using `PLACE`, `CITY`, and `STATE` placeholders for data, we code the values right into the content buffer. We then replace this buffer for the `TABLE_CONTENT` placeholder and send the HTML to the user. This method works quite well, but it has some disadvantages. First, it codes the table HTML in the code, so if we need to make changes to the HTML, we must recompile the class. Second, if we have a complex table layout, the HTML could consist of a lot of data and therefore a lot of hard-coded HTML in the code. It also could make the Java code difficult to read and maintain.

The second method for creating a dynamic table is to dynamically build the table content with nested templates. By nesting templates—that is, placing one template within another—we could create a template containing just the content for the table record layout, along with placeholders for data. For example, let's create a table record layout template called `myrecord.html` that will contain the table record and `PLACE`, `CITY`, and `STATE` placeholders. Listing 4.5 shows the relevant code.

Listing 4.5 An HTML template containing a table record layout for dynamic table content

```
<tr>
  <td><font color="#0000FF" face="Arial, Helvetica, sans-serif"
       size="2">${PLACE}</font></td>
  <td><font color="#0000FF" face="Arial, Helvetica, sans-serif"
       size="2">${CITY}</font></td>
  <td><font color="#0000FF" face="Arial, Helvetica, sans-serif"
       size="2">${STATE}</font></td>
</tr>
```

In the previous section, one of the methods we created in `HTMLTemplate` allowed us to return a `StringBuffer` object by calling the `toStringBuffer()` method. We will use this method to create the buffer of content from the second template. In this scenario the code would create two templates: one containing the main HTML of the page, as in Listing 4.4, and one containing table record data, as in Listing 4.5. The code in this scenario might look like this:

```
HTMLTemplate ht = new(HTMLTemplate(m_context.getValue("MyTemplate"));
HTMLTemplate record = new
                         HTMLTemplate(m_context.getValue("MyRecord"));

StringBuffer content = new StringBuffer();
.
.
.
// Here we begin the block of code for each record.
record.substitute("PLACE", place);
record.substitute("CITY", city);
record.substitute("STATE", state);
content.append(record.toStringBuffer());
.
.
.
ht.substitute("TABLE_CONTENT", content.toString());
ht.doHTML(out);
.
.
.
```

We need only to add the block of code that substitutes for each record and append the template's resulting string to the content buffer. This is much more readable and much simpler to implement than is coding the HTML into the servlet. In addition, the code can be maintained easily, and changes to the layout need to be made only in the record template. Again, this approach allows the content management team to change the look and feel through the HTML, possibly without coding anything.

Let's see this scenario in action. We'll create a new application called *NestedTemplate*. In this example we want the output to look similar to that of the previous example, but we want to make the table data more dynamic. As the name suggests, this example will use two templates: one for the main part of the HTML, and one for the table record. The configuration file will contain the same information as in the previous example, but we will use the templates defined in Listings 4.4 and 4.5, which will be named `myplaces.html` and `myrecord.html`, respectively. The `NestedTemplate.config` file will look like this:

```
# Configuration file
Default.Method=show
Method.show=ShowTemplate
Application.Base.URL=/servlet/NestedTemplate

# Substitute your path to the HTML in the following configuration
# file values.
MyTemplate=C:\\Book\\Chapter 04\\Example 2\\templates\\myplaces.html
MyRecord=C:\\Book\\Chapter 04\\Example 2\\templates\\myrecord.html

# Place your name in the following parameter.
MyName=Jeff
```

The rest of the configuration file is similar to the previous example, but the main dispatch servlet will be called `NestedTemplate`. This servlet has the same layout as `TemplateExample`, but we will name it accordingly. Listing 4.6 shows the relevant code.

Listing 4.6 The `NestedTemplate` main base servlet

```
import enterprise.servlet.*;
import enterprise.common.*;

import java.io.*;

public class NestedTemplate extends BaseEnterpriseServlet
{
  public void initializeApp(AppContext appContext) throws Exception
  {
  }

  public void destroyApp(AppContext appContext)
  {
  }

  public String getAppName()
  {
    return "NestedTemplate";
  }
}
```

Now we're ready to code the ShowTemplate class. In this class we will create a method called addRecord() that takes the PLACE, CITY, and STATE placeholders as parameters. This method will be responsible for loading the myrecord.html template and substituting the parameters, and will return a StringBuffer object containing the table record HTML with the substituted values. We can dynamically add table records by calling the addRecord() method. With each call we append the returned StringBuffer object to the output HTML. This method will also keep a running tally of how many records are created so that we can replace the COUNT placeholder with this value. The code for the new ShowTemplate class is shown in Listing 4.7.

Listing 4.7 The ShowTemplate class for NestedTemplate

```
import enterprise.servlet.*;
import enterprise.common.*;
import enterprise.html.*;

import java.io.*;

public class ShowTemplate extends HTTPMethod
{

  private int recordCount = 0;
  private StringBuffer sBuf = new StringBuffer();

  public void execute()
  {
    try
    {
      PrintWriter out = m_response.getWriter();

      HTMLTemplate ht = new HTMLTemplate(
                              m_context.getValue("MyTemplate"));

      addRecord("Crystal River", "Marble", "Colorado");
      addRecord("Slick Rock", "Moab", "Utah");
      addRecord("Grand Canyon", "Grand Canyon", "Arizona");
      addRecord("Frying Pan River", "Basalt", "Colorado");

      ht.substitute("NAME", m_context.getValue("MyName"));
      ht.substitute("TABLE_CONTENT", sBuf.toString());
      ht.substitute("COUNT", recordCount + "");

      ht.doHTML(out);

    } catch(Exception e)
    {
      e.printStackTrace();
    }
  }
```

```
  private void addRecord(String place, String city, String state)
    throws Exception
  {
      HTMLTemplate record = new HTMLTemplate(
                              m_context.getValue("MyRecord"));

      record.substitute("PLACE", place);
      record.substitute("CITY", city);
      record.substitute("STATE", state);

      sBuf.append(record.toStringBuffer());
      recordCount++;

  }
}
```

Let's set up the application by ensuring that the values in the configuration file are correct, registering the servlet with the servlet engine, and setting the initialization arguments so that the `ConfFile` parameter points to the configuration file. When we are executing the servlet, the browser should show output similar to that in Figure 4.4.

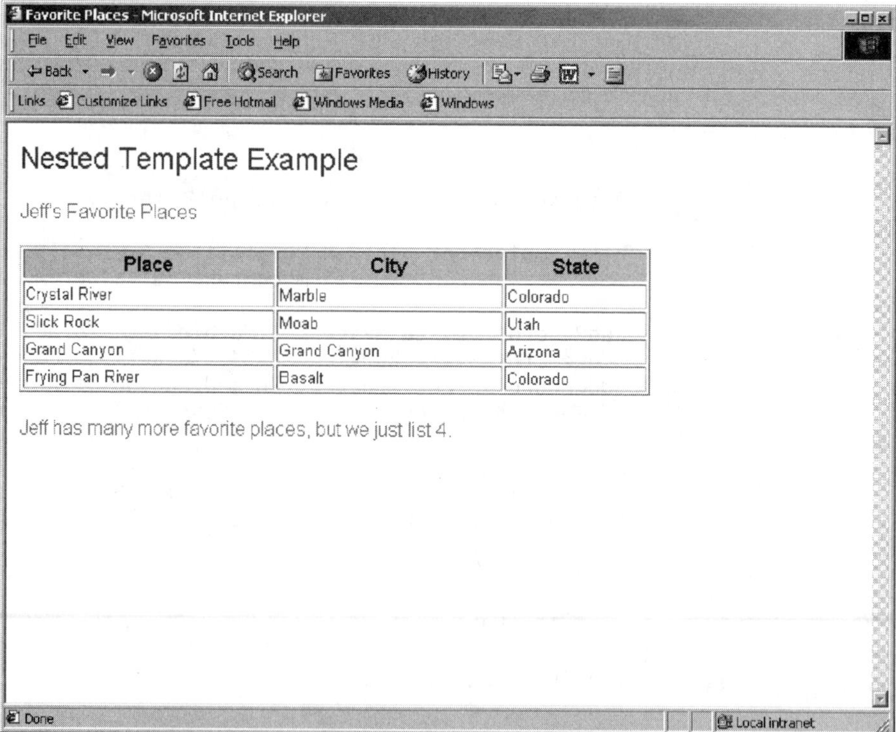

Figure 4.4 Output from `NestedTemplate`

To really appreciate how simple template objects and nested templates have made servlet development, look at the HTML source of the output from your browser. This servlet produced 47 lines of HTML. Each record contains 5 lines of HTML. Imagine having to hard-code this HTML into your servlets. In our code, we did not code even one line of HTML, so our software development was very simple.

This example showed table records with a very simple layout. In many organizations the content is so complex that table records are hundreds of lines long. Why not leave HTML development to the experts? Let the content management team be responsible for all that content! This is not to say that you will not code HTML into your servlet. Sometimes it is more efficient to code the HTML directly into the servlet, but with template objects and nested templates we can keep such coding to a minimum.

Making the Template Engine Scream: Caching Templates

When I write Web applications, I am always looking for ways to refine and streamline my applications. I know where the bottlenecks occur and look for ways to circumvent them. Our enemies in Web development are the garbage collector and input/output (I/O) operations, which slow hardware. Many of you will say, "The garbage collector is our friend, not our enemy!" This is true; it handles all the memory cleanup and lets us concentrate on the code as opposed to the memory infrastructure. It is our enemy as well, however, because it can really slow down a server if we are not careful how we code the application.

For example, earlier in this chapter `StringBuffer` objects were compared with `String` objects. The more `String` objects are created and destroyed, the more memory is fragmented and the more often the garbage collector goes into action. In an application that has not been coded correctly, a garbage collector can bring a system as powerful as a Sun Enterprise 450 with quad processors and 1GB of RAM to its knees. The idea in Java development for the Web, then, is to reuse as many objects as possible so that the garbage collector won't be called into action so often.

The other bottleneck, the I/O to hardware devices, can be an issue as well. The slowest parts of a computer system are the network and the hard drive. The fastest is the memory. The more interaction you do with the memory and the less with the other hardware, the faster your application will be.

So what is the solution? When developing Web applications, we should keep two things in mind: First, how do we keep the garbage collector from going to work often? Second, how do we minimize I/O access to the slower hardware? A good approach is to reuse as many objects as possible and to *cache* I/O into memory.

What is caching? A cache is a mechanism for storing frequently accessed data, objects, or other items from a higher-speed piece of hardware or algorithm; slower entities are accessed only as needed. For example, many companies use a caching proxy server for access to the Web by their employees. The proxy server stores the most frequently accessed Web pages on disk and in memory. When a client requests one of these Web pages, the proxy returns the one that is stored in its memory or on disk, giving the employee a sense that the Internet is very fast. The proxy server doesn't need to take the time to request the Web page. It delivers the content directly to the user without going over the Internet. When the user requests a page that is not in the cache, the proxy goes to the Internet and stores this new page in its cache for the next person who requests this URL.

Caching is an important concept that can be applied to templates as well. In previous examples we created templates and had `HTMLTemplate` objects handle substitution, loading, and parsing of the template files each time we sent a request to the servlet application. This process worked very fast, and probably it would work relatively fast under load, but is there a better way to do this?

Let's look at the bottlenecks in this process. When we load the template HTML, we are probably accessing the disk. I say *probably* because some operating systems cache the file in its own memory space, but this is not something we can count on. Each time we use a template, it executes this I/O to the disk. This is one area where we have a bottleneck. The other is the parsing of the file. When `HTMLTemplate` parses the file, it compiles the HTML into two parts: clear text and substitutable values. Each time we retrieve the template, it needs to parse the data into its subcomponents. This parsing can require a lot of overhead, and under heavy load it could be a drain on the CPU. In addition, as we create and destroy template objects we are using a lot of memory, and this could cause the garbage collector to go into action a bit more frequently than we would like.

One solution to this problem is to create a *template cache*. This cache would load all of the templates at startup of the servlet, compile the templates into their two major subcomponents only once, and store these in some type of a rapidly accessible object in memory. As classes needed to use the templates, they would look up the compiled template in the cache, substitute the values, and output the completed HTML to the client. This approach would have two major effects: It would create reusable template objects, giving the garbage collector a break, and it would use internal memory for accessing the templates, thereby bypassing the I/O to the disk. In other words, the template engine would *scream!* While minimizing object creation and destruction, we would be minimizing or nearly eliminating access to slow I/O.

How will this work? Figure 4.5 depicts the breakdown of the templates. We need to start from a template's most basic form, its subcomponents. As mentioned already, a template has two basic subcomponents: clear text (i.e., raw HTML) and placeholders.

Let's call each subcomponent of the template `HTMLTemplateItem`. An `HTMLTemplateItem` object will carry a flag that identifies itself as either clear text or placeholder. A template that has been parsed or compiled is made up of several of these `HTMLTemplateItem` objects. The number of objects depends on how many placeholders the template contains. For example, a template with no placeholders has one `HTMLTemplateItem` object, representing just clear text. A template with one placeholder has three `HTMLTemplateItem` objects: one for the first batch of clear text, one for the placeholder, and one for the rest of the clear text. A template with two placeholders has five `HTMLTemplateItem` objects: two for the placeholders and three for the clear text that surrounds the placeholders. And so on.

Therefore, an `HTMLCompiledTemplate` object is made up of a list of these `HTMLTemplateItem` objects. At the highest level is `TemplateCacheList`, a `HashSet` object containing `HTMLCompiledTemplate` objects. When we build a `TemplateCacheList` object, we compile each template as an `HTMLCompiledTemplate` object and store it in a `TemplateCacheList` object. Therefore, when we request a template by name, `TemplateCacheList` will return the `HTMLCompiledTemplate` object that is associated with that name to us. (If any of this is confusing to you, review Figure 4.5, which clearly shows the hierarchical structure just described.)

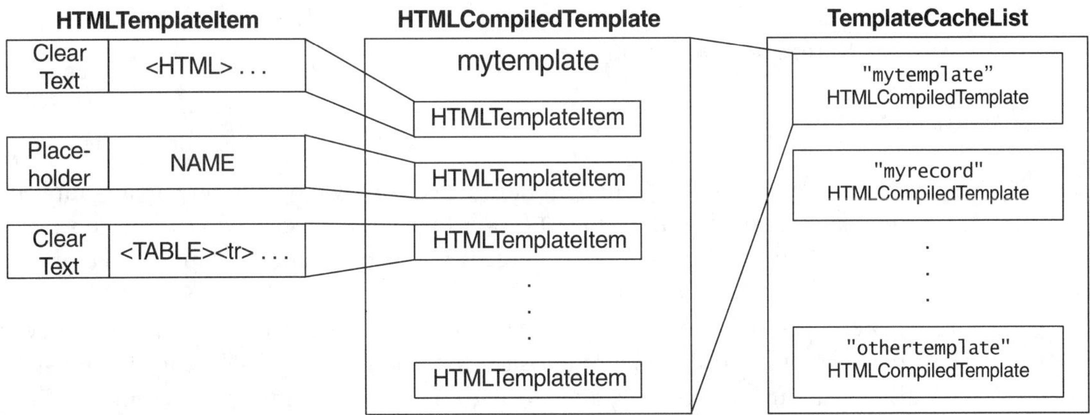

Figure 4.5 Template cache structure

Building the Template Cache

Now that we have described the structure of the cache, let's begin building it. We will start with the lowest common denominator and first develop `HTMLTemplateItem`. This object contains one of two types of components: clear text or placeholder. It stores these values as strings, so as we store the components we can pass in a `boolean` flag that describes the component type. The object will contain two member variables: `sText`, a `String` variable that holds the clear text or placeholder name, and `bClearText`, the `boolean` flag that describes the data type.

If we pass `true` to `HTMLTemplateItem`, the string contains clear text. If we pass `false`, the string contains the name of the placeholder. In the constructor we pass the string and the `boolean` flag. Let's make the member variables public so that we can easily alter them. Remember, we only want this class to be a new data type for storage, so encapsulation is not important here. Listing 4.8 shows the code for `HTMLTemplateItem`.

Listing 4.8 The `HTMLTemplateItem` class

```
package enterprise.html;

public class HTMLTemplateItem
{

  // Does sText contain unaltered text or a field name
  // to be translated?
  public boolean bClearText = false;

  // Either clear text to be passed or a field name.
  public String  sText = null;

  public HTMLTemplateItem(String text, boolean clearText)
  {
    sText      = text;
    bClearText = clearText;
  }

}
```

So we have a template item data type. Now we need to create a compiled template for storing all of the `HTMLTemplateItem` objects. We will call this template `HTMLCompiledTemplate`, which is nothing more than a vector of `HTMLTemplateItem` objects. However, because this is the actual HTML template, it needs to take on much of the role that `HTMLTemplate` had in the previous section. It needs to be responsible for reading the HTML template, parsing it into its subcomponents, and storing this data in its internal vector.

HTMLCompiledTemplate is exactly what its name suggests: a compiled template. The constructor should take in a filename and immediately parse the file. As it parses the file, instead of doing the substitution on the fly, we just want it to identify the template subcomponents and store them in its internal vector. Then when we use this object, we can spin through the vector and do the substitution at that point, reusing the compiled template over and over. Use of the HTMLCompiledTemplate object allows us to parse the file only once, thereby removing a significant amount of overhead. Let's start by declaring the class and its member variables.

```
package enterprise.html;

import java.io.*;
import java.util.*;
import java.net.*;

public class HTMLCompiledTemplate
{
  private String sFName;
  private Vector vCompiled = null;

  private static final int TEXT = 0;
  private static final int DOLLAR = 1;
  private static final int FIELDNAME = 2;
```

HTMLCompiledTemplate has the same members that HTMLTemplate had in the last section, but we also give HTMLCompiledTemplate the vCompiled vector. In this vector we will store each HTMLTemplateItem object.

Now let's define the constructor. We want the constructor to take the filename as a parameter and to parse the file immediately upon construction of the object. Because we are going to load the file immediately, the constructor will have to throw an IOException if the file is not found or cannot be read.

```
  public HTMLCompiledTemplate(String fName) throws IOException
  {
    sFName = fName;

    vCompiled = new Vector();

    parseFile();
  }
```

Let's configure HTMLCompiledTemplate not only so that it can parse a file, but also so that we can build a template with placeholders in a StringBuffer object, so that we can create our own templates on the fly without having to load them from a file. This capability could come in handy when we wish to create some very simple templates (single lines) in the servlet that may not be appropriate for a file. Examples are headers and footers that may contain information that will never change, such as copyright data or company name.

For example, we may wish all of our templates to contain *XYZ Corporation, copyright 2001, all rights reserved, developed by ${DEVELOPMENT_DEPT}* in the footer of each page. We would never want to change this information and probably wouldn't want the content management team to change it. So we could create a template that could be accessed on the fly. To do this we will create a constructor that lets us pass a `StringBuffer` object as a template parameter. The constructor will do what the previous one did, except that it will have no file to load into a `StringBuffer` object. Instead it will immediately start parsing `StringBuffer`.

```
public HTMLCompiledTemplate(StringBuffer sBuf) throws IOException
{
  sFName = "";

  vCompiled = new Vector();

  parse(sBuf);
}
```

The `parseFile()` method for `HTMLCompiledTemplate` is essentially the same as the one we developed for `HTMLTemplate`. It just reads the file into a `StringBuffer` object and calls a parse routine.

```
private void parseFile() throws IOException
{
  char cBuf[] = new char[4096];
  int  cLen = 0;
  FileReader fr;

  StringBuffer sBuf = new StringBuffer();

  try
  {
    fr = new FileReader(sFName);
  } catch(FileNotFoundException e)
  {
    throw new IOException("Cannot find file:" + sFName);
  }

  while ((cLen = fr.read(cBuf)) > 0)
  {
    for (int c = 0; c < cLen; c++)
    {
      sBuf.append(cBuf[c]);
    }
  }
```

```
    fr.close();

    parse(sBuf);
  }
```

Now the real fun begins. We will take the `parse()` method from `HTMLTemplate` and use most of the code here. The basic algorithm is the same, but instead of building the output HTML `StringBuffer` object, we will build a vector of `HTMLTemplateItem` objects. Therefore when we identify clear text, we will implement the following code:

```
vCompiled.addElement(new
HTMLTemplateItem(clearBuf.toString(),true));
```

This code appends the clear-text block to the compiled vector list.

When we have identified a placeholder, we will implement the following code:

```
vCompiled.addElement(new HTMLTemplateItem(
                               fieldBuf.toString().toUpperCase(),false));
```

Remember that we want to store the placeholder as uppercase so that when we do a lookup, we will compare by uppercase and the case of the placeholder coded in the servlet or in the HTML template will not matter. The new `parse()` method looks like this:

```
  private void parse(StringBuffer sBuf) throws IOException
  {
    int length = sBuf.length();
    StringBuffer fieldBuf = new StringBuffer();
    StringBuffer clearBuf = new StringBuffer();
    char charRead;

    int state = TEXT;

    for (int i = 0; i < length; i++)
    {
      switch (charRead = sBuf.charAt(i))
      {
        case ('$'):
          if (state == DOLLAR)
          {
            clearBuf.append("$");
          }
          state = DOLLAR;
          break;
        case ('{'):
          if (state == DOLLAR)
          {
```

```
        if (clearBuf.length() > 0)
        {
          vCompiled.addElement(new
                    HTMLTemplateItem(clearBuf.toString(),true));
        }
        clearBuf.setLength(0);
        fieldBuf.setLength(0);
        state = FIELDNAME;
      }
      else
      {
        clearBuf.append(charRead);
        state = TEXT;
      }
      break;
    case ('}'):
      if (state == FIELDNAME)
      {
        if (fieldBuf.length() != 0)
        {
          vCompiled.addElement(new HTMLTemplateItem(
                      fieldBuf.toString().toUpperCase(),false));
        }
        else
        {
          clearBuf.append("${}");
        }
        state = TEXT;
      }
      else
      {
        if (state == DOLLAR)
        {
          clearBuf.append("$");
          state = TEXT;
        }

        clearBuf.append(charRead);
      }
      break;
    default:
      if (state == FIELDNAME)
      {
        fieldBuf.append(charRead);
      }
      else
      {
        if (state == DOLLAR)
        {
          clearBuf.append("$");
          state = TEXT;
        }
```

```
            clearBuf.append(charRead);
          }
          break;
      }
    }

    if (clearBuf.length() > 0)
    {
      vCompiled.addElement(
              new HTMLTemplateItem(clearBuf.toString(),true));
    }

    clearBuf.setLength(0);
    clearBuf = null;
    fieldBuf.setLength(0);
    fieldBuf = null;
    sBuf.setLength(0);
    sBuf = null;
  }
```

Now that the template has been compiled, we should be able to create an HTMLTemplate object from this object, so we will call a protected constructor in the HTMLTemplate class. We will explain this further when we reengineer HTMLTemplate later in this chapter.

```
  public HTMLTemplate createHTMLTemplate()
  {
    return new HTMLTemplate(this);
  }
```

Finally, let's create an accessor method for other routines in the package that may want direct access to the vCompiled vector. In particular, HTMLTemplate will need to access this vector directly to build a template from the list of HTMLTemplateItem objects.

```
  protected Vector getCompiledVector()
  {
    return vCompiled;
  }

}
```

And that's the HTMLCompiledTemplate object. This object will compile templates into their basic subcomponents. If you compare this code with the code for HTMLTemplate, you will probably notice that we are missing some key methods, such as toString(), toStringBuffer(), and substitute(). Well, we aren't done yet. Although we have a compiled template, we still need an HTMLTemplate object. Its basic function should remain the same as in the last section, but it shouldn't be responsible for tasks such as parsing. We are just dividing the labor among the appropriate objects.

HTMLTemplate will be responsible for taking the compiled template, spinning through the compiled vector, substituting the placeholders, and outputting the HTML to the client. From a development perspective, its basic use will be the same as for the version we developed in the last section. The major difference is that the underlying engine will be HTMLCompiledTemplate. The member variables will remain the same as in HTMLTemplate in the previous section, but we will add an HTMLCompiledTemplate object as a member. You will understand why in a moment.

```
package enterprise.html;

import java.io.*;
import java.util.*;

public class HTMLTemplate
{
  private Properties           pList    = null;
  private String               sFName = null;
  private HTMLCompiledTemplate oTemplate = null;
```

We want two constructors: one that enables us to pass in a filename to parse on the fly if we don't want to use a compiled template, and one that allows us to pass in an HTMLCompiledTemplate object. There is a major difference between the two. If we choose to use a filename, we want the object to build an HTMLCompiledTemplate object behind the scenes because this object is what parses the templates. The HTMLCompiledTemplate object will be built when we are ready to build the string in one of our output methods (i.e., toString(), toStringBuffer(), or doHTML()). In this scenario, setting the oTemplate member variable to null in the constructor can act as a flag indicating the need to create an HTMLCompiledTemplate object. We can test for this condition when we execute one of the output methods. In other words, things will work the same as before when we use this constructor.

The second constructor will allow an HTMLCompiledTemplate object to be passed in as a parameter, and the constructor will set the oTemplate member to this object. Setting the oTemplate member to a valid HTMLCompiledTemplate object tells the output methods not to create one and instead to use oTemplate. But we want this constructor to be protected so that it cannot be created by the end developer. Why? Because this is the constructor that the method createHTMLTemplate() defined in HTMLCompiledTemplate uses to create an HTMLTemplate object. This will become clearer when we show an implementation of the template objects. In the meantime, let's put together the constructors as just described.

```
public HTMLTemplate(String fName)
{
  pList  = new Properties();
  sFName = fName;
  oTemplate = null;
}

protected HTMLTemplate(HTMLCompiledTemplate ct)
{
  pList = new Properties();
  sFName = null;
  oTemplate = ct;
}
```

The output methods—`substitute()`, `toString()`, and `doHTML()`—can remain the same, so we will leave these as they were in the `HTMLTemplate` object of the previous section.

```
public void substitute(String var, String str)
{
  if (var != null)
  {
    if (str != null)
    {
      pList.put(var.toUpperCase(), str);
    }
    else
    {
      pList.put(var.toUpperCase(), "");
    }
  }
}

public String toString()
{
  try
  {
    return toStringBuffer().toString();
  } catch(IOException e)
  {
    e.printStackTrace();
    return null;
  }
}

public void doHTML(PrintWriter out)
    throws IOException
{
  out.print(this.toString());
  out.flush();
}
```

Now we will see how all of the template objects come together as we develop the `toStringBuffer()` methods. We will create two versions of `toStringBuffer()`. One method will allow us to pass in a `StringBuffer` object that we have already created. The other one will create the `StringBuffer` object for us. We will support two methods for convenience to the developer to reuse a `StringBuffer` object that has already been allocated, or just to have the framework create one. The method that creates the `StringBuffer` object for us is probably the most common type that will be used. The implementation just creates a `StringBuffer` object and calls the other method, which takes a `StringBuffer` object parameter.

```
public StringBuffer toStringBuffer()
    throws IOException
{
  StringBuffer sb = new StringBuffer();
  Return This.toSTringBuffer(sb);
}
```

The version of `toStringBuffer()` that is not shown here is the one that does all the work. This method takes a `StringBuffer` object as a parameter and reuses a buffer that we may have already created. In this method the first thing we will do is check the `oTemplate` member variable for a value. As described already, a `null` value in `oTemplate` indicates that we used the constructor that takes a filename. This means that we need to load and parse the HTML template. Therefore, if the value of `oTemplate` is `null`, we will construct an `HTMLCompiledTemplate` object right here. Remember that constructing an `HTMLCompiledTemplate` object automatically parses the HTML template file and places it into a compiled state. If `oTemplate` already contains an object `HTMLCompiledTemplate`, then the protected-version constructor was used and `toStringBuffer()` will use this object instead.

```
public StringBuffer toStringBuffer(StringBuffer sb)
    throws IOException
{

  if (oTemplate == null)
  {
    oTemplate = new HTMLCompiledTemplate(sFName);
  }
```

At this point we have an `HTMLCompiledTemplate` object, whether it was passed as a parameter to a constructor or created in this method. We then get a copy of the vector from the `HTMLCompiledTemplate` object that contains the list of all the `HTMLTemplateItem` objects. We move step-by-step through the vector and begin creating the output HTML `StringBuffer` object. We check each HTMLTemplateItem object in the vector for its type. If it is clear text, we append it to the output buffer. If it is a placeholder, we look up the string in pList and append the resulting value to the output buffer.

```
    Vector v = oTemplate.getCompiledVector();

    for (Enumeration e = v.elements() ; e.hasMoreElements() ;)
    {
      HTMLTemplateItem ti = (HTMLTemplateItem) e.nextElement();

      if (ti.bClearText)
      {
        sb.append(ti.sText);
      }
      else
      {
        String parm = pList.getProperty(ti.sText);

        if (parm == null)
        {
          parm = "";
        }

        sb.append(parm);
      }
    }

    return sb;
  }

}
```

After spinning through all of the elements, we are able to create the final HTML from the compiled template very rapidly. As you can see, the new HTMLTemplate object can either parse an HTML template on the fly or use a precompiled HTMLCompiledTemplate object. We have objects that allow us to streamline template compilation and utilization. They offer flexibility and ease of use.

The only thing we're missing is the cache itself. The cache is nothing more than a Hashtable object that associates a template name with an HTMLCompiledTemplate object. This leads us to developing an object that is basically a wrapper around a Hashtable. We will call this object TemplateCacheList, and it will contain methods to add, delete, and get HTMLCompiledTemplate objects through the cache. The code, which is self-explanatory, is shown in Listing 4.9.

Listing 4.9 The `TemplateCacheList` class

```
package enterprise.html;

import java.util.*;

public class TemplateCacheList
{

  private Hashtable m_list;

  public TemplateCacheList()
  {
    m_list = new Hashtable();
  }

  public void add(String templateName, HTMLCompiledTemplate ct)
  {
    m_list.put(templateName, ct);
  }

  public void delete(String templateName)
  {
    m_list.remove(templateName);
  }

  public HTMLCompiledTemplate get(String templateName)
    throws IllegalArgumentException
  {
    HTMLCompiledTemplate oTemplate =
                     (HTMLCompiledTemplate)m_list.get(templateName);

    if (oTemplate == null)
    {
      throw new IllegalArgumentException(
                           "Template not found in list.");
    }

    return oTemplate;
  }

  public int getCount()
  {
    return m_list.size();
  }
}
```

Developing template and cache objects was a complex process, but all this work pays off in implementation. Typically we will use these objects by first building the cache of `HTMLCompiledTemplate` objects. In the earlier example we had two templates: `myplace.html` and `myrecord.html`. We would build our cache with the following code:

```
TemplateCacheList tcl = new TemplateCacheList();
tcl.add("MyPlace", new
            HTMLCompiledTemplate("C:\\Book\\Chapter 04\\Example 2\\
            templates\\myplace.html"));
tcl.add("MyRecord", new
            HTMLCompiledTemplate("C:\\Book\\Chapter 04\\Example 2\\
            templates\\myrecord.html"));
```

When we're ready to use the cache, we retrieve the `HTMLCompiledTemplate` object by querying the `TemplateCacheList` object with the name that we used to store it. Then we call `createHTMLTemplate()` to create an instance of `HTMLTemplate` as shown here:

```
HTMLCompiledTemplate hct = tcl.get("MyPlace");
HTMLTemplate ht = hct.createHTMLTemplate();
```

Or we could do it on one line, like this:

```
HTMLTemplate ht = tcl.get("MyPlace").createHTMLTemplate();
```

From here we use the template object as we normally would.

```
ht.substitute("NAME", "Jeff");
ht.doHTML(out);
```

So all that complex code and structure paid off. Implementing a cached and compiled template is extremely simple. All the hard work is done within the objects. It not only saves us the overhead of the increased CPU load (i.e., increased use of the garbage collector), but also decreases access to slow I/O.

Integrating the Template Objects and Cache into Enterprise Servlets

A look at the implementation of the template cache shows that we need to build the cache early in an application's execution in order to reap the benefits of using it. The idea is to reuse the compiled templates in the cache, and if they don't exist from the beginning of the application we won't be able to reuse them as the servlet serves Web requests. For this reason the application needs to build the template cache upon initialization so that the rest of the application can have access to this cache when it is ready to accept requests.

What does this mean for the enterprise servlet architecture? It means we need to build the cache either in an application's `initializeApp()` method or in the `AppContext` object. Which one should we choose? From a development perspective, most applications that serve any amount of content will have some use for templates. Coding raw HTML into a servlet can be a very labor-intensive task, so it probably makes sense to load the template cache in the

AppContext object. Doing so allows us to load the cache when AppContext initializes its members at the time the application is launched.

If we are to have AppContext load the template cache, we must examine some issues. Somehow we need to get the path and template filenames into AppContext so that it can parse and load the templates into the cache. AppContext is a conduit to the configuration stored in the configuration file, so it is probably a good idea to create a new configuration file parameter.

Because we can have many templates in a file, we should probably create a prefix-based parameter, just as we did with the *"Method."* prefix in Chapter 1. Recall that the AppContext object was able to identify all of the methods listed in a configuration file by using the *"Method."* prefix. We should implement a similar naming convention for templates. In fact, let's call this new prefix *"Template."*. Any parameters in the configuration file that begin with the *"Template."* prefix will be identified as a template. For example, the myplaces.html and myrecord.html templates may look like this in the configuration file:

```
Template.MyPlaces=C:\\Book\\Chapter 04\\Example 2\\templates\\
                      myplaces.html
Template.MyRecord=C:\\Book\\Chapter 04\\Example 2\\templates\\
                      myrecord.html
```

The configuration file could contain many of these *"Template."* lines in a large system. Most templates will probably be in the same directory or path. It may also be helpful to create a configuration file parameter that allows us to code in a default template path. Then when we move the application to another directory structure, we won't have to update a potentially large number of lines in a configuration file. Only one line will need to be updated. We can create a configuration file parameter called Default.Template.Path, which will be used to find a template. Taking this approach means that we need to list only the name of the template on the *"Template."* lines and can exclude the path. Therefore, the configuration file would contain the following:

```
Default.Template.Path= C:\\Book\\Chapter 04\\Example 2\\templates
Template.MyPlaces=myplaces.html
Template.MyRecord=myrecord.html
```

Let's look at what the AppContext object will need to do to support templates in the configuration file. First it will need to look for a Default.Template.Path parameter and store this for processing the templates. Both the Default.Template.Path parameter and any parameters beginning with the prefix *"Template."* should be optional parameters in the file because we may have applications that do not use templates, although this possibility is unlikely.

Next AppContext will need to retrieve a list of all lines that begin with *"Template."*. We need to be able both to support the default template path *and* to code a path with the template name, so we will need code in the cache-loading routine to be able to handle this case.

Finally, AppContext will compile and parse the templates and store them in a cache that is accessible to the rest of the application. Now that we know what we need the AppContext object to do to implement template caching, let's update AppContext to reflect these changes.

To begin, let's create the global constants for the object and two new member variables: one that stores the default template path, and one that stores the template cache.

```
import enterprise.html.*;
.
.
.
public class AppContext
{
.
.
.
  public static final String TEMPLATE_PREFIX          = "Template.";
  public static final String DEFAULT_TEMPLATE_PATH    =
                                          "Default.Template.Path";
.
.
.
  private String                sTemplatePath   = null;
  private TemplateCacheList  oTemplateCaches = null;
```

To comply with the way in which we developed the AppContext object in previous chapters, we will implement getters and setters for the template path and template cache. Most important is the getter for the template cache because we want the HTTPMethod objects to be able to query the cache for templates.

```
.
.
.
  protected boolean setTemplateCacheList(TemplateCacheList caches)
  {
        oTemplateCaches= caches;

        return true;
  }

  public TemplateCacheList getTemplateCacheList()
      throws ResourceNotConfiguredException
  {

        if (oTemplateCaches == null)
        {
            throw new ResourceNotConfiguredException("No HTML " +
                                 "template caches are configured.");
        }
```

```
        return oTemplateCaches;
}

protected boolean setDefaultTemplatePath(String templatePath)
{
        this.sTemplatePath = new String(templatePath);

        return true;
}

public String getDefaultTemplatePath()
{
    return sTemplatePath;
}
```

Now we need to develop the cache-building method. We will call this method `buildTemplateCache()`, and it will start by searching the configuration file for the default template path parameter. If one is found, we will set the `sTemplatePath` member variable with its value. Note that the default template path parameter may or may not have a path separator at the end of its string, depending on whether the person who maintains this file added one. Consistency is important here because we are using this string as a prefix for the template filename. We don't necessarily want the person who maintains the configuration file to have to worry about this, so we should handle the issue of consistency in the code.

We want to be sure that we always have a path separator at the end of this string. However, we may not know what platform we are running on, and the path separator could be different depending on the operating system that is executing the code: a backslash (\) on a PC, a colon (:) on a Macintosh, and and a forward slash (/) on a UNIX-based system. Luckily the folks at Sun knew this was an issue, so they have provided a method in the `System` object that lets us query this value. We will call the `System.getProperty("file.separator")` method to get the path separator and check for its existence at the end of the default template path string. If it exists, we will leave the string as is; if it does not exist, we will append the separator to the path string.

```
.
.
.
  public void buildTemplateCache()
    throws ServletException
  {
    ConfFile cf = getConfigFile();

    String defaultTemplatePath = cf.getValue(DEFAULT_TEMPLATE_PATH);
```

```
if (defaultTemplatePath != null)
{
  String dirSep = System.getProperty("file.separator");
  if (!defaultTemplatePath.endsWith(dirSep))
  {
    defaultTemplatePath += dirSep;
  }

  setDefaultTemplatePath(defaultTemplatePath.trim());
}
```

Now we are ready to build the cache within this method. We will spin through the configuration file parameters looking for names that begin with *"Template."*. If we find one that does, we will strip off the prefix, leaving the name that we want to call the template as part of the parameter name. For example, stripping the prefix off of the parameter name *Template.MyPlace* would leave us with *MyPlace,* which would become a key to the compiled template in the cache. This is essentially the same exercise as we had when we built the list of methods in Chapter 1.

For each template we will take the name and attempt to load the template file to be compiled. We want to do this verbatim, without preappending the default template path because the template may not be in the default path and thus its path may be coded in the parameter value. So we will attempt to load the template with its value first. If an exception is not thrown, the template has been found and it is parsed and compiled into an `HTMLCompiledTemplate` object. If the template is not found, `HTMLCompiledTemplate` throws an `IOException`. We will trap for this exception and again attempt to load the template, but this time we will preappend the default template location. Again, if the template is found, it is parsed and compiled into an `HTMLCompiledTemplate` object. But if it is not found, a `ServletException` is thrown stating that the template could not be loaded.

As we successfully load each template, we will add the object `HTMLCompiledTemplate` to the cache, using the parameter name without the prefix as a key. When we have spun through all of the parameters, we will set the `oTemplateCaches` member variable to the newly built `TemplateCacheList` object with the `setTemplateCacheList()` call, and the cache will be ready to be accessed by the rest of the application.

```
TemplateCacheList tcl = new TemplateCacheList();

for (Enumeration t = cf.getKeys() ; t.hasMoreElements() ;)
{
  String key = (String) t.nextElement();
```

```
        if (key.startsWith(TEMPLATE_PREFIX))
        {
          String template = key.substring(TEMPLATE_PREFIX.length());

          if (template.length() > 0)
          {
            String templateFile = cf.getValue(key);

            try
            {
              HTMLCompiledTemplate hct = new
                            HTMLCompiledTemplate(templateFile.trim());
              tcl.add(template.trim(), hct);
            }
            catch (IOException ioe)
            {
              if (defaultTemplatePath != null)
              {
                try
                {
                  templateFile = defaultTemplatePath +
                                 cf.getValue(key);
                  HTMLCompiledTemplate hct = new
                            HTMLCompiledTemplate(templateFile.trim());
                  tcl.add(template.trim(), hct);
                }
                catch (IOException ie)
                {
                  ioe.printStackTrace();
                  throw new ServletException(ioe.getMessage());
                }
              }
              else
              {
                ioe.printStackTrace();
                throw new ServletException(ioe.getMessage());
              }
            }
          }
        }
      }

      setTemplateCacheList(tcl);
    }
```

Of course, the `setTemplateCache()` method needs to be executed, and it probably should be run when the configuration file is being parsed. So we will call `buildTemplateCache()` in the `parseConfigFile()` method. We will add this call to the end of the method.

```
.
.
.
  public void parseConfigFile(String appName,String fileName)
        throws ServletException
  {
.
.
.
    buildTemplateCache();
  }
}
```

That's all there is to integrating a template cache in the enterprise servlet architecture. All we need to do is create the templates and place the appropriate "*Template.*" parameters to point toward the templates in the configuration file, and the next time the servlet is launched by the servlet engine it will load the servlets into the easily accessible template cache automatically. On paper this looks really good; let's see how it works in a real scenario.

Using the Template Cache in Enterprise Servlets

To show how powerful and easy using a cached template with enterprise servlets is, let's take the `NestedTemplate` servlet from our earlier example and convert it to use a cache. We want this example to have the same output and use the same templates as the previous example did, but now we will have it dynamically load the templates that have been registered in the configuration file. We will then use the cache instead of loading the templates in the servlet code.

Let's change the name of the application to *CachedTemplate* and create the configuration file. In the configuration file, we'll change the base URL to point toward the new application, and we'll add a default path to the templates directory, as well as a template parameter for each template. All the other parameters will remain the same.

```
# Configuration file
Default.Method=show
Method.show=ShowTemplate

Application.Base.URL=/servlet/CachedTemplate

# Substitute your path to the HTML in the following configuration
# file value.
Default.Template.Path=C:\\Book\\Chapter 04\\Example 3\\templates

Template.MyTemplate=myplaces.html
Template.MyRecord=myrecord.html
```

```
# Place your name in the following parameter.
MyName=Jeff
```

We will create the main dispatch servlet by simply changing the class name and the application name to *CachedTemplate*. Listing 4.10 shows the relevant code.

Listing 4.10 The `CachedTemplate` class

```
import enterprise.servlet.*;
import enterprise.common.*;

import java.io.*;

public class CachedTemplate extends BaseEnterpriseServlet
{
  public void initializeApp(AppContext appContext) throws Exception
  {
  }

  public void destroyApp(AppContext appContext)
  {
  }

  public String getAppName()
  {
    return "CachedTemplate";
  }
}
```

Listing 4.11 shows the code for the `ShowTemplate` object. It is basically the same as in the `NestedTemplate` example, but instead of `HTMLTemplate` loading and parsing the template every time we access this class, an instance of the object is created from the compiled cache. It retrieves the `TemplateCacheList` object from `AppContext`, queries each of the cached templates, and creates instances of `HTMLTemplate` from the compiled versions.

Listing 4.11 The `ShowTemplate` class using the template cache

```
import enterprise.servlet.*;
import enterprise.common.*;
import enterprise.html.*;

import java.io.*;

public class ShowTemplate extends HTTPMethod
{

  private int                  recordCount     = 0;
  private StringBuffer         sBuf            = new StringBuffer();
  private TemplateCacheList    tcl             = null;
  private HTMLCompiledTemplate htc             = null;
```

```
  private HTMLTemplate         MyTemplate      = null;
  private HTMLTemplate         MyRecord        = null;

  public void execute()
  {
    try
    {
      initObjects();

      PrintWriter out = m_response.getWriter();

      addRecord("Crystal River", "Marble", "Colorado");
      addRecord("Slick Rock", "Moab", "Utah");
      addRecord("Grand Canyon", "Grand Canyon", "Arizona");
      addRecord("Frying Pan River", "Basalt", "Colorado");

      MyTemplate.substitute("NAME", m_context.getValue("MyName"));
      MyTemplate.substitute("TABLE_CONTENT", sBuf.toString());
      MyTemplate.substitute("COUNT", recordCount + "");

      MyTemplate.doHTML(out);

    } catch(Exception e)
    {
      e.printStackTrace();
    }
  }

  private void addRecord(String place, String city, String state)
    throws Exception
  {
    MyRecord.substitute("PLACE", place);
    MyRecord.substitute("CITY", city);
    MyRecord.substitute("STATE", state);

    sBuf.append(MyRecord.toStringBuffer());
    recordCount++;
  }

  private void initObjects() throws Exception
  {
    tcl = m_context.getTemplateCacheList();

    MyTemplate = tcl.get("MyTemplate").createHTMLTemplate();
    MyRecord = tcl.get("MyRecord").createHTMLTemplate();
  }

}
```

This example shows that using cached templates does not create any additional code. We just need to register the templates in the configuration file, and they are automatically loaded into the cache when the application starts. The advantages of caching templates are that it streamlines the servlet and decreases the overhead of object creation and destruction, and it does not require access to slow I/O devices. However, there is a disadvantage with how we implemented this cache: If you need to change a template, you must restart the application to reload the cache. It is up to you to enhance this object if you wish, since the point here was simply to introduce templates and caching.

We could incorporate other convenient features into these objects. We could load the template's date/time stamp in the `HTMLCompiledTemplate` object, for example, and each time we used it we could check if the date/time had changed in the physical file. If it had, we would reload that template. We could also remove the template list from the configuration file and just have the template engine load all files with a *.html* extension in a particular directory. If we requested a template that did not exist in the cache, the template engine could look in this directory for the new template and load it into the cache. This would allow us to dynamically load the templates as we added them without restarting the servlet. Undoubtedly, you will think of many other interesting ways to enhance the template cache.

Summary

When we develop servlets, we find that the primary way for delivering content to the user is to code the HTML directly into the servlet. With simple HTML pages this is a reasonable task. But with the complexities of today's HTML—particularlywith the inclusion of DHTML, JavaScript, VBScript, and intricate table structures—HTML pages can be thousands of lines long. This complexity creates a difficult situation for the servlet developer because under this paradigm, coding this HTML into the servlet can be a laborious task. Not only would coding complex HTML into a servlet be time intensive, but the code would be nearly impossible to maintain. Small changes to HTML would potentially require wading through a massive amount of code.

One solution is to use a template engine to read in the bulk of HTML and replace placeholders with content. This approach allows a content management group to maintain the HTML with an editor such as Dreamweaver or FrontPage and put placeholders where dynamic content belongs. In addition, both the HTML and the servlet code are easier to maintain.

In this chapter we learned about template engines with the `HTMLTemplate` object, which parses the HTML, substitutes real data for placeholders, and outputs the final HTML to the client. We also learned a technique for nesting templates so that we can embed complex tabular data in an outer template without coding HTML into the servlet. Finally, having learned the lessons of slow I/O and unnecessary object creation and destruction, we restructured the `HTMLTemplate` object and built a robust caching template engine. We saw the advantages of implementing a compiled, memory-based template object schema and how it can streamline the execution of applications on a Web server.

CHAPTER 5

Logging and Error Handling

Logging and error handling are sensitive topics with today's developers. Many companies explicitly state internal standards for what we log and how we log it. They also specify how we handle errors. Some shops want every request to be logged—with information including who issued the request, the issuer's IP address and user ID, the requested information, and so on. Some just want error information reported, such as a stack trace. Other companies institute a robust error-handling scheme that notifies other systems of problems, sending a page to system administrators or e-mailing trouble reports to designated individuals.

At the developer level, some of us use logging as a way to debug server-side applications by dumping a trace of what is occurring in the code. We set a trace log to identify the contents of a variable when the code is executed. We then review the log to see what happened in the code. So as you can see, logging can be a critical and helpful part of an application.

In this chapter we will take a detailed look at the concept of logging and design an object that makes logging a simple task. We will build this object into the enterprise servlet architecture so that logging is readily available to our applications. We will then look at error handling and the different methods of dealing with exceptions.

Logging in a Servlet Engine

A Web server engine usually has a servlet log file or uses the Web server's log file to output logging information. When we learn about developing servlets, one of the initial concepts that is taught is that the methods—`System.out.println()` and `System.err.println()`—send information to the

Web server or servlet engine log. We also learn that we can log information by using the `HttpServlet.log()` method to send information to the log. This method not only sends the information, but also adds the servlet's name to the beginning of the message so that we can more easily identify the origination point of the message.

Listing 5.1 shows a sample servlet log. This example uses output from New Atlanta's ServletExec debugger.

Listing 5.1 Typical log from a servlet engine

```
[Tue Sep 12 08:54:06 MDT 2000] TestServlet: This is a message sent
    to the log
[Tue Sep 12 08:54:06 MDT 2000] TestServlet: This is an error
[Tue Sep 12 08:54:24 MDT 2000] java.lang.Exception
    at TestServlet.service(TestServlet.java:23)
    at javax.servlet.http.HttpServlet.service(HttpServlet.java:868)
    at com.unify.ewave.servletexec.ServletExec.CallServletService
(ServletExec.java:1703)
    at com.unify.ewave.servletexec.ServletExec.processServletRequest
(ServletExec.java:1648)
    at com.unify.ewave.servletexec.ServletExec.ProcessRequest
(ServletExec.java:1342)
    at com.unify.ewave.servletexec.ServletExec.run(ServletExec.java:358)
```

The log in Listing 5.1 is what we see when we use one of the Java Servlet API `log()` method calls. As this log file shows, the servlet that initiated this call was named *TestServlet*. The log was created from inside the `service()` method of this servlet. Just two lines of code code created this log:

```
log("This is a message sent to the log");
log("This is an error", new Exception());
```

This is a typical log created by a servlet engine, although the different servlet engines differ slightly in how they lay out the log. For example, a WebLogic server's log file will look similar to the one shown in Listing 5.1, but it will also include a log type on each line. This type helps identify what kind of log message is being sent. A WebLogic server version of the log file in Listing 5.1 is shown in Listing 5.2.

Listing 5.2 A servlet log from a WebLogic server

```
Tue Sep 12 11:12:10 MDT 2000:<I> <ServletContext-General>
    DrawCircle: This is a message
Tue Sep 12 11:12:10 MDT 2000:<E> <ServletContext-General>
    DrawCircle: This is an error
java.lang.Exception
        at DrawCircle.service(DrawCircle.java:23)
        at javax.servlet.http.HttpServlet.service
                (HttpServlet.java:865)
```

```
at weblogic.servlet.internal.ServletStubImpl.invokeServlet
(ServletStubImpl.java:124)
at weblogic.servlet.internal.ServletContextImpl.
invokeServlet(ServletContextImpl.java:760)
at weblogic.servlet.internal.ServletContextImpl.
invokeServlet(ServletContextImpl.java:707)
at weblogic.servlet.internal.ServletContextManager.
invokeServlet(ServletContextManager.java:251)
at weblogic.socket.MuxableSocketHTTP.invokeServlet
(MuxableSocketHTTP.java:369)
at weblogic.socket.MuxableSocketHTTP.execute
(MuxableSocketHTTP.java:269)
at weblogic.kernel.ExecuteThread.run(ExecuteThread.java,
Compiled Code)
```

The log created by WebLogic is not terribly different from ServletExec's log. The main differences are that the date/time stamp is not enclosed in brackets, and a log type enclosed by angle brackets is included after the date and time. For example, *<I>* indicates an information message, and *<E>* an error message. The log also states where it originated. The *<ServletContext-General>* text indicates that the log originated in a `ServletContext` object.

The point is that there are many servlet containers, and each container specifies the appearance of its log and the information the log displays. Most log files, however, have a similar flavor.

The other way to log information is with the `System.out.println()`, `System.err.println()`, and `Exception.printStackTrace()` calls. These methods typically are used to send data to the log without any question. They also do not include the name of the originating servlet, so knowing which servlet the log came from may take a little detective work. The `System` object just sends the data to the log. The `Exception.printStackTrace()` method dumps the exception stack trace to the error log.

Anomalies of a Servlet Engine Log File

The servlet log files in Listings 5.1 and 5.2, although very similar, have some definite differences. The differences are not a real concern, but they show that there are no real standards for a log file. One other area to examine is the exception stack trace when an error is encountered. Notice that in both logs, after the first few lines the date and time are not included. This can make the log somewhat difficult to read, especially when we may need to scan through many errors to find one in particular.

One major anomaly of the servlet engine log file arises as a consequence of using several applications on a single Web server. Although some servlet engines allow log files to be separated by application, many do not. The situation is difficult when multiple applications are writing to the same log file. Let's assume we have eight applications running on a Web server. On one of the many servlet containers that share a single servlet log, we may have a log file containing detailed information from each application. Imagine going through this log to try to follow a chain of events for a particular application. This could prove difficult because the log information from other applications will probably be interspersed throughout the file.

Finally, because there are no standards for the servlet log, some servlet containers allow generation log files and others do not. A *generation file* is a file that bears a different name from that of the log file, to which the log file can be copied when it exceeds a certain size. This file usually is differentiated by a numerical counter or date in the file name. For example, if we have a log file named `servlet.log`, this file will be copied to `servlet.log.1` after the log has reached a predetermined size. We continue to rename files until a certain number of generation files has been created. After we have exceeded the maximum number of generation files, the oldest one is deleted and all contents are shifted forward one file. Some servers build generation file support into their capabilities to prevent the disk from running out of space. This allows us to control how much log we want to see, while continually rolling the logging information.

The main point here is that a lack of standards means that different servlet containers handle their logging in different ways. We are thus led to review how we want our logs to be handled when we move from development to test to production. Do we want to accept a shared log or allow only a separated log? Do we want better formatting in the logs? Do we like the way ServletExec formats its logs, or do we prefer WebLogic's style?

Components of a Standardized Log File

Let's specify what an "ideal" standardized log file should look like and the components it should contain. You may have additional requirements, but the ones we will mention here cover many development needs.

To begin with, a log file should have a very readable format. The log files in Listings 5.1 and 5.2 are very well formatted until we come to the exception, at which point the date and time string is lost when the stack trace is printed. Whether the data on a particular line represents simple information or a stack trace, every line should have the date/time stamp. A consistent format or layout makes log files more readable.

WebLogic's specification of the data type being logged in the log file is also good. It is useful to differentiate among trace, information, and error log lines so that major pieces of information stand out. An ideal standard log file should identify information as follows:

- *<I>* would represent simple *information.* For instance, we might wish to send a log with the message *Application has started* or *Templates have loaded successfully.* These are examples of informational logs.
- *<T>* would represent *trace* or debug information. This type of log is most useful to programmers who are debugging an application. We would send this type of log to explain where we were in the code or to output the value of a variable.
- *<E>* would represent an *error.* Such a log would be displayed for stack traces or exception dumps to the log file.

On the basis of these criteria, an ideal standard log would look like Listing 5.3.

Listing 5.3 An ideal standard log file

```
[ 2000-09-08 11:35:21 MDT ] {I} This is a message sent to the log
[ 2000-09-08 11:35:21 MDT ] {T} This is a trace message sent to the log
[ 2000-09-08 11:35:21 MDT ] {E} TRAN ID - 968434521338-16
[ 2000-09-08 11:35:21 MDT ] {E} This is an error
[ 2000-09-08 11:35:21 MDT ] {E} java.lang.Exception
[ 2000-09-08 11:35:21 MDT ] {E} at TestServlet.service
            (TestServlet.java:23)
[ 2000-09-08 11:35:21 MDT ] {E} at HttpServlet.service
            (HttpServlet.java:868)
[ 2000-09-08 11:35:21 MDT ] {E} at CallServletService
            (ServletExec.java:1703)
[ 2000-09-08 11:35:21 MDT ] {E} at processServletRequest
            (ServletExec.java:1648)
[ 2000-09-08 11:35:21 MDT ] {E} at ProcessRequest
            (ServletExec.java:1342)
[ 2000-09-08 11:35:21 MDT ] {E} at run(ServletExec.java:358)
```

Note the third line (boldface) in Listing 5.3. An ideal standard log file should support the concept of transaction IDs (*tran IDs* for short). A tran ID is a unique identifier that we can send to a log file that is used as a bookmark to locate error information or critical information very quickly. Why would we want to bookmark errors or critical information? Say we have a high-capacity Web site that produces a lot of information in the log. All of a sudden a call comes in from a user reporting that he/she has encountered an error. Finding this error in a large log file can be difficult. But if the tran ID can be sent to the log and printed out to the end user, then when the user reports the error we can get the tran ID from the user and search the log file for it. Having the tran ID will thus allow us to find the information on the error right away.

The ideal standard log file should be specific to only one application. Every application should have its own log file. Keeping the log file specific to an application will prevent the file from becoming convoluted and difficult to follow when we're attempting to determine the flow of a set of events in a log. Imagine having eight high-capacity applications on a Web server and having to follow the flow of just one application's log in a log file containing information from all eight applications. This could be a difficult task. So we want each log file to be specific to a single application.

Finally, an ideal standard log file should support generation files. We should be able to set up the log file to specify a maximum size and a maximum number of generations. Therefore, when the log file has reached a predetermined size, a number will be appended to its name, and any other generation files that already exist will also be renamed. Once the maximum number of

Case Study

Employee White Pages, Automated Expense, and Travel Reservation applications were sharing a single Web server at a large telecommunication organization. All three were high-capacity applications. The most widely used of the three, the Employee White Pages application, had a hit rate of over 1 million hits per day because it was used by 77,000 employees. This application alone had the capability of filling a server's log with 250MB of data each day.

The developers built all three applications using the logging facilities that were part of the servlet API. As a result, each application sent its information to the Web server log. The three applications worked flawlessly until one day an executive vice president of finance hit a snag in the Automated Expense application. He called the development team to find out why he was getting an error message, and he wanted answers very quickly.

Reviewing the servlet engine log proved futile. The team had to go through 200MB of logs from the three different applications. When the approximate location of the error was found in the log file, the team had to trace back to identify the events that had led to the problem. Because the logs for three high-capacity applications were intermixed, reviewing the chain of events was a very difficult chore, and it took a day and a half to get answers for the VP of finance.

> To solve the problem of a complex and confusing log file, the development group built a robust logging object specific to each application. To find errors more rapidly, they integrated the *transaction ID* concept; that is, they gave each error the ability to send a tran ID to the log and return it to the program. This capability allowed the developer to send the tran ID to the user so that the user could report this ID to the support group. With this information in hand, the development group was able to find a problem in the log file very quickly and to more easily follow the chain of events that may have led to the problem.

generation files has been reached, the oldest one will be deleted before the next generation file is created. This mechanism allows us to "roll" the contents of the log files so that the most current information is retained. (From this point forward we'll refer to this process as the *generation roll.*) Having a log file support generations prevents us from constantly having to monitor the log file size so that it does not fill the hard disk.

The EnterpriseLog Object

We have just established criteria for an ideal standardized log file. Let's briefly review these specifications:

- The log file should be in standardized readable format, each line with a date/time stamp.
- The log file should support three basic types of logged data: information (<*I*>), trace data (<*T*>), and errors (<*E*>). Each line should be stamped with its associated type.
- The log file should support transaction IDs.
- Each application should have its own log file.
- The log file should support generation log files.

With these specifications in mind, let's build a log file object that handles each of these requirements. Because this will be a robust object that will eventually become a significant member of the enterprise servlet framework, we will call it `EnterpriseLog`. This is a common type of object, so we will put it in the `enterprise.common` package. Let's begin by declaring the object and its member variables.

```
package enterprise.common;

import java.io.*;
import java.util.*;
import enterprise.common.*;
import enterprise.servlet.AppContext;
import java.text.SimpleDateFormat;

public class EnterpriseLog
{
  private String           m_logFilePath    = null;
  private RandomAccessFile m_logFile        = null;
  private long             m_maxSize        = 0;
  private int              m_generations    = 0;
```

The log file will have objects representing the filename and its path, the number of generations we want the log file to support, and the maximum ssize of the log file. So we need to create member variables for these items. In particular, we want to use `RandomAccessFile` for the file object instead of `FileWriter` or `FileOutputStream` because `RandomAccessFile`'s output typically does not get buffered in the operating system when we need to write out to the file. Why is this important? If we are using generation files and specifying the maximum size of the log file, we consistently want to check the file size after writing to the log to find out if we have exceeded it and if it is time to do a generation roll. When we use `FileWriter` or `FileOutputStream`, depending on the platform, the output may not be written to disk. If not, then the reading we get when we check the file's size will not be accurate. By using a `RandomAccessFile` object, we are guaranteed to get an accurate file size on each reading.

Let's declare a few more member variables to support the `EnterpriseLog` object. Because we want each line to display the date and time, we need a `SimpleDateFormat` member to contain the date/time string. Each line in the log file also ends with a line separator. On a Windows or DOS machine, a line separator is a carriage return and a line feed. On a UNIX machine it is just a line feed. So we need a member variable to hold the line separator for the current operating system that is executing the object. We also want to create a locking object that controls synchronized access to writing to the log file because this object will be used in a multithreaded environment. We make this object public so that any outside code that needs access to the locking object will have it.

```
  private SimpleDateFormat m_logDateFormat = null;
  private String           m_separator     = null;

  public  Object           m_lock          = new Object();
```

Because we are going to log three types of information—trace data (<*T*>), simple information (<*I*>), and errors (<*E*>)—we probably want to be able to filter these types of log requests out of the logging facility. For instance, we may have heavy trace logs in the application to aid in debugging, but when we go to production, we may not wish to have all of this trace data in the log files. We need to be able to filter out these logs as they are being created, so we will create a filter mask that specifies what kind of data will be logged to the log file. We'll go into more detail on this in a moment.

```
private int             m_filterMask    = 0;
```

Finally, we will create a counter to make the transaction ID unique. When we develop the code that produces the trans ID, we will see exactly how this works. For now, we will just create the member variable.

```
private static int      m_nIncrement    = 0;
```

Next we need to create some important global constants that are an integral part of the logging object. We will create the log type and filtering constants that we will use when setting a log message type and how we want to filter it. Building these types of filters on the basis of binary data is an extremely effective way of creating filters because it easily allows us to execute the OR, AND, and other logical operations when building a filter. For example, we can create constants for our three data types: `TRACE`, `INFO`, and `ERROR`. If we build these constants with binary numbers, we can combine data types to create a filter by using the OR operator—for example, `INFO | ERROR`. Using binary data thus makes it easy to customize and build filters, and the results are very readable.

```
public static final int INFO   = 0x01;
public static final int TRACE  = 0x02;
public static final int ERROR  = 0x04;
```

For the sake of readability when we write the code, let's redundantly create *FILTER* constants of the log types just shown, as well as a `FILTER_ALL` constant to offer a simple way to filter all log types. Notice that we create the `FILTER_ALL` constant by using the OR operator, |, to combine all the log types.

```
public static final int FILTER_INFO  = INFO;
public static final int FILTER_ERROR = ERROR;
public static final int FILTER_TRACE = TRACE;
public static final int FILTER_ALL = FILTER_INFO |
                                     FILTER_ERROR |
                                     FILTER_TRACE;
```

Having declared the member variables and global constants, we are now ready to build the constructors for the `EnterpriseLog` object. As stated at the beginning of this section, we want the capability to make log generation files optional. If we don't want generation files, we have no need to pass parameters to the logging object. These possibilities lead us to develop two constructors for the EnterpriseLog object: one that takes generation file setup parameters and one that does not.

Let's examine the more complex constructor and decide what we need to create a log file. First, of course, we need a filename and a path, so we will make the parameter containing this information required. To set up generation files, we need a maximum file size so that the object knows when to do a generation roll, as well as the total number of generation files that we wish to create. These are all the parameters required for this constructor.

Because this is the more complex constructor, it should also be the main constructor that is called by all other constructors. Therefore we need to think about the implications of the parameters that are passed. We can make a rule that if the maximum file size is 0 or the generation number is 0, we will not create generation files. Anything less than 0 would be considered illegal. In addition, to keep things simple, let's specify the maximum file size in kilobytes. A value of 100 will thus be construed as 100KB; a value of 1,000 as 1MB, and so on. Here's the constructor:

```
public EnterpriseLog(String logFilePath, long maxSize,
                     int generations)
  throws IllegalArgumentException
{
```

Now let's test the generation file parameters for legal arguments; that is, let's make sure that their values are 0 or greater. If the values are less than 0, we'll throw an IllegalArgumentException.

```
  if (maxSize < 0)
  {
    throw new IllegalArgumentException(
             "maxSize parameter argument is less than 0.");
  }

  if (generations < 0)
  {
    throw new IllegalArgumentException(
             "generations parameter argument is less than 0.");
  }
```

At this point we'll initialize the member variables. The parameter values we pass in will establish member variables for the filename and path, the maximum log file size, and the maximum number of generation files. Let's also create the formatted date/time string that we will use when logging data.

```
  m_logFilePath = logFilePath;
  m_maxSize = maxSize;
  m_generations = generations;
```

```
    m_logDateFormat =  new SimpleDateFormat(
                                "[ yyyy-MM-dd hh:mm:ss zzz ] ");
```

In addition, we want to set the line separator for the operating system that is hosting this object. Luckily, we can query the correct line separator with the `System` object. In reponse to a query of `line.separator` with the `getProperty()` method, the Java framework will return the line separation string:

```
    m_separator = System.getProperty("line.separator");
```

To complete the constructor, we want to set a default filter. We should allow all types of log data to be sent to the log file as a default, so we will call a setter that we will create later in this object and pass it the `FILTER_ALL` constant value.

```
    setLogFilter(EnterpriseLog.FILTER_ALL);
  }
```

As stated earlier, this constructor should be the main constructor that is called by all other constructors. Other constructors we create will call the one we just developed with default parameters. In addition, we want a constructor that does not require generation file parameters because we want the generation file to be optional. So we will create a constructor that a path and filename as its only parameter. This constructor will call the main constructor with 0 values for its maximum file size and number of generation files. Remember that if either of these values is 0, the object will not create a generation file.

```
  public EnterpriseLog(String logFilePath)
    throws IllegalArgumentException
  {
    this(logFilePath, 0, 0);
  }
```

Now let's create the getters and setters for the log filter. In these methods we want to access the `m_filterMask` member variable, either by setting it with a value or by retrieving the value for the end user. Here's where we begin using a centralized locking object, `m_lock`. Whenever we use *any* shared resource with this object, we want to be sure we have a traffic cop that says, "One at a time." Synchronizing methods is not good enough because only the methods themselves are synchronized. We need a semaphore, `m_lock`, that controls locking for the *entire* class.

Why is this important? A good example is that if we have more than one logging method (which we will in this object) and we synchronize them, each method can attempt to log concurrently (i.e., method `logInfo()` can run at the same time as `logError()`). Synchronizing the methods prevents more than one thread from running the same method at the same time, but it does not prevent separate methods from running concurrently. By using a semaphore such as `m_lock`, we can be sure that only the thread that has the lock on `m_lock` can run any code in the *entire* class. So we will use the `m_lock` semaphore heavily when accessing shared resources in the `EnterpriseLog` class.

```
public int setLogFilter(int filterMask)
{
  synchronized(m_lock)
  {
    int oldMask = m_filterMask;

    m_filterMask = filterMask;

    return oldMask;
  }
}

public int getLogFilter()
{
  synchronized(m_lock)
  {
    return m_filterMask;
  }
}
```

Other getters include methods to retrieve the formatted date/time string for the log file and a tran ID. The `getDateTimeString()` method will return the formatted current date/time string that is placed on each logged line in the file. The `getTranId()` method will return a unique transaction ID. The tran ID is the number of milliseconds since January 1, 1970, and it is made unique by incrementation of the `m_nIncrement` member variable.

We need the incrementor in case two threads access this code in the same millisecond. Is this possible? Maybe not, but we will include this code just to be sure. We will also return the incrementor to 0 after it has reached 9,999 because there is very little chance that this code will be executed by 10,000 threads in the same millisecond. The `getTranId()` method will be static so that any code can get a transaction ID without having to create an `EnterpriseLog` object. Tran IDs could come in handy in many different development efforts.

```
private String getDateTimeString()
{

  return m_logDateFormat.format(new Date());

}
```

```
public static synchronized String getTranId()
{
  StringBuffer sb = new StringBuffer();
  Date now = new Date();
  sb.append(now.getTime());
  sb.append("-");
  sb.append(++m_nIncrement);

  if (m_nIncrement > 9999)
  {
         m_increment = 0;
  }

  sb.toString();
  return sb.toString();
}
```

The logging class must be able both to create and to open or close the log file. For these functions we will create `openLog()` and `closeLog()` methods. The `openLog()` method will open or create the log file and set the file-write pointer at the end of the file, thus allowing the logger to append itself to any previously existing log file.

```
public void openLog()
  throws IOException
{
  m_logFile = new RandomAccessFile(m_logFilePath, "rw");
  m_logFile.seek(m_logFile.length());
}

public void closeLog()
  throws IOException
{
  m_logFile.close();
}
```

Now we're ready to develop the main engine of the `EnterpriseLog` object: the logger itself. The `logMessage()` method will be responsible for logging most messages because single-line messages are what we want sent to the log. It will take two parameters: a log type (`TRACE`, `INFO`, or `ERROR`) and the message to be logged. The first thing we want to do is lock the semaphore, `m_lock`. Every time we log something, we want to retrieve a transaction ID. We will pass this tran ID back to the user because it can be used as an acknowledgment for an action when we return from this method.

The next thing we'll do is check the requested log type against the filter mask. By using the logical AND (&) operator to test the log type with the filter mask, we can decide whether we send the message to the log or simply skip it. If we do wish to log the message, we build the log line by combining the date/time string, the log type, and the message and sending the combination to the log file. After writing to the log, we will call the `checkLogSize()` method, which is responsible for monitoring the generation files and maximum file size.

```
public String logMessage(int logType, String str)
{
  synchronized(m_lock)
  {
    String tranId = getTranId();
    StringBuffer buffer = new StringBuffer();

    if ((logType & m_filterMask) == logType)
    {

      buffer.setLength(0);
      buffer.append(getDateTimeString());

      switch(logType)
      {
        case(ERROR):
          buffer.append("{E} ");
          break;
        case(INFO):
          buffer.append("{I} ");
          break;
        case(TRACE):
          buffer.append("{T} ");
          break;
        default:
          buffer.append("{?} ");
          break;
      }

      buffer.append(str);
      buffer.append(m_separator);

      try
      {
        m_logFile.writeBytes(buffer.toString());
        checkLogSize();
      } catch (IOException ioe)
      {
        ioe.printStackTrace();
      }

    }

    return tranId;
  }
}
```

The checkLogSize() method is called whenever something is written to the log so that we can constantly keep an eye on the log's size. Here's where we check for the maximum file size and generation number values. If either one is 0, we exit the method without doing anything. If both are not greater than 0, we test the log file for its size. If the size is greater than or equal to the maximum log size, we do a generation roll.

```
private void checkLogSize() throws IOException
{

  // If there is no maximum size for generations, ignore creating
  // generation files.
  if ((m_maxSize == 0) || (m_generations == 0))
  {
    return;
  }

  // If we have reached the maximum size, then generate.
  if (m_logFile.length() >= m_maxSize * 1024)
  {
    closeLog();
    for(int i = m_generations; i > 0; i--)
    {
      String oldFilePath = m_logFilePath;
      if ((i - 1) > 0)
        oldFilePath += "." + (i-1);

      File oldFile = new File(oldFilePath);
      if (oldFile.exists())
      {
        String newFilePath = m_logFilePath + "." + i;
        File newFile = new File(newFilePath);
        newFile.delete();
        oldFile.renameTo(new File(newFilePath));
      }
    }

    openLog();
  }
}
```

Now let's create some helper methods that allow the user to create trace and information logs.

```
public String logInfo(String str)
{
  return logMessage(INFO, str);
}
```

```
public String logTrace(String str)
{
  return logMessage(TRACE, str);
}
```

We need a special class that handles errors or exceptions. Why? When we get an exception, we usually like to see the stack trace. The stack trace is usually a multiline string, which is why when an error occurs in a servlet engine log, we lose the date/time information. The servlet engine just prints the stack trace. In the logging object, we want errors formatted so that readability is enhanced. This means that we want to break each line in a stack trace into separate lines and format them as usual. This method will need to call a function that is a part of the logging object called `splitTrace()`. Its sole purpose is to take an exception, break the stack trace into individual lines, and return a `String` array in which each line is a separate element.

Now that we have established how we will break out the stack trace, let's build the `logException()` method. We want the main error-logging method to take a `String` object and an `Exception` object as parameters. Again we will start by locking the semaphore so that we have an exclusive lock on the log file. This is especially critical here because we will be sending multiple lines to a log and we don't want the lines interrupted by other information or trace logs. Locking the semaphore ensures that nobody else can write to the log at the same time. We will get a tran ID and decide whether we are logging errors by checking the filter mask. If we are, then we will first break the exception into multiple lines through a call to `splitTrace()`. We will then write the tran ID to the log. With this information in the log file, we can find the exact place the error occurred by searching for its tran ID. Typically we will send the tran ID back to the user in HTML, who will report it to us, thus giving us the information we need to find the error very rapidly.

After writing the tran ID, we'll see if we need to write the `String` message that we originally passed into the method. If the `String` message is `null`, we ignore it; otherwise we write it to the log. Finally, we spin through the `String` array of stack trace lines and send each one to the log. By doing this we format the stack trace so that the log file is more readable.

```
public String logException(String msg, Exception e)
{
  synchronized(m_lock)
  {
    String tranId = getTranId();
    StringBuffer buffer = new StringBuffer();

    if ((ERROR & m_filterMask) == ERROR)
    {
```

```
        String dateTime = getDateTimeString();
        String errors[] = splitTrace(e);

        buffer.setLength(0);

        buffer.append(dateTime);
        buffer.append("{E} TRAN ID - ");
        buffer.append(tranId);
        buffer.append(m_separator);

        if (msg != null)
        {
          buffer.append(dateTime);
          buffer.append("{E} ");
          buffer.append(msg);
          buffer.append(m_separator);
        }

        for (int i = 0; i < errors.length; i++)
        {
          buffer.append(dateTime);
          buffer.append("{E} ");
          buffer.append(errors[i]);
          buffer.append(m_separator);
        }


        try
        {
          m_logFile.writeBytes(buffer.toString());
          checkLogSize();
        } catch (IOException ioe)
        {
          ioe.printStackTrace();
        }

      }

      return tranId;
    }
  }
```

Because we may not always want to pass a `String` message when reporting an error, we will create a helper method that does not take a string as a parameter and allows us just to log the error.

```
  public String logException(Exception e)
  {
    return logException(null, e);
  }
```

Finally, we need to develop the `splitTrace()` function. This method will take an exception as a parameter, and break each line in the stack trace into individual lines, returning the result in a `String` array. The `splitTrace()` method captures the output of the `Exception.printStackTrace()` method through a `StringWriter` object and ultimately places the stack trace in a `String` array.

```
private String[] splitTrace(Exception e)
  {
    StringWriter sw = new StringWriter();
    PrintWriter pw = new PrintWriter(swtrue);
    Vector v = new Vector();

    e.printStackTrace(pw);
```

We take the stack trace `String` and tokenize the line separators within the `String` with the `StringTokenizer` object. As we find a separator, we add the line to a `Vector` object.

```
    StringTokenizer st = new StringTokenizer(
                             sw.toString(), m_separator);

    while(st.hasMoreElements())
    {
      v.addElement((String)st.nextElement());
    }
```

When we are finished building the `Vector` object with lines, we convert it to a `String` array and send it back to the user.

```
    String[] retArray = new String[v.size()];

    v.copyInto(retArray);

    try
    {
        pw.close();
        sw.close();
    }
    catch(Exception ex)
    {}
    finally
    {
        pw = null;
        sw = null;
        v = null;
    }

    return retArray;
  }

}
```

There we have it: the EnterpriseLog object. That was a lot of code for a simple logging object! Well, the object wasn't so simple, so meeting all the requirements required all this code. Despite the complexity of the code, however, the object itself is simple to use. That was the real reason for all the code. Ultimately we want this object to be very simple for a developer to use, so that developers can concentrate on writing business logic and not worry about the application infrastructure.

How do we use the EnterpriseLog object? We start by creating the object and opening the log file. We can use the simple form if we don't want generation files:

```
EnterpriseLog el = new EnterpriseLog("C:\\Book\\Chapter 05\\
                       Example 1\\logs\\mylog.log");
el.openLog();
```

Or we can use the constructor that allows us to define generation files:

```
// Define a maximum log size of 1MB (1,000*1,024 = 1MB) and
// a maximum of 10 generation files.
EnterpriseLog el = new EnterpriseLog("C:\\Book\\Chapter 05\\
                       Example 2\\logs\\mylog.log", 1000, 10);
el.openLog();
```

We can set the filter mask at any time if we want to create only certain types of logs, or we can skip this step if we want to log everything, which is the default.

```
// Don't log trace data.
el.setFilter( EnterpriseLog.FILTER_INFO | EnterpriseLog.
              FILTER_ERROR );
```

To log data, then, we use one of the four logging methods:

1. `el.logTrace("This is a trace log")`
2. `el.logInfo("This is an info log")`
3. `el.logException("This is an error", new Exception() )`
4. `el.logException(new Exception() )`

When we're finished and the application is shutting down, we close the log. (Although closing the log is not necessary, because the Java Virtual Machine will close any open files when it shuts down, it is good coding etiquette.)

```
el.close();
```

As you can see, the EnterpriseLog object allows us to create a robust logging mechanism that supports formatted log text, log typing, and generation files. This object can be used within the enterprise servlet architecture or in a standard servlet.

Logging in Enterprise Servlets

We have seen how simple it is to create and use the `EnterpriseLog` object. But how do we use it in the enterprise servlet architecture? Because one of our objectives is to have one log file per application, `EnterpriseLog` fits into the architecture very well. Typically we will want almost every application to have a log, so it should be easy for you to guess the appropriate place (object) for `EnterpriseLog` to be; it is `AppContext`, of course.

Because the `EnterpriseLog` object will exist in the `AppContext` object, the application will have access to the log throughout the code. This means that we can also configure the log through the configuration file. The parameters we want to configure are the filename and path, the maximum log file size, the maximum number of generation files, and the log filter mask. Why would we want these configurable in the configuration file? In development we probably will not have a heavy load of users, so we probably don't care about generation files, and we will probably want to have the trace as part of the log filter so that we can see debug statements that we place in the code. When we go to production, however, we probably will want generation files and we may be interested in only the information and error data in the logs. Making these parameters configurable in the log file gives us the flexibility to change how the logging works in different environments.

Essentially we want to support the following four new configuration file parameters:

1. **`Log.File.Path`**. The path and the filename of the log file.
2. **`Log.Generation.Count`**. The maximum number of log generation files.
3. **`Log.Max.Size`**. The maximum log file size in kilobytes (e.g., 100 = 100KB).
4. **`Log.Filter`**. The log filter mask of the types of data we want to log. Legal values are `TRACE`, `INFO`, `ERROR`, and `ALL`. We can mix and match different types by delimiting them with a comma. For example, if we wanted to log information and error data, we would make the value `INFO, ERROR`.

Of course, we will make these parameters optional. If the developer really doesn't want a log file, then he/she shouldn't be required to have one.

To integrate EnterpriseLog into AppContext, we will follow the methodology we have implemented in previous chapters when adding common parameters and objects to AppContext. We will create global constants, create a parser to verify and move the configuration file parameters into values that we can work with, and provide the proper getters and setters to give us access to the objects. In this case, however, instead of giving direct access to the EnterpriseLog object with getters and setters, let's provide helper methods that allow the developer to log information directly from the AppContext object. This approach to logging data in the applications should be considerably better than getting references to the log object itself. In addition, if the developer attempts to use the logger and it has not been configured in the configuration file, this approach to logging information allows us to throw errors when he/she attempts to use the log.

Let's begin by taking AppContext and declaring the String constants that we look for in the configuration files, as well as the EnterpriseLog object.

```
public class AppContext
{
.
.
.
  public static final String LOG_FILE_PATH    = "Log.File.Path";
  public static final String LOG_GENERATION   =
       "Log.Generation.Count";
  public static final String LOG_MAX_SIZE     = "Log.Max.Size";
  public static final String LOG_FILTER       = "Log.Filter";
.
.
.
  private EnterpriseLog      oAppLog         = null;
.
.
.
```

Now let's create accessor methods so that we can use the EnterpriseLog object. We only really need to set and get the filter and provide access to the logging type functions. We'll build each of these methods, but let's also check if the EnterpriseLog object has been created and initialized. We will add a method, isLog(), that allows us to query if a log has been set up and initialized in the application. Essentially we check if the log object is null. If it is, we return false; otherwise (i.e., if the log object exists) we return true. In the accessor methods, the fact that a log object has not been created will signify that the proper information has not been set up in the configuration file for the log, and we will throw a ResourceNotConfiguredException.

```
.
.
.
public boolean isLog()
{
  return (oAppLog != null);
}

public synchronized int setLogFilter(int filterMask)
      throws ResourceNotConfiguredException
{

  if (isLog())
  {
    throw new ResourceNotConfiguredException(
                              "The log file is not configured.");
  }

  return oAppLog.setLogFilter(filterMask);
}

public synchronized int getLogFilter()
      throws ResourceNotConfiguredException
{

  if (oAppLog == null)
  {
    throw new ResourceNotConfiguredException(
                              "The log file is not configured.");
  }

  return oAppLog.getLogFilter();
}

public synchronized Object getLogLockSemaphore()
      throws ResourceNotConfiguredException
{

  if (oAppLog == null)
  {
    throw new ResourceNotConfiguredException(
                              "The log file is not configured.");
  }

  return oAppLog.m_lock;
}

public synchronized String logTrace(String msg)
{
  String transId = "";

  if (isLog())
  {
```

```
      try
      {
        transId = oAppLog.logTrace(msg);
      }
      catch (Exception e)
      {
        System.err.print(sAppName + " can't generate log : " +
                                               e + " IOException");
      }
    }

    return transId;
  }

  public synchronized String logInfo(String msg)
  {
    String transId = "";

    if (isLog())
    {
      try
      {
        transId = oAppLog.logInfo(msg);
      }
      catch (Exception e)
      {
        System.err.print(sAppName + " can't generate log : " +
                                               e + " IOException");
      }
    }

    return transId;
  }

  public synchronized String logError(Exception exp)
  {
    String transId = "";

    if (isLog())
    {
      try
      {
        transId = oAppLog.logException(exp);
      }
      catch (Exception e)
      {
        System.err.print(sAppName + " can't generate log : " +
                                               e + " IOException");
      }
    }

    return transId;
  }
```

```
public synchronized String logError(String msg, Exception exp)
{
  String transId = "";

  if (isLog())
  {
    try
    {
      transId = oAppLog.logException(msg, exp);
    }
    catch (Exception e)
    {
      System.err.print(sAppName + " can't generate log : " +
                                        e + " IOException");
    }
  }

  return transId;
}
```

We need a parser method to read log parameters from the configuration file, verify them, and if all are valid, create the logging object.

```
.
.
.
  private void parseLogInfo(ConfFile cf)
    throws ServletException
  {

    int                  nLogGenerations = 0;
    long                 nLogMaxSize     = 0;
    int                  nFilter         = 0;

    // Set the maximum number of log generations.
    String sLogGen = cf.getValue(LOG_GENERATION);
    if ((sLogGen != null) && (sLogGen.trim().length() > 0))
    {
      try
      {
        nLogGenerations = Integer.parseInt(sLogGen);
      }
      catch(NumberFormatException nef)
      {
        throw new ServletException(LOG_GENERATION +
                             " contains a non-numeric value.");
      }
    }

    // Set the maximum log file size.
    String sLogSize = cf.getValue(LOG_MAX_SIZE);
    if ((sLogSize != null) && (sLogSize.trim().length() > 0))
    {
```

```
    try
    {
      nLogMaxSize = Long.parseLong(sLogSize);
    }
    catch(NumberFormatException nef)
    {
      throw new ServletException(LOG_MAX_SIZE +
                " contains a non-numeric value.");
    }
  }

  // Get the logging filter.
  String sLogFilter = cf.getValue(LOG_FILTER);
  if ((sLogFilter != null) && (sLogFilter.trim().length() > 0))
  {
    StringTokenizer st = new StringTokenizer(sLogFilter, ",");
    while (st.hasMoreTokens())
    {
      String sFilter = st.nextToken();
      if (sFilter.trim().toUpperCase().equals("ALL"))
      {
        nFilter = nFilter | EnterpriseLog.FILTER_ALL;
      } else if (sLevel.trim().toUpperCase().equals("INFO"))
      {
        nFilter = nFilter | EnterpriseLog.FILTER_INFO;
      } else if (sFilter.trim().toUpperCase().equals("TRACE"))
      {
        nFilter = nFilter | EnterpriseLog.FILTER_TRACE;
      } else if (sFilter.trim().toUpperCase().equals("ERROR"))
      {
        nFilter = nFilter | EnterpriseLog.FILTER_ERROR;
      } else
      {
        throw new ServletException(LOG_FILTER +
                      " contains an invalid value.");
      }
    }
  } else
  {
    nFilter = EnterpriseLog.FILTER_ALL;
  }

  // Get the log file to activate logging.

  String logFilePath = cf.getValue(LOG_FILE_PATH);

  if (logFilePath != null)
  {
    try
    {
```

```
        oAppLog = new EnterpriseLog(logFilePath, nLogMaxSize,
                                    nLogGenerations);
        oAppLog.setLogFilter(nFilter);

        oAppLog.openLog();
      }
      catch(Exception e)
      {
        e.printStackTrace();
        throw new ServletException(e.getMessage());
      }
    }
.
.
.
```

Finally, we need to call the log parser from the `parseConfigFile()` method. We should do this early in the method so that the log is available to the initialization code if we need it. The best place to put this call is probably just after the `setAppName(appName)` call.

```
  public void parseConfigFile(String appName,String fileName)
        throws ServletException
  {
.
.
.
    setAppName(appName);

    parseLogInfo(cf);
.
.
.
  }
}
```

`AppContext` is now ready to parse the new configuration file logging parameters and integrate the log in the enterprise servlet architecture.

Just for kicks, if the servlets start properly let's send the message *Application has started* to the log. In `BaseEnterpriseServlet`, we want to add the following code to the end of the `init()` method. If we reach the end of the `init()` method without any exceptions, it's safe to say that the servlet has started properly. We will check if we have a log object, and if so, we'll log the information message.

```
public final void init(ServletConfig config) throws ServletException
{
.
.
.
```

```
    if (m_ac.isLog())
    {
      m_ac.logInfo("***********************************************");
      m_ac.logInfo(getAppName() + " Application has started.");
    }

}
```

Now the EnterpriseLog object is completely integrated in the enterprise servlet architecture, so we are ready to develop enterprise servlet–based applications and use this robust logging object. This object is worth all the code it required, as the example in the next section will show.

A Logging Example

Our example will be an enterprise servlet architecture application that has one purpose: to log data. To show how simple the EnterpriseLog object is to configure and use in the enterprise servlet architecture, we will develop an application that logs all the different kinds of errors. The application will log text that is placed into a text field, and one of three buttons may be pressed to set the log type. The application will also dump the log to the screen so that we can see the log being updated each time we submit the form. Figure 5.1 shows the output from the sample logger application.

In this example we will use the concept of a *half template*. A half template is simply an incomplete template that has most of the HTML layout but does not end with </body></html>. Instead, we have the servlet end the HTML with the proper text. Why do we do this? We do this when we want to stream large amounts of data to the browser. It is extremely inefficient to create a large StringBuffer object every time we want to display the log. Keep in mind that a log file can become very large—many times bigger than the computer's memory. So allocating the log to a StringBuffer object could potentially be disastrous. It is much more feasible to stream the data directly to the browser as it is produced. Hence in our application we want to dump the contents of the log to the user. By using a half template, we are able to format the upper part of the template, stream the log to the user, and then close the HTML by outputting the </body></html> tags. The template that produces the upper portion of Figure 5.1 is shown in Listing 5.4.

Listing 5.4 The logger.html template, a good example of a half template

```
<html>
<head>
<title>Show Log</title>
</head>
```

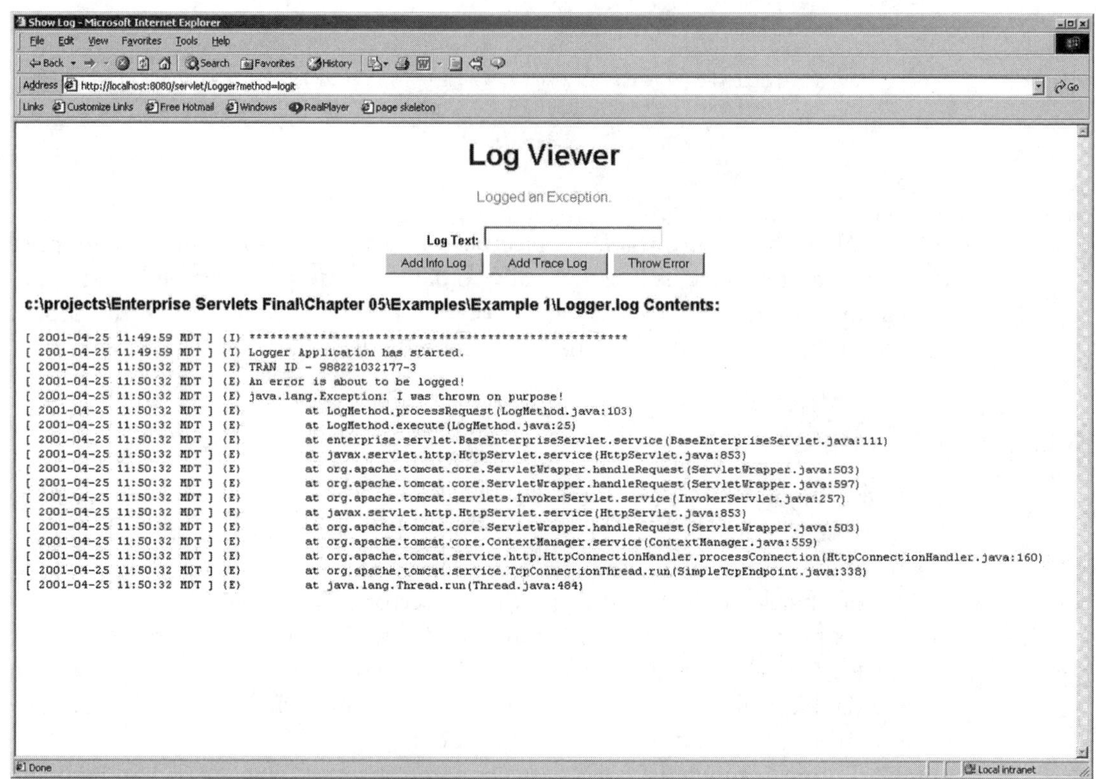

Figure 5.1 Sample logger application output

```
<body bgcolor="#FFFFFF">
<center>
  <h1><font face="Arial, Helvetica, sans-serif">Log Viewer</font> </h1>

  <p><font face="Arial, Helvetica, sans-serif"
      color="green">${MESSAGE}</font> </p>

  <form method="post" action="${BASEURL}?method=logit">
    <table border="0" cellspacing="0" cellpadding="3">
      <tr>
        <td valign="bottom">
          <b><font face="Arial, Helvetica, sans-serif" size="2">Log
            Text: </font></b>
        </td>
        <td valign="bottom">
          <input type="text" name="logtext" size="30" maxlength="70">
        </td>
      </tr>
    </table>
    <table border="0" cellspacing="0" cellpadding="3">
```

```
        <tr>
          <td>
            <input type="submit" name="button" value="Add Info Log">
          </td>
          <td>
            <input type="submit" name="button" value="Add Trace Log">
          </td>
          <td>
            <input type="submit" name="button" value="Throw Error">
          </td>
        </tr>
      </table>
    </form>
</center>
<h3><font face="Arial, Helvetica, sans-serif">${LOGFILE}
Contents:</font> </h3>
```

Let's call our new application *Logger* and set up the configuration file. The application will consist of a single dispatch method that we will call `LogMethod`. After setting up the usual parameters—such as dispatch methods, the base URL, and the template—we'll configure the logging parameters.

`Log.File.Path` will point at where we want the log file to exist and to be named. We'll set `Log.Generation.Count` to 5 (for five generations). To keep the maximum log file size small so that we can observe the file generation roll, we'll set `Log.Max.Size` to 3 (for 3K). We want to show all types of logs, so we'll set `Log.Filter` to `all`. Listing 5.5 is an example of the configuration file.

Listing 5.5 Configuration file for Logger

```
Application.Base.URL=/servlet/Logger

Default.Method=logit
Method.logit=LogMethod

# Place the default template path here.
Default.Template.Path=c:\\Book\\Chapter 05\\Example 1\\templates
Template.logger=logger.html

# Place the log file path here.
Log.File.Path=c:\\Book\\Chapter 05\\Example 1\\Logger.log

# Place the maximum number of log generation files here.
Log.Generation.Count=5

# Place the maximum size of the log file here.
# Value is in 1K bytes (i.e 10 = 10K)
Log.Max.Size=3
Log.Filter=all
```

Like the application, the main dispatch servlet is called `Logger`. Listing 5.6 shows the code for the `Logger` class.

Listing 5.6 The `Logger` class, the main dispatch servlet

```
import enterprise.servlet.*;
import enterprise.common.*;

import java.io.*;

public class Logger extends BaseEnterpriseServlet
{
  public void initializeApp(AppContext appContext) throws Exception
  {
  }

  public void destroyApp(AppContext appContext)
  {
  }

  public String getAppName()
  {
    return "Logger";
  }
}
```

The dispatch method that we listed in the configuration file is called `LogMethod`. This class is responsible for loading the template, substituting the proper values, opening the log file, and streaming the log file contents to the user. Here's where we use the half template.

The class begins by initializing the objects—i.e., loading the templates. It then processes the request by looking at the query parameters sent from the browser. In particular, it looks for the string to send to the log and the type of log to write. For the `INFO` and `TRACE` types, it just calls the `logInfo()` and `logTrace()` methods from `AppContext`. However, to get the `logException()` method to work properly, we need an `Exception` object. So we will throw an exception, but we also catch it so that we can log it.

To read the log file, we must convert the log to HTML. We do this by reading each line in the log file; appending an HTML line break, `<br>`, to the line; and streaming the line to the user. Streaming or writing each line as we read it prevents us from creating too large a `StringBuffer` object. When we are finished streaming the output to the user, we end the HTML with `</body></html>`, which ultimately closes the HTML created by the half template. Listing 5.7 shows the code for `LogMethod`.

Listing 5.7 The `LogMethod` class

```
import enterprise.servlet.*;
import enterprise.common.*;
import enterprise.html.*;
```

```
import java.io.*;

public class LogMethod extends HTTPMethod
{

  private PrintWriter         out           = null;
  private TemplateCacheList   tcl           = null;
  private HTMLTemplate        logTemplate   = null;
  private String              button        = null;
  private String              logText       = null;
  private String              message       = null;

  public void execute()
  {
    try
    {
      initObjects();

      PrintWriter out = m_response.getWriter();

      processRequest();

      processHTML();

    } catch(Exception e)
    {
      e.printStackTrace();
    }

  }

  private void processHTML() throws Exception
  {

    // Lock the log file while reading it so that the logging engine
    // does not have trouble with open file pointers to the log.
    Object lock = m_context.getLogLockSemaphore();
    synchronized(lock)
    {
      BufferedReader br = new BufferedReader(
                          new FileReader(
                                m_context.getValue(
                                m_context.LOG_FILE_PATH)));

      logTemplate.substitute("BASEURL", m_context.getAppBaseURL());
      logTemplate.substitute("MESSAGE", message);
      logTemplate.substitute("LOGFILE", m_context.getValue(
                                          m_context.LOG_FILE_PATH));
      logTemplate.doHTML(out);

      out.println("<pre>");
      String logLine = null;
```

```
        while((logLine = br.readLine()) != null)
        {
          out.println(logLine);
        }
        out.println("</pre>");

        // We know that the template shouldn't have a closing </body>
        // and </html> because we are streaming out the data.

        out.println("</body>");
        out.println("</html>");

        br.close();

        out.close();
      }
    }


    private void processRequest()
    {
      button = m_request.getParameter("button");
      logText = m_request.getParameter("logtext");

      if (button == null)
      {
        return;
      }

      if ((logText == null) || (logText == ""))
      {
        logText = "N/A";
      }

      if (button.equals("Add Info Log"))
      {
          m_context.logInfo(logText);
          message = "Logged Info Message: \"" + logText + "\"";
      } else if (button.equals("Add Trace Log"))
      {
          m_context.logTrace(logText);
          message = "Logged Trace Message: \"" + logText + "\"";
      } else if (button.equals("Throw Error"))
      {
        message = "Logged an Exception.";
        try
        {
          throw new Exception("I was thrown on purpose!");

        } catch(Exception e)
        {
          m_context.logError("An error is about to be logged!", e);
        }
```

```
    }
  }

  private void initObjects() throws Exception
  {
    out = m_response.getWriter();

    tcl = m_context.getTemplateCacheList();

    logTemplate = tcl.get("logger").createHTMLTemplate();
  }

}
```

Now that all the code has been written, we are ready to set up and run the application. At this point you are probably used to the drill. We set up the servlet engine with the `Logger` servlet and set the initialization arguments to contain *ConfFile=<Path to the Logger config file>*. The browser output of this servlet should look similar to what Figure 5.1 shows. After several additions to the log file, the browser may come back with a blank log screen. Did it log the submission? Is it a bug? No! The file generation code kicked off and placed the log in the first generation file. The framework simply saw that the log file had exceeded the maximum size and therefore did a generation roll. If you look in the directory where you created your log file, you should see a generation file that contains your logged information.

Try different testing scenarios. Edit your configuration file with different combinations of the log filter. Remember to restart the servlet engine each time you update the configuration file. Notice that as we change the filter, the log object sends only the specified logs to the log file.

Also try bombarding the log file with many logs. We want to force the generation files to roll. In the previous example 3K was set as the maximum log size to force a generation roll with a small number of logs. Submitting error logs places a large amount of data in the log file and will force a generation roll much more quickly. Notice that the application creates only the number of generation files that we define in the configuration file. Notice also that when we again force a generation roll, the oldest generation file is deleted. No more worries about logs eating up our hard drives!

Error Handling

We have just learned about how we gracefully handle errors inside a program: We log them. But what about externally? What do end users see on their browsers when they encounter errors? Too often I have used an application on a corporate intranet and received a stack trace when I have encountered an error. Although this type of error is something that *I* can understand, it can be quite frightening for the average user. To understand how a stack trace may affect an end user, ask yourself, "How would my grandmother react if she encountered a stack trace?"

We must never assume too much about the user. In fact, we should do the opposite and assume nothing. Our users may be very unknowledgeable and thus intimidated by a stack trace. On the other hand, a stack trace may be a security breach that tells a lot about the code and may provide too much information for a sophisticated and malicious user. Letting end users know that an error has occurred and telling them how to report the error without giving them too much technical information is crucial.

How do we handle the issue of error handling in terms of the end user? One of the first things to consider is how we want to report the error to the user. First and foremost, the error message should very simply explain that an error has occurred. Depending on the audience, in some cases we may not even wish to state that an error has occurred. If the audience is not technically sophisticated, we may just tell the user to contact someone. In any case, the error message that the end user sees should be friendly, yet give detailed instructions about what to do next.

Earlier we introduced the concept of the transaction ID. Here's where we really see the value of a tran ID. When we log something in `EnterpriseLog`, we are always returned a tran ID. The tran ID is a code guaranteed to be unique that is stamped in the log when we log an error, and it is returned to the developer.

When we developed that code, you may have asked, "Why do I want the tran ID?" We get it so that we can return it to the user in the HTML. Therefore when we encounter an error, we log it, get the tran ID, and produce a "friendly" error message to the user with the tran ID as part of the message. The message can be something like this: *An error has occurred at the server. Your transaction ID is 9373774878374-3. Please contact the help desk and refer to this ID number to help diagnose the problem.* Figure 5.2 shows a good example of an error screen that contains the tran ID.

Although the description of the problem in Figure 5.2 could be much more detailed, the idea is clear. You should now understand why the tran ID is returned from the logging methods.

How do we integrate this type of error handling in our code? To begin with, an error-handling schema should be developed that gives the developer the freedom to create a simple or a robust HTML page, or to be offered a default HTML page to use. Should the error-handling code be duplicated and integrated within each class, or should there be a centralized error-handling

Figure 5.2 Typical error screen with a tran ID

engine? Why not both? Let's offer a centralized error-handling engine that allows us to configure our own error HTML or provides a default error page. It should also be flexible enough that we can create our own error handling within our classes. Remember that the whole point of enterprise servlets is to make software development very simple so that we do not have to worry about issues like error handling. We can let the framework handle this for us.

The code we have developed thus far allows only customized error handling in each `HTTPMethod` object. That is, if we want to handle errors with the enterprise library in its current state, we need a `try/catch` block within the `execute()` method and would probably output the HTML in the `catch` section. Listing 5.8 shows the relevant code.

Listing 5.8 Error-handling code in the `execute()` method

```
Public void execute()
{
  try
  {
  .
  .
  .
  } catch (Exception e)
  {
    String tranId = m_context.logError(e);
    out.println("<html><body>");
    out.println("<h1>An error occurred at the server. ");
    out.println("Your tran id is " + tran Id + "</h1><br>");
    out.println("Please contact a System Admin.");
    out.flush();
  }
}
```

We could use the code in the `catch` block to produce the HTML, or we could use a template to create a robust error page and substitute the tran ID into the HTML. This approach works fine, but it means that we must copy this code into each of our dispatch classes. What we want to do is have a centralized *default* error-handling scheme, yet also be able to develop code such as that shown in Listing 5.8 when we need different error handling.

The DefaultErrorHandler Object

Before centralizing the error-handling code, let's build an object that will handle errors. Why do we need such an object? Can't we simply create code that is similar to what Listing 5.8 shows? Not if we want it to be robust. By *robust,* I mean that we want to support both templates and default hard-coded HTML. In other words, if we supply a template, the object will look for its existence and use it. If we don't supply a template, the object will simply produce some default text.

Here's how it could work. We reserve a template name—*defaulterror,* for example—that we place in the configuration file. This template is loaded in the cache as usual when the enterprise servlet application initializes. If we hit an error, the default error handler checks the cache for the name *defaulterror.* If it exists, the object creates the template from the cache and substitutes the value `TRANID` with the transaction ID that we received from logging the error. If the template doesn't exist, the object just combines some basic text with the tran ID and outputs this text to the user.

The object needs to support the fact that a log has not been set up, and if it hasn't, direct the error to the standard output, or the servlet engine log. The template will support two substitution strings: `TRANID` and `BASEURL`. `TRANID` is self-explanatory; `BASEURL` is there so that we can substitute the application's base URL if we want a link on the error template to another part of our application (remember that it's a bad idea to hard-code links to the application when we're moving to different platforms).

Let's call this object `DefaultErrorHandler`. Because this object will be used primarily in servlets, we'll place it in the `enterprise.servlet` package. It should be very simple to use. We construct this object with `AppContext` and the `PrintWriter` object to output the HTML to the user. We need `AppContext` so that we can access the application's resources. In particular, we need access to the application log and the template cache.

`PrintWriter` is the writer we get by calling the servlet object that we use to output HTML. When we're ready to write the error, we simply call `writeError()` and pass in the `Exception` object as a parameter. `DefaultErrorHandler` handles all the actual logging and checking for whether to use a template or the standard HTML. Listing 5.9 shows the code for `DefaultErrorHandler`.

Listing 5.9 The `DefaultErrorHandler` class

```
package enterprise.servlet;

import enterprise.common.*;
import enterprise.html.*;
import java.io.*;
import java.util.*;
import javax.servlet.*;
import javax.servlet.http.*;

public class DefaultErrorHandler
{

  private AppContext m_ac = null;
  private PrintWriter m_out = null;

  public DefaultErrorHandler(AppContext ac, PrintWriter out)
  {
    m_ac = ac;
    m_out = out;
  }

  public void writeError(Exception e)
  {

    String tranId = null;

    // Check if we have a log.
    if (m_ac.isLog())
    {
```

```
        // We do, so log the error.
        tranId = m_ac.logError(e);
      } else
      {
        // We don't, so send the error to the servlet
        // engine log and write a default error message.
        tranId = EnterpriseLog.getTranId();

        System.out.println("ERROR - TRAN ID " + tranId);
        e.printStackTrace();

        writeDefaultMessage(tranId);
        return;
      }

      try
      {
        TemplateCacheList tcl = m_ac.getTemplateCacheList();

        HTMLCompiledTemplate hct = tcl.get("defaulterror");

        HTMLTemplate ht = hct.createHTMLTemplate();

        ht.substitute("TRANID", tranId);
        ht.substitute("BASEURL", m_ac.getAppBaseURL());

        ht.doHTML(m_out);

      } catch (Exception rce)
      {
        // An exception occurred when we were trying to use the cache
        // either because the "defaulterror" template does not
        // exist or because another error prevented us from
        // using a template. Instead we will use the default text.
        writeDefaultMessage(tranId);
      }
    }

    private void writeDefaultMessage(String tranid)
    {
      StringBuffer sb = new StringBuffer();

      sb.append("<html>\n");
      sb.append("<body>\n");
      sb.append("<center>\n");
      sb.append("<h1>System Error TRAN-ID: ");
      sb.append(tranid);
      sb.append("</h1><br>\n");
      sb.append("<b>An error has occurred at the server.</b><br>\n");
      sb.append("Please contact a System Administrator with ");
      sb.append("the tran id.\n");
      sb.append("</center>\n");
```

```
    sb.append("</body>\n");
    sb.append("</html>\n");

    m_out.println(sb.toString());
  }
}
```

Now that we have a default error handler, how do we centralize it? The best place to centralize is `BaseEnterpriseServlet`. It manages all dispatching and runs the `HTTPMethod.execute()` method. To make this work, we need `HTTPMethod.execute()` to be able to throw an exception. Let's add this capability to the declaration in the `HTTPMethod` object. We just need to change the `execute()` declaration to throw an exception, as shown here:

```
public abstract class HTTPMethod
{
.
.
.
  public abstract void execute() throws Exception;
.
.
.
}
```

In `BaseEnterpriseServlet` we need to place a `try/catch` block around the `methodInstance.execute()` call in the `service()` method. Doing so allows us to catch any error that is thrown in the `HTTPMethod.execute()` method. When we catch the exception, an instance of `DefaultErrorHandler` is created and writes the error to the user. The following is how we need to change `BaseEnterpriseServlet`:

```
public abstract class BaseEnterpriseServlet extends HttpServlet
{
.
.
.
 public void service(HttpServletRequest req, HttpServletResponse res)
      throws ServletException, IOException
  {
.
.
.
      try
      {
        methodInstance.execute();
      } catch (Exception e)
      {
```

```
            DefaultErrorHandler deh = new DefaultErrorHandler(m_ac,
                                                getPrintWriter(res));
            deh.writeError(e);
        }
  .
  .
  .
   }
  .
  .
  .
}
```

Now we have integrated centralized error-handling code into the enterprise servlet framework. To use this centralized error handler, we just build dispatch method classes as we always have, except that the `execute()` method must be declared as being able to throw an exception. For any errors that we want to let the default error handler catch, we just allow exceptions to be thrown and the centralized code will deal with them. If we wish to do customized error handling for a particular dispatch class, we just catch the error *within* the `execute()` method so that it is not passed on to the centralized handler. By building the `DefaultErrorHandler` object and integrating it into `BaseEnterpriseServlet`, we have effectively provided

- A centralized error-handling mechanism
- Flexibility to support a customized error template
- Flexibility for customized error handling within the dispatch method

Now the developer can concentrate on the business at hand: developing business objects and logic for the code. He/she does not need to worry about the error-handling framework.

The Logger Application with Error Handling

We have just integrated a centralized error-handling scheme into the enterprise servlet framework. Now let's see it work. We'll implement the centralized error-handling capabilities in the Logger application. First let's create customized default error HTML as shown in Figure 5.2. We will create a template called `defaulterror.html` that will contain the HTML shown in Listing 5.10.

Listing 5.10 The `defaulterror.html` template

```
<html>
<body>

<center>
<h1><font color="green">Logger Application</font></h1><br>
The Logger Application has experienced an error.  Your error <br>
```

```
has been given the following transaction id:<br><br>
<b>${TRANID}</b><br><br>
Please contact the IT Department Help desk and tell them your
transaction id.

<form>
<input type="button" value="Click Here To Return To Logger"
 OnClick="location='${BASEURL}';">
</form>

</center>

</body>
</html>
```

Now we need to add a template to the Logger configuration file. We need this template to be named *defaulterror* so that the `DefaultErrorHandler` object will find the template in the cache. So we will add the following line to the configuration file:

```
Template.defaulterror=defaulterror.html
```

Now let's make the necessary changes to the `LogMethod` class to use the central error handler. As stated already, we need to change the `execute()` declaration to throw an exception. Let's change the declaration with the class.

```
public class LogMethod extends HTTPMethod
{
.
.
.
  public void execute() throws Exception
  {
.
.
.
  }
.
.
.
}
```

To make this work, we need to allow the `exception` to pass through to the framework. In the previous version of this example, we did customized error handling. In the `processRequest()` method, we implemented a `try/catch` block around the exception so that we could catch it and log it. The code (see Listing 5.7) looked like this:

```
try
{
  throw new Exception("I was thrown on purpose!");
```

```
} catch(Exception e)
{
  m_context.logError("An error is about to be logged!", e);
}
```

In the current example we don't want to catch the error. We want the error to flow to the centralized default error handler. Therefore we should replace the preceding code in the `processRequest()` method of the `LogMethod` class with the following:

```
throw new Exception("I was thrown on purpose!");
```

That's all we need to change in the example to make it use the centralized error handler. A full listing of the Logger example and its changes can be found on the CD that accompanies this book. Try running the application and see what happens when you select the **Throw Error** button. You should get the screen shown in Figure 5.2. Now try taking out the line in the configuration file that declares the `defaulterror.html` template and see what happens. You should see thedefault text displayed that we embedded in the `DefaultErrorHandler` object.

Centralized error handling was simple to integrate into the enterprise servlet framework, and it releases the developer from the burden of coding error handling into every dispatch method. With enterprise servlet applications, centralized error handling allows us to concentrate on the most important development issues: the business objects.

Summary

This chapter described the importance of logging and error handling in the enterprise. Many of the logs in servlet engines look similar, but each has its own intricacies. As we move from platform to platform, we begin to see the usefulness of a standardized log format that is recognizable across platforms. We find that it is also beneficial to have one log per application, especially on a high-capacity site that runs several applications concurrently. On high-capacity sites we also find that creating generation files means that we don't need to worry about running out of disk space.

These needs led us to develop the `EnterpriseLog` object, which supports single-application logging, standardized format, and generation files. The `EnterpriseLog` object helps us handle internal errors, but we need a way to show errors to external users without scaring them with a Java stack trace. We developed the `DefaultErrorHandler` object so that we could handle errors centrally and would not have to code error handling throughout an application.

Centralized error handling helps the developer concentrate on business objects instead of the supporting framework.

The `DefaultErrorHandler` object aids us in providing a "friendly" interface to the end user by using an HTML template or default text that contains a transaction ID (tran ID) that we send to the user. With a friendly message to the user along with the tran ID, we are able to locate an error rapidly within a log and diagnose the problem in a much more efficient manner.

CHAPTER 6

Security

Security is extremely critical in the enterprise. Sensitivity about executive information systems can become a legal issue if not handled properly. Human resources applications containing payroll data and personal information about employees, such as social security numbers, are common in many corporations, and restriction to this data is a necessity. Financial information throughout the course of a corporate reporting period could do detrimental things to a company's stock if the information fell into the wrong hands. For these reasons corporations take extra steps to ensure adherence to proper security policies.

Implementing security policies is a topic that we will encounter many times throughout our development careers. In fact, very few Web projects do *not* require some type of security. We use security to protect applications from unauthorized users. It allows us to control who has access to whole applications and to the different components of applications. We can detail a complex hierarchy of user access, or we can keep it simple and have only a single tier of access to the components of an application.

In this chapter we will examine how security fits into Web development. We will look at the different types of security and how they are handled in the Web server. We will also look at the two major security types—Web authentication and form-based authentication—and show how they can be integrated into the enterprise servlet framework.

Types of Security

There are several types of security with respect to the Web. These types fall into different categories, ranging from data encryption to user authentication. Security on a Web server is layered; that is, multiple security methods can be used on top of each other. For example, we may have a Web site that not only requests access through a user ID and password, but also encrypts the data.

There are only two basic types of security authentication methods for Web applications: Web authentication and form-based authentication. The term *Web authentication* (which comes from the *WWW_Authenticate* header in an HTTP security handshake) encompasses several security mechanisms that result in the browser displaying the typical user ID/password dialog box. In *form-based authentication,* the user enters his/her security information on a Web page, which is submitted as an HTML form, and the security is usually tracked via a cookie. We will examine both of these security types later in this chapter. But for now, let's look at security from a bird's-eye view.

You may ask, "What about SSL (Secure Sockets Layer)?" The *Secure Sockets Layer* is more or less a way to encrypt HTTP traffic so that it won't be "sniffed" to extract information from the communication. This is the reason you may see *https* in the address of a site when you are conducting a credit card transaction. Most sites that care about protecting their customers from fraudulent activities typically use SSL during the transaction phase of e-commerce. Encrypting the data between the Web server and the user makes extracting the information very difficult, if not nearly impossible. Although SSL can be used to authenticate users through the creative use of certificates, it is used primarily to encrypt the line between the user and the Web server. However, using SSL along with other security mechanisms will result in a very secure Web site.

Security on a Web server requires a layered approach, which is depicted in Figure 6.1. The first layer, if used, is SSL. It encrypts all inbound and outbound traffic and is used to garble the data from the communication between client

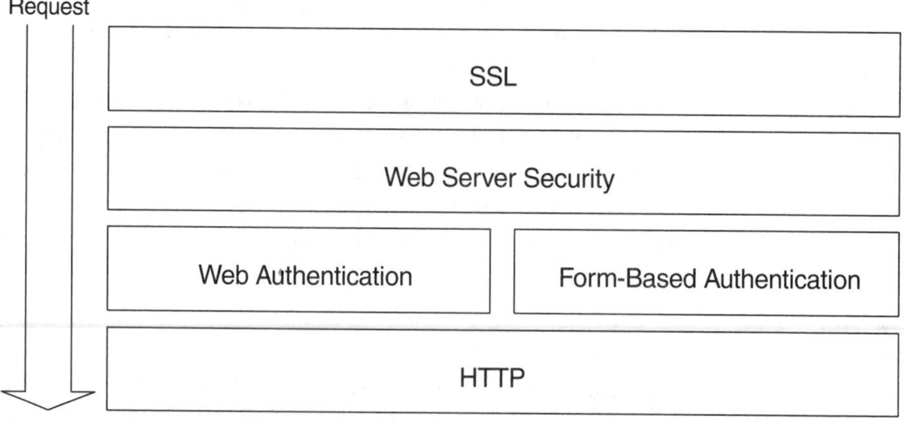

Figure 6.1 Security layers in a Web server

and server so that anyone who is sniffing the communication over the wire cannot view it. In addition, it prevents anyone from viewing user IDs and passwords that are sent in clear text. All traffic traveling through SSL will be encrypted, so SSL is a good layer to implement when line sniffing is feared.

The second layer is Web server security. Most Web servers offer some form of Web authentication. Web server security usually protects documents via a security zone or "realm." We will discuss this in detail later in the chapter, but the point here is that most Web servers support Web authentication. Web authentication is what causes the user ID/password box to pop up when you are accessing a secured document.

There are many different kinds of Web authentication, the most common of which are basic, digest, and NTLM (Windows NT LAN Manager). Basic authentication, which is supported by most Web servers, sends the user ID and password in base64-encoded clear text. If we are worried about the user ID and password being sniffed over the wire, this is not a very reliable way of implementing security (which is why we would use this type of security in conjunction with SSL). Most Web servers implement basic Web authentication by using hooks to an internal database or table structure. IIS uses the NT user database; Apache uses a text list or DBM database; Netscape/iPlanet uses a text file or can also use LDAP. No matter which server is used, it usually has one or two methods to store user ID and password information.

The final layer of security is custom Web authentication or form-based authentication. Customized Web authentication is very similar to Web server security, except that we perform our own security user ID and password implementation. We may store user IDs and passwords in an Oracle or Sybase database. However, because most Web servers do not directly support Oracle or Sybase as a data store for user IDs and passwords, we would need to create our own access to the database. We would also need to implement HTTP to show the user ID/password dialog box to the user. Many Web servers contain an API that allows us to do this. IIS uses the ISAPI SDK; Netscape/iPlanet uses the NSAPI SDK; Apache includes its C API with its distribution. Java's SDK requires a little creativity to get this to work.

Form-based authentication is also customized, but the interface is controlled through the HTML. The user ID and password are entered on an HTML form, and authentication is handled programmatically. Typically, the user authenticates through one page, known as a *doorway,* before being allowed to continue through the rest of the application. The user's authentication is continually verified through the use of a session cookie in the browser that is set by the application.

The types of security that interest us most from a development standpoint are Web authentication and form-based authentication because when we want to implement a customized security structure, these will most likely be the two choices for developing a security schema. The rest of this chapter will be devoted to these two security implementations. Let's begin by looking at Web authentication.

Web Authentication

Web authentication is a term that encompasses several types of security mechanisms, all of which present the same results to the end user. Upon accessing a Web site that is protecting its pages with Web authentication, the user will receive from the browser a dialog box like the one shown in Figure 6.2. The user then will type in his/her user ID and password and, if they are validated, will receive the proper Web page. Figure 6.2 shows a typical authentication pop-up window requesting authentication using Microsoft's Internet Explorer.

The user probably is most interested in the **User Name** and **Password** fields, the fields that will hold the authentication information. Depending on the browser that is used, the user may or may not receive the **Site** and **Realm** information fields. The **Site** field typically displays the site to which the user is going.

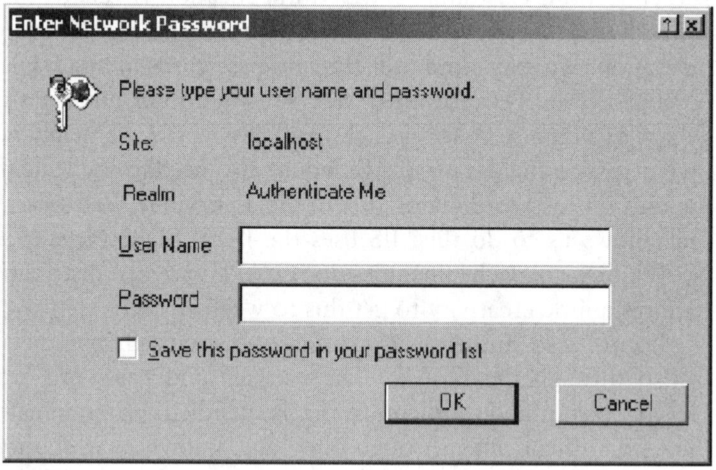

Figure 6.2 The browser's security authentication pop-up window with Web authentication

The realm is considered a security zone on the site. Because a site may host multiple Web applications or different security zones within a Web server, the realm describes the zone to which the authentication applies.

Presenting multiple realms to the user allows different levels of security. For instance, a Web server may be running an accounting application and a human resources application on a site called `www.myapplications.com`. If both applications shared the same realm, then theoretically the user would have instant access to both systems. However, if each had its own separate realm, the user would need to authenticate separately to both applications. The realm is nothing but a unique string for a particular security zone. You can name your realm anything you want.

As stated already, Web authentication encompasses several types of security mechanisms. Although all follow a similar HTTP protocol, the way the data is encrypted and how it is handled are different. The following are the three most common types of Web authentication.

1. **Basic.** This is the original authentication scheme that was defined in HTTP. It is named *basic* because of its simplistic approach to security. It passes the user ID and password back to the server in a base64-encoded text, which for all intents and purposes is clear text because it is easy to decode. Although this is not the most secure form of authentication (the user ID and password can be easily sniffed over the wire), it is probably the most popular and widely used authentication scheme on the Net. When used with SSL, basic authentication is a very secure and safe method for authenticating users.

2. **Digest.** This mode of authentication is a more secure rendition of the basic authentication in that the password is hashed with encryption routines and is never actually sent to the server. Digest authentication became a standard in the HTTP 1.1 specification. The server creates a random string and sends it to the browser. The browser hashes the string with the password and sends the hashed string back to the server. The server also hashes the original string internally with the stored password. It then compares the internally hashed string with the one that was sent by the browser. If they both match, the password entered by the browser was correct. Although digest authentication is much more secure than basic authentication, many server vendors do not support it. sApache is one of the few vendors who at the time of this writing offer digest authentication as an alternative to basic. On the client side, Microsoft's Internet Explorer did not support digest authentication until version 5.0.

3. **NTLM.** This is Microsoft's proprietary authentication scheme for authenticating the browser to the server. Only Microsoft's Internet Explorer

and IIS Web Server currently support this method. It works by sending a public token to the browser to encrypt the user ID and password. The browser sends the encrypted string back to the IIS server, where it is decrypted with a private key and authenticated against an NT domain. Its main advantage is that if the user is using Internet Explorer (IE), the user ID/password dialog box will not pop up if the user is valid. IE takes the user name and password from the login to the operating system and passes this information along silently during the challenge/response period of the Web conversation. Because this mode of authentication allows *single sign-on*—that is, users can sign on to the system just once and do not need to provide their user names and passwords each time they access something different—it is a big hit in corporate environments.

Under the Hood

How does Web authentication work? It is an exchange of challenge/response headers between the server and the client. Let's take a closer look at Web authentication and see what's happening behind the scenes when we go to a site that uses this kind of security. We'll look at basic authentication because this type of authentication is the easiest to understand.

Let's look at exactly what happens during the basic authentication challenge/response exchange. It's pretty simple. The client requests a document at a secured site. The request is a standard `GET` request. Let's assume that the client wants to request the `/servlet/WWWSecureExample` document. The HTTP request looks like this:

```
GET /servlet/WWWSecureExample HTTP/1.1
Accept: */*
Accept-Language: en-us
Accept-Encoding: gzip, deflate
User-Agent: Mozilla/4.0 (compatible; MSIE 5.5; Windows NT 5.0)
Host: localhost:8080
Connection: Keep-Alive
```

This document (or servlet) is secured, so the server will attempt to challenge the client for his/her credentials. The server sends back a "401" response, which states simply *Unauthorized.* By sending this response along with a `WWW-Authenticate` header, the server provokes the browser to show the user ID/password dialog box, such as the one shown in Figure 6.2. The `WWW-Authenticate` header states the kind of security that the server will be using and the realm. In this exchange, the server is requesting basic authentication (BASIC), and the security is for the *Authenticate Me* realm. In addition, the server sends some HTML that is shown if the user presses the **Cancel** button.

```
HTTP/1.0 401 Unauthorized
Date: Fri, 06 Oct 2000 01:40:21 GMT
Server: Unify eWave ServletExec Debugger 3.0C
Content-Type: text/html; charset=iso-8859-1
Pragma: No-cache
Cache-Control: no-cache
Expires: Thu, 01 Jan 1970 00:00:00 GMT
WWW-Authenticate: BASIC realm="Authenticate Me"

<HTML><HEAD>
<TITLE>401 Authorization Required</TITLE>
</HEAD><BODY>
<H2>Authorization Required!</H2>
You are not authorized to access this
server and have not supplied the proper
user ID and password. <BR><BR>
Please contact the system administrator
to give you the proper credentials to
access this system.
</BODY></HTML>
```

After the user has entered the security information, the client again requests the page, but this time the browser packages the user ID and password in the header on an Authorization line. In this exchange we entered “open” as the user name and “sesame” as the password. The browser packages this information into a single string by combining the user name and the password with a colon as separator. In this case the string would be *open:sesame.* It then encodes this information with base64 encoding, and the resulting string sent to the server is *b3BlbjpzZXNhbWU=*. The browser packages the Authorization line with the type of security to which it is responding (in this case basic) and the base64-encoded user name and password.

```
GET /servlet/WWWSecureExample HTTP/1.1
Accept: */*
Accept-Language: en-us
Accept-Encoding: gzip, deflate
User-Agent: Mozilla/4.0 (compatible; MSIE 5.5; Windows NT 5.0)
Host: localhost:8080
Connection: Keep-Alive
Authorization: Basic b3BlbjpzZXNhbWU=
```

The server receives this request and checks for an Authorization header. If it exists, the server decodes and separates the user ID and password into its separate parts and verifies this information with a user ID/password data store. If the user ID and password are validated, the server responds with the document that was requested. If the user ID and password are not validated, the server responds with the 401 challenge (*Unauthorized*) as shown earlier.

With this type of authentication scheme, the browser passes the `Authorization` line for all subsequent calls to that particular server. The browser stores the authorization information in memory and indexes this information by the Web site name. This is why when you browse a secure Web site, you usually have to authenticate only while your browser is running. This is also why you may notice that sites that change the Web site name on some of their links (i.e., using a DNS alias name for their Web site) may require you to reauthenticate. This storage of the host, user name, and password by the browser is cleared when you exit or shut down the browser.

Customizing Web Authentication

Web authentication is quite interesting, but it also seems complex. Is it hard to implement? Absolutely not! Its implementation is incredibly simple. The enterprise servlet framework lends itself to allowing a very customizable implementation of Web authentication, or just about any other security scheme. It is important to remember that everything is dispatched centrally from `BaseEnterpriseServlet`, and all of the HTTP output comes from `HTTPMethod`. By enhancing these two objects, we should be able to allow pluggable security modules that provide the developer with the tools to build just about any kind of custom security scheme.

How do we do this? We need `BaseEnterpriseServlet` to check for `HTTPMethod`'s authorization, if there is one, before dispatching to `HTTPMethod`. `HTTPMethod` by itself does not provide authentication capabilities, but we can create our own inherited versions of `HTTPMethod` that do. Then when we create dispatch methods, we extend the inherited secure version of `HTTPMethod` instead of the base `HTTPMethod` object, and we will have a secure application.

To do this, we need to start by creating an `Authentication` interface that `HTTPMethod` will implement, as shown in Listing 6.1. The `Authentication` interface calls for having a method called `authorize()`, which returns a `boolean` value. If it returns `true`, the user has been authenticated. If it returns `false`, authentication has failed.

Listing 6.1 The `Authentication` interface

```
package enterprise.servlet;

public interface Authentication
{
  public boolean authorize() throws Exception;
}
```

We will have `HTTPMethod` implement this interface, thereby forcing `HTTPMethod` to declare a version of the `authorize()` method, which allows us to create a default implementation of `authorize()`. Because `HTTPMethod` by itself would never need to authenticate credentials, we can have it always return `true` so that it passes any challenge to authorization. Listing 6.2 shows `HTTPMethod` implementing the `Authentication` interface.

Listing 6.2 Adding implementation of the `Authentication` interface to `HTTPMethod`

```
public abstract class HTTPMethod implements Authentication
{
.
.
.
  public boolean authorize() throws Exception
  {
    return true;
  }
}
```

Now let's make the necessary changes to `BaseEnterpriseServlet`. The only thing we need to do here is check the results of the `authorize()` call. If we are authenticated, we dispatch the `execute()` call as we normally would. If `authorize()` returns `false` (indicating that we are not authenticated), we just return and do not dispatch the `execute()` call. Therefore, place this authorization testing code just before we call `execute()` in `BaseEnterpriseServlet`. Listing 6.3 shows the changes (marked by boldface) that we need to make to `BaseEnterpriseServlet`.

Listing 6.3 Adding the `authorize()` call to `BaseEnterpriseSevlet`

```
public abstract class BaseEnterpriseServlet extends HttpServlet
{
.
.
.
  public void service(HttpServletRequest req, HttpServletResponse res)
      throws ServletException, IOException
  {
.
.
.
      try
     {
        if (!methodInstance.authorize())
          return;

        methodInstance.execute();
      } catch (Exception e)
      {
```

```
            DefaultErrorHandler deh = new DefaultErrorHandler(m_ac,
                                                 getPrintWriter(res));
            deh.writeError(e);
        }
.
.
.
    }
.
.
.
}
```

Is that it? Do we have security now? Not exactly. We have changed the enterprise servlet framework in order to create our own pluggable security components. What does this mean? Normally the dispatch methods are inherited or extended from `HTTPMethod`. We created a default implementation of `authorize()` inside `HTTPMethod` that always returns `true`. We just changed `BaseEnterpriseServlet` to always check for the `authorize()` method and check its result. Because the dispatch methods that extend `HTTPMethod` inherit the default implementation of `authorize()`, they will continue to work as they always have because they always authenticate.

However, because we implemented the `Autenticate` interface on the `HTTPMethod`, we have enforced virtuality on `HTTPMethod` and can extend this to build a custom and secure version of `HTTPMethod`. In other words, we can create an object that extends `HTTPMethod` and implements its own `authorize()` method, and that does verify the user in some way. Then the dispatch methods can extend this new object instead of `HTTPMethod`, and the new object's `authorize()` method will be executed by `BaseEnterpriseServlet`.

To put this more directly, we could create a new class that is called the `MySecureHTTPMethod` that would extend `HTTPMethod`. We would then create an `authorize()` method that would check for a user ID and password. This method would test the validity of the user ID and password and would report `true` if they were validated, or `false` if not.

Let's say we create a dispatch class called `Main`. Normally `Main` would extend `HTTPMethod`. But instead we will have it extend `MySecureHTTPMethod`. Everything else is the same. When `BaseEnterpriseServlet` calls the `authorize()` method, it calls the `MySecureHTTPMethod` version instead of the default `HTTPMethod` version, and hence we have secured the `Main` class. To put it succinctly, for any of the dispatch classes in this sample application that need security, we extend from `MySecureHTTPMethod`; otherwise we extend from `HTTPMethod`. This is the magic of using interfaces in the code.

To clarify what has just been described, let's look at an example of a pluggable security model.

An Example Using Pluggable Security Components

Let's build a small application that implements basic Web authentication. Because the most confusing part of what we just discussed was the extension of HTTPMethod, let's build a secure version of HTTPMethod that is called the MySecureHTTPMethod. We will start by declaring the object and extending HTTPMethod.

```
import enterprise.common.*;
import enterprise.servlet.*;

import java.util.*;
import java.io.*;
import javax.servlet.http.*;
import javax.servlet.*;

import sun.misc.*;

public abstract class MySecureHTTPMethod extends HTTPMethod
{
```

Because we want this version of HTTPMethod to have control over security, we will create an authorize() method to do the authentication. Remember that BaseEnterpriseServlet needs this method to return true if authenticated or false if not. But in this object, getting to this result is not that simple. As described earlier, basic authentication requires a challenge/response exchange to go on with the HTTP, so we must code this into the method. First we want to see if the client has sent us an Authorize header in the request. We call a function (which we will develop in a moment) called checkUser() that checks the Authorization string for a user ID and password.

```
  public boolean authorize() throws Exception
  {

    String authString = m_request.getHeader("Authorization");

    if (!checkUser(authString))
    {
```

If checkUser() cannot authenticate, or an Authorization header was not included in the client request, we set up a 401 response (*Unauthorized*) to be sent to the browser. This will always happen on the first request a client makes to the application because it has not authenticated yet. We set a WWW-Authenticate header with BASIC as the authentication type and a realm, which for this example we will call *Authenticate Me.*

```
      m_response.setHeader("WWW-Authenticate",
                           "BASIC realm=\"Authenticate Me\"");
```

We also need to set the response status to 401. We do that by calling the `setStatus()` method from the `HttpServletResponse` object with the `SC_UNAUTHORIZED` constant as a parameter. Making this call forces the response to begin with *HTTP/1.0 401 Unauthorized,* which provokes the client to display the user name/password dialog box.

```
m_response.setStatus(m_response.SC_UNAUTHORIZED);
```

Although we could have called the `HttpServletResponse.setError()` method, which in addition would have sent out some plain text explaining the lack of authorization, here we do it manually. The text that comes from `setError()` is rather boring and plain and does not offer any detailed description. By calling `setStatus()` instead, we can create our own HTML. If we wanted to, we probably could create a robust template with images and so on. But for this example, we will just output some HTML explaining the lack of authentication.

```
        PrintWriter out = m_response.getWriter();

        // Output text when the user hits the Cancel button
        // or cannot authenticate.
        out.println( "<HTML><HEAD>");
        out.println( "<TITLE>401 Authorization Required</TITLE>");
        out.println( "</HEAD><BODY>");
        out.println( "<H2>Authorization Required!</H2>");
        out.println( "You are not authorized to access this ");
        out.println( "server and have not supplied the proper ");
        out.println( "user ID and password. <BR><BR>");
        out.println( "Please contact the system administrator ");
        out.println( "to give you the proper credentials to ");
        out.println( "access this system.");
        out.println( "</BODY></HTML>");

        return false;

    } else
    {

        return true;

    }
}
```

The `checkUser()` method decodes the base64-encrypted user name and password from the `Authorization` line, and it splits the user ID and password into their respective parts. Because `checkUser()` is called on each request, we may not initially have an `Authorization` line. The `authorize()` method, shown earlier, first checks for the word *Authorization* in the header. If it is not there, the resulting String object has the value null, and this value is passed to this routine. Therefore, we must check for null first in checkUser(). We then need to check if the authentication is basic. If the header line yields the value null, or if the word *BASIC* is not in the header, we return false, indicating not authenticated.

```
private boolean checkUser(String basicLine) throws Exception
{

  if (basicLine == null)
  {
    return false;
  }

  if (!basicLine.toUpperCase().startsWith("BASIC "))
  {
    return false;
  }

  String encodedAuthString = basicLine.substring(6);
```

We then decode the base64-encoded string into the user ID and password. Sun included a Base64Decoder object in the sun.misc package, which is part of the Java SDK. After decoding the string, we break it up into the user ID and password by adding a colon as delimiter. Finally, with the user ID and password separated, we call the isAuthenticated() method, which is what actually validates the user ID and password.

```
  BASE64Decoder decoder = new BASE64Decoder();
  String clearAuthString = new
                String(decoder.decodeBuffer(encodedAuthString));

  int pos = clearAuthString.indexOf(':');
  String userid = clearAuthString.substring(0, pos);
  String password = clearAuthString.substring(pos + 1);

  return isAuthenticated(userid, password);
}
```

The isAuthenticated() method will validate the user. Here we will just check for the user ID *open* and the password *sesame*. You can alter this method to do anything you want to validate the user. You can look at a text list, go to a database, or do an LDAP lookup. This is where you can create your own validation scheme. Keep in mind that this method needs to return true if the user is validated, and false if not.

```
private boolean isAuthenticated(String userid, String password)
{
  if (userid.equals("open") && password.equals("sesame"))
  {
```

```
            return true;
        }

        return false;
    }

}
```

NOTE: Whenever you are using Web authentication, the Web server must authenticate the client on every call. This means that validation routines will be called for every request because every time a page is requested, the server must see an `Authorization` header in the request and must do a lookup of the user ID and password. This requirement may raise some issues that may need to be considered when you are validating users. If you're using a database, you will call the database on every client request. On a high-capacity site this could create a bottleneck in the system. Consider writing a `Cache` object or using a `Hashtable` object to store valid user IDs and passwords of the last 100 (or any number you choose) unique clients who have visited the site. This way, only the first time do expensive calls to the database need to be made. You then store the user ID and password in the cache, and on subsequent calls the lookup for the user ID and password is stored in memory, enabling much faster validation of the user. This is how the big server vendors implement their validation routines.

Now that the `MySecureHTTPMethod` class has been developed, we can say that we have security. Now let's develop an application that uses the `MySecureHTTPMethod` object. The application will be very simple—a one-page servlet that just displays a message that, if we can read it, indicates we have been validated. The application will be called *WWWSecureExample,* so we will give the dispatch servlet this name. The main page object will be called `MainForm`, and we will dispatch it with the name *main.* As we have in all other examples, let's begin with the configuration file. We will create a configuration file named `WWWSecureExample.config`. We will set up the base URL, the modules, and a log file. Listing 6.4 shows the configuration file.

Listing 6.4 Configuration file for `WWWSecureExample`

```
Application.Base.URL=/servlet/WWWSecureExample

Default.Method=main
Method.main=MainForm

# Place the log file path here
Log.File.Path=c:\\Book\\Chapter 06\\Example 1\\WWWServletExample.log
```

The dispatch servlet is simple, without any customized initialization or destruction. We just set the application name to *WWWSecureExample* in the `getAppName()` method. Listing 6.5 shows the relevant code.

Listing 6.5 The `WWWSecureExample` dispatch servlet

```
import enterprise.servlet.*;
import enterprise.common.*;

import java.io.*;

public class WWWSecureExample extends BaseEnterpriseServlet
{
  public void initializeApp(AppContext appContext) throws Exception
  {
  }

  public void destroyApp(AppContext appContext)
  {
  }

  public String getAppName()
  {
    return "WWWSecureExample";
  }
}
```

The `MainForm` dispatch method class (that is shown in Listing 6.6) just returns some text to the user. The point is that `MainForm` is extending the custom `MySecureHTTPMethod` class instead of `HTTPMethod`. Everything else is the same, as if we were extending `HTTPMethod`.

Listing 6.6 The `MainForm` dispatch method

```
import enterprise.servlet.*;
import enterprise.common.*;
import enterprise.html.*;

import java.io.*;

public class MainForm extends MySecureHTTPMethod
{

  public void execute() throws Exception
  {

    PrintWriter out = m_response.getWriter();

    out.println("<html>");
    out.println("<body>");
    out.println("<h1>Welcome to My Application</h1>");
    out.println("<p>If you see this page then you have ");
```

```
        out.println("a valid user ID and password!</p>");
        out.println("</body>");
        out.println("</html>");

    }

}
```

Now that the example has been developed, we need to set it up and execute it. First register the servlet in the servlet engine and set the initialization arguments to point at the configuration file with the `ConfFile` parameter. After executing the servlet engine, go to the `WWWSecureExample` servlet with your browser. You should get a user name/password dialog box similar to the one shown in Figure 6.2. To see the main page, enter "open" for the user name and "sesame" for the password. Also try hitting the **Cancel** button in the dialog box so that you can see the *Unauthorized* message.

Wasn't that simple? We created a customized `HTTPMethod` object that handles authentication for us, and we just have the dispatch method classes extend this object instead of `HTTPMethod` itself. Voilà! We have security. Another interesting thing we can do is create several different security `HTTPMethod` objects to set different kinds of security for an application. We may also wish to have a few dispatch classes inherit directly from `HTTPMethod` to create FAQ pages or contact information for people who may not already have security.

By coding our own security, we have much more control over what the user can see, whether we choose a hierarchical security structure or no security at all. This gives us granular control over which classes are protected and which are not. Doing our own coding is much better than using the default Web security of a Web server. We also have the freedom to choose any type of data store for the validation routines.

We have just learned about Web authentication and how it works within an application. In particular we showed how to create a pluggable security component and secure the parts of the application that require authorization to access. This pluggable style of developing security modules can be applied to just about any type of security scheme. Now let's take a look at the other common security method: form-based authentication.

Form-Based Authentication

Form-based authentication is exactly as the name implies: security through an HTML form. This has become a very common security method over the last few years, and it is being used more and more every day. The reason this authentication scheme is fairly recent is that it requires the Web server to make use of cookies and/or session management. Many Web servers did not support sessions until the last few years (for more information on sessions, see Chapter 3). Authentication works with sessions as follows. The client goes to a login screen similar to the one shown in Figure 6.3. The user enters his/her credentials and submits the form. The Web server processes the request, checking to see if the client has a valid session by reading the cookies from the header. Because this is the client's first time visiting this site, there is no valid session, so the Web server creates one. It checks the user's credentials against a data store and stores the validity of the credentials in an internal variable that is associated with the session (in Java the `getAttribute()` and `setAttribute()` methods of the `HttpSession` object would perform these tasks). The server may store a `boolean` variable named `authenticated`. It sends the session ID back to the client to be stored as a cookie. On subsequent requests by the client within the timeout period of the session, the `authenticated` variable will be checked, and if the authentication is valid, the secure page will be displayed. All of the

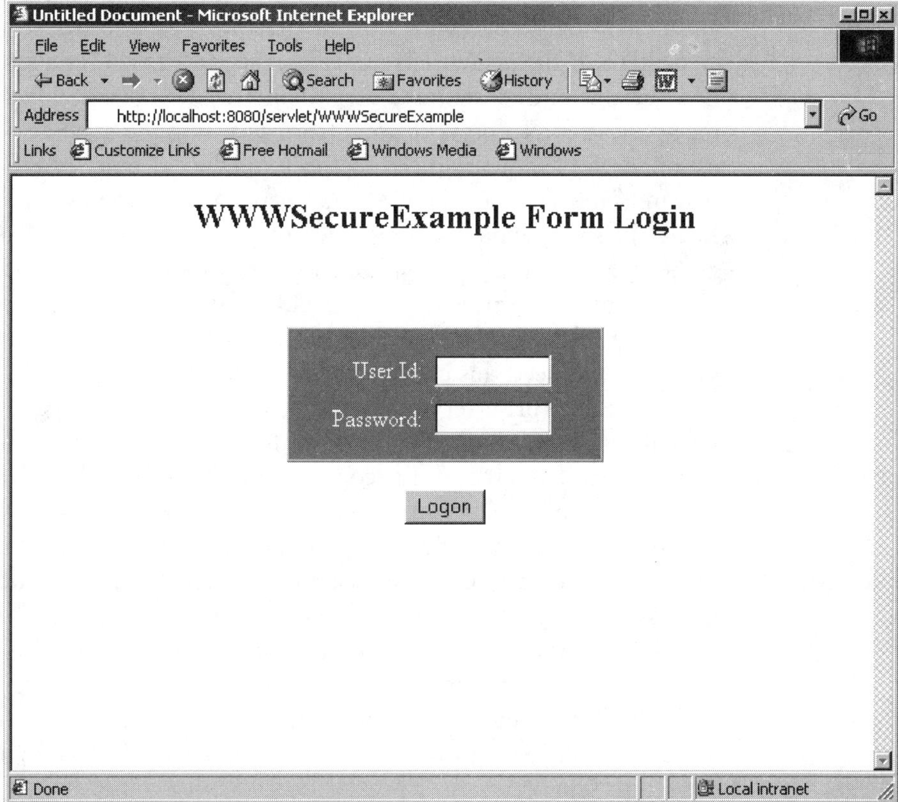

Figure 6.3 A form-based login screen

session management for storing and maintaining the security variable is handled by the Web server environment.

In an application that implements form-based authentication, nearly all of the pages are secured through this mechanism. However, a minimum of one page must *not* be secured. This would be the login page. Users need to be able to access this page to submit their credentials to the application. I call these types of pages *doorways*. The doorway is a page that gives a user minimal access to an application. Logon pages are always considered doorways and should have no authentication layer. Other types of doorway pages that should not contain security are FAQ pages, contact pages, and sometimes general information pages. Such pages tell the user how to access additional information on the Web site.

Integrating Form-Based Authentication into Enterprise Servlets

In a standard servlet environment, to implement form-based security we write an HTML login page with a form that posts to another servlet that verifies credentials. If the credentials are valid, the servlet will set a session authentication variable and redirect the user to another URL, probably the main page of the application. To prevent users from accessing the servlets without authentication, each page would need to check for the existence of the session variable that indicates whether the user is authenticated. If the user were not authenticated, the server would redirect the user to the login page. A user with a valid authentication variable would proceed unhindered. In a standard servlet development environment, each servlet could have a lot of code that would need to be secure. To prevent unauthorized users from using the application, each servlet would need this code to check session variables.

In the enterprise servlet model we can develop a pluggable security component that does all of the validation for us. The layout of the code is not all that different from that of the code required for Web authentication. Instead of checking for an `Authorization` line in the header, we check for the existence of a session variable that checks authentication. If the variable does not exist or if the user has not been authenticated, we need to check if the user is in the process of being authenticated. We check for the existence of a query string if the user ID and password have been sent. If the string exists, we attempt to authenticate it. If it doesn't exist, the user has not been through the login page, so we will authenticate him/her. This flow is quite similar to that of Web authentication, but in this case we are responsible for the login screen, so we use redirection.

To use this type of an implementation, as a minimum we will need a login page and the pluggable security component. Listing 6.7 shows the code for a login template that we can use to build a login page. We use a template because we can substitute the application base URL for the `BASEURL` string. This ability makes the application portable to other platforms (see Chapter 3 for information on the base URL). The main page of the application will be the `MainForm` class, which we built in the previous example. The login form should go to the main page (assuming that it passes security), so we will create a hidden input tag with *main*, the name of the `MainForm` dispatch identifier that we defined in the configuration file (see Listing 6.4).

Listing 6.7 The `login.html` template

```
<html>
<head>
<title>Untitled Document</title>
</head>
<body bgcolor="#FFFFFF">
<center>
  <h2>WWWSecureExample Form Login</h2>
  <h2> </h2>
  <form method="post" action="${BASEURL}">
  <input type="hidden" name="method" value="main">
    <table width="0%" border="1" cellspacing="0" cellpadding="10"
      bgcolor="#009933">
      <tr valign="middle" align="center">
      <td>
        <table width="200" border="0" cellspacing="3"
         cellpadding="3">
          <tr>
            <td>
              <div align="right"><font color="#FFFFFF">
               User Id:</font></div>
            </td>
            <td>
              <input type="text" name="userid" size="10"
               maxlength="10">
            </td>
          </tr>
          <tr>
            <td>
              <div align="right"><font color="#FFFFFF">
               Password:</font></div>
            </td>
            <td>
              <input type="password" name="password" size="10"
               maxlength="10">
            </td>
          </tr>
        </table>
      </td>
```

```
    </tr>
  </table>
  <p>
    <input type="submit" name="Submit" value="Logon">
  </p>
</form>
</center>
</body>
</html>
```

The most important pieces of the template are the input fields: user ID and password. These input text fields will trap the user's credentials and will be used to validate the user. Listing 6.8 shows the code for the `Login` class, which displays the template for the user. Notice that this class extends the `HTTPMethod` class because we do not want it to implement any security here. The login screen is a doorway that is an entry point into the system. This is the main conduit by which the user will enter the application, so this class should not be secure.

Listing 6.8 The `Login` class that displays the `login.html` template

```
import enterprise.servlet.*;
import enterprise.html.*;

import java.io.*;

public class Login extends HTTPMethod
{

  public void execute() throws Exception
  {

    PrintWriter out = m_response.getWriter();
    TemplateCacheList tcl = m_context.getTemplateCacheList();

    HTMLCompiledTemplate hct = tcl.get("login");
    HTMLTemplate ht = hct.createHTMLTemplate();

    ht.substitute("BASEURL", m_context.getAppBaseURL());

    ht.doHTML(out);
  }
}
```

Now let's build a pluggable security component that supports form-based authentication. Taking the previous example, let's rewrite `MySecureHTTPMethod`. The `authorize()` method will start by grabbing an `EnterpriseSession` object and checking for the existence of a `boolean` session variable that we will call `authenticated`. If the variable doesn't exist, we'll create it.

```
import enterprise.common.*;
import enterprise.servlet.*;

import java.util.*;
import java.io.*;
import javax.servlet.http.*;
import javax.servlet.*;

public abstract class MySecureHTTPMethod extends HTTPMethod
{

  public boolean authorize() throws Exception
  {

    PrintWriter out = m_response.getWriter();
    EnterpriseSession es = getEnterpriseSession();

    // See if the user has been authenticated before.
    boolean authenticated = (boolean)es.getAttribute(
                                          "authenticated");
    if (authenticated == null)
    {
      // The user hasn't been authenticated, so create a new object.
      authenticated = new boolean(false);
    }
```

At this point we want to check the value of `authenticated`. The user has been authenticated before if it is `true`, and then we can return `true` to `BaseEnterpriseServlet`.

```
    // Check the authentication status.
    if (authenticated.booleanValue() == true)
    {
      // The user has already been authenticated, so leave
      // here gracefully by returning a positive
      // authentication status to BaseEnterpriseServlet.
      return true;
    }
```

If the value of `authenticated` is `false`, the user has not yet been authenticated. So we check to see if we have user ID and password query parameters. If we do not have these parameters, then we redirect the user to the login page and return `false` (indicating that the user has not been authenticated) to `BaseEnterpriseServlet`.

```
    // See if there are user ID and password parameters.
    // If there are, then we are being asked to authenticate the
    // user.
    String userId = m_request.getParameter("userid");
    String password = m_request.getParameter("password");
```

```
if ((userId == null) && (password == null))
{
  // No parameters, so the user is requesting a page while not
  // being authenticated, so redirect to the login page.
  m_response.sendRedirect(m_context.getAppBaseURL() +
                          "?method=login");
  return false;
}
```

If we got to this point, then the user has not been authenticated and we do have a user ID and a password in the query string. We take the user ID and password and check the credentials by calling the `isAuthenticated()` method. We save the results of the authentication in the session variable `authenticated` for the next request by the client. We then check to see if the user was authenticated. If not, we display a message that tells the user that he/she was not authenticated. If the user was authenticated, we return `true` to `BaseEnterpriseServlet`, which means that the client's credentials were valid.

```
// Check to see if the user has a valid user ID and password.
authenticated = new boolean(isAuthenticated(userId, password));
es.setAttribute("isAuthenticated", authenticated);
if (!authenticated.booleanValue())
{

  // Bad user ID and password, so display a failure message
  // to the user.
  out.println( "<HTML><HEAD>");
  out.println( "<TITLE>Authorization Failed</TITLE>");
  out.println( "</HEAD><BODY>");
  out.println( "<H2>Authorization Failed!</H2>");
  out.println( "You are not authorized to access this ");
  out.println( "server and have not supplied the proper ");
  out.println( "user ID and password. <BR><BR>");
  out.println( "Please contact the system administrator ");
  out.println( "to give you the proper credentials to ");
  out.println( "access this system.");
  out.println( "<FORM>");
  out.println( "<input type=\"button\" value=\"Try Again\" ");
  out.println( "OnClick=\"location='" +
               m_context.getAppBaseURL() +
               "'\">");
  out.println( "</FORM>");
  out.println( "</BODY></HTML>");

  // Leave with a negative result.
  return false;

}
```

```
        // If we got here, then the user ID and password have been
        // authenticated.
        return true;

    }
```

We also need to develop the `isAuthenticated()` method that was called by `authorize()`. This is where we would check the user ID and password against a data store. In this example we will do as we did before and make only the user ID (*open*) and the password (*sesame*) valid credentials. Just as before, we return `true` for valid credentials, and `false` if the user ID and password are not correct.

```
    private boolean isAuthenticated(String userid, String password)
    {
        if ((userid == null) || (password == null))
            return false;

        if (userid.equals("open") && password.equals("sesame"))
        {
            return true;
        }

        return false;
    }

}
```

We will reuse the same `MainForm` class that we had earlier for the application's main screen. We see this screen only if we have validated correctly. Remember from the last example that we extended from `MySecureHTTPMethod` instead of `HTTPMethod`. This time, however, we will use the `MySecureHTTPMethod` class that we developed earlier, which is a form-based security module.

Now let's finish this up by putting together the configuration file (shown in Listing 6.9). We need to add the `Login` class to the dispatch methods, so let's name one of these methods *login*. Because the login screen is probably the first screen that the user will see, let's also make `login()` the default method. In addition, we need to set up the `login.html` template and its template path.

Listing 6.9 Configuration file for the form-based authentication example

```
Application.Base.URL=/servlet/WWWSecureExample

Default.Method=login
Method.login=Login
Method.main=MainForm
```

```
# Place the default template path here.
Default.Template.Path=c:\\Book\\Chapter 06\\Examples\\
                     Example 2\\templates\\Template.login=login.html

# Place the log file path here.
Log.File.Path=c:\\Book\\Chapter 06\\Example 2\\WWWServletExample.log
```

Now we are ready to run the application. We can leave the registered servlet in the servlet engine the same as in the previous example, as long as we are replacing the old configuration file with the one in Listing 6.9. Otherwise, we need to update the `ConfFile` parameter in the servlet's initialization parameter arguments to point at the new configuration file path and name. After executing and viewing the application, the browser should display a login screen similar to the one in Figure 6.3. Try to enter invalid credentials to see the *Unauthorized* screen. Then try to enter the user name *open* and the password *sesame* to see the main screen.

Another thing to try is to see how the security traps the authentication when the user attempts to go directly to the main page of the application. Shut down your browser so that you force the security cookie to be flushed. You should then reopen it and go directly to the following link: `http://{Path Your ServletEngine}/WWWSecurityExample?method=main`. The security module should intercept the call and redirect you to the login screen.

As you can see, implementing form-based authentication is not that much more complex than implementing Web authentication, especially when we use enterprise servlets. We simply create the security module by extending `HTTPMethod`. We make our own customized `HTTPMethod` object, which implements form-based authentication, and we extend the servlet's classes from this object. By adding a login screen without security, we will then have a form-based security framework for our applications. Using this technique saves us from the hassle of duplicating security code throughout our applications.

Summary

Security is a critical function in the enterprise because unauthorized access to corporate data can severely damage a company's reputation and financial health. This is why security is at the top of requirements for applications developed in the enterprise.

Security requires a layered approach on a Web server. It begins with SSL to encrypt any communication between the client and the server. Next is the Web server's internal security that protects an entire site with one security model and is usually based on a user access list. This layer may not be robust enough for corporate or Internet demands, depending on the Web server vendor. Also depending on the vendor, the authentication method may support only a limited or proprietary data store. This leads us to the final layer, which is customized security. Customized security comes in two flavors: Web authentication and form-based authentication. These types of security schemes allow the developer to customize the way in which security is handled and the type of validation mechanism to use.

Web authentication is an HTTP type of authentication that uses HTTP headers for challenge/response exchanges between the server and the client. The most common types of Web authentication are basic, digest, and NTLM. Web authentication is what makes the browser display the user ID/password dialog box when going to a site that is secured with this scheme. Form-based authentication is HTML form based and is controlled by the session mechanism of a Web server. Form-based authentication may be used only if the Web server supports sessions. This type of authentication is more programmatic in nature, and it uses a cookie with a security token after validating the client to track the user's validation status in the system.

In the enterprise servlet framework, we learned that we can extend the `HTTPMethod` object to create custom authentication schemes and support either Web authentication or form-based authentication. By creating a customized `HTTPMethod` object, we can extend from this new object when building dispatch classes, and this process automatically secures Web pages that the objects create. Customizing allows us to choose which parts of an application to secure and which to leave open. It also allows us to create a hierarchy of security controls in an application just by extending from a customized security `HTTPMethod` class. This type of a model keeps security in a central location and allows the developers to concentrate on the bulk of an application's development: the business logic.

CHAPTER 7

Pools

Scalability is nearly the top issue of every corporate Web site, for both intranets and extranets. How do the companies scale to a growth in traffic? Corporations constantly need to be prepared for growth because their business plans dictate growth over time. The concerns are, How is a surge in traffic handled as business grows? Do systems need to be rewritten? Do bigger computers with more horsepower need to be deployed? Will current systems built on current technology scale to accommodate new growth?

Sometimes growth comes a little too unexpectedly. In July of 2000, for example, Qwest Communications had approximately 10,000 employees. Qwest bought out US West, which had 67,000 employees. Qwest's systems needed to scale up from handling 10,000 to 77,000 employees overnight. In terms of the Internet, Qwest's Web sites went from handling only network access customers to handling a 13-state local telephone region. Use of Qwest's Web sites grew from thousands of hits per day to hundreds of thousands of hits per day. Scalability was a critical issue for this organization.

If you are reading this book, you must be about to develop your Web systems in Java, or perhaps you already have. You have made a very good decision because Java runs on many different kinds of platforms, so hardware options help on one side of the scalability equation. The other side of the equation is software—that is, building applications that scale well. More horsepower takes scalability only so far. Designing the software correctly can be even more critical to scalability.

The key to building scalability into an application is object reuse. By *object reuse* we don't mean taking an object-oriented approach to development, but rather reusing resources such as database connections and memory buffers. We call this *pooling* resources. Through pooling, we can create a specific number of resources, borrow resources when we need them, and put them back into the pool when we have finished with them, allowing another process or user to use them.

In this chapter we will examine the concept of pooling and why it is important to scalability. We will build a base pool object that allows us to reuse all kinds of resources. We will then look at how to manage pools and how pools fit into the enterprise servlet framework.

What Is a Pool?

When we talk about pools with respect to Web development, we are not talking about relaxing in a warm, small body of water, sipping a margarita, and getting a nice tan. We are talking about pooling together resources to be "borrowed" by different processes. A *pool* is a readily available supply—a finite supply from which resources are borrowed, used, and returned for reuse. To clarify, let's look at a familiar real-world example of a pool.

Most of us have been to a video store at one time or another. Imagine that your local video store, Freddy's Video Rentals, ordered five copies of a particular video, thus creating a pool of videos. The owner, Freddy, figured that by having five copies of a particular video on hand, he would be able to keep his customers happy because almost never are five copies of the same movie checked out at once. You go to Freddy's to check out this video, and you notice that two videos are left. After you check out the movie, only one copy is left. But during the transaction, your friend Jerry walks through the door to return the same movie that you're checking out. "Hey Jerry, how did you like the movie?" you ask. He says, "It was great. I'm just returning it now." Now again two movies are left. You go home, watch the movie, and return it the next day. As you return the movie, you notice that there are three movies on the shelf, so with the addition of your returned copy, four copies are available. Then you spy your friend Pete, who is standing in line with the same movie. You call out, "Hey Pete! Awesome movie!" Pete says, "Yeah, I'm going to watch it tonight. I hear it's good." Pete has the fifth movie.

Freddy purchased five copies of the same movie, creating a pool of that particular movie. His customers (or users) check out and borrow the movie as illustrated in Figure 7.1. After watching the movie, each customer returns the video to the pool so that another customer can use it. Freddy has done an excellent job of pooling his resources to fit his customer's needs.

Would it have been prudent for Freddy to purchase a new video for each of his customers, then let them check out the video and return it? Absolutely not. Such an approach would have been too expensive, and Freddy would have

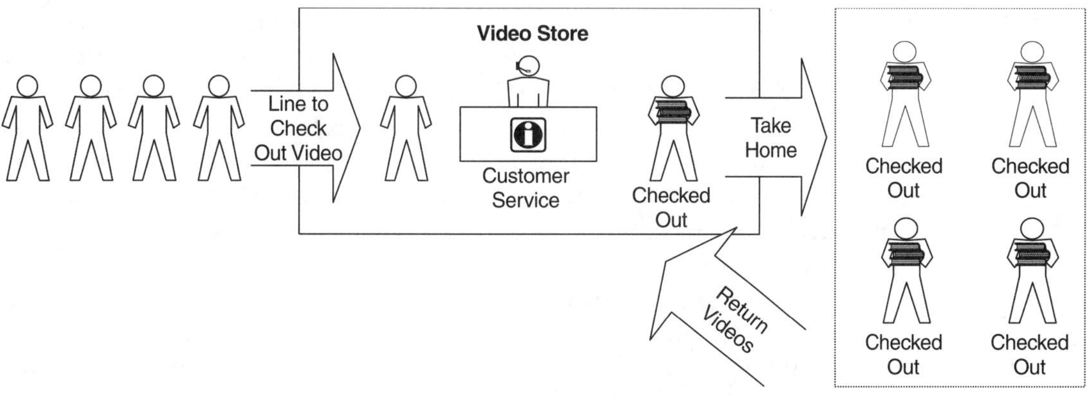

Figure 7.1 Pooling at a video store

gone out of business. Freddy gauged his customer traffic and was able to pool the right number of videos so that all of his customers were happy.

Now let's see where scalability fits into this scenario. Say that the year's Academy Award Best Picture comes out on video. Although the movie has received rave reviews, many people have been very busy and haven't had the chance to see it in the movie theaters. Others have seen the movie and liked it so much that they can't wait to see it on video. Freddy knows that this movie will be a hit, so he orders 10 copies of it for his store, instead of the usual 5. But Freddy hasn't anticipated just how popular the movie will be; all 10 copies are checked out in the first ten minutes after the shipment is received from the distribution company. In addition, 20 people are waiting for the video. Freddy needs to scale his business to meet the demand of his customers.

Freddy places a rush order for 20 more videos. When they arrive, he has a total of 30 copies of the movie. The next day, 2 copies are left on the shelf. Freddy has scaled his business very well for the increased growth in demand for the video. What happens when the fury is over and Freddy has a lot of videos taking up space on his shelf? He has a fire sale and sells the excess videos at a great discount!

Web development is not so different from the video store scenario. Just as Freddy would not order a new video for each of his customers, we would not want to assign a new database connection to each user going to a Web site. With thousands of users hitting a Web site, the database would not be able to handle all the concurrent connections. Just as thousands of videos are too expensive for Freddy, thousands of database connections are too expensive for us, but in this case in terms of memory resources and CPU usage.

We can scale resources just as Freddy scales his business with videos. If our Web site is hit by only a few people at any given moment, we need only a few database connections. If the Web site is high capacity and is hit by as many as 30 users at any given moment, we should be prepared to have a pool of 30 database connections. If customers have to wait a long time for a connection, they will complain about the performance of the Web application. So a good approach is to pool a number of resources that matches the largest spike in hits to the Web server.

The advantages of pools do not stop at scalability. In Java, continual creation and destruction of objects are bad things. These operations increase the rate at which the garbage collector executes, and for a high-capacity Web site, they could freeze a Web server for a period of time. An application with less destruction and more reuse of objects will manage memory better and run more efficiently. Scalability, object reuse, and refined memory management are all good side effects of object pooling.

Using Pools in Web Development

What kinds of resources do we pool when we build applications? Just about any kind of resource can be pooled. If you have a CD-ROM farm, for example, you can pool each of the CD-ROM drives to serve data. As in the Web example just described, database connections are one of the most commonly pooled resources. Large memory blocks are also an excellent candidate to pool as a resource.

So how do we pool objects? An *object pool* is a list or group of objects, usually stored in an array. The array keeps track of each object's state—either in use and unavailable, or available for use. The array also provides the methods to allow the child threads to "check out" and "check in" the objects. Such a pool is not very different from the pool of videos in a video store. Typically, a developer or administrator sets the number of objects that the pool will contain. The pool creates these objects at startup of the application or server. As each thread, process, or user requires a resource from the pool, it calls a *checkout* method on the pool. When the pool receives this call, it moves a pointer along the object array and looks for an object that is available. The pool then marks the object as unavailable and passes it back to the calling thread. The thread uses the object as it needs; then it calls the *checkin* method and passes the object back to the pool. The pool finally takes the object and marks it as available so that may be used by other threads.

When all objects are checked out, the threads wait and retrieve the first available object on a first come, first served basis. This is very similar to how the video store pool works. The video store has a certain number of videos.

Each person checks out a video, watches it, and checks it back in after using it. If the number of people who want to watch the video exceeds the number of available videos, some people must wait until a copy is checked back in. Most video stores have a waiting list that is on a first come, first served basis, so they let the first customer on the list know when a copy of the video becomes available.

Just as in the video store, our pool needs to be *scalable*. In the earlier video store example, for instance, Freddy purchased more copies of a particularly popular movie so that nobody would have to wait for it. We should do the same when we use pools. Ultimately we want just enough objects in the pool that we maximize the resources without being wasteful and without making any thread wait.

When threads wait, end users wait. The results are slow sites and angry customers. With scalability, we can grow the system to meet the demands of users. Therefore, we need to choose a pool size that fits the users' needs and increase the size of the pool as the needs increase.

There are two different ways of doing this. The first is the *manual* method: We choose a pool size based on our expectations of the users' demands. Then we monitor the peaks and valleys of the users' demands and size the pool accordingly. As users' demands grow, we increase the pool size. The second method is *dynamic* pool growth. We build a pool that constantly grows according to the needs of the users. If the pool objects are all checked out, the next user who comes along is given a brand-new object as the pool automatically grows by one.

Although the second method may appear better because it requires no monitoring and the pool is responsible for its own scaling, it has some disadvantages. An outsider who knows that objects are being dynamically created in the application could maliciously attack a Web site by making hundreds of calls to the application at once. This tactic could force the servers to run out of memory very quickly as the pool continually added objects to itself in an attempt to scale to the load. The disadvantage of the first method is that it requires constant monitoring of the pools to be sure users are not waiting. So each method has its advantages and disadvantages for scaling pools.

Object reuse seems like a great concept, but is there a time when we do not want to use a pool? Absolutely! Pools do not solve all problems when we're building Web applications. One instance in which a pool should *not* be used is for a long-running process. Using an object that takes ten minutes to run a process, such as a large database query, could be detrimental to a site. With many users, and thus many of these long-running processes running at the same time, the pool could be used up very quickly. As a result, the Web server would appear to hang, or we might be forced to send an error message to the user stating that all connections were in use and to try again later. Just as the video store might lose customers who are not willing to wait a long time for a video to come back and thus go to another video store, so might we lose users of our Web sites. So one rule of thumb in deciding whether an object is a good candidate for a pool is that should not belong to a long-running process.

The Base Pool Object

Let's look more closely at a pool and what it will take to build a pooling object. From what we understand of pools so far, it's clear that each pool minimally needs an object array that contains flags to describe each object's availability. It needs methods to create and initialize the objects, and methods to check in and check out the objects. But this is a lot of code to build for each object. Extend that idea to an application that has two database pools and three memory pools, and the amount of code required becomes unmanageable.

The answer to this problem is to create a *base pool object* that can be extended to create any sort of object pool. This base pool object would allow us to create a very minimal amount of code when developing an object pool. In September 1999, while looking to build such a base pool object. I read an article[1] about creating a base pool object for a graphics pool for the Java Abstract Windows Toolkit (AWT). This article gave me an idea about building a generic base pool that can be used for any kind of object. The key requirements for any pool are that it must

1. Maintain each of the object's states—through a generic `Object` array.
2. Be able to create its own objects.
3. Have means for checking objects out and back in.
4. Be able to perform operations just before an object is checked out or in (such as initializing an object before it is checked out and cleaning it up before it is checked in).
5. Be able to replace an object with a newly created object. This capability could be helpful if the object became invalidated for some reason and the pooled object needed to be re-created. One such scenario would be an invalidated database connection, which would mean that we would have to re-create the connection on the fly and replace the old with the new.

Let's begin developing a base pool object with the interface that it may implement. The base pool needs to allow object pools to perform operations on

1 "Java 2 Graphics Rendering: An Architecture for Extreme Animation," by Torpum Jannak, in *Dr Dobb's Journal*, September 1999 (online, available at `http://www.ddj.com/articles/1999/9909/9909a/9909a.html`).

an object before it is checked out and before it is checked back in. For example, if we have a memory object that needs to be intialized or to have its internal data set to particular values before it is used, the framework needs to allow the pool to perform these actions on the object. The same capability may be needed just before the object is checked back in. For instance, if we have a pool of `StringBuffer` memory areas, we might wish to have the framework automatically reset the size of `StringBuffer` and empty it before checking it in.

We do this by creating an interface with the `beforeCheckin()` and the `beforeCheckout()` methods. By creating an interface, we can create default implementations of these methods in the base pool. That way the developer's pool does not need to create its own versions if no operations have to be performed on the object before checkin or checkout. In other words, if the developer decides to override these methods, the framework will call the developer's version instead of the default version. Let's call this interface `PoolInterface`. Listing 7.1 shows the code for `PoolInterface`.

Listing 7.1 The `PoolInterface` class

```
package enterprise.common;

public interface PoolInterface
{

  public void beforeCheckin(Object object);

  public Object beforeCheckout(Object object) throws Exception;

}
```

A technical description of the various methods of `PoolInterface` is necessary because it is important to understand what's going on here. The `beforeCheckout()` method takes an object (`Object`) as a parameter. The object that is passed to this method is the same one that was checked out by the framework. But we want this method to return `Object` as the return type. Why? Why not just claim the return type as `void` and use the parameter referenced `Object`? Requirement number 5 for pools states that we may need to re-create an object, so the object reference could change. By passing `Object` as a parameter, the reference point to the framework remains the same, so there would be no way to return a new object to the user unless we return `Object` as a return type.

Why would we need to re-create an object? A database connection is a perfect example. If the database administrator needs to restart the database, all of the connections in the database will become invalid. A `beforeCheckout()` method could detect a bad connection, re-create the `Connection` object, and internally replace the old one with the new. Because `Connection` is passed as a parameter to `beforeCheckout()`, we must return the new `Connection` object to be used. Only by having the `beforeCheckout()` method return an `Object` type can we do this.

The `beforeCheckin()` method is a little simpler. It does not need to have a return type, so we can declare it as `void`. Because we are checking in an object, the framework will need to use this object's reference to find its place in the array. We cannot simply change the object at this point, or the reference will change and we will not be able to check in the object. Besides, we are done with the object, so we really aren't interested in creating new versions. With this method we just want to clean up the object.

Now we are ready to develop the base pool object. Because this is a generic pool, we can simply call this class `Pool`. The `Pool` class will be declared abstract for two reasons. First and foremost it is a base pool. Without an implementation of code that pools some kind of an object, this class is completely unusable. Therefore, by declaring the `Pool` class abstract, we ensure that it cannot be used directly. Rather, this class must be extended as a part of an object to create the pool. The second reason that the `Pool` class must be abstract is that we plan to force the declaration of some methods in a subclass. By declaring the class abstract and declaring abstract methods, we can ensure that subclasses implement these abstract methods.

The whole concept behind a pool is to manage an array of objects. We manage this array by setting a flag upon checkin and checkout of an object to state whether the object is currently available or not. Each stored object must have one of these flags (which we will call `isUsed`). The easiest way to implement a one-to-one correlation between the flag and the object is to create a nested class that contains the `isUsed` flag and `Object` as member variables. We will call the private class `PoolObject`, thereby forcing a one-to-one correlation between the flag and the object when we create an array of `PoolObject` objects.

```
package enterprise.common;

public abstract class Pool implements PoolInterface
{

  private class PoolObject
  {
    public boolean isUsed;
    public Object object;

    public void setObject(Object o)
    {
      object = o;
    }
  }

  private PoolObject objectArray[];
```

We will declare a couple of constants to use within the class. These will be described when we get to the code that uses them.

```
private static final int SLEEP_MILLISECONDS = 100;
private static final int MAX_NUMBER_OF_TRIES = 10;
```

The following are some member variables that are used in managing the pool. The number of objects in the internal array will be kept in the `capacity` variable. The `indexPointer` variable will contain the index element in the array that identifies the next object in the array that will be checked out.

```
private int capacity;

private int indexPointer;
```

Next we will create the abstract method that all pools that extend the `Pool` class must implement. All pools must somehow create objects for the pool. Therefore, each pool should implement a `createObject()` method that returns an object. We want the framework to call the `createObject()` method for each object that will be placed into the array. By making this method abstract, we can force the inherited classes to include it and guarantee that the version in the subclass will be executed when the pool is being created. We will see how this works when we get to the pool initialization code. For now, let's declare an abstract class for `createObject()`.

```
public abstract Object createObject() throws Exception;
```

The default constructor will be declared protected and is used only when we want an inherited class to create its own constructor. This protection will allow certain inherited classes to compile.

```
protected Pool()
{
}
```

The directly usable constructor takes a parameter for the size of the pool. The constructor then calls the internal `createPool()` method.

```
public Pool(int maxSize) throws Exception
{
  createPool(maxSize);
}
```

The `createPool()` method is what creates the object array. We first want to be sure that we have a pool size of at least one. We do this because a pool size with no objects is no good. Such a pool would be completely unusable, so we require the pool size to be 1 or greater, or an exception is thrown. The first thing we do is create a `PoolObject` array of the requested pool size. Then we create the objects. This is where we call the abstract createObject() method mentioned earlier. Because it is abstract, it actually calls the version of createObject() that is in the inherited class. As you can see, for each element in the array, createObject() is called to retrieve a new object and place it in this array.

```
protected void createPool(int maxCapacity) throws Exception
{
  if (maxCapacity < 1)
  {
    throw new Exception("maxCapacity is less than 1.");
  }

  // Create the pool
  this.capacity = maxCapacity;
  objectArray = new PoolObject[capacity];

  // Create the objects
  for ( int i = 0; i < capacity; i++)
  {
    objectArray[i] = new PoolObject();
    objectArray[i].isUsed = false;
    objectArray[i].object  = createObject();
  }
}
```

We will also create some helper functions that return the array size (the capacity) and a method that allows the developer to free all of the pool connections.

```
public synchronized int getCapacity()
{
  return (capacity);
}

public synchronized void openAll()
{
  int i = 0;
  for ( i = 0; i < capacity; ++i)
    objectArray[i].isUsed = false;
}
```

Here we will declare the default implementations of beforeCheckin() and beforeCheckout() methods as required by PoolInterface. These methods will be called if the inherited pool class does not declare its own versions.

```
public void beforeCheckin(Object object){};

public Object beforeCheckout(Object object) throws Exception
{
  return object;
}
```

Now let's develop the real meat of the base pool: the checkin and checkout methods. These methods will be synchronized because they are publicly accessible and only one thread at a time should be allowed access to the object array. This prevents the possibility of multiple requests at the same time to retrieve the same object.

Let's start with checkout because it is more complex than checkin. We'll call this method `checkOutPoolObject()`, and it will be responsible for going through the array in a round-robin fashion until it finds an available object (in other words, an object whose `isUsed` flag is set to `false`). It works by incrementing the `indexPointer` flag and checking the `PoolObject.isUsed` variable. Whenever it finds a `PoolObject` element in the array whose `isUsed` flag is set to `false`, `checkOutPoolObject()` knows that that object is available and it sets the `isUsed` flag to `true` (making the object unavailable), calls the `beforeCheckout()` method on the object, and returns the resulting object to the user.

However, if `indexPointer` has gone through the entire array a full time, the thread goes to sleep for the amount of time specified by the constant `SLEEP_MILLISECONDS`, and then wakes up and tries again. During the sleep period, it is hoped that another thread will check in an object, and the original thread will then have access to this available object. If not, the original thread will continue this process for the number of tries specified by another constant defined in this class, `MAX_NUMBER_OF_TRIES`. If the value specified by `MAX_NUMBER_OF_TRIES` has been reached, the exception `PoolObjectNotAvailableException` is thrown.

The code for `PoolObjectNotAvailableException` is shown in Listing 7.2 on page 253. In a nutshell, when we want to check out an object and none are available, we try as many times as specified by `MAX_NUMBER_OF_TRIES` and sleep for the amount of time specified by `SLEEP_MILLISECONDS`. If we cannot get an object, `checkOutPoolObject()` throws the `PoolObjectNotAvailableException` exception. If we do get an object, it executes the `beforeCheckout()` method on the object and returns the resulting object.

```
public synchronized Object checkOutPoolObject() throws Exception
{
  Object object = null;

  int tryCount = 0;
  int elementCounter = 0;

  while (tryCount < MAX_NUMBER_OF_TRIES)
  {

    // We are about to go through all the array elements once, so
    // we will set elementCounter = 0
```

```
        elementCounter = 0;
        while( elementCounter < capacity)
        {
            // Find an object that is not being used
            if (!objectArray[indexPointer].isUsed)
            {
                // Found one! Now let's reserve it.
                object = objectArray[indexPointer].object;
                objectArray[indexPointer].isUsed = true;
            }

            // Let's increment the index pointer
            indexPointer++;

            // Wrap the pointer around if we reached the top
            if (indexPointer == capacity)
              indexPointer = 0;

            // Increment the number of elements we have looked at
            elementCounter++;

            // If we have an object, exit the element loop
            if (object != null)
            {
              break;
            }
        }

        // Did we get an object?
        if (object == null)
        {
          // No, so let's increment the try count and sleep
          // to allow someone to check in a value
          tryCount++;
          try
          {
              wait(SLEEP_MILLISECONDS);
          }
          catch (java.lang.InterruptedException ie)
          {
          }
          break;
        } else
        {
          // We have an object, so get out of the loop
          break;
        }
      }

      // If we couldn't get an object after trying
         MAX_NUMBER_OF_TRIES,
      // then we will throw an exception
```

```
    if (object == null)
    {
      throw new PoolObjectNotAvailableException(
                           "Cannot get object from pool.");
    }

    return beforeCheckout(object);
  }
```

Our checkin method, `checkInPoolObject()`, takes the object that we want to check in as a parameter. When we check in the object, we look for its place in the array. When we find its place, we call the `beforeCheckin()` method with the object passed as a parameter to perform any custom cleanup actions on the object, if this method is defined in the inherited pool class. Ultimately, then, we check in the object by setting the associated `isUsed` variable to `false`. If the object is not found in the array, the method throws the exception `IllegalArgumentException`.

```
  public synchronized void checkInPoolObject( Object object )
    throws IllegalArgumentException
  {
    boolean found = false;
    for (int i=0; i < capacity; ++i)
    {
        if (objectArray[i].object == object)
        {
            beforeCheckin(object);

            objectArray[i].isUsed = false;
            found = true;
            break;
        }
    }

    if (! found)
    {
        throw new IllegalArgumentException(
                           "Object does not belong to pool");
    }
  }
```

Finally, we need a method that allows us to replace an object in the pool array. This method will take two parameters—the old object and the new object—and it works very similarly to how `checkInPoolObject()` works. It looks in the array for the old object. If it finds it, it replaces the `PoolObject.object` reference with the new object. We make this a public synchronized method because once again we are potentially altering the array. It is public so that the inherited pool classes have the power to replace objects in the pool.

```
  public synchronized void replacePoolObject( Object oldObject,
                                              Object newObject)
    throws IllegalArgumentException
  {
    boolean found = false;
    for (int i=0; i < capacity; ++i)
    {
        if (objectArray[i].object == oldObject)
        {
            objectArray[i].object = newObject;
            found = true;
            break;
        }
    }

    if (! found)
    {
        throw new IllegalArgumentException(
                    "Object does not belong to pool");
    }
  }

}
```

As stated earlier in the chapter, if we try to check out an object and after `MAX_NUMBER_OF_TRIES` no such object is available to be retrieved, we will receive the exception `PoolObjectNotAvailableException`. Listing 7.2 shows the code for `PoolObjectNotAvailableException`.

Listing 7.2 The `PoolObjectNotAvailableException` class

```
package enterprise.common;

public class PoolObjectNotAvailableException extends Exception
{
  public PoolObjectNotAvailableException()
  {
        super();
  }

  public PoolObjectNotAvailableException(String msg)
  {
        super(msg);
  }

}
```

Using the Pool Object

Now that we have a base pool object (`Pool`), how do we use it? Before creating a pool, we need an object that will be pooled. Let's build a simple object that may be useful in building Web pages. On a high-capacity Web site that uses a lot of rich and robust templates, we would create and destroy many `StringBuffer` objects. Although it is much better to use `StringBuffer` objects than to use `String` objects, over time the hunt for memory during the dynamic building of large instances of `StringBuffer` could create havoc with the garbage collector.

Default initialization of a `StringBuffer` object allocates a size of 16 characters. A typical template in an application may be approximately 4,000 characters (4K). If we create a `StringBuffer` object and build a template in it, the virtual machine needs to allocate an additional 3,984 characters when building the template. Each time we call the `append()` method on the `StringBuffer` object, the virtual machine needs to find space to allocate room for the buffer piece by piece.

On a high-capacity site, many threads may be doing this at the same time—creating a workload that can heavily fragment memory and keep the garbage collector busy. If we can pool `StringBuffer` objects and preallocate the buffer size, we can reuse these objects. This approach prevents memory fragmentation, and the garbage collector practically does not need to execute because no objects are being destroyed. Let's create an object called `SBObject` as a wrapper class for `StringBuffer`. This object will preallocate 4,000 characters for `StringBuffer`. We will include an `int` variable that contains an identifier for the buffer when we create the pool. Listing 7.3 shows the code for `SBObject`.

Listing 7.3 The `SBObject` class as a `StringBuffer` object

```
import java.util.*;

public class SBObject
{

  public StringBuffer sb = new StringBuffer(4000);
  public int bufferId = 0;

}
```

To pool all the `SBObject` objects, we start by extending the `Pool` object. Only a couple of rules apply to creating a pool in this scenario. The first is that the constructor must call the `super()` method with an `int` parameter for the size of the pool. We do this so that the superclass can create the object array and all of the objects. It's a good idea to create a constructor that takes an `int` variable as a parameter so that the pool size can be defined outside the object.

Second, because the Pool class is abstract, it forces the inherited class to implement the createObject() method, so the pool will need to create the objects in this class. The createObject() method will create a new instance of SBObject, which automatically allocates a size of 4,000 characters for its internal StringBuffer object, and will set the bufferId parameter to an integer that uniquely identifies the object. When we use the pool, bufferId will show us which object is being used.

These are the two required rules for creating a pool. The two optional rules are to create beforeCheckin() or beforeCheckout() methods. Remember that these methods are used when we need to perform actions on the object before checking in or checking out an object. In this example, we want to clean up an instance of SBObject and its internal StringBuffer object before checking it in. Therefore we will implement the beforeCheckin() method. In this method we will set the length of StringBuffer to zero. This does not deallocate the size, but instead makes the StringBuffer contents disappear, preparing the StringBuffer object for the next user. Because we are creating a pool of SBObject objects, let's call the pool SBOPool. Listing 7.4 shows the code for SBOPool.

Listing 7.4 The StringBuffer object pool, SBOPool

```
import enterprise.common.*;

public class SBOPool extends Pool
{

  private static int counter = 0;

  public SBOPool(int maxSize)
      throws Exception
  {
    super(maxSize);
  }

  public Object createObject() throws Exception
  {
    SBObject sbo = new SBObject();
    sbo.bufferId = ++counter;

    return sbo;
  }

  public void beforeCheckin(Object o)
  {
    SBObject sbo = (SBObject) o;

    sbo.sb.setLength(0);
  }
}
```

As Listing 7.4 shows, creating the pool is quite simple, but how do we use it? Where do we create it? How do we check objects out and check them back in? We usually initialize the pool when the application starts. This is a one-time action. Somewhere in the application's initialization we would declare the following:

```
SBOPool sboPool = new SBOPool(10);
```

This declaration creates the pool and ten objects in the pool's object array. When we are ready to use an object, we will want to check it out and check it back in when we are finished. The following code would be used to retrieve and use the pooled objects:

```
SBObject sbo = null;

try
{
  sbo = (SBObject) sboPool.checkOutPoolObject();

  // Use the object
  . . .

} finally
{
  // If we have an object, then we check it back in
  if (sbo != null)
  {
    sboPool.checkInPoolObject(sbo);
  }
}
```

This construct is required when we need a pooled object. What we are doing is checking out an object within a `try` block. We do this to guarantee that the object will be checked back in, no matter what happens. If an exception is thrown, or the user needs to exit the method, the `finally` clause is guaranteed to execute, so we can also guarantee that the object will be checked back in.

As you can see, creating a pool and using a pool are very simple with the `Pool` base class. Let's see the pool work in an example.

Using the Pool: An Example

In the previous section we created a `StringBuffer` object and an associated pool that preallocates a certain size for `StringBuffer`. Let's implement a sample application to use this pool and object. The goal of this example is to show where we would create a pool and where we would use it. This example will use the `SBObject` and `SBOPool` classes that we created earlier. The reason we created SBObject was to reuse the internal StringBuffer object for potentially large templates. So we will create an HTML template that allows us to show what pool we are using (now you see why we have a buffer identifier in the object).

Let's name this application (and thus also the base dispatch servlet) PoolExample. The application will have one page and thus one dispatch class, which we will call PoolPage. We will use one template, which we will call pool.html. We'll begin with the configuration file, as shown in Listing 7.5.

Listing 7.5 The configuration file for PoolExample

```
Application.Base.URL=/servlet/PoolExample

Default.Method=pool
Method.pool=PoolPage

# Place the default template path here
Default.Template.Path=c:\\Book\\Chapter 07\\Example 1\\templates
Template.pool=pool.html

# Place the log file path here
Log.File.Path=c:\\Book\\Chapter 07\\Example 1\\PoolExample.log
```

Now let's build the base dispatch servlet, PoolExample. This servlet isn't too different from the base servlets that we have developed in other chapters, except that we will create a static member as the pool object and initialize it in the initializeApp() method (see Listing 7.6). Normally, having accessible member variables in a servlet is not good, unless they are thread-safe through synchronization. Of course, our pools are thread-safe because all of the accessor methods that we use in the pool are synchronized. In this example, we will use a pool size of five objects.

Listing 7.6 The PoolExample main dispatch servlet with pool initialization

```
import enterprise.servlet.*;
import enterprise.common.*;

import java.io.*;

public class PoolExample extends BaseEnterpriseServlet
{
  public static SBOPool sboPool = null;

  public String getAppName()
  {
    return "PoolExample";
  }
```

```
  public void initializeApp(AppContext appContext)  throws Exception
  {
    sboPool = new SBOPool(5);
  }

  public void destroyApp(AppContext ac)
  {
  }
}
```

`PoolExample` has one page, called `PoolPage`. This page will check out one instance of `SBObject` and use the `pool.html` template with that object's `StringBuffer`. The checkout and checkin code is used in the `try/finally` block shown earlier (at the end of the section titled Using the Pool Object). The substitution for the template will place `SBObject.bufferId` in the string, so you may see which pool object is being used for displaying the page. Listing 7.7 shows the code for `PoolPage`.

Listing 7.7 The `PoolPage` class

```
import enterprise.servlet.*;
import enterprise.html.*;

import java.io.*;

public class PoolPage extends HTTPMethod
{

  public void execute() throws Exception
  {
    SBObject sbo = null;

    try
    {
      PrintWriter out = m_response.getWriter();
      TemplateCacheList tcl = m_context.getTemplateCacheList();

      HTMLCompiledTemplate hct = tcl.get("pool");
      HTMLTemplate ht = hct.createHTMLTemplate();

      sbo = (SBObject) PoolExample.sboPool.checkOutPoolObject();

      ht.substitute("poolno", sbo.bufferId + "" );
      ht.substitute("BASEURL", m_context.getAppBaseURL());
      ht.toStringBuffer(sbo.sb);

      out.println(sbo.sb.toString());
    } finally
    {
      if (sbo != null)
      {
```

```
            PoolExample.sboPool.checkInPoolObject(sbo);
          }
        }
      }
    }
```

Finally, we need the template—pool.html—that PoolPage will use. Listing 7.8 shows the code for pool.html.

Listing 7.8 The pool.html template

```
<html>
<head>
<title>PoolExample</title>
</head>

<body bgcolor="#FFFFFF">
<center>
  <h2>This HTML Page has been created using....</h2>
  <br>
  <br>  <h3><font color="#3333FF">StringBuffer Object Pool
         Number ${poolno}.</font></h3>
  <br>
  <br>
<form>
  <input type="button" name="Button"
         value="Click here to get another Pool Object"
         onClick="document.location='${BASEURL}'">
</form>
</center>
</body>
</html>
```

Now we are ready to set up and execute the application. The setup program registers the servlet and the ConfFile parameter in the servlet engine to point to the configuration file that we defined in Listing 7.5. When the application is being run, the output should be similar to what Figure 7.2 shows. Notice that we get the SBObject object in round-robin fashion. As we get the fifth object, notice also that the pool wraps around to the first one in the array.

Another idea is to have a friend test the servlet out with you on another browser. Try hitting the server several times at the same time as your friend. You will notice that the server still distributes objects in a round-robin fashion. If you hit the reload button on your browser—very rapidly—it may appear to you that the server is skipping complete blocks of the pool. In reality it is not; it is just rapidly checking the SBObject objects in and out.

You can try with a few friends hitting the server at the same time. See if you can get the server to "wait" for an available connection. This may be difficult to do because the object is used for only a very short time and is checked in and out very rapidly. This test helps show the power of pooling heavily used and

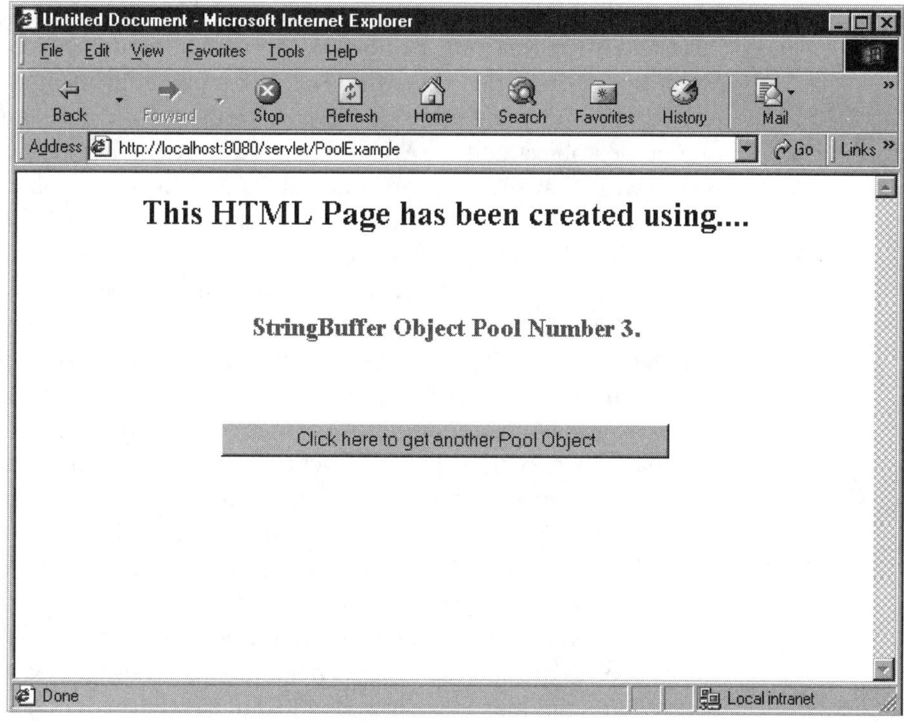

Figure 7.2 Output of the sample application

large objects. Appreciation for a pool becomes really clear on a high-capacity site, where you will notice that the memory usage of your application remains static and the garbage collector does not have to work as hard to clean up after the objects.

The Pool Anomaly

The information about pools presented in the previous section is very valuable for the use of pooled resources. With this knowledge, however, comes a huge burden. The `try/finally` block that we must use when we check objects in and out must be present when a pooled object is being used. This is a critical requirement because we cannot guarantee that the object will be checked back in without it. The anomaly in this scenario is that the developer bears the responsibility of ensuring that the checkin is implemented in the object. We are placing trust in the developer that this code will be executed in every piece of code that uses a pooled object.

It is very easy to check out an object and forget to check it back in. Doing so may cause the Web servers to freeze up very fast as they wait for an object.

Many of the pool object APIs that are available today, including open-source APIs and APIs that are included as part of a vendor's Web server, such as WebLogic, require this `try/finally` block to be implemented in code when a pooled object is being used. However, too often this code is missed during use of a pooled object and the Web server freezes. Generally both users and developers swear that the problem is not theirs and that the problem is the fault of the servlet engine vendor. After many attempts to find the problem, the culprit almost always turns out to be a piece of code that forgot to check in an object. Such coding errors are very difficult to find and debug.

One reason for implementing the constant `MAX_NUMBER_OF_TRIES` in the base `Pool` object is that it allows us to trap the condition when all of the objects have been used up. Receiving the `PoolObjectNotAvailableException` exception is a reasonably good indication that some of the code is not checking in objects. This exception helps prevent the appearance that the Web server is freezing up. However, the best scenario would be to avoid this situation altogether. If we rely on developers to execute the `try/finally` block, we risk running into code that does not comply with use of a pool. Is there something we can do to relieve the developer of this burden?

The answer is a resounding yes! In the enterprise servlet architecture, everything revolves around the base-servlet concept. By using a base servlet, we can ensure that pool management is handled in `BaseEnterpriseServlet` and make sure that any objects checked out of pools are checked back in. In other words, we need to have a centrally located pool manager that monitors which objects are checked out and ensures that the objects are checked back in. To monitor the pools, such a manager would need a list of all available pools. The pool manager will handle requests for objects to be checked out of each pool and then make sure those objects are checked back into their respective pools.

To understand this concept, let's examine the video store example again. The pool manager would be the customer service person (CSP). A movie belongs to one pool of videos. A different movie belongs to another pool of videos. Therefore we have many pools of videos in the video store—one for each movie. When a customer wants a particular movie, the CSP literally checks out the video and hands it to the customer. A customer who forgets to bring the borrowed movie back to the video store after watching it usually gets a call from the CSP—a reminder that the video needs to be checked back in. The CSP is ensuring that the video is checked back into the pool so that it can be reused by others. When the video is returned, the CSP places it back in its respective pool on the shelf so that it can be checked out again. In the development world, the pool manager is analogous to the video store's CSP, and the pool list is analogous to the list of movies. In the next section we will create objects to handle these two roles.

Case Study

The Marketing Department of a large corporation hired a very well-known consulting company to create an executive information system product. This product was a Web-based application that allowed the executives to drill down sales data at any given moment to analyze departmental sales quota and revenue bases.

The application had a polished interface and was the type that would be expected from this consulting firm. However, the Web server appeared to "freeze up" at random intervals. The only way to get the application running again was to restart the Web server. This became a real problem because the server was freezing up many times a day, and the executives were becoming concerned about the viability of the product.

The consulting company investigated and found no problems with its code. The consultants blamed the Web server and asked the Web server's vendor to look into the problem.

After investigating, the vendor stated that there was no problem with the server. Frustrated, the Marketing Department asked IT's crack Java team to analyze the problem.

The Java team interviewed the consultants and asked if they were using any pools. The consultants replied that they were using pools for connections to the database. The Java team had seen this kind of behavior before and instantly believed the culprit was that some code was not checking in objects.

Because there were hundreds of servlets in this application, the consultants had to comb through many lines of code. Four days later, they had found seven servlets that were not checking in code. The consulting company quickly made the change to the code and the server never froze up again.

This example shows that a lot of responsibility falls on the shoulders of the developer to be sure to check in pooled objects after using them. Having learned a lesson, the consulting company and the client's Java team worked together to design a way for objects to be automatically checked back in after use.

PoolList and PoolObjectManager

Let's start with the pool list. We need an object that contains a list of all the available pools from which to check out objects for the application. We will call this object `PoolList`. This object is nothing more than a glorified `Hashtable` object. It will store the pools by name. For example, we may have three pools in one application. We would name the Oracle connection pool *OraPool,* the graphics pool *ImagePool,* and the `StringBuffer` pool *SBPool.* When we create a pool, we will add it to the pool list by calling the `PoolList.add()` method, and when we want to retrieve a pool, we will call `PoolList.getPool()` and use the name of the pool as a unique identifier. Listing 7.9 shows the code for `PoolList`.

Listing 7.9 The `PoolList` class

```
package enterprise.common;

import java.util.*;

public class PoolList
{
  private Hashtable m_poolList = new Hashtable();

  public synchronized void add(String name, Pool pool)
    throws IllegalArgumentException
  {
    if (pool == null)
    {
      throw new IllegalArgumentException("Pool object is null.");
    }

    if (name == null)
    {
      throw new IllegalArgumentException("name is null.");
    }

    if (m_poolList.containsKey(name))
    {
      throw new IllegalArgumentException(name + " already exists.");
    }

    m_poolList.put(name, pool);
  }

  public synchronized Pool getPool(String name)
          throws IllegalArgumentException
  {
    if (name == null)
    {
      throw new IllegalArgumentException("name is null.");
    }
```

```
    if (m_poolList.containsKey(name) == false)
    {
      throw new IllegalArgumentException(name +
                                 " does not exist in list.");
    }

    return (Pool) m_poolList.get(name);
  }
}
```

Now we need the equivalent of a customer service representative—a pool manager—to manage this pool list, monitoring which objects are checked out from which pool and ensuring that objects are checked back in. We'll call the object we create for this purpose `PoolObjectManager`. It will field all requests to check out and check in objects from a pool, rather than the pool fielding such requests directly. `PoolObjectManager` will keep track of all the objects that have been checked out by storing them in a list. As the user requires another object, `PoolObjectManager` will check out the object and add it to its internal array. If the user manually checks in an object, `PoolObjectManager` will remove the object from the internal list.

When the developer is done executing the call, the `checkInAll()` method is executed in `PoolObjectManager`, which goes through the internal object list and checks in any objects that have not already been checked in. The object `PoolObjectManager` ensures that the developer never directly accesses a pool. Instead, the developer requests a pool by a particular name (such as *SBPool*) from `PoolObjectManager` and gets an object back. When the the code is finished executing, `PoolObjectManager` checks in all checked-out objects. Listing 7.10 shows the code for `PoolObjectManager`.

Listing 7.10 The `PoolObjectManager` class

```
package enterprise.common;

import java.util.*;

public class PoolObjectManager
{

  private Hashtable m_checkedOut = new Hashtable();

  private PoolList m_poolList = null;

  public PoolObjectManager(PoolList pl)
  {
    m_poolList = pl;
  }

  public Object checkOut(String name) throws Exception
  {
```

```
    Pool p = m_poolList.getPool(name);

    Object poolObject = p.checkOutPoolObject();

    if (poolObject != null)
    {
      m_checkedOut.put(poolObject, p);
    }

    return poolObject;
  }

  public void checkIn(Object o)
  {
    Pool p = (Pool)m_checkedOut.get(o);

    p.checkInPoolObject(o);

    m_checkedOut.remove(o);
  }

  public void checkInAll()
  {
    Enumeration e = m_checkedOut.keys();
    while (e.hasMoreElements())
    {
      Object o = e.nextElement();
      checkIn(o);
    }
  }
}
```

Now that we have created `PoolList` and `PoolObjectManager`, what do we do with them? How do we use pools with them? The only way we can use these objects is to locate them centrally. `PoolList` is specific to an application. Each application has its own list of pools, just as a video store has its own list of videos. This makes `PoolList` a good candidate to be a member of `AppContext`. So let's create a `PoolList` member in `AppContext`, as well as a getter for the object. These additions to `AppContext` are shown in Listing 7.11.

Listing 7.11 Changes to `AppContext` to provide access to `PoolList`

```
public class AppContext
{
.
.
.
  private PoolList oPoolList = new PoolList();
.
.
.
```

```
  public PoolList getPoolList()
  {
    return oPoolList;
  }
.
.
.
}
```

PoolObjectManager is where we go when we want to check out an object; therefore we must have access to this object from our dispatch methods. For such access to be possible, the HTTPMethod object needs a member variable of type PoolObjectManager. This member variable, which we will call m_poolObjMgr, will be set by BaseEnterpriseServlet when it calls HTTPMethod.registerMethod(). We will create the member variable and alter the registerMethod() method to accept PoolObjectManager as one of its parameters, and set the member variable from within this method. Listing 7.12 shows these changes.

Listing 7.12 Changes to the HTTPMethod class to provide access to the PoolObjectManager object

```
public abstract class HTTPMethod implements Authentication
{
.
.
.
  protected PoolObjectManager m_poolObjMgr;
.
.
.
  public void registerMethod(HttpServletRequest  req,
                             HttpServletResponse res,
                             AppContext          context,
                             PoolObjectManager   pom)
  {
.
.
.
      m_poolObjMgr   = pom;
  }
.
.
.
}
```

Now we'll see the real magic happen. The main engine for PoolList and PoolObjectManager is in BaseEnterpriseServlet. We will take a little closer look at BaseEnterpriseServlet to see what changes need to be made so that

PoolList and PoolObjectManager can be used. Because the dispatching occurs in the service() method of BaseEnterpriseServlet, we will start there.

```
public abstract class BaseEnterpriseServlet extends HttpServlet
{
.
.
.
  public void service(HttpServletRequest req,
                      HttpServletResponse res)
      throws ServletException, IOException
  {
.
.
.
```

We know that all pools require a try/finally clause of some sort. There is no exception here. In this method there is already a large try/catch block, so we will reuse this block with the pool code. Right before the try clause we want to create a PoolObjectManager object so that any checked-out objects can be monitored.

We create PoolObjectManager and use PoolList to construct the object. Understand that PoolObjectManager needs to know about all available pools, which is why we pass PoolList to it. By doing this, the developers can ask PoolObjectManager if it can check out *SBPool, ImagePool,* or any other specific pool that may have been created in the application. Because PoolList is accessible through AppContext, we would create PoolObjectManager with the following code:

```
PoolObjectManager pom =
                  new PoolObjectManager(m_ac.getPoolList());
try
{
```

The rest of the try block and code are the same, until we get to registerMethod(). In the try clause, we will call registerMethod() with PoolObjectManager added as one of the parameters because we changed HTTPMethod's version to accept this parameter. This gives HTTPMethod access to PoolObjectManager.

```
.
.
.
      methodInstance.registerMethod(req, res, m_ac, pom);
.
.
.
```

At the end of the catch blocks we want to add a finally block because we are allowing the dispatched methods to check out any object they want from PoolObjectManager, and PoolObjectManager must clean up afterward, even if an exception is thrown in the dispatch method. The finally clause takes PoolObjectManager and calls the checkInAll() method, which checks in any objects that were checked out by the dispatch method.

```
    }finally
    {
      // Close up the connections
      pom.checkInAll();
    }
}
```

For monitoring checkout of objects, we may want to give access to PoolObjectManager in the initializeApp() and destroyApp() methods of BaseEnterpriseServlet. When we extend BaseEnterpriseServlet, we may want the initialization and destruction code to have access to any pools. Although we will create most pools in the initializeApp() method, when we get into databases and pooling, we may offload some of this work to AppContext, so initalizeApp() may need access to some pools that have already been created. For this reason we will allow the initializeApp() and destroyApp() methods to take PoolObjectManager as a parameter. Of course, the code that calls these methods will need the usual try/finally block, and it will need to create and pass PoolObjectManager to the initializeApp() and destroyApp() methods. The changes are as follows:

```
  public abstract void initializeApp(AppContext appContext,
                                     PoolObjectManager pom)
                                throws Exception;

  public abstract void destroyApp(AppContext appContext,
                                  PoolObjectManager pom);
.
.
.
  public final void init(ServletConfig config) throws
                             ServletException
  {
.
.
.
      m_ac.parseConfigFile(getAppName(),sConf);

      PoolObjectManager pom = new
                             PoolObjectManager(m_ac.getPoolList());
```

```
        try
        {
          initializeApp(m_ac, pom);
        }
        finally
        {
          pom.checkInAll();
        }
  .
  .
  .
  }
  .
  .
  .
  public final void destroy()
  {
    if (getAppName() != null)
    {
      m_appManager.removeApp(getAppName());
    }

    PoolObjectManager pom =
                         new PoolObjectManager(m_ac.getPoolList());

    try
    {
      destroyApp(m_ac, pom);
    }
    finally
    {
      pom.checkInAll();
    }
  }
  .
  .
  .
}
```

What does all this code do for us? It takes the burden of having to check in pool objects away from the developer and puts it in the hands of `BaseEnterpriseServlet`. To use a pool with this framework, we would create the pool and add it to the list with the following code:

```
SBOPool sboPool = new SBOPool(5);
appContext.getPoolList().add("SBOPOOL", sboPool);
```

In the dispatch class, we check out an object like this:

```
SBObject sbo = (SBObject) m_poolObjMgr.checkOut("SBOPOOL");
```

That's all there is to it! No need for any try/finally blocks, and more importantly, no need to remember to check the object back into the pool. BaseEnterpriseServlet and PoolObjectManager do all the dirty work.

Using PoolList and PoolObjectManager: An Example

Creating and using pools with PoolList and PoolObjectManager is really easy, but don't take my word for it. Let's take the PoolExample application that we developed earlier in the chapter and change it so that it uses PoolList and PoolObjectManager. We'll start with the PoolExample base dispatch servlet. We no longer need the SBOPool static member in the class. Remember that we now store the pools in the application's PoolList object. We still initialize the pool in the initializeApp() method, but we also add the pool to PoolList through AppContext. We need to give the pool a string name when we add it to the list, so we will call it SBOPool. Listing 7.13 shows the code for the new PoolExample class.

Listing 7.13 The new PoolExample class

```
import enterprise.servlet.*;
import enterprise.common.*;

import java.io.*;

public class PoolExample extends BaseEnterpriseServlet
{
  public String getAppName()
  {
    return "PoolExample";
  }

  public void initializeApp(AppContext appContext,
                             PoolObjectManager pom)  throws
                             Exception
  {
    SBOPool sboPool = new SBOPool(5);
    appContext.getPoolList().add("SBOPOOL", sboPool);
  }

  public void destroyApp(AppContext ac, PoolObjectManager pom)
  {
  }
}
```

The only other code we need to change is in the PoolPage class. We can strip out the try/finally block and request the object SBObject from the PoolObjectManager member variable m_poolObjMgr. We request the pool by the name that we gave it when we created it. We call checkout() with this string as a parameter, and it gives us the object we requested. Listing 7.14 shows the code for the new PoolPage class.

Listing 7.14 The new PoolPage class

```
import enterprise.servlet.*;
import enterprise.html.*;

import java.io.*;

public class PoolPage extends HTTPMethod
{

  public void execute() throws Exception
  {

    PrintWriter out = m_response.getWriter();
    TemplateCacheList tcl = m_context.getTemplateCacheList();

    HTMLCompiledTemplate hct = tcl.get("pool");
    HTMLTemplate ht = hct.createHTMLTemplate();

    SBObject sbo = (SBObject) m_poolObjMgr.checkOut("SBOPOOL");

    ht.substitute("poolno", sbo.bufferId + "" );
    ht.substitute("BASEURL", m_context.getAppBaseURL());
    ht.toStringBuffer(sbo.sb);

    out.println(sbo.sb.toString());
  }
}
```

Notice that the revised code for PoolPage does not check in the SBObject object. PoolObjectManager takes care of this. We could check in the object by calling the PoolObjectManager.checkIn() method, but this is not necessary because the object will clean up after us. Although nothing prevents us from creating or accessing pools directly, using pools in conjunction with PoolList and PoolObjectManager ensures that the developer does not forget to check in objects. In addition, as this example shows, a lot less code needs to be implemented in the dispatch classes, so this approach speeds up development time.

Summary

In this chapter we learned about object pools and developed the base pool object that allows us to create a pool with just about any kind of object. We also learned that creating a pool places responsibility on the developer to make sure that each piece of code that uses a pooled object checks used objects back in. If objects are not checked back in, the pool becomes depleted of available resources, and the Web server eventually gives the impression of freezing up as the threads wait for available objects.

We created `PoolList` and `PoolObjectManager` to help alleviate this burden. When using pools with these objects in the enterprise servlet framework, we no longer need to worry about checking in pooled objects when we're done using them. `PoolObjectManager` monitors and checks in the checked-out objects after we're done using them.

As this chapter showed, object creation and destruction can sometimes be considered the enemy in Java programming. Large blocks of memory resources or lengthy connection processes can hinder a Web server's performance. The garbage collector can also slow things down. By pooling resources and reusing objects, we can streamline applications and provide scalability to servlets.

CHAPTER 8

Database Connectivity

Databases are a necessary part of most Web applications. Many applications need a place to store and retrieve information. Corporations store massive amounts of data in data warehouse databases and need access to the summary information. Human Resources stores employee information in databases. Finance tracks expenses and revenue (as well as payroll information) in databases. It is no wonder, then, that nearly every project's specification includes access to one or more databases. For this reason just about every developer has encountered a database at least once in his or her development career.

Database development in server-based applications can be tricky. In Java we connect to databases through the Java Database Connectivity (JDBC) API, and there are many ways to execute database queries. But implementing database connectivity in a server application and managing this connectivity are two entirely different issues. Although making a connection and executing a query are simple tasks, we will run into scalability issues for high-capacity sites, such as how to keep from running out of cursors on database connections, and how to ensure that we are always using a valid connection. This chapter will focus on how to properly manage a database connection in a servlet-based application, and we'll discuss the typical problems that developers encounter.

JDBC: A Quick Review

Although you should have a firm knowledge of JDBC, SQL, and relational databases before reading this chapter, we will give you a quick refresher of JDBC and how it works. JDBC is a standardized API layer that allows a common means of connecting to a relational database. Its driver converts JDBC calls into calls that are native to the database. Therefore, theoretically, we could use the same JDBC code to connect to any database, just by changing its driver.

The JDBC database driver is the base of all database activity. Sun includes the JDBC-ODBC bridge driver with J2EE. (ODBC stands for Object Database Connectivity.) Most drivers can be obtained from the database vendor, and usually they can be downloaded for free from the Web vendor's Web site. Using JDBC and a driver requires adding the driver (usually packaged in a ZIP or JAR file) and the JDBC API (which is included in the Java SDK) to the class path. For the information shown here and in the rest of the chapter, we will use the Oracle thin database driver. The Oracle database was chosen because it is one of the most widely used databases in Internet and intranet technologies. It is also a database that has more intricacies when it is being used for development in a servlet environment. This driver can be obtained from Oracle's Web site, at `http://technet.oracle.com`.

Loading the Driver and Connecting to the Database

The first thing we need to do before attempting to connect to a database is to load the database driver. This is a simple task and can be done in one of two ways. The first way is to load the driver through the `Class.forName()` call. For example, if we wanted to load the Oracle thin driver, we would execute the following command:

```
Class.forName("oracle.jdbc.driver.OracleDriver");
```

The other way to load the database driver is to instantiate and create the driver object directly through the `DriverManager` object, as shown here:

```
DriverManager.registerDriver(
                    new oracle.jdbc.driver.OracleDriver());
```

Both methods for loading the driver prepare `DriverManager` to make connections with the database—which is the second step in using JDBC. We need to create a connection before executing SQL statements against the database. We create a connection by calling the `DriverManager.getConnection()` method, which returns a `Connection` object.

The `getConnection()` call can take several parameters and is able to be called in a variety of ways. These variations can be viewed through Sun Microsystems's JavaDoc (`http://java.sun.com/j2ee/tutorial/api/javax/servlet/http/HttpSession.html`) for JDBC, but for the sake of this explanation we will use the one that takes a connection URL, user ID, and password. The URL is usually defined by the database vendor. It usually defines some information that is necessary when we are connecting to a database.

With Oracle, the URL begins with *jdbc:oracle:thin:* and is followed by @ and the IP address or domain name of the machine that is running the Oracle server. This is followed by a colon and the port on which the Oracle TNSListener is listening—normally port 1521. The URL also has a colon and the name of the Oracle database service ID appended to the string. One example of a URL string is `jdbc:oracle:thin:@localhost:1521:ORCL`. In this case when we made a connection, we would implement the following code:

```
String userId = "scott";
String password = "tiger";
String url = "jdbc:oracle:thin:@localhost:1521:ORCL";

Connection cn = DriverManager.getConnection(url,
                                            userId,
                                            password);
```

This code is what will make the connection to the database, assuming that the URL, the user ID, and the password are all correct.

The JDBC Statement and ResultSet Objects

In JDBC, the `Statement` object is used to interact with the database. It allows the end user to enter SQL statements and execute them. We use the `Connection` object to create a `Statement` object, as in the following code:

```
Statement stmt = cn.createStatement();
```

With a `Statement` object we can execute SQL statements with the database. There are a few ways of doing this with the `Statement` object, but two are more widely used. We use the first method when we want to perform an updating type of action against the database—for example, inserting, updating, or deleting data. To execute an update type of SQL statement, we call the `executeUpdate()` method. For example, if we wanted to insert data into the `DEPT` table, we would execute the following code:

```
String sql = "insert into DEPT (deptno, dname, loc) " +
                    "values(50, 'HR', 'DENVER')";
stmt.executeUpdate(sql);
```

The second type of SQL statement we could execute is a query type of statement. This type of SQL statement is usually a `select` statement. It returns tabular data in a `ResultSet` object that is created by a call to the `executeQuery()` method of the `Statement` object. The following code executes a query and returns a `ResultSet` object:

```
String sql = “select deptno, dname, loc from DEPT”;
ResultSet rs = stmt.executeQuery(sql);
```

When it is returned, `ResultSet` is initially set before the first record in the cursor, and we get the records by processing the result set. We process a result set by calling the `next()` method. When we call `next()`, it will return `true` if it moves the record pointer forward one record, and `false` when it has reached the end of the `ResultSet` object. Acessing the fields within a result set is simple. It is a matter of calling the *getXXX()* methods. The *XXX* is associated with the type of data the field represents and the type of data to be returned from the method call. For example, if it is a `String` type we want to retrieve, we will want to call the `getString()` method. We know which particular field to access by passing to the method either the name of the field or an `int` parameter representing the number of the field in the query's field order. The following code shows how we would proceed through a `ResultSet` object from where the preceding snippet code left off:

```
while(rs.next())
{
    int    deptNo = rs.getInt("deptno");
    String dName = rs.getString("dname");
    String loc = rs.getString("loc");

    System.out.println("DEPTNO - " + deptNo);
    System.out.println("DNAME - " + dName);
    System.out.println("LOC - " + loc);
}
```

The PreparedStatement and CallableStatement Objects

The `PreparedStatement` and `CallableStatement` objects provide some additional functionality compared to a standard `Statement` object. These objects allow us to precompile SQL statements so that they may be used efficiently multiple times. The two objects are used similarly, but `CallableStatement` is used primarily to execute stored procedures.

One of the more important aspects of these objects is that they allow us to bind values to placeholders in the SQL statement; that is, they allow us to substitute values such as `int`, `String`, or `Date` for question mark placeholders. Values are set with *setXXX()* methods, where *XXX* is the Java data type that is being set. These methods take two parameters: (1) an `int` parameter representing the question mark placeholder (*?*) in the SQL statement that will be substituted (the first *?* is 1, the second is 2, and so on) and (2) the value to be set. The `PreparedStatement` object and the *setXXX()* methods are used in the following manner:

```
int    deptNo = 50;
String dName = "HR";
String loc = "DENVER";
```

```
String sql = "insert into DEPT (deptno, dname, loc) " +
             "values(?, ?, ?)";
PreparedStatement ps = cn.prepareStatement( sql );
ps.setInt(1,  deptNo);
ps.setString(2,  dName);
ps.setString(3,  loc);
ps.executeUpdate();
```

The `CallableStatement` object is used for stored procedures. With respect to parameter placeholders it is used like `PreparedStatement`, but instead it executes a stored procedure. The main difference is how it is declared, as shown here:

```
String sql = "{call execSomeProc(?)}";
CallableStatement cs = cn.prepareCall( sql );
```

NOTE: Using question mark placeholders (?) in SQL code when we're using JDBC is the preferred method for passing values to a SQL statement. This is called *binding* the variable to the SQL statement. Binding allows us to pass variables that normally couldn't be a part of the SQL string. For example, in Oracle the single quotation mark signifies the beginning or end of a string. If we place any string with a single quotation mark in it in an Oracle SQL statement—such as *I wouldn't place this text directly in an Oracle SQL string*—the program will send us an error when it attempts to process the query. But if we pass this string to a SQL statement as a bound variable with the ? placeholder, the database will process the statement with no problem.

Transactions

Transactions are an important part of many database development efforts. They allow us to take an all-or-nothing approach to saving pieces of information. When we create a `Connection` object in JDBC, if the database supports transactions we are automatically in an autocommit state. This means that anytime we execute and update, insert, or delete a SQL command, the action will automatically be committed to the database. Other users accessing that database at that moment will instantly see all of these changes. In JDBC, we can turn off the autocommit mode and control transactions with the following command:

```
cn.setAutoCommit( false );
```

When we are not in autocommit mode, if we make a change to the database we can call the `commit()` method to permanently save the change.

```
cn.commit();
```

At the same time we would call `rollback()` to throw away any changes made since the last transaction.

```
cn.rollback();
```

We do this to allow several changes to take place or none at all. The classic master/detail relationship—of which invoices are a good example—demonstrates this. We can insert the invoice header record into one table and line items in another. Then if an insertion fails, we can roll back the entire save operation to prevent the situation of having only partial data.

Closing the Connection

Closing the connection is a matter of cleaning up any `ResultSet` and `Statement` objects and finally closing the connection itself. Closing the `ResultSet` and `Statement` objects when they are no longer needed is important because the garbage collector may not clean these up until it deems necessary. If these objects are not explicitly closed, the maximum number of allowed cursors may be exceeded in some databases. Closing these objects is a matter of calling the `close()` method, as shown here:

```
rs.close();
stmt.close();
cn.close();
```

At a high level, we have just reviewed JDBC. Although there is a lot more to it than has been covered here, this code is what is used 90 percent of the time. Using JDBC involves loading the driver, creating a connection, creating a statement, executing a query, and closing the connection.

Managing the Connection in a Server Environment

The title of this section will immediately have some of you asking, "Why do I need to manage my connections? My application server does it for me!" True, some enterprise application servers do help manage the database connections through built-in pooling and connection management mechanisms. WebLogic is a perfect example. However, even the servers that do provide a connection-pooling facility do not monitor how the connection is used or automatically clean up the resources. In addition, not all application servers have their own internal database-pooling facilities, and most servlet engines have no connection support at all (the exceptions are servlet engines that are implemented by the developer). So there is a lot of merit to managing connections yourself. Even if you choose to use the connection management facilities of your application server (if it has them), this section can at least give you insight into some of the issues you may run into when managing a connection.

Using and implementing JDBC is simple, but in a server environment there are a few issues you should consider when developing servlets with database connections. Many servlet-based database applications create a connection when going to a page, implement the query, and then close the connection at the end of the page. Think of the implications of this design. With a high-capacity site receiving perhaps 20 hits per second, this approach would open and close 20 database connections at any given moment. Is this efficient? No. The memory will fragment, and both the database server and the servlet application could have problems managing their own memory.

Databases were not made to efficiently withstand heavy loads of opening and closing database connections. In addition, creating a connection to a database server on another machine creates additional traffic and can be slow to initiate. In some Oracle installations, connections to the database take as long as eight to ten seconds. Do you want your users to wait that long for every Web page they access on your system? Probably not. A good solution, then, is to pool connections.

Just about every Web-based system that is developed—whether it is developed in servlets, C++, ASP, or another language of choice—should make use of some form of database connection pooling. In fact, this should be a design requirement in most server-based systems. However, sometimes it is not good to pool a database connection. Such is the case for long-running queries. If a query takes more than a few seconds to execute, pooling is not a good option because you will probably have users waiting for available connections. You should think about this issue when you're developing an application. However, most applications should implement refined and tuned SQL queries, so pooling should be the first consideration.

Because connection pooling is critical in any Web application, we must consider some other important pooling issues. Many applications that have implemented connection pooling need to be sure that the developers are checking connections back in after they have been used. Forgetting to check in connections makes other threads wait for connections that will never become available because they are "permanently" checked out. As a result, the server will appear as though it has locked up. This issue was discussed at great length in Chapter 7. Being sure to use a pool manager (e.g., the `PoolObjectManager` object that we developed in Chapter 7) will prevent developers from failing to check in their connections when finished with them.

Another consideration for development with databases is how to avoid running out of cursors. For Oracle developers, running out of cursors produces the dreaded ORA-1000 error: *Maximum number of cursors exceeded.* Many developers who have properly implemented a connection pool and have used Oracle as a database server have repeatedly run into this problem.

The error is difficult to debug and usually results in a call to Oracle's technical support. The solution is to close the `ResultSet` and `Statement` objects after using them. Forgetting to close these objects keeps the memory spaces open until the garbage collector cleans them up. That is, the Oracle database considers the cursors valid until the garbage collector does its job. By not closing these objects, we eventually run out of available cursors in the Oracle database and receive the ORA-1000 error.

This problem is not limited to Oracle; other production-level databases also have a maximum number of cursors. Just as with checking other objects in and out, the problem here is that we must trust the developer to close his or her `ResultSet` and `Statement` objects after using them. We need to build a database management object that can ensure that the `ResultSet` and `Statement` objects are closed after being used. This object would work very much like the object `PoolObjectManager` of Chapter 7. We will build a database connection manager in the next section to tackle this issue.

Another consideration has to do with transactions. If the database supports transactions and we use database connections in a pooled environment, we must be sure that the transactions are closed properly before we check the connection back into the pool. It we are using a connection, we want to be sure that we commit or roll back the transactions when we are done with the connection. If we do not, the transaction remains open for the next client thread to use, potentially causing all sorts of problems—from errors stating that a transaction is already open, to unintended changes to the database. With the `ResultSet` and `Statement` objects, we need a process that makes sure we close any open transactions.

The final consideration is ensuring that connections are always up. The server may create a database connection pool on startup, but there may be a break in the network connection to the database, or the database may be restarted at some point while the Web server application is running. Such scenarios cause the database connection objects to become invalid, and errors are generated when we attempt to use those objects. For many users, this means restarting the Web server to reinitiate the connections.

This situation is unacceptable because it means that we must always monitor the connection, network, and database status to be sure the Web application is working at all times. The goal is to have the connection pool manager test the connection by "pinging" the database to see if the connection is active. This ping would be a simple database query, such as *select 1 from dual* on an Oracle database. Such a statement in Oracle is a lightweight type of query that requires no overhead or resources to execute. Nearly every database has a query similar to this one.

When we execute this type of ping query, if no errors are thrown the connection is valid, and the connection pool manager hands the connection off to the calling process to use. If the connection is invalid, the connection pool manager could reinitiate the connection to the database and then hand the new connection to the user. This testing, or pinging, of the database should be optional because some databases cannot be shut down but instead are a file system, such as Microsoft Access. There would be no need to ping an Access database because it is not based on a network connection; rather it is accessed as a file.

Be sure to take all of these issues into consideration when you're building a Web server application that accesses a database. As you can see, there are many facets to managing a database connection. Now that we have a good idea of what this connection management involves, let's design and build a connection manager that we can use with the pool objects we developed in Chapter 7.

Understanding Connection Management

We have just identified the issues we must consider in building connection management into applications. Let's look at these considerations in a more succinct format. To manage connections in an efficient manner, we need to keep in mind the following issues:

1. Pooling should be used except when we expect queries to last more than a few seconds.
2. We should use pool management to ensure that connections are checked back into the pool.
3. We must ensure that `ResultSet` and `Statement` objects are properly closed to avoid running out of cursors on the database.
4. We must ensure that any open transactions are properly closed before being checked back into the pool.

5. We can optionally support reliable connections by providing a mechanism to "ping" the database to be sure the database connection is valid, and we should be able to reinstate the database connection if it is not valid.

In this list, issues 1 and 2 are supported by managment of the connection pool through use of the `PoolObjectManager` and `PoolList` objects as described in Chapter 7. When we build the database connection pool, we will use these objects to manage the pool. For issues 3, 4, and 5, however, we will need to build a connection manager. Before doing this, let's be sure we have a firm understanding of what a connection manager is and how it relates internally to the JDBC objects.

Connection management will be performed not by one particular object, but by a group of objects that work together. Three basic objects will work together. The main object, `JDBCManager`, will manage the connection and encapsulate the `Connection` object. It will be in charge of watching the state of the connection, such as transactions (commit and rollback if desired), and the list of `SQLCursor` objects. `JDBCManager` will also be responsible for creating `SQLCursor` objects when requested and removing them when they are no longer needed. This is very similar to how `PoolObjectManager` manages pool objects, except in this case `SQLCursor` objects are being managed.

What is a `SQLCursor` object? It is one of the management objects that encapsulates a `Statement` object and a `ResultSet` object, combining them into a single object. `SQLCursor` is the object with which we will execute the SQL statements. It reproduces most of the calls that we use on any one of the several `Statement` types (that is, `Statement`, `PreparedStatement`, and `CallableStatement`). This means that this is the object with which we will set SQL statements, substitute placeholder parameters, execute queries and updates, and run stored procedures.

The `DBConnection` object is the front end for `JDBCManager`. It acts as the constructor for the entire connection management structure. It is also responsible for the "ping" code that checks the connection validation. `DBConnection` is an extension of `JDBCManager`. The relationships among the `DBConnection`, `JDBCManager`, and `SQLCursor` objects are depicted in Figure 8.1.

The objective of this design structure is to give a more real-world description of connections and cursors. In this design we have an object that is a connection manager. It manages certain aspects of a connection and components that have to do with a connection—for example, whether the connection supports transactions, transactional states, and closing of the entire connection. This connection manager object then manages the creation and destruction of SQL cursors. It knows how many SQL cursors are open, and it is responsible

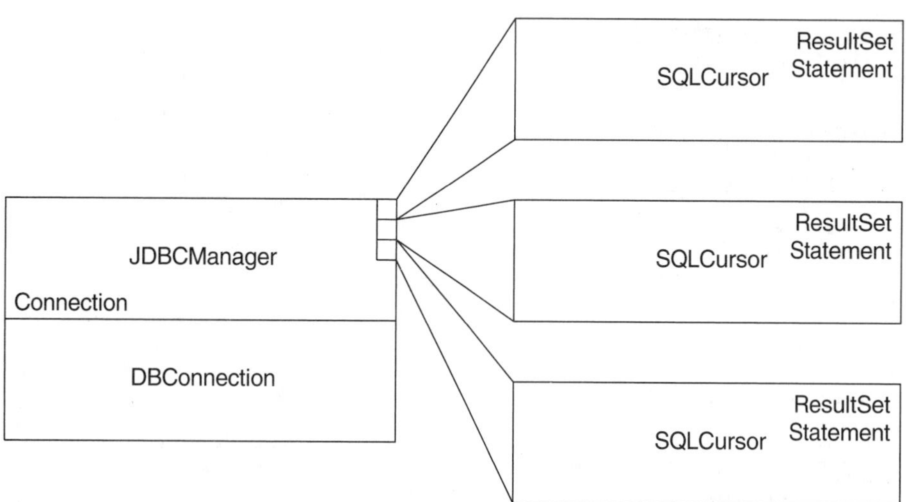

Figure 8.1 A graphical view of connection management objects

for closing them when we are finished using them. This is exactly how Oracle manages its own connections and cursors.

`DBConnection`, which extends `JDBCManager`, is the user's conduit to this structure. It is in charge of constructing `JDBCManager`, and it has the responsibility of pinging to ensure that the connection is good because this method belongs outside of the central database management. We use this design structure to mimic Oracle's connection management in the database because Oracle does not care if the connection is active or not; it is up to the client to be sure the connection is active. So we keep the connection active by having the ping on the front side, and out of `JDBCManager`.

Although here we would normally begin building these objects, this time let's do things a little differently so that you understand this object management structure before we develop the objects themselves. A graphical Unified Modeling Language (UML) description of the objects and their relationship to one and other will help us in this endeavor. Figure 8.2 depicts the objects and their associated properties and methods. Take a good look at them. Try to pinpoint where the methods are, as well as where we use SQL operations such as `executeQuery()`, *setXXX()*, and *getXXX()*.

If you have used a production-level database such as Oracle in the past, you can probably see that this object mimics a connection/cursor structure. This design strictly defines a separation between the connection and the SQL cursor.

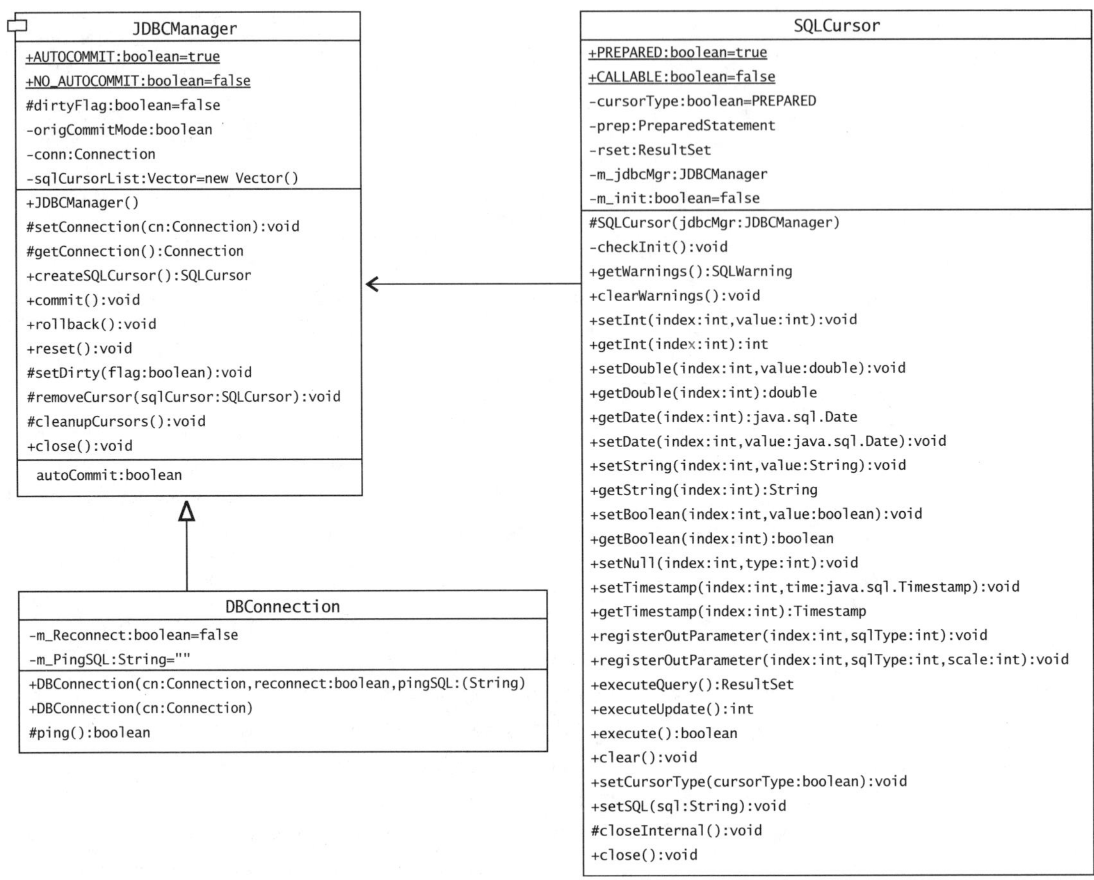

Figure 8.2 UML class relationships, with properties and methods

Building Connection Management

You should now have a good feel for the object relationships and how they interact, so let's begin building these objects. Following a description of each object, the relevant code will be presented. The code is self-explanatory, but the way it works will become very clear when we use the objects and place them in a pooled environment. We'll start with `JDBCManager`.

The JDBCManager Object

This object has three main objectives: (1) to encapsulate the `Connection` object, (2) to manage the transactional state, and (3) to manage the list of `SQLCursor` objects. With this object we will allow the user to set the autocommit mode, commit or roll back a transaction, and create a `SQLCursor` object. The whole idea behind the `JDBCManager` object is that it will reset the `Connection` object to its original state when we're done using it. That is, it will reset the `Connection` object's transactional state and close any open `SQLCursor` objects. Listing 8.1 gives the code for `JDBCManager`.

Listing 8.1 The `JDBCManager` object

```
package enterprise.db;

import java.sql.*;
import java.util.*;

public abstract class JDBCManager
{
  public static final boolean AUTOCOMMIT = true;
  public static final boolean NO_AUTOCOMMIT = false;

  protected boolean dirtyFlag = false;

  private boolean origCommitMode;

  private Connection conn = null;

  private Vector sqlCursorList = new Vector();

  public JDBCManager()
  {
  }

  public void setAutoCommit(boolean flag) throws SQLException
  {
    conn.setAutoCommit(flag);
  }

  protected void setConnection(Connection cn) throws SQLException
  {
    conn = cn;
    origCommitMode = conn.getAutoCommit();
  }

  protected Connection getConnection()
  {
    return conn;
  }

  protected void setDirty(boolean flag)
  {
    dirtyFlag = flag;
  }
```

```
public SQLCursor createSQLCursor() throws SQLException
{
  SQLCursor sqlCursor = new SQLCursor(this);

  sqlCursorList.add(sqlCursor);

  return sqlCursor;
}

public void commit() throws SQLException
{
  setDirty(false);

  if (conn != null)
    conn.commit();
}

public void rollback() throws SQLException
{
  setDirty(false);

  if (conn != null)
    conn.rollback();
}

public void reset()
{
  cleanupCursors();

  try
  {
    // If we are not autocommitting and we have executed queries,
    // then roll back to avoid data errors if the connection is
    // dirty. (Of course, it wouldn't be dirty if the programmer
    // hadn't forgotten to commit or roll back the connection.)
    if ((conn.getAutoCommit() == NO_AUTOCOMMIT) &&
        (dirtyFlag == true))
      conn.rollback();

    // Set back to original commit mode.
    conn.setAutoCommit(origCommitMode);

    // Be sure we mark this object as "clean."
    setDirty(false);
  }
  catch( SQLException e )
  {
    // Do nothing; we are resetting the connection, so it
    // doesn't matter.
  }
}
```

```
    protected void cleanupCursors()
    {
      int i = (sqlCursorList.size() - 1);
      for(; i >= 0; i--)
      {
        SQLCursor sqlCursor = (SQLCursor)sqlCursorList.elementAt(i);
        sqlCursor.closeInternal();
        sqlCursorList.removeElementAt(i);
      }
    }

    protected void removeCursor(SQLCursor sqlCursor)
    {
      int i = sqlCursorList.indexOf(sqlCursor);

      // If it's not found, then ignore it.
      if (i == -1)
        return;

      sqlCursorList.removeElementAt(i);
    }

    public void close()
    {
      cleanupCursors();

      if( conn != null )
      {
        reset();
        conn = null;
      }
    }
  }
```

The SQLCursor Object

`SQLCursor` is the object that we will request from `JDBCManager` and use for interaction with the database. `SQLCursor` is created by a call to `JDBCManager.createSQLCursor()`. It encapsulates the objects `ResultSet` and `Statement`. This object redeclares and exposes the same SQL actions that the objects `Statement`, `PreparedStatement`, and `CallableStatement` contain. Therefore we can call any of the JDBC methods—*getXXX(), setXXX()*, `execute()`, and so on—that we would normally execute with a `Statement` type object. The main difference between using this object and using the `Statement` type objects directly is that instead of passing the SQL statement to the `execute()` methods, we set the SQL statement through the `setSQL()` method, and we call the `execute()` methods without any parameters.

We will use this object by declaring the kind of cursor we wish to use: PREPARED or CALLABLE. The initial setting is PREPARED; that is, SQLCursor's underlying object is PreparedStatement. We will create a method called setCursorType() that allows us to pass the kind of Statement object we wish to use: PREPARED or CALLABLE. This parameter will change how the SQLCursor object is used and allow us to make the same object capable of executing stored procedures. You will understand how SQLCursor operates when we use it. Listing 8.2 shows the code for SQLCursor.

Listing 8.2 The SQLCursor object

```
package enterprise.db;

import java.sql.*;
import java.util.*;

public class SQLCursor
{
  public static final boolean PREPARED = true;
  public static final boolean CALLABLE = false;

  private boolean cursorType = PREPARED;

  private PreparedStatement prep;

  private ResultSet rset;

  private JDBCManager m_jdbcMgr;

  private boolean m_init = false;

  protected SQLCursor(JDBCManager jdbcMgr) throws SQLException
  {
    m_init = true;
    m_jdbcMgr = jdbcMgr;
    clear();
  }

  private void checkInit() throws SQLException
  {
    if (m_init == false)
    {
      throw new SQLException("SQLCursor has not been initialized. " +
                             "Call the JDBCManager " +
                             "createSQLCursor to create an " +
                             "initialized instance.");
    }
  }

  public SQLWarning getWarnings() throws SQLException
  {
```

```
        checkInit();
        if (prep == null)
            return null;

        return prep.getWarnings();
    }

    public void clearWarnings() throws SQLException
    {
        checkInit();
        if (prep == null)
            return;

        prep.clearWarnings();
    }

    public void setInt( int index, int value ) throws SQLException
    {
      checkInit();
      prep.setInt( index, value );
    }

    public int getInt( int index ) throws SQLException
    {
      checkInit();
      return ((CallableStatement)prep).getInt( index );
    }

    public void setDouble( int index, double value )
       throws SQLException
    {
      checkInit();
      prep.setDouble( index, value );
    }

    public double getDouble( int index ) throws SQLException
    {
      checkInit();
      return ((CallableStatement)prep).getDouble( index );
    }

    public java.sql.Date getDate( int index ) throws SQLException
    {
      checkInit();
      return ((CallableStatement)prep).getDate( index );
    }

    public void setDate( int index, java.sql.Date value )
       throws SQLException
    {
      checkInit();
      prep.setDate( index, value );
    }
```

```
public void setString( int index, String value )
   throws SQLException
{
  checkInit();
  prep.setString( index, value );
}

public String getString( int index ) throws SQLException
{
  checkInit();
  return ((CallableStatement)prep).getString( index );
}

public void setBoolean( int index, boolean value )
   throws SQLException
{
  checkInit();
  prep.setBoolean( index, value );
}

public boolean getBoolean( int index ) throws SQLException
{
  checkInit();
  return ((CallableStatement)prep).getBoolean( index );
}

public void setNull( int index, int type ) throws SQLException
{
  checkInit();
  prep.setNull( index, type );
}

public void setTimestamp( int index, java.sql.Timestamp time )
   throws SQLException
{
  checkInit();
  prep.setTimestamp( index, time );
}

public Timestamp getTimestamp( int index ) throws SQLException
{
  checkInit();
  return ((CallableStatement)prep).getTimestamp( index );
}

public void registerOutParameter( int index, int sqlType )
      throws SQLException
{
  checkInit();
  ((CallableStatement)prep).registerOutParameter( index, sqlType );
}
```

```
public void registerOutParameter( int index, int sqlType, int
                                  scale )
      throws SQLException
{
  checkInit();
  ((CallableStatement)prep).registerOutParameter( index, sqlType,
                                                  scale );
}

public ResultSet executeQuery() throws SQLException
{
  checkInit();
  m_jdbcMgr.setDirty(true);
  rset = prep.executeQuery();
  return( rset );
}

public int executeUpdate() throws SQLException
{
  checkInit();
  m_jdbcMgr.setDirty(true);
  return( prep.executeUpdate() );
}

public boolean execute() throws SQLException
{
  checkInit();
  m_jdbcMgr.setDirty(true);
  return( prep.execute() );
}

public void clear() throws SQLException
{
  checkInit();
  closeInternal();
  setCursorType( PREPARED );
}

public void setCursorType( boolean cursorType )
      throws SQLException
{
  checkInit();
  this.cursorType = cursorType;
}

public void setSQL( String sql ) throws SQLException
{
  checkInit();
  if( cursorType == PREPARED )
  {
    prep = m_jdbcMgr.getConnection().prepareStatement( sql );
  }
```

```
      else
      {
        prep = m_jdbcMgr.getConnection().prepareCall( sql );
      }
    }

    protected void closeInternal()
    {
      if( rset != null )
      {
        try
        {
          rset.close();
        }
        catch( SQLException e )
        {
          e.printStackTrace();
        }
        finally
        {
          rset = null;
        }
      }
      if( prep != null )
      {
        try
        {
          prep.close();
        }
        catch( SQLException e )
        {
          e.printStackTrace();
        }
        finally
        {
          prep = null;
        }
      }
    }

    public void close() throws SQLException
    {
      checkInit();
      closeInternal();
      m_jdbcMgr.removeCursor(this);
      m_init = false;
    }

  }
```

The DBConnection Object

The final connection management object is DBConnection. This is the front end for JDBCManager. That is, we do not create JDBCManager directly. Instead we extend JDBCManager in DBConnection. DBConnection sets the internal variables of JDBCManager so that it is usable. Its constructors take the Connection object as a parameter, and the "ping" SQL statement and reconnection test request if the developer wants this capability. DBConnection implements a ping() method that does the ping to test the connection to the database. This method sends a simple query (the one we passed to the constructor) to the database. If the query executes properly, we return true to the calling function. If it does not, we return false. We will see exactly how this works when we implement this in a pool. Listing 8.3 shows the code for DBConnection.

Listing 8.3 The DBConnection object

```
package enterprise.db;

import java.sql.*;

public class DBConnection extends JDBCManager
{

  private boolean m_Reconnect = false;

  private String m_PingSQL = "";

  public DBConnection(Connection cn, boolean reconnect,
                      String pingSQL)
    throws SQLException
  {
    setConnection(cn);
    m_Reconnect = reconnect;
    m_PingSQL = pingSQL;
  }

  public DBConnection(Connection cn)
    throws SQLException
  {
    this(cn, false, "");
  }

  protected boolean ping() throws SQLException
  {
    if (m_Reconnect == false)
    {
      return true;
    }
```

```
      boolean rc;
      Statement s = null;
      ResultSet r = null;

      try
      {
        s = getConnection().createStatement();
        String SQL = m_PingSQL;
        r = s.executeQuery(SQL);

        // If we made it here, then no error, so the ping was
        // successful.
        rc = true;
      } catch (SQLException e)
      {
        rc = false;
      } finally
      {
        if( r != null )
          r.close();

        if( s != null )
          s.close();
      }

      return rc;
    }
  }
```

Using the Connection Management Objects

The previous section showed the code for the connection management objects. Although it was quite a bit of code, it was not explained in the same depth as the code for other objects that we have developed in this book because it is generally self-explanatory. But more importantly, explaining the code would not illustrate how the objects work as well as specific examples can. To use the objects, we start by creating a `Connection` object. For now, since we are not using `DBConnection` in a pool, we will not worry about reconnecting or pinging the database. We start by creating a `Connection` object and pass it to the constructor of `DBConnection`.

```
String userId = "scott";
String password = "tiger";
String url = "jdbc:oracle:thin:@localhost:1521:ORCL";

Connection cn = DriverManager.getConnection(url,
                                            userId,
                                            password);
DBConnection dbc = new DBConnection(cn);
```

This code creates the `Connection` object and requests that this object manage the connection. From here we are ready to create a `SQLCursor` object and execute a SQL query. We do this by calling `createSqlCursor()` from the `DBConnection` object.

```
SQLCursor sc = dbc.createSQLCursor();
```

To execute a SQL query, we set it with the `setSQL()` method, use the *setXXX()* methods if we want parameter replacement, and call one of the `execute()` methods.

```
sc.setSQL("insert into DEPT (deptno, dname, loc) values(?, ?, ?)");
sc.setInt(1, 50);
sc.setString(2, "HR");
sc.serString(3, "DENVER");
sc.executeUpdate();
```

We can use the `SQLCursor` object over and over by calling the `reset()` method when we are ready to execute more SQL. This method clears the underlying `Statement` and `ResultSet` objects and removes any substitution parameters from them.

```
sc.reset();
```

To execute a query we would execute code similar to that given earlier for `executeUpdate()` (see Listing 8.2). This code returns a `ResultSet` object just as if we were using a `Statement` object.

```
sc.setSQL("select deptno, dname, loc from DEPT");
ResultSet rs = sc.executeQuery();
```

To execute a stored procedure, we simply set the cursor type by calling the `setCursorType()` method. `SQLCursor.PREPARED` or `SQLCursor.CALLABLE` are the two possible parameters. When we create a `SQLCursor` object or we call `reset()` on a cursor, the object is in `PREPARED` mode. To change the type, we call `setCursorType()` with the type of the statement as a parameter.

```
sc.reset();
sc.setCursorType(SQLCursor.CALLABLE);
sc.setSQL("{call execSomeProc(?)}");
sc.setString(1, "myParam");
sc.execute();
```

Normally, when we pass in a `Connection` object to `DBConnection` and we do not change to autocommit mode, the mode is automatically changed to autocommit. To switch to autocommit mode, we call the `setAutoCommit()` method on the `DBConnection` object. To change the transaction mode, we pass this method DBConnection.AUTOCOMMIT for autocommit mode, or DBConnection.NO_AUTOCOMMIT for non-autocommit mode. When we are in non-autocommit mode, we need to call commit() or rollback() when we have completed executing the SQL statements.

```
dbc.setAutoCommit(DBConnection.NO_AUTOCOMMIT);
//
// Execute SQL statements with the SQLCursor objects here.
//
dbc.commit();
```

When we are finished with the SQLCursor objects and we want to clean up DBConnection, we call the reset() method with DBConnection as a parameter, which does the following:

- Closes all ResultSet and Statement objects associated with every SQLCursor object that was opened.
- Checks if DBConnection was in non-autocommit mode. If it was, reset() checks if the developer called commit() or rollback() on DBConnection to clean up the transaction. If neither method was called, DBConnection executes an obligatory rollback to clean up the transaction for the developer.
- Resets the connection to the original autocommit mode.

In other words, the reset() call places the connection back into its original state.

```
dbc.reset();
```

To close a connection, we just call the close() method. This method does everything that the reset() command does, but it also closes the JDBC connection.

```
dbc.close();
```

As you can see, using connection management objects is quite simple. But what does this scheme do for us? At this point it cleans up for us after we execute SQL, and it gives us a single object to use for SQL queries instead of the three different Statement types. Most important is the cleanup. But wait! We still have to call reset() to clean up, and what about this "ping" reconnection business? As mentioned earlier, these connection management objects show their true colors when they are being used in conjunction with a pooling object. This is where the framework takes care of calling reset() for us, as well as the ping test and database reconnection. Let's look at a database connection pool and see what the connection management objects really can do.

Database Pooling with the Connection Management Objects

Let's build a generic database-pooling object that allows us to pool the `DBConnection` objects. The term *generic* here means that we want the object to support any kind of database. This pool should allow for several different kinds of configurations. A database connection pool that supports the connection management objects must be able to take the following parameters:

- Pool size
- Database driver
- Connection URL
- User ID
- Password
- Autocommit flag (if we want the connections set in autocommit mode)
- Ping SQL (SQL that is used to test if the database connection is valid)

The pool should require at least a pool size, a database driver, and a connection string because all database connections require these elements. The user ID and password should be optional so that this pool can create connections to databases that may not require a user ID and password. The connections that are created are normally in autocommit mode, but we may wish to create a pool of connections whose default mode is non-autocommit. So we will want to optionally allow this pool to accept an autocommit mode selection type. Finally, this pool will also optionally need to support reconnectivity. We will allow it to accept a reconnection flag and "ping" SQL to use for the reconnection test.

Let's create a `DBConnectionPool` object that extends the `Pool` object developed in Chapter 7. We'll start by declaring the object and create member variables to store the parameter values just described. We will also create a few constructors that take different combinations of these parameters.

```
package enterprise.db;

import enterprise.common.*;
import java.sql.*;

public class DBConnectionPool extends Pool
{
  private String      m_ConnStr       = "";
  private String      m_UserId        = "";
  private String      m_Password      = "";
  private boolean     m_Reconnect     = false;
  private boolean     m_AutoCommit    = true;
  private String      m_PingSQL       = "";
```

```
public DBConnectionPool(int maxSize, String driver,
                        String connStr, String userId,
                        String password, boolean auto_commit,
                        boolean reconnect, String pingSQL)
    throws Exception
{

  m_ConnStr = connStr;
  m_UserId = userId;
  m_Password = password;
  m_Reconnect = reconnect;
  m_PingSQL = pingSQL;
  m_AutoCommit = auto_commit;

  try
  {
    Class.forName(driver);
  } catch (ClassNotFoundException e)
  {
    throw new Exception("Driver '" + driver +
                        "' not found in classpath.");
  }

  createPool(maxSize);
}

public DBConnectionPool(int maxSize, String driver,
                        String connStr)
    throws Exception
{
  this(maxSize, driver, connStr, "", "", true, false, "");
}

public DBConnectionPool(int maxSize, String driver,
                        String connStr,
                        String userId, String password)
    throws Exception
{
  this(maxSize, driver, connStr, userId, password, true, false, "");
}

public DBConnectionPool(int maxSize, String driver,
                        String connStr,
                        String userId, String password,
                        boolean auto_commit)
    throws Exception
{
  this(maxSize, driver, connStr, userId, password,
      auto_commit, false, "");
}
```

The createObject() method is one of the methods that the Pool object requires us to implement. This method will take the variables that we set through the constructors and create the DBConnection object.

```
public Object createObject() throws SQLException
{

  Connection conn =
        DriverManager.getConnection(m_ConnStr, m_UserId,
        m_Password);

  conn.setAutoCommit(m_AutoCommit);

  DBConnection dbc = new DBConnection(conn, m_Reconnect,
        m_PingSQL);

  return dbc;
}
```

We will implement a beforeCheckin() method to be sure that the DBConnection object is cleaned up before being checked back into the pool. We will call reset() to close all of the SQLCursor objects, clean up any open transactions, and reset the connection to its original state.

```
public void beforeCheckin(Object o)
{
  DBConnection dbc = (DBConnection) o;
  dbc.reset();
}
```

We will implement a beforeCheckout() method to test the connection before handing it to the client. This method does the ping test of the database connection, if it is set up to do so. It calls the DBConnection.ping() routine that we developed earlier. If the ping() method returns false, we will create a new DBConnection object and replace it in the pool, and we'll return this new object to the user.

```
public Object beforeCheckout(Object o) throws Exception
{
  DBConnection dbc = (DBConnection) o;

  if (!dbc.ping())
  {
    DBConnection new_dbc = null;

    try
    {
      // No ping (for whatever reason), so attempt a reconnect.
      new_dbc = (DBConnection) createObject();
    }
```

```
            catch(Exception e)
            {
              // Can't get a connection, so put the old one away.
              this.checkInPoolObject(dbc);
              throw e;
            }

            // Replace the old with the new.
            replacePoolObject(dbc, new_dbc);

            dbc = new_dbc;
          }

          return dbc;
        }

    }
```

Now that we have a pool, what do we do next? We instantiate the pool as we have done with other pools, but this time we use the required constructors. Let's build a small sample enterprise servlet application that uses this pool so that we can see the pool in action.

Using the DBConnectionPool Object

Let's create a simple application that queries the Oracle sample scott/tiger tables that come with every Oracle installation. We will create a page that queries the `DEPT` table and shows its contents in HTML format to the user.

We will call this application DBExample. The main dispatch servlet, `DBExample`, will have one dispatch class that will produce the screen shown in Figure 8.3. We will call this class `MainScreen`. Let's start with the configuration file, `DBExample.config`, which is shown in Listing 8.4.

Listing 8.4 Configuration file for `DBExample`

```
Application.Base.URL=/servlet/DBExample

Default.Method=main
Method.main=MainScreen

# Place the log file path here.
Log.File.Path=c:\\Book\\Chapter 08\\Example 1\\DBExample.log
```

The main dispatch servlet, `DBExample`, will create the `DBConnectionPool` object in the `initializeApp()` method. As stated earlier in this chapter, it is very beneficial to add `DBConnectionPool` to the `PoolList` object, so that the `PoolObjectManager` object can keep tabs on the connection pool. This will ensure that the pool is checked back in when we're finished using it. Let's name

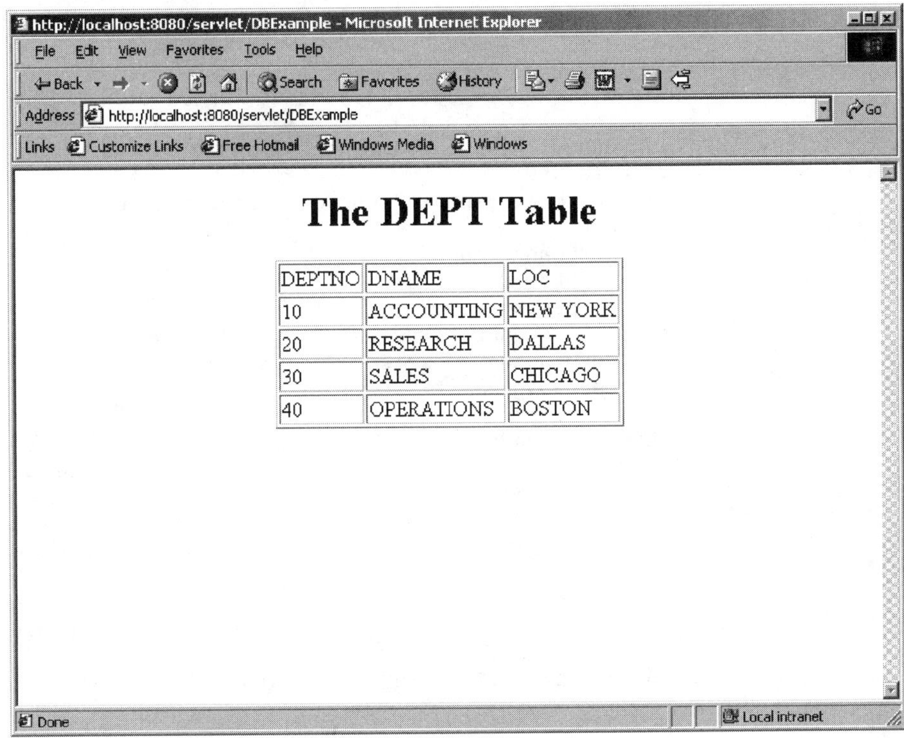

Figure 8.3 Query screen of the Oracle sample DEPT table

the pool *Oracle* in `PoolList`. When we initialize the `DBConnectionPool` object, we will specify that the connection reconnect itself and use a low-overhead SQL statement as a ping to test the connection before it is checked out. We will use *select 1 from dual* as the ping SQL statement. Of course we will request that the pool is created with autocommit mode. The code for `DBExample` is shown in Listing 8.5.

Listing 8.5 The `DBExample` dispatch servlet

```
import enterprise.servlet.*;
import enterprise.common.*;
import enterprise.db.*;

import java.io.*;

public class DBExample extends BaseEnterpriseServlet
{
  public String getAppName()
  {
    return "DBExample";
  }
```

```
  public void initializeApp(AppContext appContext,
                            PoolObjectManager pom)  throws Exception
  {
    String driver = "oracle.jdbc.driver.OracleDriver";

    // Change this to the connection string for your Oracle
    // database.
    String connection = "jdbc:oracle:thin:@localhost:1521:ORCL";

    int maxConnections=5;
    String userId = "scott";
    String password = "tiger";
    boolean reconnect=true;
    String pingsql = "select 1 from dual";
    boolean autoCommit= true;

    DBConnectionPool dbcp = new DBConnectionPool(maxConnections,
                                                 driver,
                                                 connection,
                                                 userId,
                                                 password,
                                                 autoCommit,
                                                 reconnect,
                                                 pingsql);

    appContext.getPoolList().add("Oracle", dbcp);
  }

  public void destroyApp(AppContext ac, PoolObjectManager pom)
  {
  }
}
```

The `MainScreen` class (see Listing 8.6) will represent the main screen that we are shown in this application. It works by checking out the `DBConnection` object from the pool, creating a `SQLCursor` object, and executing a query on the `DEPT` table. `MainScreen` cycles through the `ResultSet` object created by the query to produce the HTML.

Listing 8.6 The `MainScreen` class

```
import enterprise.servlet.*;
import enterprise.html.*;
import enterprise.db.*;

import java.io.*;
import java.sql.*;

public class MainScreen extends HTTPMethod
{
```

```
  public void execute() throws Exception
  {

    PrintWriter out = m_response.getWriter();
    DBConnection dbc = (DBConnection) m_poolObjMgr.checkOut
                         ("Oracle");
    SQLCursor sc = dbc.createSQLCursor();

    sc.setSQL("select deptno, dname, loc from dept");

    out.println("<html>");
    out.println("<body>");
    out.println("<center>");
    out.println("<h1>The DEPT Table</h1>");
    out.println("<table border=1>");
    out.println("<tr>");
    out.println("<td>DEPTNO</td>");
    out.println("<td>DNAME</td>");
    out.println("<td>LOC</td>");
    out.println("</tr>");

    ResultSet rs = sc.executeQuery();
    while(rs.next())
    {
      out.println("<tr>");
      out.println("<td>");
      out.println(rs.getInt(1));
      out.println("</td>");
      out.println("<td>");
      out.println(rs.getString(2));
      out.println("</td>");
      out.println("<td>");
      out.println(rs.getString(3));
      out.println("</td>");
      out.println("</tr>");
    }

    out.println("</table>");
    out.println("</center>");
    out.println("</body>");
    out.println("</html>");

  }
}
```

Notice in the `MainScreen` class that we are not checking in any objects or choosing the `ResultSet` object that we use to cycle through the records. The `DBConnectionPool` object is doing it for us. We no longer need to worry about cleaning up after ourselves. The framework does all this for us!

Now that we have completed the example, register the servlet in your servlet engine and set the `initArgs` parameter to have the `ConfFile` parameter point at the `DBExample.config` file. Run the application, and you should get the same results as shown in Figure 8.3. One major test is to shut down the Oracle database and restart it, thereby invalidating the connections, and then without restarting the servlet engine or Web server, to go to the DBExample application and see what happens. Notice that it appears as though the application is unaware that the database has gone down or that the connections in the pool have become instantly invalid. Well, that's true. The connections became invalid, and when DBExample tried to communicate with the database with the `ping()` method in the `DBConnection` object, it re-created the `DBConnection` object and replaced the bad connection with the good one in the pool. This is an extremely important concept if we want to keep applications up and running 24 hours a day, 7 days a week.

Making the DBConnectionPool Object Easier to Create

Most applications that we develop will probably have access to a database. Hence most of our applications will use the `DBConnectionPool` and connection management objects. Looking at the previous example, we needed to supply a database driver, connection URL, user ID, password, reconnect flag, and ping SQL query. We hard-coded these elements into the main dispatch servlet. But this is not the best way to do things because it is very likely that some of these parameters will change when we move the application from development to testing, and from testing to production. Many development shops have different databases for the different environments, which means that we might need to change these parameters every time we move to a different platform.

The first thought is to create custom parameters in the configuration file and then retrieve them with the `AppContext.getValue()` method. This approach would be very effective, but let's take this a step further and create a new standard configuration file parameter, let the framework parse this parameter to extract the values we need, *and* have the framework automatically create the database pool. The reason for making this a standard configuration file parameter is that most applications probably will require connections to a database. If we can declare database pools in the configuration file, we won't need to set up any database connection pools; we will just need to use them. WebLogic allows developers to set up very powerful connection pool objects in its version of a configuration file, the `weblogic.properties` file. Such pool objects would be a very beneficial for enterprise servlets.

To implement these changes, we must figure out what we need to look for in a configuration file. If we create an object that sets up database connection pools from the configuration file, it must be able to support multiple pools. This object should operate much as templates do. The template parser looks for the *"Template."* prefix, and the name that follows this prefix is the name of the template. Let's do the same for the database pools. Let's look for the *"DB.ConnectionPool."* prefix to let the parser know we wish to create a database pool, and the name that follows the prefix will be the name of the pool that is stored in the `PoolList` object. For example, if we had a configuration file parameter named `DB.ConnectionPool.MyPool`, the pool would be accessed through the `PoolObjectManager` object with the *MyPool* string.

The value of the *"DB.ConnectionPool."* parameter needs to be handled differently from the way we have handled other parameters. For other parameter/value pairs in the configuration file, we had a single parameter and a single value. However, our database connections require multiple parameters, so just taking the entire value will not work. We need to have multiple name/value pairs for the *"DB.ConnectionPool."* parameter. We do this by taking a name value, such as *Driver,* followed by an equal sign, followed by the value. We delimit name/value pairs with commas. So a typical line in a configuration file would look like this:

```
DB.ConnectionPool.Oracle=\
        driver=oracle.jdbc.driver.OracleDriver,\
        connection=jdbc:oracle:thin:@localhost:1521:ORCL,\
        maxconnections=5,\
        userid=scott,\
        password=tiger,\
        reconnect=true,\
        pingsql=select 1 from dual,\
             autocommit= true
```

The name of this pool is *Oracle.* We have several name/value pairs, and each one has its own particular meaning. Notice that the name/value pairs are separated by commas.

NOTE: What does the backslash mean at the end of each line in a configuration file or properties file? A backslash followed by a carriage return means "continue the line." The line that follows this construct is read as a continuation of the previous line.

Let's look at the different name/value pairs that we have shown here and the values they can take:

- **`driver`**. The JDBC driver that is used for the database connection—for example, `oracle.jdbc.driver.OracleDriver` for an Oracle driver. This is a required parameter.

- **connection**. The connection string to connect to a database—for example, `jdbc:oracle:thin:@localhost:1521:ORCL`. See the database vendor instructions for the exact string. This is a required parameter.
- **maxconnections**. The maximum number of connections to store in the pool. The value must be 1 or greater. This is a required parameter.
- **userid**. The user ID to log in to the database. This is an optional parameter but is necessary if the database requires authentication.
- **password**. The password to log in to the database. This is an optional parameter but is necessary if the database requires authentication.
- **autocommit**. A parameter that allows the developer to set the default commit mode for the `DBConnection` objects in the pool. The values allowed are `true` and `false`. `True` turns the default commit mode on, and `false` turns it off. If the default commit mode is off, it is the developer's responsibility to call `commit()` to make any updates to the database or `rollback()` to throw away changes. If this parameter is omitted from the configuration file, the commit mode of the the pool's `DBConnection` object is set to autocommit. This parameter is optional.
- **reconnect**. A parameter that tells the pool to attempt a reconnection if the current connection goes bad. This parameter is used so that the framework can attempt to reconnect to the database without having to restart the servlet process or reinitialize the `DBConnection` objects. The valid values are `true` and `false`. If `true`, then the framework will expect a value in the `pingsql` parameter to know how to detect a bad connection. If `false`, it will not attempt to reconnect. This is an optional parameter. If omitted, it defaults to `false`.
- **pingsql**. The SQL query that is used to test the database connection; it should be a lightweight SQL command. An example would be *select 1 from dual* for an Oracle connection. This is normally an optional parameter, but it is required if the value of the `reconnect` parameter is `true`.

The NameValuePair Object

To parse the line, we must first handle name/value pairs. We need to take a string such as *userid=scott* and break it into *userid* and *scott*. We will create a utility called `NameValuePair` to do just that. We will place this utility in the `enterprise.common` package because it can be useful in many different applications. We construct the object with the *name=value* string, and it tokenizes the string into a public name string and a public value string. The `NameValuePair` object would work with the following code:

```
String nvPair = "userid=scott";
NameValuePair nvp = new NameValuePair(nvPair);
String name = nvp.name;
String value = nvp.value;
```

`NameValuePair` is a useful object that we will use when parsing the "*DB.ConnectionPool.*" configuration file parameter. The code for the object `NameValuePair` is shown in Listing 8.7.

Listing 8.7 The `NameValuePair` class

```
package enterprise.common;

import java.util.*;

public class NameValuePair
{
  public String name = "";
  public String value = "";

  public NameValuePair(String nvString)
  {
    StringTokenizer st = new StringTokenizer(nvString.trim(), "=");
    name = "";
    value = "";

    if (st.hasMoreTokens())
    {
      name = st.nextToken().trim();
    }

    if (st.hasMoreTokens())
    {
      value = st.nextToken().trim();
    }
  }
}
```

The DBPoolParser Object

We have just defined the kinds of name/value pairs that we will encounter in a "*DB.ConnectionPool.*" configuration value. Now we need to find each "*DB.ConnectionPool.*" line in a configuration file, parse each of these pool name/value pairs, verify that they all contain valid values, create the `DBConnectionPool` object with these values, and add the pool to the `PoolList` object. We will do this through the `DBPoolParser` object. `DBPoolParser` will be completely responsible for these actions. The code for `DBPoolParser` is shown in Listing 8.8.

Listing 8.8 The `DBPoolParser` class

```
package enterprise.db;

import java.util.*;
import java.io.IOException;
import javax.servlet.*;

import enterprise.common.*;
import enterprise.io.*;
import enterprise.db.*;

public class DBPoolParser
{

  private static final String DB_POOL_PREFIX = "DB.ConnectionPool.";
  private static final String DRIVER = "DRIVER";
  private static final String CONNECTION = "CONNECTION";
  private static final String USERID = "USERID";
  private static final String PASSWORD = "PASSWORD";
  private static final String MAXCONNECTIONS = "MAXCONNECTIONS";
  private static final String RECONNECT = "RECONNECT";
  private static final String PINGSQL = "PINGSQL";
  private static final String AUTOCOMMIT = "AUTOCOMMIT";
  private static final String TRUE = "TRUE";
  private static final String FALSE = "FALSE";

  private ConfFile cf = null;
  private PoolList pl = null;

  public DBPoolParser(ConfFile config, PoolList poolList)
  {
    cf = config;
    pl = poolList;
  }

  public void buildConnectionPools()
    throws ServletException
  {
    // Get the list of DB pools.

    for (Enumeration m = cf.getKeys() ; m.hasMoreElements() ;)
    {
      String key = (String) m.nextElement();

      if (key.startsWith(DB_POOL_PREFIX))
      {
         String poolName = key.substring(DB_POOL_PREFIX.length());

         if (poolName.length() > 0)
         {
```

```
          // Get the pool name.
          String poolConfig = cf.getValue(key);
          // Now parse the values.
          parseValues(poolName, poolConfig);
        }
      }
    }
  }

  private void parseValues(String poolName, String poolConfig)
    throws ServletException
  {
    String userId = "";
    String password = "";
    String driver = "";
    String connection = "";
    boolean reconnect = false;
    boolean autoCommit = true;
    String pingSQL = "";
    int maxConnections = 0;

    StringTokenizer st = new StringTokenizer(poolConfig, ",");
    while(st.hasMoreTokens())
    {
      String parameter = st.nextToken();
      NameValuePair nvp = new NameValuePair(parameter);

      if (nvp.name.toUpperCase().equals(DRIVER))
      {
        driver = nvp.value;
      }

      if (nvp.name.toUpperCase().equals(USERID))
      {
        userId = nvp.value;
      }

      if (nvp.name.toUpperCase().equals(PASSWORD))
      {
        password = nvp.value;
      }

      if (nvp.name.toUpperCase().equals(CONNECTION))
      {
        connection = nvp.value;
      }

      if (nvp.name.toUpperCase().equals(MAXCONNECTIONS))
      {
        try
        {
```

```
        maxConnections = Integer.parseInt(nvp.value);
      } catch (NumberFormatException nfe)
      {
        throw new ServletException(invalidMessage(poolName,
                                   nvp.name, nvp.value));
      }
    }

    if (nvp.name.toUpperCase().equals(RECONNECT))
    {
      String sReconnect = nvp.value.toUpperCase();

      if (sReconnect.equals(FALSE))
      {
        reconnect = false;
      } else if(sReconnect.equals(TRUE))
      {
        reconnect = true;
      } else
      {
        throw new ServletException(invalidMessage(poolName,
                                   nvp.name, nvp.value));
      }
    }

    if (nvp.name.toUpperCase().equals(PINGSQL))
    {
      pingSQL = nvp.value;
    }

    if (nvp.name.toUpperCase().equals(AUTOCOMMIT))
    {
      String sAutoCommit = nvp.value.toUpperCase();

      if (sAutoCommit.equals(FALSE))
      {
        autoCommit = false;
      } else if(sAutoCommit.equals(TRUE))
      {
        autoCommit = true;
      } else
      {
        throw new ServletException(invalidMessage(poolName,
                                   nvp.name, nvp.value));
      }
    }

    }
```

```
    // Test that the values are good.
    checkValues(poolName, userId, password, driver, connection,
                      reconnect, pingSQL, maxConnections);

    this.setupPool(poolName, userId, password, driver, connection,
                   reconnect, pingSQL, maxConnections,
                   autoCommit);
}

private void checkValues(String poolName, String userId,
                         String password, String driver,
                         String connection, boolean reconnect,
                         String pingSQL, int maxConnections)
                throws ServletException
{
  if (driver.length() == 0)
    throw new ServletException(errNoExistMessage(poolName,
                                                  DRIVER));

  if (connection.length() == 0)
    throw new ServletException(errNoExistMessage(poolName,
                                                  CONNECTION));

  if (maxConnections < 1)
    throw new ServletException(
                     errMessage(poolName, MAXCONNECTIONS,
                     "is less than 1 or does not exist."));

  if (reconnect == true)
  {
    if (pingSQL.length() == 0)
    {
      String errMsg = errNoExistMessage(poolName, PINGSQL) +
                      "You must have a " + PINGSQL +
                      " parameter when the " + RECONNECT +
                      " is true.";
      throw new ServletException(errMsg);
    }
  }


}

private void setupPool(String poolName, String userId,
                       String password, String driver,
                       String connection, boolean reconnect,
                       String pingSQL, int maxConnections,
                       boolean autoCommit)
                throws ServletException
{
  try
  {
```

```
        DBConnectionPool dbp = new DBConnectionPool(maxConnections,
                                                     driver,
                                                     connection, userId,
                                                     password, autoCommit,
                                                     reconnect, pingSQL);

        pl.add(poolName, dbp);

      } catch (Exception e)
      {
        throw new ServletException(e);
      }
    }

    private String invalidMessage(String poolName, String name,
                                  String value)
    {
      String errMsg = errMessage(poolName, name,
                                 "with a value of " + value +
                                 " is invalid.");
      return errMsg;
    }

    private String errNoExistMessage(String poolName, String name)
    {
      String errMsg = errMessage(poolName, name,
                                 "does not exist or is empty.");
      return errMsg;
    }

    private String errMessage(String poolName, String name,
                              String message)
    {
      String errMsg = "In " + DB_POOL_PREFIX + poolName +
                      ", the " + name + " parameter " + message;
      return errMsg;
    }

}
```

To use `DBPoolParser`, we have to integrate it into the enterprise servlet framework. Because most configuration file parameters are parsed through the `AppContext` object, this is probably the best place to execute `DBPoolParser`. In fact, we will place the parsing code in the `parseConfigFile()` method.

The first thing that we need to do is import the `enterprise.db` package. Then we will construct the `DBPoolParser` object in the `parseConfigFile()` method. We will place the code after the call to `parseLogInfo()` and before the call to `buildMethodList()`. The changes to `AppContext` are shown in Listing 8.9. The text in bold is the code that is to be added to the `AppContext` object.

Listing 8.9 Changes to AppContext to integrate DBPoolParser

```
import enterprise.db.*;
.
.
.
public class AppContext
{
.
.
.
  public void parseConfigFile(String appName,String fileName)
        throws ServletException
  {
.
.
.
    parseLogInfo(cf);

    // Parse DBConnectionPool objects.
    DBPoolParser dpp = new DBPoolParser(cf, this.getPoolList());
    dpp.buildConnectionPools();

    buildMethodList();
.
.
.
  }
.
.
.
}
```

Using DBPoolParser in Enterprise Servlets

Let's see how DBPoolParser works within the enterprise servlet framework and how easy it is to create database connection pools. We will take the previous example and alter it so that DBPoolParser creates the database pool. Let's add the following configuration file parameter to the DBExample.config file (you may wish to change the connection parameter to match your particular configuration):

```
DB.ConnectionPool.Oracle=\
        driver=oracle.jdbc.driver.OracleDriver,\
        connection=jdbc:oracle:thin:@localhost:1521:ORCL,\
        maxconnections=5,\
        userid=scott,\
        password=tiger,\
        reconnect=true,\
        pingsql=select 1 from dual,\
             autocommit= true
```

The only other change we must make is to remove the initialization code for DBConnectionPool in the initializeApp() method of the DBExample dispatch servlet class. We no longer need to create the pool because the framework will read the database connection pool parameters from the configuration file and create the pool itself. The new version of DBExample is shown in Listing 8.10.

Listing 8.10 The new DBExample servlet

```
import enterprise.servlet.*;
import enterprise.common.*;
import enterprise.db.*;

import java.io.*;

public class DBExample extends BaseEnterpriseServlet
{
  public String getAppName()
  {
    return "DBExample";
  }

  public void initializeApp(AppContext appContext,
                            PoolObjectManager pom)  throws Exception
  {
  }

  public void destroyApp(AppContext ac, PoolObjectManager pom)
  {
  }
}
```

The results of the program should be the same as in the previous example. Notice that we do not need to worry about creating database connection pools any more. The framework finds the necessary information in the configuration file, and voilà! We have a fully featured, robust database connection pool with complete connection management.

In order to cover all the bases with respect to connection management, this chapter showed a huge amount of code. But it was worth it. Although a very large amount of information was covered, in the end we discovered how simple it is to create an enterprise solution for server database application development.

Summary

In this chapter we learned about connecting servlets to back-end databases. We learned about the different facets of database connectivity and about the various issues that we must consider when developing applications for a database, including the following:

- Pooling should be used except when we expect queries to take longer than a few seconds.
- We should use pool management to ensure that connections are checked back into the pool.
- To avoid running out of cursors on the database, we must ensure that `ResultSet` and `Statement` objects are properly closed.
- We must ensure that any open transactions are properly closed before they are checked back into the pool.
- We should optionally support reliable connections by providing a mechanism to "ping" the database to be sure the database connection is valid, and we should be able to reinstate the database connection if it is not valid.

With these considerations in mind, we developed three connection management objects: `JDBCManager`, `SQLCursor`, and `DBConnection`. These objects help manage database connections in a server environment. We created the `DBConnectionPool` object specifically to handle the connection management objects, thus completing a solution that addressed all of the issues listed here. Using these objects while connecting to a database offers a robust and solid framework for developing servlet applications.

CHAPTER 9

LDAP Connectivity

Lightweight Directory Access Protocol, otherwise known as LDAP, is quickly becoming the rage at many corporations. More and more companies are moving their public employee information, such as work location, e-mail addresses, telephone, position, and other employee-centric data to a centralized location. LDAP is being used for hierarchical management chaining, work flow management, and a verification mechanism for corporate applications. Its centralized location of employee user name and password data is becoming standard for authentication to gain entry into internal corporate systems and is used as vehicle for "single sign-on." Centralized employee information also aids in rapid application development and supports a high degree of data integrity. These reasons demonstrate why LDAP is one of the fastest-growing technologies today.

Because of the success of LDAP in the corporate environment and its open standards, it has spread to become part of many client applications, including integration with e-mail, security certificates, and work flow management products. As a result, many corporations now require that their applications utilize an LDAP server's services. Therefore, as Java developers, at some point we may be asked to develop to an LDAP server.

This chapter will cover some of the aspects of developing with LDAP, and using Sun's Java Naming and Directory Interface (JNDI) API to access an LDAP server with Java. We'll discuss some techniques, and we'll build an LDAP connection pool that may be integrated with the enterprise servlet framework. The concepts in this chapter will be based on the Netscape Directory Server (NDS) because this is one of the more common servers found in the corporate environment. We will make heavy use of the Airius.com company LDIF (LDAP Data Interchange Format) example that comes with the NDS product.

If you do not have access to Netscape Directory Server, you can obtain a trial version from the iPlanet Web site, at `www.iplanet.com`. However, the concepts that are shown in this chapter will work with just about any LDAP server. Let's start by taking a look at the basics of LDAP and some of its history.

A Little History of LDAP

LDAP was developed at The University of Michigan, in partnership with the Internet Engineering Task Force (IETF). It was based on X.500 Directory Access Protocol and was developed as a lighter version of this standard. X.500 was a hierarchical and tree-based model for storing directory information and was envisioned as the panacea for integrating distributed global directories.

LDAP was originally intended to be used as a *lightweight* version of X.500 for testing X.500 directory queries, especially across the Internet, and to extend beyond the UNIX environment. The standard needed to be open so that clients on any platform could communicate with X.500 servers. The open standard was a solution to the problem of integrating the countless diverse and heterogeneous directories that were available at that time.

LDAP allowed clients to add, update, remove, and query directory information via an open standard. It was refined to make queries and data retrieval faster than in any relational database management system (RDBMS). The tradeoff was that updates were slow, but the update speed did not matter because the intent with LDAP was to make most transactions query based.

Two versions of the LDAP specification have been introduced over the years: LDAPv2 and LDAPv3. LDAPv2 was a basic specification that provided the access protocol but left out some of the more important features, such as referral capabilities to other servers, the ability to provide extensions, limited internationalization support, and even minimal security.

LDAPv3 improved on the LDAPv2 weaknesses, and it was developed as a better fit in the Internet world. LDAPv3 supports full referral capabilities to other LDAP servers, internationalization support, strong security, and extensions such as server-based sorting and other data control options. Only some servers support the LDAPv3 specification, and it is still a work in progress.

How LDAP Works

LDAP stores its data in a tree type of structure. Entries belong to nodes known as *objects* within these trees. The storage of an object dictates the subobject entry to which it belongs. The top of the tree, or *root node,* is usually the country, such as *us* for United States. Most environments do not consider this the root node because the company in question is the root. The *.com* name of the company—for example, Airius.com—is usually used for the root node. This is a great root node for starting a tree because every object will belong to an organization. To comply with standards, Figure 9.1 depicts an LDAP tree with the country as the node.

You may notice that LDAP was made for the Internet and based on a tree-like organization. DNS (domain name service) is built this way and provides for very fast querying speeds, but updates can be slow, taking days to propagate through the Internet. LDAP's updates are quite a bit faster, but although the tree-based structure provides for lightning-fast queries, the updates are not so rapid.

Each object or entry contains a set of *attributes*, which are akin to fields in a database. The main difference is that a database record contains every field, whether it is used or not. An LDAP entry may not have an attribute if that

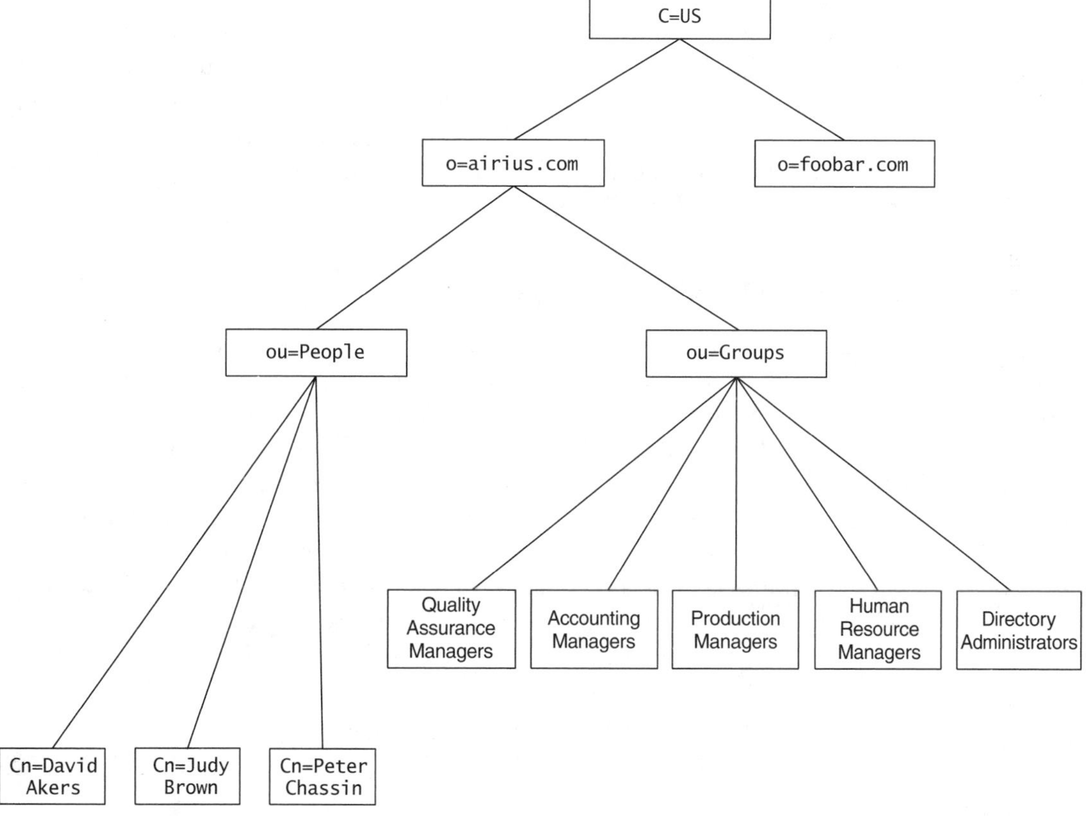

Figure 9.1 A sample LDAP tree

attribute is not required in one of the hierarchical objects. The object hierarchies define which attributes may be part of an entry. Each attribute may contain one or more values, as well as a descriptor that defines the attribute's type.

Distinguished Names

To facilitate the searching of entries, each entry in an LDAP server has an *LDAP* name associated with it. This name may be considered a primary key of the entry, and it mimics a file in an operating system. In a file system, we normally refer to the file by its filename or relative path name, such as `notepad.exe` or `readme.txt`. But when we need to find the file, we need to know the entire path. `C:\WINNT\SYSTEM32\notepad.exe` may be the true path and filename of `notepad.exe`. If we place the file in a directory below `SYSTEM32`, this additional path becomes part of the file's full path and name. This type of tree structure and referencing method allows the operating system to find files very rapidly.

LDAP works in the same way. As an example, let's look at employee David Akers from Figure 9.1. His user ID (`uid`) may be *dakers*. His relative distinguished name (RDN) would be this user ID, `dakers`. But his full distinguished name (DN) would be `DN: uid=dakers, ou=People, o=airius.com`. This entry states that `dakers` (i.e., David Akers) belongs to the `People` organizational unit, and is a part of the organization `airius.com`. As you can see, whereas a file system's path/filename is read hierarchically from left to right, the path of a DN is read from right to left.

Advantages and Disadvantages of LDAP

At first glance, an LDAP server appears to be an excellent replacement for a database. However, the structure and layout of LDAP were meant for very fast reads but not so speedy updates. In addition, LDAP does not support transactions, and it has virtually no relational capabilities. Looking under the hood of an LDAP server confirms that it was never developed to replace an RDBMS.

LDAP has one primary application, which is for directory services. It is meant to allow a user to look up a piece of information, such as employee contact information, very quickly and securely. LDAP contains no cross-referencing or reporting capabilities in its queries. It lacks the ability to do robust joined queries. If these capabilities are necessary for your organization, then an LDAP server is not for you. But if you need lightning-fast access to employee and contact information, single sign-on capabilities, and an open standard for information retrieval by many different kinds of client software, then LDAP is the technology of choice.

LDAP with Java: The JNDI

When developers first learn about the Java Naming and Directory Interface, many of them think about how to access EJBs (Enterprise JavaBeans), RMI (Remote Method Invocation) services, and even Common Object Request Broker Architecture (CORBA). But one area that the JNDI supports particularly well is directory services. The *D* in JNDI stands for *directory,* so it is little surprise that one of the main reasons the JNDI exists is to support directory services. The JNDI supports not only LDAP, but also DNS (domain name service), NIS (Network Information System), and Novell Directory Services, to name a few. In this chapter we'll look at just LDAP.

The JNDI works with pluggable service providers to support the different naming and directory implementations. In this chapter we will be using the JNDI and the LDAP 1.2.2 service provider, both of which are accessible through Sun's Web site (`www.javasoft.com`). The JNDI can be downloaded separately, or it can be used directly through J2EE, which may be preferable because J2EE is packaged with just about every Java API imaginable, and managing one JAR file is easier than managing many. The LDAP 1.2.3 service provider is not part of J2EE and must be downloaded separately. This API is what gives us access to LDAP and its extension controls. Most of the objects described in this chapter can be found in the packages `javax.naming`, `javax.naming.ldap`, and `javax.naming.directory`.

Connecting to LDAP

Connecting to LDAP means simply creating a socket connection to the LDAP TCP/IP port and letting the communication occur, just as it would for any TCP service. JNDI hides all of the necessary TCP/IP socket communication and LDAP communication protocol for us. It is simply an abstraction of the communication layer so that we can concentrate on developing the software and communicate with LDAP through an API. In JNDI we connect to an LDAP server by obtaining an initial context. In fact, we cannot do anything in JNDI without one. Specifically, we will obtain an `LdapContext` object.

To obtain an initial `LdapContext` object, we need to select a service provider and place it inside a `Hashtable` object along with the URL of the LDAP server. The URL contains the following syntax: the string *ldap://,* followed by the server name, followed by a colon and the port on which the LDAP server is listening (usually 389). A typical connection URL would be `ldap://localhost:389`. This `Hashtable` object is called an environment

Hashtable. It allows us to set up a variable number of parameters to create an initial context, as shown here:

```
Hashtable env = new Hashtable();
env.put(Context.INITIAL_CONTEXT_FACTORY,
        "com.sun.jndi.ldap.LdapCtxFactory");
env.put(Context.PROVIDER_URL, "ldap://localhost:389");
```

These parameters alone are enough for us to initiate an "anonymous" connection to an LDAP server that contains no authentication. Sometimes we may wish to connect as a particular user to be able to add and update information. To do this we add three additional parameters to the environment Hashtable object. The SECURITY_AUTHENTICATION parameter specifies the type of authentication. There are several types, but in this case we will just use *simple* authentication. The SECURITY_PRINCIPAL parameter specifies the user that we are going to authenticate as. This parameter usually is a declaration of the common name (cn) followed by an equal sign and then the user's common name. We could have also used the user ID following *uid=*. The SECURITY_CREDENTIALS parameter specifies the password string.

```
env.put(Context.SECURITY_AUTHENTICATION,"simple");
env.put(Context.SECURITY_PRINCIPAL, "cn=Directory Manager");
env.put(Context.SECURITY_CREDENTIALS, "mysecretpassword");
```

To obtain an initial context, we would make the following call:

```
LdapContext ctx = new InitialLdapContext(env, null);
```

The initial context is basically the connection to the LDAP server. It is the equivalent of the Connection object for a database and will be used for all operations we do with an LDAP server.

Searching LDAP for Values

There are many different ways to search LDAP through JNDI: straightforward lookups, matches, and filtered searches. Although each has its own advantages and disadvantages, the filtered search is the most flexible in allowing you to search for specific data and particular attributes to return.

First let's talk about LDAP search filters. An LDAP search filter is very simple. All filters are usually placed in parentheses. To search for a last name (the sn attribute in LDAP), we place the search string—for example, *sn=Akers*—in parentheses:

```
(sn=Akers)
```

To do a wild-card search on an attribute, we simply place an asterisk where we want the wild card. The following filter, for example, will search for all entries whose last name (`sn`) starts with *Ak:*

```
(sn=Ak*)
```

For searches based on multiple attributes, each attribute filter is encased in its own set of parentheses. The operator, such as AND or OR, precedes the filters, and the entire string is encased in its own set of parentheses. If this seems confusing, look at the following filter, which searches for the last name (`sn`) *Akers* and the first name (`givenname`) *Dan:*

```
(&(sn="Akers")(givenname="Dan"))
```

The next search looks for the last name (`sn`) *Campaigne* and the first name (`givenname`) *Jeffrey* or *Jody:*

```
(&(sn=" Campaigne")(|(givenname=" Jeffrey") (givenname=" Jody")))
```

These examples show that the syntax of search filters is very simple. A full description of LDAP search filters and syntax rules can be found in the RFC 2254 specification and at Netscape's Web site (`developer.netscape.com`).

To do a search with LDAP using the `LdapContext` object, search filters offer the most powerful and flexible method. Before searching, we define a parameter called `SearchControls` that defines the scope of the search, whether to retrieve the data or just the object class identifier, and which attributes to retrieve. There are a few different scopes, but `SUBTREE_SCOPE` allows the search to look for the data everywhere below the search base (which will be described shortly). This scope also lets us see whether we retrieve just the name of the object or the entire entry's data.

Usually we want the entry's data to be returned so that we may access the attribute information. We do this by calling the `setReturningObjFlag()` method with `true` as a parameter. Finally, we state what parameters we want returned to us. Some calls will return all parameters, but this is wasteful because it is very rare that we need all the attributes. To declare the attributes we want returned, we create a `String` array, with each element containing the name of an attribute that we want returned in its own element. The following code shows a `SearchControls` setup:

```
String retAttrs = { "sn", "gn", "uid" };
SearchControls ctls = new SearchControls();
ctls.setReturningObjFlag (true);
ctls.setSearchScope(SearchControls.SUBTREE_SCOPE);
ctls.setReturningAttributes(retAttrs);
```

To do the actual search, we call search() with the LdapContext object as a parameter. There are a few variations of this call, but I like to use the simplest one, which takes a search base string, the filter, and SearchControls as parameters. The *search base* string is the base object from where we wish to search. For example, if we choose to search from the root object—that is, if we want to search the entire tree—we pass in o=airius.com if airius.com is the root.

When search() finds a match, it returns a NamingEnumeration object with the results. NamingEnumeration is an enumeration of SearchResult objects that holds each entry found. We call the SearchControls.getAttributes() method to return an Attributes object, and from there we call get() with the attribute name as a parameter to get the Attribute object. With the Attribute object we call get() and cast it as the Java type that we want returned to retrieve the attribute value.

This next bit of code searches for everyone whose last name begins with *Ca* and prints out the last name, first name, and e-mail address for each:

```
String retAttrs = { "sn", "gn", "mail" };
SearchControls ctls = new SearchControls();
ctls.setReturningObjFlag (true);
ctls.setSearchScope(SearchControls.SUBTREE_SCOPE);
ctls.setReturningAttributes(retAttrs);

String baseDN = "o=airius.com";
NamingEnumeration ne = ctx.search(baseDN, "(sn=Ca*)", ctls);

while(ne.hasMore())
{
  SearchResult sr = (SearchResult) ne.next();
  Attributes attrs = sr.getAttributes();

  Attribute  attr = attrs.get("sn");
  String lastname = attr.get();
  attr  = attrs.get("givenname");
  String firstname = attr.get();
  attr  = attrs.get("mail");
  String email = attr.get();
  System.out.println(firstname + " " +
                     lastname + " (" + email + ")");

}
```

There are many ways to implement a search, and many different kinds of operations can be done on the SearchResult, Attributes, and Attribute objects. A good review of the JavaDoc for JNDI and the LDAP service provider can identify the many different options available.

Sorting Results

One of the great things about LDAPv3 is that its specifications allow for sorting on the server. In other words, the server handles all of the sorting for us. With LDAPv2 we need to do the sorting ourselves, so there is a lot more code and we must be creative with Sun's Java tools and APIs to do rapid sorting on the fly. With the LDAPv3 controls, we can let the server do all the dirty work, so when we receive the `NamingEnumeration` object, the results are nicely sorted for us.

To sort the results we use the `SortControl` object that is included in the LDAP service provider library. First we create a `String` array of the attributes on which we wish to sort. The elements of this array must contain the names of the attributes, and the order in which they appear in the array is the order in which the results will be sorted. After creating this array, we create a `Control` array using the `SortControl` object as one of the parameters.

Creating the `SortControl` object is simply a matter of passing in the `String` array containing the attribute names to sort on, and a `Control.CRITICAL` parameter. The `Control.CRITICAL` parameter indicates that the control that is being used is critical and that the server cannot ignore it. If the server does not support the control, it will throw an `OperationNotSupportedException`. After setting the control, we call the `setRequestControls()` method on the `LdapContext` object and pass the `Control` array as a parameter. This call will sort all subsequent searches.

```
Control[] ctxCtls = new Control[]{
                        new SortControl(attrs, Control.CRITICAL)
};

ctx.setRequestControls(ctxCtls);
```

Because all of the subsequent searches will be sorted according to the last `setRequestControls()` call, creating a new `Control` array with the `SortControl` object will change the sorting to a new structure. If you wish to remove the sorting all together, passing `null` as a parameter to `setRequestControls()` will do the trick, as shown here:

```
ctx.setRequestControls(null);
```

Adding and Removing an Entry

An entry is nothing more than an object in an LDAP server—an object with a name as its main identifier. This name is the DN. To add an entry, we must build the attributes, include the minimum of attributes that are required for the parent object, and bind the attributes to the LDAP server with the DN.

NOTE: Before adding, removing, or modifying any data, remember that you must have supplied some of the security parameters when obtaining an initial context. If you are logged in anonymously, you will not be able to modify any data, and you will likely receive a `NamingException` stating that you do not have rights to change data.

We create the `Attributes` interface by declaring a `BasicAttributes` object. We add attributes to the object either directly through the `put()` method or by creating a `BasicAttribute` object. Why create a `BasicAttribute` object instead of adding the attribute directly? We would do this if we had multiple values for an attribute. In the `airius.com` schema, each `People` entry requires multiple `objectclass` values and can have multiple organizational units (`ou`). For these attributes, we would create `BasicAttribute` objects. Once we have added all of the attributes with the `put()` method, we execute the `bind()` call. In this call we pass the DN and the attributes. The following code creates a new entry in the `airius.com` schema:

```
Attribute oc = new BasicAttribute("objectclass");
oc.add("inetOrgPerson");
oc.add("organizationalPerson");
oc.add("person");
oc.add("top");

Attribute ouSet = new BasicAttribute("ou");
ouSet.add("People");
ouSet.add("Product Development");

BasicAttributes bas = new BasicAttributes(true);
bas.put(oc);
bas.put(ouSet);
bas.put("uid", "jgenender");
bas.put("cn", "Jeff Genender");
bas.put("sn", "Genender");
bas.put("givenname", "Jeff");
bas.put("mail", "jgenender@airius.com");
bas.put("l", "Denver");
bas.put("telephonenumber", "+ 1 303 555 1234");
bas.put("facsimiletelephonenumber", "+ 1 303 555 9876");
bas.put("roomnumber", "1234");
bas.put("userpassword", "enterprise");
lpo.getLdapContext().bind("uid=jgenender, ou=People, o=airius.com",
                          null, bas);
```

To remove an entry, we just call `unbind()` on the `LdapContext` object and use the DN as a parameter.

```
ctx.unbind("uid=jgenender, ou=People, o=airius.com");
```

Modifying Attributes within an Entry

For any particular entry we may choose to add, update, or remove an attribute. We use the `ModificationItem` object for these operations. We create an array containing `ModificationItem` objects in which the number of objects matches the number of attributes to add, change, or remove. Each `ModificationItem` object is set with the attribute and a `DirContext` action field. The three possible `DirContext` action values are `REPLACE_ATTRIBUTE`, `REMOVE_ATTRIBUTE`, and `ADD_ATTRIBUTE`. A final call to `LdapContext.modifyAttributes()` with the DN and the `ModificationItem` array as parameters submits the changes to the LDAP server. The sample code that follows updates, removes, and adds attributes in a single submission.

```
ModificationItem[] mods = new ModificationItem[3];

Attribute loc = new BasicAttribute("l","Chicago");
Attribute roomno = new BasicAttribute("roomnumber");
Attribute pager = new BasicAttribute("pager", "+ 1 888 555 1111");

mods[0] = new ModificationItem(DirContext.REPLACE_ATTRIBUTE, loc);
mods[1] = new ModificationItem(DirContext.REMOVE_ATTRIBUTE, roomno);
mods[2] = new ModificationItem(DirContext.ADD_ATTRIBUTE, pager);

ctx.modifyAttributes("uid=jcampai2,ou=People,o=airius.com", mods);
```

Closing the LdapContext Object

Closing the LDAP connection is just as simple as calling `close()` on the `LdapContext` object. Executing this method closes the connection and immediately releases any resources associated with the context.

```
ctx.close();
```

LDAP Considerations in a Server Application

We have just learned about how to make Java interact with a LDAP server. But how do we use the JNDI in a Web-based application? Do we just create a context, use it, and close it on each page? Not exactly. Remember that we are making a connection to an outside server. Creation and destruction of the context on a regular basis would create havoc with the garbage collector. The short delay in making the LDAP connection is probably something we want to leave out of our applications because the faster the Web server is, the happier the customer will be.

Managing an LDAP connection is not too different from managing a database connection. First we should pool the `LdapContext` objects. There is no question about this. *All* LDAP connections should be pooled. In fact, we do not have the "long-running query" excuse that we had with the database for not pooling a connection. There is no such thing as a long-running query in LDAP. If a query is taking a long time, then either there is a problem with the filter or the attributes being searched are not indexed.

We can remedy both of these problems either by fixing the filter string or by adding an index to the attribute. This is why there is no reason *not* to pool the LDAP connection. We also need to be sure that the connections are checked back into the pool when we're done using them. This is a pool management issue, and once again, by using LDAP connections with `Pool`, `PoolObjectManager`, and `PoolList`, we can ensure that the connections are checked back in.

The LDAP connection has no transaction capabilities, so there is no reason to monitor or have to set transactions. But the pool does need to monitor the state of `SearchControls`. Remember that once the value of `SearchControls` is set, all subsequent queries will sort on the setting. Therefore, we need to reset `SearchControls` so that no searches are active before we check in the object.

Just as we did with the database connections, we need to "ping" the connections to be sure that they are active before we use them. LDAP is vulnerable to the same problems as a database when it comes to active connections. If the LDAP server is restarted or there is a break in the connection, we will need to reinitiate the connection. We do not need to pass it any "ping" filter to do the low-overhead LDAP query. Instead we can use a built-in `lookup()` method call with `LdapContext`. The parameter we use is the root object.

In the case of the Airius company, we would pass `o=airius.com` to the connection. This simply looks up the object. Because the object is the root object, a heavily indexed search is not used; instead, the connection uses the DN to look up the object, which is the fastest method for finding information. Thus this is a low-overhead call. If no exception occurs, we can assume we have a good connection. If an exception does occur, we need to reconnect. What's nice about this is that we do not need to pass a ping filter because it is built into the managed object.

Finally, you probably remember that when we built the database connection management objects, we needed to monitor the `ResultSet` and `Statement` objects with `SQLCursor`. Is a `SQLCursor` type of object needed with an LDAP connection? Yes and no. The closest thing we have to a `ResultSet` object is the `NamingEnumeration` object. Does a `NamingEnumeration` object need to be closed? Yes, closing the `NamingEnumeration` object is highly advised.

To help ensure that this happens, we can provide a simple search utility to use with an LDAP connection. If this utility is used, the `NamingEnumeration` will be cleaned up. If it is not used, the developer should close the object directly.

You might wonder why we wouldn't simply close up everything for the developer and wrap a `SQLCursor` type of object around it all. There are two reasons. First, the JNDI is too expansive to have a front-end API that replicates everything it does as we did with the `SQLCursor` and JDBC. It could be done, but the amount of code required would be tremendous.

Second, it just is not worth it in this situation. Failing to close a `NamingEnumeration` object does not keep a "cursor" open for any length of time. It simply reserves some memory until the garbage collector comes along to clean it up, which does eventually happen. In other words, failing to close a `NamingEnumeration` object does not harm an application or make it inoperable.

Therefore it really is not worth the trouble of developing a full front-end API for `NamingEnumeration`. As stated in the JNDI JavaDoc, the `NamingEnumeration` object should be closed in order to give the garbage collector a "hint" that it may be cleaned up right away, but close monitoring is not necessary.

Building the LDAP Connection Management Objects

On the basis of what we have discussed so far, and remembering what we learned in Chapter 8 about database connections, we are beginning to formulate how the LDAP connection management objects should look. Because we have no "cursor," we end up with an `LDAPManager` object and an `LDAPConnection` object. `LDAPManager` is an encapsulation of the `LdapContext` object. This object will contain a few generic helper functions that make using the JNDI a little easier. It also will watch for any `NamingEnumeration` objects that were opened through it and be sure that it closes them before releasing the connection back to the pool. In addition, it will clear any `SearchControls` objects before checking in the object.

`LDAPConnection` is the front end to `LDAPManager`. The difference between this object and `DBConnection` is that we will make `LDAPConnection` responsible for creating the connection instead of passing the connection as a construction argument as we did with `DBConnection`. Just as with `DBConnection`, however, `LDAPConnection` will contain the `ping()` routine.

The LDAPManager Object

Of the two LDAP connection management objects, we'll start by building `LDAPManager`, the object that will manage the connection. There is not much to managing this connection, except that as it creates `NamingEnumeration` objects, we want to provide the ability to close them.

We'll have a `Vector` object that contains a list of `NamingEnumeration` objects that are open. A method called `reset()` will ensure that this `Vector` object is processed and all `NamingEnumeration` objects are closed. The `reset()` method also will reset any `SearchControls` objects by setting the request controls to `null` on the connection. In addition to the cleanup code, we will develop a few helper functions to aid in searching the LDAP server for information. We will use the more common types of searches because, as shown earlier in the chapter, using the JNDI can be very code intensive. Let's start by declaring the `LDAPManager` object and its member constants and variables.

```
package enterprise.db;

import java.util.*;

import javax.naming.*;
import javax.naming.ldap.*;
import javax.naming.directory.*;

import com.sun.jndi.ldap.ctl.*;

public class LDAPManager
{
  private final static String USER_ID_FILTER_PREFIX    = "uid=";
  private final static String COMMON_NAME_ATTRIBUTE    = "cn";
  private final static String MANAGER_ATTRIBUTE        = "manager";
  private final static String SECRETARY_ATTRIBUTE      = "secretary";

  protected String m_baseDN                            = "";
  protected String m_Host                              = "";
  protected int    m_Port                              = 0;
  protected String m_cn                                = null;
  protected String m_password                          = null;

  protected LdapContext ctx;
  private Vector m_NE_List = new Vector();

  protected LDAPManager()
  {
  }
```

We want to allow the developer to have full use of LdapContext, so we will expose this object by creating a getter for it.

```
public LdapContext getLdapContext()
{
  return ctx;
}
```

The reset() method will clean up any open NamingEnumeration objects to help the garbage collector, and it will remove any sorts on LdapContext. This method will most likely be called by the LDAP connection pool before the object is checked back into the pool.

```
public void reset()
{
  cleanupNamingEnumerations();
  if (ctx != null)
  {
    try
    {
      ctx.setRequestControls(null);
    } catch (Exception e)
    {
    }
  }
}
```

The cleanupNamingEnumerations() method does the dirty work of closing all open NamingEnumeration objects. It goes through the contents of the internal Vector object, calling the close() method on each NamingEnumeration object.

```
protected void cleanupNamingEnumerations()
{
  int i = (m_NE_List.size() - 1);
  for(; i >= 0; i--)
  {
    NamingEnumeration ne = (NamingEnumeration)
    m_NE_List.elementAt(i);
    try
    {
      ne.close();
    } catch (NamingException e)
    {
      // Do nothing because we are cleaning up.
    }
    m_NE_List.removeElementAt(i);
  }
}
```

We will provide an easy method, `close()`, for closing the LDAP connection and releasing the resources on `LdapContext`.

```
public void close()
{
  if( ctx != null )
  {
    try
    {
      ctx.close();
    }
    catch( NamingException e )
    {
      e.printStackTrace();
    }
    ctx = null;
  }
}
```

Let's provide a simple method that performs an LDAP search and returns a `NamingEnumeration` object to us. This method, which we'll call `ldapSearch()`, will take a filter string, a `String` array of attribute names to return, and a search base. The routine will set up a `SUBTREE_SCOPE` search, which is the most common type of search. Before being returned, the `NamingEnumeration` object will be added to the internal `Vector` object for cleanup by the `reset()` method. It is strongly recommended that developers use this method to search the LDAP server for information because the object cleans up after itself.

```
public NamingEnumeration ldapSearch(String filter,
                                    String attrs[],
                                    String searchBase)
    throws Exception
{

  // Perform the search.
  SearchControls ctls = new SearchControls();
  ctls.setReturningObjFlag (true);
  ctls.setSearchScope(SearchControls.SUBTREE_SCOPE);
  ctls.setReturningAttributes(attrs);

  NamingEnumeration ne = ctx.search(searchBase, filter, ctls);

  if (ne != null)
    this.m_NE_List.add(ne);

  return ne;

}
```

A method to easily set the sort attributes would be very handy in this object. This method will take the `String` array that contains the list and order of the attributes, and it will do all the dirty work of creating and setting the `SortControl` object.

```
public void setSortAttr(String[] attrs) throws Exception
{
  // Create the critical sort control that sorts on "cn".
  Control[] ctxCtls = new Control[]{
      new SortControl(attrs, Control.CRITICAL)
  };
  ctx.setRequestControls(ctxCtls);
}
```

That's really all there is to managing an LDAP connection. But let's also build some routines that will take the drudgery out of using the JNDI. We will develop some helper routines that quickly return common information. The routines listed here are searches that have proven useful in my development efforts. You are encouraged to add and change these routines to fit your environment. No modification routines are included because these can be very customized to the application and very code intensive. It's a good idea to create customized objects to handle modification.

One common search we do is to get the common name (`cn`) from the user ID. We just pass in a `uid` parameter and a search base, and we get back the `cn` if the information was found, or `null` if it was not.

```
public String getCNfromUID(String uid, String searchBase)
    throws Exception
{
   String[] attrIDs = {COMMON_NAME_ATTRIBUTE};
   SearchControls ctls = new SearchControls();
   ctls.setCountLimit(1);
   ctls.setReturningObjFlag (true);
   ctls.setSearchScope(SearchControls.SUBTREE_SCOPE);
   ctls.setReturningAttributes(attrIDs);

   String filter = "(" + USER_ID_FILTER_PREFIX + uid + ")";
   NamingEnumeration answer = ctx.search(searchBase, filter, ctls);

   if (answer.hasMoreElements())
   {
      SearchResult sr = (SearchResult)answer.next();
     return
       (String)sr.getAttributes().get
       (COMMON_NAME_ATTRIBUTE).get();
    }
    return null;
}
```

The following routine, getStringAttribute(), will return a value of any attribute identified by the uid parameter. The uid attribute is probably one of the most heavily used for such searches. We pass getStringAttribute() the uid attribute, the name of an attribute we wish to have returned, and the search base. If the search is successful, getStringAttribute() will return the attribute's value; if the specified user ID is not found, it will return null. Keep in mind that getStringAttribute() will not return multiple values, but only the first one found.

```
public String getStringAttribute(String uid,
                                 String attrName,
                                 String searchBase)
    throws Exception
{
  String[] attrIDs = {attrName};
  SearchControls ctls = new SearchControls();
  ctls.setCountLimit(1);
  ctls.setReturningObjFlag (true);
  ctls.setSearchScope(SearchControls.SUBTREE_SCOPE);
  ctls.setReturningAttributes(attrIDs);

  String filter = "(" + USER_ID_FILTER_PREFIX + uid + ")";
  NamingEnumeration answer = ctx.search(searchBase, filter, ctls);

  try
  {
    if (answer.hasMoreElements())
    {

      SearchResult sr = (SearchResult)answer.next();
      Attributes attrs = sr.getAttributes();
      Attribute attr = attrs.get(attrName);

      if (attr == null)
        return null;

      return (String)attr.get();

    }
  } finally
  {
    if (answer != null)
      answer.close();
  }

  return null;

}
```

The getAttributes() method returns all of the attributes associated with a uid parameter. It returns an Attributes object that may be processed by the developer. This method takes a uid attribute and a search base as parameters. As with the other methods, if the search is successful, getAttributes() returns an Attributes object; if the search is not successful, it returns null.

```
public Attributes getAttributes(String uid,
                                String searchBase)
     throws Exception
  {
    SearchControls ctls = new SearchControls();
    ctls.setCountLimit(1);
    ctls.setReturningObjFlag (true);
    ctls.setSearchScope(SearchControls.SUBTREE_SCOPE);

    String filter = "(" + USER_ID_FILTER_PREFIX + uid + ")";
    NamingEnumeration answer = ctx.search(searchBase, filter, ctls);

    try
    {
      if (answer.hasMoreElements())
      {

        SearchResult sr = (SearchResult)answer.next();
        return (Attributes)sr.getAttributes();

      }
    } finally
    {
      if (answer != null)
        answer.close();
    }

    return null;
  }
```

The getManager() and getAssistant() methods are very helpful. MANAGER_ATTRIBUTE and SECRETARY_ATTRIBUTE, the manager and secretary attributes, typically contain the DN of the user. Often this information does not help us because we need the user ID, and we would need to parse the DN to get this information. The getManager() and getAssistant() methods call an internal method, getDNfromAttr(), that searches for a user ID and gets the DN of the secretary or manager. It then extracts the user ID from the DN and returns this user ID to the user.

Although the Airius.com example that comes with the Netscape Directory Server does not contain a management or assistant structure, many organizations do use these attributes. These methods can come in very handy when we are searching through a management tree for work flow applications.

```
public String getManager(String uid,
                         String searchBase)
  throws Exception
{
  return getDNfromAttr(uid, MANAGER_ATTRIBUTE, searchBase);
}

public String getAssistant(String uid,
                           String searchBase)
  throws Exception
{
  return getDNfromAttr(uid, SECRETARY_ATTRIBUTE, searchBase);
}

private String getDNfromAttr(String uid,
                             String attr,
                             String searchBase)
  throws Exception
{
  String[] attrIDs = {attr};
  SearchControls ctls = new SearchControls();
  ctls.setCountLimit(1);
  ctls.setReturningObjFlag (true);
  ctls.setSearchScope(SearchControls.SUBTREE_SCOPE);
  ctls.setReturningAttributes(attrIDs);

  String filter = "(" + USER_ID_FILTER_PREFIX + uid + ")";
  NamingEnumeration answer = ctx.search(searchBase, filter, ctls);

  try
  {

    if (answer.hasMoreElements())
    {

      SearchResult sr = (SearchResult)answer.next();
      Attributes attrs = sr.getAttributes();
      Attribute atr = attrs.get(attr);
      if (atr == null)
      {
        return null;
      }
      String DN = (String)atr.get();
      if (DN.equals(""))
      {
        return null;
      }

      StringTokenizer st1 = new StringTokenizer(DN,",");
      String uidStr = st1.nextToken();

      StringTokenizer st2 = new StringTokenizer(uidStr,"=");
      st2.nextToken();
```

```
          String DN_uid = st2.nextToken();

          return DN_uid;
        }

      } finally
      {
        if (answer != null)
        {
          answer.close();
        }
      }
      return null;
    }
  }
```

The LDAPConnection Object

The `LDAPConnection` object is an extension of `LDAPManager`. It will be responsible for creating the connection through its constructors and supplying the `ping()` routine for the connection pool. The constructors will support both anonymous and authenticated connections.

```
package enterprise.db;

import java.util.*;
import javax.naming.*;
import javax.naming.ldap.*;
import javax.naming.directory.*;

public class LDAPConnection extends LDAPManager
{

  public LDAPConnection(String baseDN, String host, int port,
                        String cn, String password)
    throws NamingException
  {
    super();

    m_baseDN = baseDN;
    m_Host = host;
    m_Port = port;
    m_cn = cn;
    m_password = password;

    Hashtable env = new Hashtable();
    env.put(Context.INITIAL_CONTEXT_FACTORY,
           "com.sun.jndi.ldap.LdapCtxFactory");
    env.put(Context.PROVIDER_URL, "ldap://" + m_Host + ":" +
           m_Port);
```

```
      if (m_cn != null)
      {
        env.put(Context.SECURITY_AUTHENTICATION,"simple");
        env.put(Context.SECURITY_PRINCIPAL, "cn=" + m_cn);
        env.put(Context.SECURITY_CREDENTIALS, m_password);
      }

      ctx = new InitialLdapContext(env, null);

    }

    public LDAPConnection(String baseDN, String host, int port)
         throws NamingException
    {
      this(baseDN,host,port,null,null);
    }
```

The ping() routine just does a lookup of the base DN or the root object. If the lookup() call does not return a NamingException, the connection is considered good and ping() returns true; otherwise it returns false. If ping() returns false, it is up to the calling routine (which will probably be a connection pool) to reestablish the connection.

```
  protected boolean ping()
  {
    try
    {
      // Do a simple nonoverhead lookup of an object.
      // If we don't get an error, then we have a valid connection.
      ctx.lookup(m_baseDN);
      return true;
    } catch(NamingException ne)
    {
      return false;
    }
  }
}
```

Using the LDAP Connection Management Objects

Using the objects we just created is easy. For starters, we need to create an LDAP connection. By simply declaring an LDAPConnection object and passing in the appropriate parameters, we initialize and create an LDAP connection and the underlying LdapContext object.

```
LDAPConnection lc = LDAPConnection("o=airius.com",
                                   "localhost",
                                   389,
                                   "Directory Manager",
                                   "mysecretpassword");
```

We can retrieve the underlying LdapContext object with the following code:

```
LdapContext ctx = lc.getLdapContext();
```

With the context we can execute any JNDI operation. For search operations, however, a good choice is the ldapSearch() routine because it will monitor the NamingEnumeration object and make sure it is cleaned up when reset() is called.

```
String attrs[] = {"sn","givenname","mail"};
NamingEnumeration ne = lc.ldapSearch("(sn=A*)", attrs,
                                     "o=airius.com");
```

To sort searches, we call the setSortAttr() method and pass in the String array of attributes. We initiate this call before executing a search.

```
String sortAttrs = {"sn", "givenname"};
lc.setSortAttr(sortAttrs );
```

Now let's take a look at some of the helper functions we developed. The getStringAttribute() method will return the value of any attribute found for a particular user ID. This example finds the value mail for Dan Akers's user ID, dakers:

```
String dansMail = lc.getStringAttribute("dakers", "mail",
                                        "o=airius.com");
```

The next example uses the getCNfromUID() method to return a common name (cn) from a user ID (uid):

```
String dansCN = lc. getCNfromUID ("dakers", "o=airius.com");
```

We can also get the attributes from a uid search with the following helper function:

```
Attributes dansEntry = lc.getAttributes("dakers", "o=airius.com");
String sn = dansEntry.get("sn").get();
String givenname = dansEntry.get("givenname").get();
. . .
```

Finally, we can retrieve the manager and secretary attribute values from a search on an ID. Although the airius.com schema does not include managers or secretaries, the following code will show how to extract this information if it exists:

```
String dansManager = lc.getManager("dakers", "o=airius.com");
String dansAssistant =  lc.getAssistant("dakers", "o=airius.com");
```

These LDAP connection management objects are meant to be only a stepping-stone that you can enhance to fit your needs. There are all sorts of ways to enhance these objects, such as by integrating entry modification objects that fit your application's needs. For example, wouldn't it be neat just to pass the `uid`, `givenname`, and `sn` attributes, along with a few other attributes, to the method and have the framework automically create the entry? This is just one of many ideas that can be integrated into these objects. Before we get too caught up in enhancing these objects, however, let's shore up the framework and look at building a pooling class for the connection management objects because these objects are not very useful without a connection pool of some kind.

The LDAPConnectionPool Object

The LDAP connection management objects don't really show their true colors without a connection pool. The connection pool is what enforces the rules for reusability and cleans up after us. Just like `LDAPConnection`, the pool must support both an anonymous and an authenticated connection pool. To create a pool, the constructors will need to take a pool size, the host name of the server on which the LDAP server is running, the port on which the server is running, and the base DN or root object name (such as `o=airius.com`).

One of the constructors will need to support user authentication, so the connections can be bound to the LDAP server as a particular user so that modifications can be made to LDAP. In addition, this constructor will need to take the `cn` attribute and password as parameters to implement the authentication. The main constructor will be responsible for setting the member variables with the passed-in arguments and creating the pool; the other constructor will just call the main constructor.

Not surprisingly, we'll call this connection pool `LDAPConnectionPool`. Because we want the enterprise servlet framework to manage `LDAPConnectionPool`, this class will extend the `Pool` object. Let's declare the `LDAPConnectionPool` object and create the constructors.

```
package enterprise.db;

import enterprise.common.*;
import javax.naming.*;
import javax.naming.ldap.*;
import javax.naming.directory.*;
import java.util.*;

public class LDAPConnectionPool extends Pool
{
```

```
    private String m_Host        = "";
    private int    m_Port        = 0;
    private String m_base        = "";
    private String m_cn          = null;
    private String m_password    = null;

  public LDAPConnectionPool(int    maxSize,
                            String ldapHost,
                            int    ldapPort,
                            String baseDN)
      throws Exception
  {
    this(maxSize, ldapHost, ldapPort, baseDN, null, null);
  }

  public LDAPConnectionPool(int    maxSize,
                            String ldapHost,
                            int    ldapPort,
                            String baseDN,
                            String cn,
                            String password)
      throws Exception
  {
    m_cn = cn;
    m_password = password;
    m_Host = ldapHost;
    m_Port = ldapPort;
    m_base = baseDN;

    createPool(maxSize);
  }
```

Using the `Pool` object means that we must implement the `createObject()` method. It is in the `LDAPConnectionPool` class that we create the object `LDAPConnection` object, which we return to the framework to be added to the pool. Notice the `retry` loop in this code. This is included because LDAP servers can be a little finicky in creating connections. Sometimes it takes more than one try to establish a connection. We give the server a one-second breather between tries, and we allow three tries to make the connection before throwing an error.

```
  public Object createObject() throws NamingException
  {
    int retry = 0;

    LDAPConnection ctx = null;

    while (true)
    {
      try
      {
```

```
          ctx = new LDAPConnection(m_base, m_Host, m_Port,
                                   m_cn, m_password);
          break;

        } catch (NamingException ne)
        {

          retry++;
          if (retry >= 3)
          {
            throw ne;
          }

          try
          {
            Thread.sleep(1000);
          } catch (InterruptedException ie)
          {
          }

        }
      }

      return ctx;

    }
```

Just as we did in Chapter 8 with the `DBConnection` object, we want to have the framework automatically clean up the connection before checking the object in, and we want to ensure that we have a valid connection before checking the object out. So we will implement the `beforeCheckin()` and `beforeCheckout()` methods. The `beforeCheckin()` method will call `reset()` on the `LDAPConnection` object, which will close all the open `NamingEnumeration` objects created by the object and will clear any sorting operations that we declared on the connection. As a result, `LDAPConnection` will be returned to its original state.

```
public void beforeCheckin(Object o)
{
  LDAPConnection lc = (LDAPConnection) o;
  lc.reset();
}
```

The `beforeCheckout()` method tests the connection before handing it to the developer. It executes the `ping()` call and checks the answer. If the ping was successful, `beforeCheckout()` passes the connection to the developer. If not, it creates a new `LDAPConnection` object and replaces the old object with the new one in the pool and then passes the new `LDAPConnection` object to the developer.

```
public Object beforeCheckout(Object o) throws Exception
{
  LDAPConnection lc = (LDAPConnection) o;

  if (!lc.ping())
  {
      LDAPConnection new_lc = null;

      try
      {
          // No ping (for whatever reason), so attempt a
          // reconnect.
          new_lc = (LDAPConnection) createObject();
      }
      catch(Exception e)
      {
         // Can't get a connection, so just put the old one away.
         this.checkInPoolObject(lc);
         throw e;
      }

      // Replace the old object with the new one.
      replacePoolObject(lc, new_lc);

      lc = new_lc;
  }

  return lc;
}

}
```

Now that we have developed all of the connection management objects, as well as the LDAP connection pool, let's see them in action. We'll develop an enterprise servlet application that uses these objects and see how easy it is to integrate LDAP into servlets.

Putting the Connection Management Objects to Use

To see the LDAP connection management objects work in a real application, let's build an example. We'll assume that we work for the Airius company and have been handed a set of specifications to develop an online directory of employees. This directory must allow employees to find each other by the first character of the last name. When an employee selects a letter, the directory should display all employees whose last name begins with that letter, sorted by their last name and first name.

NOTE: This example requires Netscape Directory Server and the Airius.com LDIF file to be installed on the server. The `Airius.ldif` file can be found in the `slapd-yourserver/ldif` directory of the NDS installation. Netscape should include instructions on loading LDIF files in the documentation that accompanies the server. This example also requires the J2EE and the LDAP 1.2.2 service provider JAR files—`j2ee.jar`, `ldap.jar`, and `ldapbp.jar`—to be included in the class path.

A screen layout has been submitted to us; it is a one-page application with the selectable letters at the top of the screen and the employees at the bottom. A mock screen was submitted along with the HTML to the development team, and the screen looks like the one shown in Figure 9.2.

The final requirement is that this application must use the company's LDAP server because this is the standard for centralizing employee contact informa-

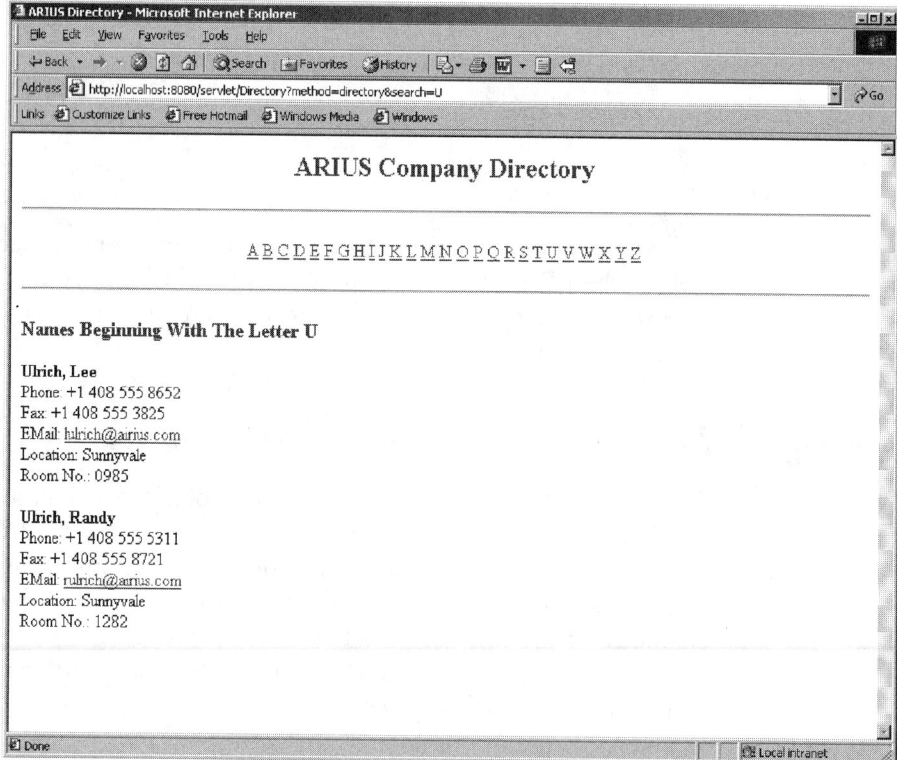

Figure 9.2 The Airius employee directory application

tion. Because we just finished developing the LDAP objects, we know we're ready to tackle this application.

Knowing that this is a one-page application, we figure that the application will have two classes: the main dispatch servlet and the directory screen. We'll call the main dispatch servlet `Directory` and the main screen `DirectoryScreen`. We will use the template we were given: `directory.html`. The initial configuration file is shown in Listing 9.1.

Listing 9.1 Configuration file for the Directory application

```
Application.Base.URL=/servlet/Directory

Default.Method=directory
Method.directory=DirectoryScreen

# Replace your path to the HTML in the following configuration file
# value.
Default.Template.Path=C:\\Book\\Chapter 09\\Example 1\\templates\\

Template.directory=directory.html

# Place the log file path here.
Log.File.Path=c:\\Book\\Chapter 09\\Example 1\\Directory.log
```

The HTML that we were given will be used as a template. We just need to put the placeholders in the proper locations. Because we want this application to be portable from development to test to production, we will place the `BASEURL` substitution parameters in the template anywhere a link is required. We also want an area where we can place messages and employee information, so we will create `message` and `employees` substitution parameters. Listing 9.2 shows the template.

Listing 9.2 The `directory.html` template

```
<html>
<head>
<title>ARIUS Directory</title>
</head>

<body bgcolor="#FFFFFF">
<h2 align="center"><b><font color="#0000FF">
ARIUS Company Directory</font></b></h2>
<hr>
<p align="center">
  <a href="${BASEURL}?method=directory&search=A">A</a>
  <a href="${BASEURL}?method=directory&search=B">B</a>
  <a href="${BASEURL}?method=directory&search=C">C</a>
  <a href="${BASEURL}?method=directory&search=D">D</a>
  <a href="${BASEURL}?method=directory&search=E">E</a>
  <a href="${BASEURL}?method=directory&search=F">F</a>
```

```
  <a href="${BASEURL}?method=directory&search=G">G</a>
  <a href="${BASEURL}?method=directory&search=H">H</a>
  <a href="${BASEURL}?method=directory&search=I">I</a>
  <a href="${BASEURL}?method=directory&search=J">J</a>
  <a href="${BASEURL}?method=directory&search=K">K</a>
  <a href="${BASEURL}?method=directory&search=L">L</a>
  <a href="${BASEURL}?method=directory&search=M">M</a>
  <a href="${BASEURL}?method=directory&search=N">N</a>
  <a href="${BASEURL}?method=directory&search=O">O</a>
  <a href="${BASEURL}?method=directory&search=P">P</a>
  <a href="${BASEURL}?method=directory&search=Q">Q</a>
  <a href="${BASEURL}?method=directory&search=R">R</a>
  <a href="${BASEURL}?method=directory&search=S">S</a>
  <a href="${BASEURL}?method=directory&search=T">T</a>
  <a href="${BASEURL}?method=directory&search=U">U</a>
  <a href="${BASEURL}?method=directory&search=V">V</a>
  <a href="${BASEURL}?method=directory&search=W">W</a>
  <a href="${BASEURL}?method=directory&search=X">X</a>
  <a href="${BASEURL}?method=directory&search=Y">Y</a>
  <a href="${BASEURL}?method=directory&search=Z">Z</a>
</p>
<hr>
<h3><font color="#0000FF">${message}</font></h3>
<p>${employees}</p>
</body>
</html>
```

Now on to development. The main dispatch servlet, `Directory`, will need to create the `LDAPConnection` pool in the `initializeApp()` method. We will choose a pool size of 5 because five connections appear to be enough to support the load. We will add this pool to the `PoolList` to keep track of, and we'll name the pool *LDAP*. Listing 9.3 shows the code for the `Directory` dispatch servlet.

Listing 9.3 The `Directory` dispatch servlet class

```
import enterprise.servlet.*;
import enterprise.common.*;
import enterprise.db.*;

import java.io.*;

public class Directory extends BaseEnterpriseServlet
{
  public String getAppName()
  {
    return "Directory";
  }

  public void initializeApp(AppContext appContext,
                            PoolObjectManager pom)  throws Exception
  {
```

```
      // Be sure to replace the directory host name of ldap.airius.com
      // and the port with your LDAP server's information.
      LDAPConnectionPool lcp = new LDAPConnectionPool(5,
                                        "ldap.airius.com",
                                        389, "o=airius.com");
      appContext.getPoolList().add("LDAP",lcp);
    }

    public void destroyApp(AppContext ac, PoolObjectManager pom)
    {
    }
  }
```

The DirectoryScreen class does all of the work for us. It looks for a search parameter on the HTML query screen. If it doesn't find one, it displays the message *Select a letter to view the employee directory* on the directory screen. If it finds a letter, it passes that letter to the getEmployees() method, which does the LDAP search and returns a StringBuffer object with the content. The class uses the template and substitutes the placeholders with the necessary content.

```
import enterprise.servlet.*;
import enterprise.html.*;
import enterprise.db.*;

import java.io.*;
import java.sql.*;
import javax.naming.*;
import javax.naming.directory.*;

public class DirectoryScreen extends HTTPMethod
{

  public void execute() throws Exception
  {
    String message = "Select a letter to view " +
                     "the employee directory.";
    String employees = "";

    PrintWriter out = m_response.getWriter();
    TemplateCacheList tcl = m_context.getTemplateCacheList();
    HTMLTemplate ht = tcl.get("directory").createHTMLTemplate();

    String searchLetter = m_request.getParameter("search");
    if ((searchLetter != null) && (
         searchLetter.trim().length() > 0))
    {
      searchLetter = searchLetter.trim().substring(0,1).
      toUpperCase();
      message = "Names Beginning With The Letter " + searchLetter;

      employees = getEmployees(searchLetter);
    }
```

```
  ht.substitute("employees", employees);
  ht.substitute("message", message);
  ht.substitute("BASEURL", m_context.getAppBaseURL());
  ht.doHTML(out);
}

String getEmployees(String letter) throws Exception
{
  StringBuffer sb = new StringBuffer();
  LDAPConnection lc =
       (LDAPConnection) m_poolObjMgr.checkOut ("LDAP");

  String attrList[] = {"sn","givenname", "telephonenumber",
                       "mail", "l", "roomnumber",
                       "facsimiletelephonenumber"};
  String sortList[] = {"sn","givenname"};
  String filter = "sn=" + letter + "*";
  lc.setSortAttr(sortList);

  boolean bFoundEmployees = false;
  NamingEnumeration ne = lc.ldapSearch(filter, attrList,
                                       "o=airius.com");
  while(ne.hasMore())
  {
    bFoundEmployees = true;
    SearchResult sr = (SearchResult) ne.next();
    Attributes attrs = (Attributes)sr.getAttributes();

    sb.append("<p>");
    sb.append("<b>");
    sb.append(getAttrValue(attrs, "sn"));
    sb.append(", ");
    sb.append(getAttrValue(attrs, "givenname") + "</b><br>\n");
    sb.append("Phone: " + getAttrValue(attrs, "telephonenumber") +
              "<br>\n");
    sb.append("Fax: " + getAttrValue(attrs,
                                "facsimiletelephonenumber") +
                                "<br>\n");
    String mail = getAttrValue(attrs, "mail");
    sb.append("EMail: <a href=\"mailto:");
    sb.append(mail);
    sb.append("\">");
    sb.append(mail);
    sb.append("</a><br>\n");
    sb.append("Location: " + getAttrValue(attrs, "l") +
              "<br>\n");
    sb.append("Room No.: " + getAttrValue(attrs, "roomnumber") +
              "<br>\n");
    sb.append("</p>\n\n");
  }

  if (!bFoundEmployees)
  {
```

```
            return "<p><b>No employees found for the letter " +
                    letter + "</b></p>";
        }

        return sb.toString();
    }

    String getAttrValue(Attributes attrs, String id) throws Exception
    {
        Attribute attr = attrs.get(id);
        if (attr == null)
          return "";

        return (String)attr.get();
    }
}
```

After coding the application, we set it up by registering the `Directory` servlet with the servlet engine and have the `ConfFile` parameter in the initialization arguments point at the `Directory.config` file. The output from the application looks exactly as shown in Figure 9.2.

Summary

LDAP is becoming one of the fastest-adopted technologies today. It has become a standard in directory services management and is an essential part of software development in accessing centralized employee information. It provides solutions for contexts ranging from work flow and and management chaining applications to single sign-on possibilities.

In this chapter we learned how to access an LDAP server with the JNDI API and the LDAP service provider. We learned how to query an LDAP server and how to modify its contents. Because accessing an LDAP server requires a physical connection, it makes sense to pool these connections. In pooling LDAP connections, we must take into consideration many of the same issues that we addressed for database connections.

Thus we developed LDAP connection management objects that help administer LDAP connections and aid the pooling mechanism to clean up these connections after we're done using them. We found that using the JNDI with the LDAP connection management objects and in a pooled framework makes development of a robust and scalable Web-based solution easy.

CHAPTER 10

Dynamic Graphics

The Internet existed many years before the World Wide Web took hold. What was it about the Web that captivated people and unleashed their imagination? What made them want to turn this government experiment into something the masses could use? It wasn't the idea of a global network; the Internet goes back to the 1960s, and the global network expanded gradually without the masses climbing aboard. It wasn't the ability to access content from any point on the planet; FTP, news, and Gopher provided access to content long before the World Wide Web (WWW). So what was new about the WWW? Quite simply, it mixed content with graphical images. In this chapter we'll talk more about the use of graphical images—particularly dynamic images—to expand the capabilities of any Web site.

"A picture's worth a thousand words," goes the old saying. The combination of text and graphics gave content producers a medium with which they could comfortably work—one that married text and images over the computer. That's when the Web took off, when companies began to realize that a whole new medium was born—a medium that had the same advantages of existing media (text and images), as well as the ability to supply content to anyone, anywhere in the world.

Nearly every Web site today provides content mixed with graphics; this is now a standard way of presenting information. Most images are used to make a site more attractive; some are used to depict statistics and other useful information in a format that is easy to read and understand. Many people think visually, so a Web site that presents a data summary in a visual format is more desirable than one that presents a data summary in text format.

Pie charts and bar charts are often used in business to summarize data—to depict the information in a way that's easy for people to understand. Web sites, particularly intranet sites, should employ images whenever their use will improve understanding. The Web site will then serve the customer better by providing content in a way that's easier to understand and use.

Unfortunately, static images are limiting; a static pie chart has to be replaced every time the data changes. Any static image that is based on dynamic data is a burden on the Web team. The team must do frequent updates to swap out the static images, or provide a collection of similar but different images and a mechanism to control their display. Unfortunately, the maintenance required with such a solution is prohibitive. It would be better to generate the images dynamically.

This chapter will provide a basic understanding of dynamic Web graphics and will cover the following topics:

- How browsers and servers handle images
- How dynamic images are created
- How images are managed in memory

How a Browser Requests Images

When users request a Web page, they assume that only one request was made to the server. The user enters a URL, and the page seems to appear almost instantly in the browser. In a typical Web page, however, the server receives multiple simultaneous requests for information. The most common type of request is a request for an image.

The user is unaware of the additional requests a browser makes while loading a page. The user doesn't really need to know what the browser is doing, so the browser does all the work behind the scenes. The browser performs the following steps:

1. It requests the page from the server.
2. It parses the page, searching for requests for different components, such as images, JavaScript files, Cascading Style Sheets, and so on. The browser issues a request for each component needed to fully render the page.
3. It renders the finished page after all JavaScript files and Cascading Style Sheets have been received, but often before all images have been received because images are typically much larger than the text portions of the page and take longer to load. In addition, JavaScript files and Cascading Style Sheets are required for proper rendering of the textual content of the page and for proper execution of any JavaScript on the page.

Listing 10.1 shows the code for a simple HTML page that displays two images. The browser requests the HTML page, parses it and finds references to images/bg.jpg, images/first_image.jpg, and images/another_image.jpg. The browser issues a separate request to the server for each image and then renders the page, thus ensuring that the user can start reading the content while waiting for the images to load.

Listing 10.1 A simple HTML page

```
1.      <html>
2.
3.      <body background="images/bg.jpg">
4.
5.      <table>
6.        <tr>
7.          <td><img src="images/first_image.jpg">
8.        </tr>
9.        <tr>
10.         <td> </td>
11.       </tr>
12.       <tr>
13.         <td><img src="images/another_image.jpg">
14.       </tr>
15.     </table>
16.
17.     </body>
18.     </html>
```

The HTML page in Listing 10.1 requires four separate requests: one for the HTML page, and three more for the images on the page. The browser issues a GET request to the server for each file and waits for the content to be returned. The browser knows what kind of content it's requesting (text, images, multimedia files, and so on) and will render it accordingly or send the data to another program for processing.

The browser requests the file from the server and receives back a stream of data. It doesn't know if the data originated from a static file on the server or if the server is generating the image dynamically, nor does it care. The browser simply makes the request so that it can render the page properly and then handles the returned data appropriately. The server sends back a header with each file—to describe the format of the file, the length, the date the file was last altered, and other file characteristics.

On line 7 in Listing 10.1, the reference doesn't have to be for a static image on the server. It could be written as a request to a servlet for image data, provided that the servlet also set the header information properly. We could rewrite line 7 like so:

```
<td><img src="/servlet/DynamicImageServlet">
```

The servlet, called `DynamicImageServlet`, on the server would have to return image data and a properly formatted header for the page to render correctly. Notice that in this URL we didn't specify a file type or the name of an image on the server; we're expecting the servlet to return image data. In this way we can create a servlet that returns dynamic images that we create on the fly. However, before we go into detail about how to return images from a servlet, let's take a closer look at browser and server communication.

Handling Image Types

When the browser requests an image, it's requesting a file; it has no idea about what type of image is going to be returned. Even though the extension of the file may be *.gif* or *.jpg,* the browser doesn't assume the type. So how does the browser know how to display the image and what type of image to return? The server returns a header with a content-type statement along with other information before sending the actual image data. In the HTML of Listing 10.1, one file requested by the browser is `/images/bg.jpg`. Even though the browser is requesting a background type of image, it has absolutely no idea what type of file it is requesting. The file could be another HTML document, a word document, or an Adobe Acrobat (PDF) file. Let's take a look at the request the browser makes when it requests this file.

Listing 10.2 shows the communication the browser makes to the server to request the image. Although each of the lines has a certain significance, line 1 is the actual request for the file on the server. The HTML file tells the browser to retrieve a file located at `/images/bg.jpg` when it parses the data. Line 1 shows the `GET` command that is directed to the server.

Listing 10.2 A browser's request

```
1.     GET /images/bg.jpg HTTP/1.0
2.     If-Modified-Since: Mon, 16 Aug 1999 17:18:15 GMT;
3.        length=1845
4.     Proxy-Connection: Keep-Alive
5.     User-Agent: Mozilla/4.7 [en] (WinNT; U)
6.     Pragma: no-cache
7.     Host: localhost
8.     Accept: image/gif, image/x-xbitmap, image/jpeg,
9.        image/pjpeg, image/png, */*
10.    Accept-Encoding: gzip
11.    Accept-Language: en,pdf
12.    Accept-Charset: iso-8859-1,*,utf-8
```

In Listing 10.3 we show the server's response—minus the image data. The response contains the normal HTTP header information from a server response. Line 8 is where the server tells the browser what kind of file type is being returned.

Listing 10.3 A server's response

```
1.     HTTP/1.1 200 OK
2.     Date: Sat, 05 Feb 2000 23:37:41 GMT
3.     Server: Apache/1.3.6 (Unix)
4.     Last-Modified: Mon, 16 Aug 1999 17:18:15 GMT
5.     Accept-Ranges: bytes
6.     Content-Length: 5595
7.     Connection: close
8.     Content-Type: image/jpeg
9.
10.    <Image data will go here…>
```

Most browsers allow the user to set up an application according to MIME type. The MIME type is a standard encoding that allows programs to exchange data over the Internet and notify each other of the type of data that is passed along a stream. When an application receives a stream, it is typically notified of the MIME type and the data to follow. Browsers are no exception.

In Listing 10.3 the server responds with `image/jpeg` on line 8, which tells the browser that the data that follows will be of a JPEG type. When the browser receives this request, it looks up the `image/jpeg` MIME type in its internal application/MIME reference list. Normally the browser handles images internally, and the browser uses itself to display the image. After retrieving the image type and data, the browser attempts to display the data through one of its internal programs or external viewer, depending on its application setup.

Dynamic Images

Now that you know how a browser requests an image, note that the browser does not know what type of image is being requested. So the browser doesn't have to request a static image on the server; it could be simply a reference to a URL that will return image data. In the next example we will build a servlet that will draw a JPEG image on the fly and return the image to the browser.

Let's start by talking about the graphics engine. In Java 2.0 (version 1.2.x) and later versions, Sun included the Java 2D package with the standard Java implementation. In particular, Sun included an engine that can generate, encode, and decode JPEG graphics. This engine is extremely fast and very easy to use, so we will use it to produce dynamic JPEG images.

Although GIF files are used heavily on the Internet for Web graphics, GIF is a copyrighted image type that is owned by CompuServe. That's why it is difficult to find GIF-rendering engines. There are a few good freeware, pure Java implementations of GIF encoders on the Internet that were written by independent developers. One such engine is a GIF-rendering API that can be found at `www.acme.com`. However, in an effort to keep this chapter simple, we will use the Sun version for the following reasons:

- It is an open implementation that is included in nearly all Java 2.0 distributions.
- Sun built a solid native interface underneath the JPEG engine, which increases the speed of rendering.
- We don't want to upset the folks at CompuServe. For those developers who wish to use one of the freeware engines or write their own, the concepts presented can be applied to almost any type of rendering engine.

NOTE: For those users who wish to generate dynamic graphics on a UNIX/X Windows–based platform, there are some very important considerations to keep in mind. The Java graphics engine requires an available X session to render images. Therefore, you will need to start your server from an X session. You may have difficulty making an X session available to your application at all times. However, a program called Xvfb (X virtual frame buffer) allows you to have an "invisible" X session running in the background and fakes the Java engine into believing that it is being run in a normal X session. This program can be found on various sites on the Internet. Xvfb should be run in the background before you execute your Web server or Java VM.

Creating a dynamic image in a servlet is fairly straightforward and is accomplished in the following five simple steps:

1. Create a `java.awt.image.BufferedImage` object as the image memory area.
2. Implement the proper drawing functions on the `BufferedImage` object.
3. Set the image quality.
4. Encode the image in JPEG format.
5. Send the JPEG image to the output stream.

The steps in creating an image are quite simple; the complexity lies in what you do with the image. How complex do you want the image to be? Will the image be a simple bar graph, or will you need to implement 3D-to-2D conversion functions to create a three-dimensional pie or point graph? We'll keep things simple in our example so that you get the basic idea.

We are going to focus solely on the basics of creating an image from a servlet. We will use a simple servlet rather than `BaseEnterpriseServlet` to do this. In a later example we'll use `BaseEnterpriseServlet` and configuration files to control and generate a dynamic image. For this example, however, we will keep things as simple as possible. We'll display an HTML page that includes a graphic that is actually a call to the image-generating servlet.

The goal with this example will be to return a circle image to a browser, as shown in Figure 10.1. Because the goal is to draw a circle, let's call the servlet *DrawCircle*. We will begin with a quick view of the HTML code. Note that in line 10 of Listing 10.4 we have an image tag that references the servlet rather than a static image on a Web server. Where normally we might use `<IMG SRC="/images/circle.jpg">` to reference a static image on the Web server, in this case we use `<IMG SRC="/servlet/DrawCircle">` to call a servlet that will return a JPEG image.

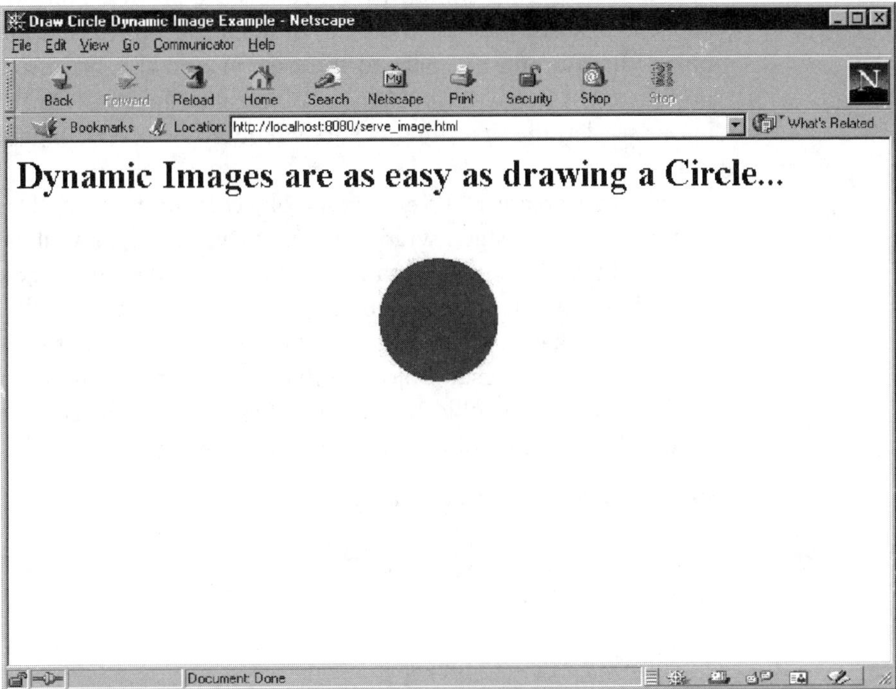

Figure 10.1 Dynamic circle image

Listing 10.4 Image request page (`serve_image.html`)

```
1.     <HTML>
2.     <HEAD>
3.     <TITLE>Draw Circle Dynamic Image Example</TITLE>
4.     </HEAD>
5.     <BODY BGCOLOR="#FFFFFF">
6.     <H1>Dynamic Images are as easy as drawing a Circle...</H1>
7.
8.     <BR><BR>
9.     <CENTER>
10.    <IMG SRC="/servlet/DrawCircle">
11.
12.    </BODY>
13.    </HTML>
```

When the Web browser parses the HTML page in Listing 10.4, it will make a call to the servlet when it is ready to load the image. Keep in mind that you may need to change the link on line 10 to point at the servlet you develop. Remember, not all engines require the text */servlet* in a servlet call.

Now for the servlet. Let's look at each of the five steps in creating the image. Listing 10.5 contains the `DrawCircle` servlet. Note that we are using the `getOutputStream()` call instead of the `getPrintWriter()` method to get the object that outputs the data to the user. We do this because the JPEG engine prefers to use a raw `OutputStream` object instead of a `PrintWriter` object. So in our servlet, the first thing we do is request the servlet engine's `OutputStream` object.

Next we create a `BufferedImage` object from the Java 2D graphics package and declare the image's width and height in pixels, as well as the image type, which will be RGB (red-green-blue). We use a `BufferedImage` object instead of a standard AWT `Image` object because, once again, the Java JPEG engine prefers this type of image in its rendering. Once we have created the object, we request a `java.awt.Graphics2D` object so that we may perform drawing functions on the `BufferedImage` object. With the `Graphics2D` object, we clear the background by filling it with white and then drawing a blue circle.

Listing 10.5 The `DrawCircle` servlet

```
import javax.servlet.*;
import javax.servlet.http.*;
import java.io.*;

import java.awt.*;
import java.awt.image.*;
import com.sun.image.codec.jpeg.*;

public class DrawCircle extends HttpServlet
{
```

```
  public static final int TOP      = 0;
  public static final int LEFT     = 0;
  public static final int WIDTH    = 100;
  public static final int HEIGHT   = 100;

  public void service(HttpServletRequest req,
                      HttpServletResponse res)
       throws ServletException
  {

    try
    {
      // Get the output stream.
      OutputStream out = res.getOutputStream();

      // Create an image object.
      BufferedImage bi = new BufferedImage(WIDTH, HEIGHT,
                                 BufferedImage.TYPE_INT_RGB);

      // Get a graphics object.
      Graphics2D g = bi.createGraphics();

      // Clear the background.
      g.setColor(Color.white);
      g.fillRect(TOP, LEFT, WIDTH, HEIGHT);
      g.setColor(Color.blue);
      g.fillOval(TOP, LEFT, WIDTH, HEIGHT);
      g.dispose();

      // Set the MIME type.
      res.setContentType("image/jpeg");

      // Convert the image to a JPEG image.
      JPEGImageEncoder jpg = JPEGCodec.createJPEGEncoder(out);
      JPEGEncodeParam param = jpg.getDefaultJPEGEncodeParam(bi);
      param.setQuality(.75f,true);
      jpg.encode(bi, param);

      // Send out the JPEG image.
      out.close();

    } catch (IOException ioe)
    {

      System.out.println("An error occurred");
      ioe.printStackTrace();

    }
  }
}
```

Now we are ready to convert the `BufferedImage` object to a JPEG image and send it out to the user. Before doing this, we need to declare the MIME type so that when the browser receives the stream, it knows it is an image and it knows how to display the image. The MIME type for a JPEG image is `image/jpeg`, and we set this type with the `setContentType()` method. We begin converting the `BufferedImage` object to a JPEG image by using the `com.sun.image.codec.jpeg` package and creating a `JPEGImageEncoder` object. This object is stream based, so when we create it we pass in the stream to which we want the JPEG image to flow. In this case we pass in the `OutputStream` object that we retrieved with the `getOutputStream()` call in the beginning of the servlet.

We also need to define the parameters indicating how we want the JPEG image to be created. We can set many kinds of parameters, but image quality and compression are our biggest concerns. We retrieve a `JPEGEncodeParam` object from `JPEGImageEncoder` by calling the `getDefaultJPEGEncodeParam()` method with `BufferedImage` as a parameter. From the `JPEGEncodeParam` object we can set the quality to .75, a high value. (Quality values range from .01, lowest quality, to 1.0, perfect quality.) Remember that JPEG is a lossy compression image-rendering scheme, so the lower the quality, the more of the image is lost and the more its rendering is degraded. There is a tradeoff between image size (bytes) and quality. The higher the quality, the bigger the file. You may experiment with these values to find the right balance between size and quality.

Finally, we do the actual encoding of the image. We call the `encode()` method of the `JPEGImageEncoder` object. We pass in the `BufferedImage` and `JPEGEncodeParam` objects to the method. Calling this method encodes and sends the JPEG image out to the `OutputStream` object. Because the data can be large, we also want to close the `OutputStream` object to flush the buffer so that the entire image is sent to the end user.

That was very simple. An image was created dynamically in only a few lines of code. Of course, the more complex the image, the more drawing functions will be called with the `Graphics2D` object. But conceptually, dynamic image creation can be done in just a few lines of code. When running this example, be sure that the image servlet is properly coded in the HTML (i.e., remember that different servlet engines have different base URLs for servlets), and be sure you load the HTML directly from an HTTP URL call to the servlet engine, and not from the file system. This will simulate a Web call from the client, and you won't have problems finding your image servlet from a relative URL in the HTML.

Memory Management

The previous example showed how simple it is to create a dynamic image. We also learned that it really is *that* simple to generate on-the-fly graphics. This is true; it is simple to create dynamic content. But there definitely are some gotchas to consider. In the example you may have noticed that it took a second or two or three, maybe even five, depending on the machine, for the image to be drawn on the browser's screen. What took so much time? You would probably guess that it was the drawing of the image and the image rendering, but that's not even close. The drawing routines are memory based and are very fast. The image encoding that Sun includes for the JPEG library consists of typically native calls, which are also very fast. So where did all that time go in calling the servlet? It went to the creation of the `BufferedImage` object.

Each time the `DrawCircle` servlet is called, it creates a 100×100, or 10K, data area, along with the additional memory needed for color and overhead of managing the `BufferedImage` object. But this isn't the bad news. The bad news is that Java needs to clean up all this memory and return it to the heap. That's where garbage collection becomes a factor. If you were to take this servlet in its current form and use it on a high-traffic Web site, after a while the Java garbage collector would clean up the unused objects, and you might very well bring a Sun E450 quad processor with 1GB of RAM to its knees. It wouldn't cause the machine to crash, but it might very well slow the machine to a crawl while Java used all of its CPU resources to clean up the heavily fragmented memory.

Creating Objects Is Your Worst Enemy

The goal in writing server-based code is to keep from creating and destroying objects. In our beginning Java courses we were told not to continually create and concatenate strings. We were told to use the `StringBuffer` object and use the `append()` method to add or create a large string, and then call the `toSting()` method when we needed to convert it to a `String` object.

We did this because the `StringBuffer` object blocked out a memory area and we could manipulate the `String` data all we wanted, yet the `String` object was created only once because we wanted to prevent the garbage collector from becoming inundated with objects to clean up. This concept is more important in a server environment, where potentially many objects can be created in a short period of time. The concept becomes even more critical when we are dealing with fairly large memory objects, such as `BufferedImage` objects.

Pooling Memory Buffers

With server-side Java development, when we work with objects we want to create them once and never destroy them. This is especially true with large objects. We essentially need to recycle memory. How do we do this? We use the `Pool` object that we introduced in Chapter 7.

Case Study

Company A was merging with company B, and the employee base was going to grow from 12,000 to 77,000 employees. Company A was on a mission-critical development schedule to create a building-mapping application to use in conjunction with its directory services. This application was needed so that employees could not only look up contact information for other employees, but also be able to pinpoint a person's office within a specific building. The development team had 30 days to develop this application, and it was to be released on day one of the merger. The team was working 12 hours a day along with the graphics designer to load all the buildings and floors in the application. Under development, the application ran relatively well. Although there was some delay in graphics generation, the development server seemed to be generating the maps in a reasonable amount of time.

A week before the deadline, the application went to QA for testing with capacity stressing. To the developers' surprise, the test servers failed and the image generation took too long to be considered acceptable. The development team profiled the code and found that the brunt of the time was being consumed in creating the memory for the images on each call, and that the garbage collector was being kept very busy creating and destroying all of these memory areas.

The development team developed a reusable image pool that allowed the images to be recycled through each request for an image. They implemented the pooling code in the application and saw the image-rendering speed increase substantially. When the application was delivered for testing, the images continued to display rapidly, and the application ran as it was originally intended. The application was installed on day one of the merger and was able to run with a high degree of reliability and speed, with hundreds of thousands of images created each day.

We want to create a pool of reusable memory objects that we can check out to generate graphics and check back in after sending the graphics stream to the user. To be more specific, we use the `Pool` object to create a pool of `BufferedImage` objects. Let's build this pool and see how it fits in the enterprise servlet architecture. We will start by creating a `BufferedImage` pool and call the object `ImagePool`. Because we will use this pool in an example, we will have it contain a pool of BufferedImage objects with a height of 400 pixels and a width of 400 pixels, and we will stamp each object with an identification number so that we may watch the pool in action in the example.

```
import enterprise.common.*;

import java.awt.*;
import java.awt.image.*;
import java.awt.geom.*;

public class ImagePool extends Pool
{

  private static final int WIDTH = 400;
  private static final int HEIGHT = 400;
  private static int counter = 0;
```

We declare the width and the height as constants, and we create a static counter that we will use as the unique identifier for each pooled object. Each time we create a pool object, we will draw the incremented counter number at the bottom of the image so that it will display its ID. The constructor will be the usual pool constructor and will call the superclass with the size so that the pool will be initialized and created.

```
  public ImagePool(int maxSize)
      throws Exception
  {
    super(maxSize);
  }
```

The createObject() method, which is required by all pools, will create the BufferedImage object, clear the background, get the unique identifier from the counter, and draw the unique ID on the bottom of the image.

```
  public Object createObject() throws Exception
  {
    BufferedImage bi = new BufferedImage(WIDTH, HEIGHT,
                                  BufferedImage.TYPE_INT_RGB);
    Graphics2D g = bi.createGraphics();

    // Clear the background.
    g.setColor(Color.white);
    g.fillRect(0, 0, WIDTH, HEIGHT);
    g.setColor(Color.blue);
    g.drawString("Image Pool Object " + (++counter), 5, HEIGHT-5);
    g.dispose();

    return bi;
  }
```

We will create a beforeCheckin() method, which is an optionally overridden method for Pool objects. We want to clean up the object before we release it back to the pool. That is, we want to clear the background but leave the identifier at the bottom of the image, thus providing a clean image before others use the BufferedImage object.

```
  public void beforeCheckin(Object o)
  {
    BufferedImage bi = (BufferedImage) o;

    Graphics2D g = bi.createGraphics();

    // Clear the background, but leave the text at the bottom.
    g.setColor(Color.white);
    g.fillRect(0, 0, WIDTH, HEIGHT - 20);

  }

}
```

That's all there is to the ImagePool object. We will let the enterprise servlet architecture manage the pool, and all we have left to do is draw on the images as we use them. Let's create an example that uses this new ImagePool object with enterprise servlets.

Random Pie Chart Example

In this example we will create an application that randomizes the slice of a pie chart and displays this pie chart to the user. It will not only be responsible for creating the image, but we will use the template engine to have it produce the HTML as well. Our goal in this example is to show how to use a pool of images (the ImagePool object) in dynamic image creation and to show that reusing the memory areas speeds up the cycle time associated with rendering the image. We will also draw some complex information on the image to show that the drawing functions are incredibly fast. So let's not create a simple pie chart. Let's create a three-dimensional pie chart. The output will look like Figure 10.2.

The application will be made up of three classes: the dispatch servlet, a class to render the image, and a class to generate the HTML. We will call this application *ImagePoolExample,* and to remain consistent, we will give the dispatch servlet the same name. We will call the HTML generator ImageHTML, and the pie chart image renderer PieChart. We will also create a template named imagehtml.html that will be used by the ImageHTML class when generating the HTML for the output.

Let's start with the configuration file, which is shown in Listing 10.6. We will attach the dispatch method html to the ImageHTML class and the method

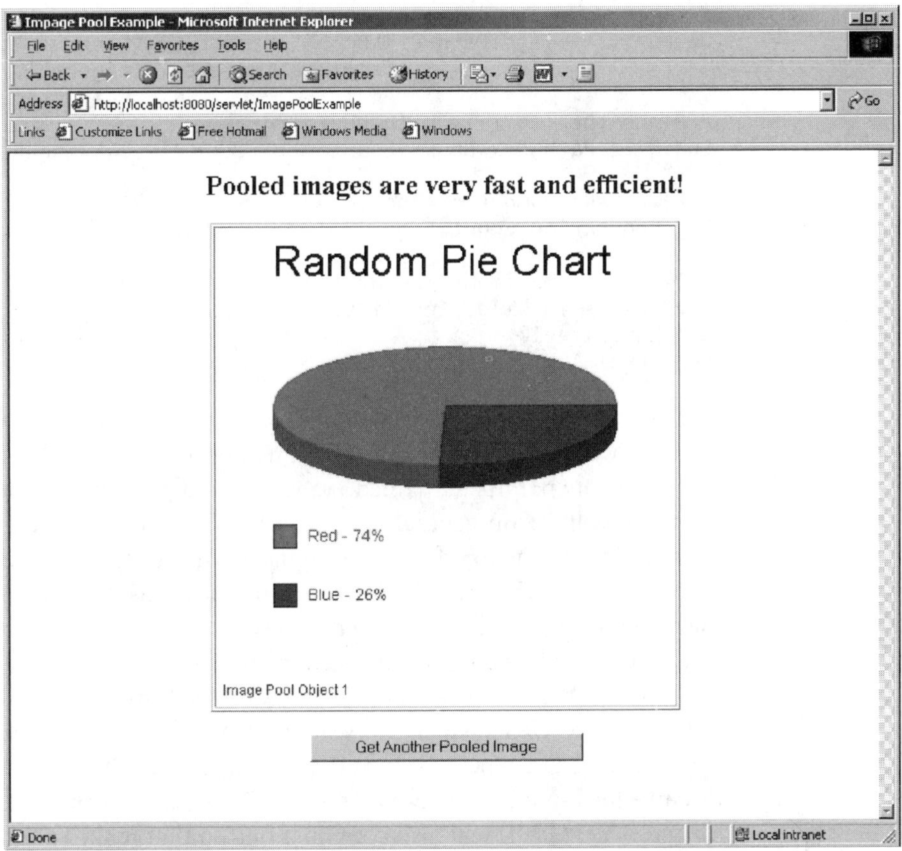

Figure 10.2 Random pie chart output using an image pool

piechart to the PieChart class. Because typically we want to generate the HTML before the image, we will want to dispatch to the ImageHTML class first. For this reason we will make the default method html. We want to generate the HTML first so that it can embed the image in a nice layout, such as the one in Figure 10.2. If we don't do this, the browser will show just the image, as if we were viewing a JPEG image without the HTML.

Listing 10.6 Configuration file for the pie chart application

```
# Configuration file
Default.Method=html
Method.html=ImageHTML
Method.piechart=PieChart

# Place the application's base URL here.
Application.Base.URL=/servlet/ImagePoolExample
```

```
# Place your template location here.
Default.Template.Path=c:\\Book\\Chapter 10\\Example 2\\templates\\
                        Template.imagehtml=imagehtml.html

# Place the log file path here.
Log.File.Path=c:\\Book\\Chapter 10\\Example 2\\ImagePool.log

# Place the number of log generation files you want here.
Log.Generation.Count=5

# Place the maximum size of the log file here.
# Value is in kilobytes (i.e., 10 = 10K).
Log.Max.Size=10
Log.Level=ALL
```

We will set up the default template path. (This isn't necessary in this case because we are using only one template, but it's a good habit.) We will also set up a template parameter named `imagehtml` and point it at the template. In addition, we will set up general logging. Again, although logging is probably not terribly important for this small application, setting up these parameters is a good habit for when we develop larger applications. Logging is a good thing to have in any application because it is very handy for trying to see why an application is not producing the expected results.

Now let's develop the HTML template (see Listing 10.7). This template will take the base URL, which we will substitute from the application base URL that we stored in `AppContext`, and dispatch a call to the `PieChart` class. The call is embedded in an `<IMAGE>` tag, so the browser thinks that it is going to get an image. The HTML will also contain a button that makes a call to the `html` dispatch method, which reexecutes the HTML and image so that we get a new random pie chart.

Listing 10.7 The `PieChart` template, `imagehtml.html`

```
<html>
<head>
<title>Impage Pool Example</title>
</head>

<body bgcolor="#FFFFFF">
<center>
<h2>Pooled images are very fast and efficient!</h2>
<table border="1">
  <tr>
    <td><img src="${BASEURL}?method=piechart" width="400"
    height="400">
</td>
  </tr>
</table>
<form method="post" action="">
```

```
  <input type="button" name="Button"
         value="Get Another Pooled Image"
         onClick="document.location='${BASEURL}'">
</form>
<center>
</body>
</html>
```

Now that we have the configuration file and template, we are ready to develop the application. We'll start with the `ImagePoolExample` dispatch servlet and create the required methods. The `getAppName()` method will return the application's name, *ImagePoolExample*. The `destroyApp()` method has nothing to do, so we will just create a stub here. However, the `initializeApp()` method will have a job to do. It needs to create the `ImagePool` object and register the pool with `PoolList` so that it can be managed by the object `PoolObjectManager`.

In this example we will create a pool of five objects. As a design recommendation, the number of pool objects to create is a good candidate for a configuration file custom parameter, so that we may increase the pool for scalability purposes without having to recompile. But in this example we will just hard-code five objects in the `initializeApp()` method. The base dispatch servlet is shown in Listing 10.8.

Listing 10.8 The `ImagePoolExample` main dispatch servlet

```
import javax.servlet.*;

import enterprise.common.*;
import enterprise.servlet.*;

public class ImagePoolExample extends BaseEnterpriseServlet
{

  public String getAppName()
  {
    return "ImagePoolExample";
  }

  public void initializeApp(AppContext appContext,
                            PoolObjectManager pom) throws Exception
  {
    ImagePool ip = new ImagePool(5);
    appContext.getPoolList().add("IMAGE", ip);
  }

  public void destroyApp(AppContext ac, PoolObjectManager pom)
  {
  }

}
```

The ImageHTML class does nothing more than loading the template from the template cache, creating template objects, replacing the base URL in the template, and spitting out the HTML to the end user. Why are we creating an HTML generator instead of just creating an HTML page that is accessed through the Web server? The answer lies in the substitution call. The base URL is the answer.

Although we could have easily created a static HTML page that is accessed through the Web server, our HTML contains a call to a servlet, and it is better to allow us to change the application base URL for portability purposes. In the previous example you may have had to change the link in the static HTML so that the example would work with your servlet engine. As a general rule of thumb, anytime there is a link to a servlet, the HTML should be coded as a template and BASEURL as a substitution parameter. This will ensure that the application can be made portable by a change to a single configuration file parameter (Application.Base.URL). Listing 10.9 shows the ImageHTML HTML-rendering class.

Listing 10.9 The ImageHTML HTML-rendering class

```
import enterprise.common.*;
import enterprise.html.*;
import enterprise.servlet.*;

import java.io.*;

public class ImageHTML extends HTTPMethod
{
  public void execute()
  {
    try
    {
      PrintWriter out = m_response.getWriter();

      TemplateCacheList tcl = m_context.getTemplateCacheList();
      HTMLTemplate ht = tcl.get("imagehtml").createHTMLTemplate();

      ht.substitute("BASEURL", m_context.getAppBaseURL());
      ht.doHTML(out);

    } catch (Exception e)
    {
      e.printStackTrace();
    }
  }
}
```

For the code that is the meat of the application, we will develop the PieChart class. This class is responsible for dynamically generating the pie chart. As stated earlier, we will develop a three-dimensional depiction of a pie chart with a single slice whose size is randomly predetermined. Instead of showing this code as one large piece of source, let's go through the class step by step so that you can clearly see what it's doing. We will start by declaring the class and some constants that are used within the code.

```
import enterprise.common.*;
import enterprise.html.*;
import enterprise.servlet.*;

import java.io.*;
import java.util.*;
import java.net.*;
import java.awt.*;
import java.awt.image.*;
import java.awt.geom.*;
import javax.servlet.http.*;
import com.sun.image.codec.jpeg.*;

public class PieChart extends HTTPMethod
{
```

We will create a couple of fonts for drawing text on an image. We want to draw a title and a legend. The title is usually larger than the other text, so we will create a big font for the title and a small font for the legend.

```
  public static final Font bigFont =
                              new Font("SanSerif",Font.PLAIN, 36);
  public static final Font smallFont =
                              new Font("SanSerif",Font.PLAIN, 14);
```

We will also declare some colors to use in the pie chart. We will use red and blue as the slice and the pie colors, respectively, but we need to use slightly darker colors for the pie's sides to create the three-dimensional effect.

```
  public static final Color red = Color.red;
  public static final Color darkerRed = red.darker();
  public static final Color blue = Color.blue;
  public static final Color darkerBlue = blue.darker();
```

The `execute()` method is where the image-streaming code will go. The first thing we do is retrieve the `OutputStream` object from the servlet. Then we request that a `BufferedImage` object be checked out from the `ImagePool` object through `PoolObjectManager`. From the image buffer we can retrieve the `Graphics2D` object from which we will be able to draw on the `BufferedImage` object.

```
public void execute()
{
  OutputStream out = null;

  try
  {
    out = m_response.getOutputStream();

    BufferedImage destImg =
              (BufferedImage)m_poolObjMgr.checkOut("IMAGE");

    // Get the graphics object.
    Graphics2D g = destImg.createGraphics();
```

Our drawing begins with creating the title *Random Pie Chart* above the image. This title uses the large font, and we want it to be black.

```
    // Draw the title.
    g.setFont(bigFont);
    g.setColor(Color.black);
    g.drawString("Random Pie Chart",50,40);
```

Next we will randomize the arc angle. Because there are 360° in a circle (the pie chart is basically a circle), we retrieve a random number between 0 and 359. We determine the arc of the rest of the pie chart by taking the random arc value and subtracting it from 360.

```
    // Get the random angles for the PieChart object.
    int arcAngle = (int) (Math.random() * 360);
    int restAngle = 360 - arcAngle;
```

When we draw the pie chart, we want it to be three-dimensional. Therefore, we want to give it some perspective. We want to view the pie chart at an angle, and we want it to have some height. To give the pie chart the effect of viewing it at an angle, we draw a flattened circle, or oval. To give it height, we draw it 20 times and move up a pixel each time we draw it. We use the darker colors for the first 19 times we draw the chart to add depth and shadow to the sides of the pie chart. When we draw the twentieth pie chart, we use the normal red and blue. Putting all of these images together renders a three-dimensional pie chart.

```
    // Draw the pie chart.
    for (int i = 120; i >= 100; i--)
    {

      if (i > 100)
        g.setColor(darkerRed);
      else
        g.setColor(red);
```

```
    // Draw the slice.
    g.fillArc(50, i, 300, 100, 0, arcAngle);

    if (i > 100)
      g.setColor(darkerBlue);
    else
      g.setColor(blue);

    // Draw the rest of the pie chart.
    g.fillArc(50, i,300,100, arcAngle, restAngle);
  }
```

Now we need to draw the legend. We will draw a red and a blue box and place text next to each color that depicts the percentage of the pie chart that the red and the blue, respectively, comprise.

```
// Draw the legend.
g.setFont(smallFont);
int redPercent = (int)(((float)arcAngle/360)*100);
int bluePercent = 100 - redPercent;
g.setColor(Color.red);
g.fillRect(50,250,20,20);
g.drawString("Red - " + redPercent + "%", 80, 265);
g.setColor(Color.black);
g.drawRect(50,250,20,20);
g.setColor(Color.blue);
g.fillRect(50,300,20,20);
g.drawString("Blue - " + bluePercent + "%", 80, 315);
g.setColor(Color.black);
g.drawRect(50,300,20,20);

// Free up the graphics objects.
g.dispose();
```

Now we are ready to encode and render the image into JPEG format. We do exactly as we did in the previous example in creating a JPEG image. First we want to set the MIME type for a JPEG image so that the browser knows the kind of data it will be receiving. We then declare the `JPEGImageEncoder` and `JPEGEncodeParam` objects to set the quality of the image. Finally we encode the JPEG image and send it out to the user.

```
m_response.setContentType("image/jpeg");

// Convert the image to JPEG format.
JPEGImageEncoder jpg = JPEGCodec.createJPEGEncoder(out);
JPEGEncodeParam param =
    jpg.getDefaultJPEGEncodeParam(destImg);
param.setQuality(1.0f,false);
jpg.encode(destImg, param);
```

```
        // Send out the JPEG image.
        out.close();

      }
      catch(Exception exp)
      {
```

Here's where logging becomes especially important. When we create an image, telling the user that an error has occurred is difficult. If an exception occurs, we cannot just send back a page saying, *An error has occurred. Please contact the system administrator.* Remember that the browser is expecting an image. If we send back text, the browser will just consider the image invalid and display either nothing or an error icon. If we get some form of an error, we need to log it so that if we get a complaint, we can check the log to see what may have occurred.

```
        m_context.logError(exp);
      }
    }
  }
```

As you may have noted, we did not check the `BufferedImage` object back in. Since `PoolObjectManager` takes care of this in `BaseEnterpriseServlet`, and this is automatically done for us. When this class has finished executing, `BaseEnterpriseServlet` regains control and `PoolObjectManager` cleans up and checks in any objects that have been checked out from the pool, making them available for the next request.

Now that we have coded the application, let's set it up and execute it. Register the servlet with the servlet engine and set the `initArgs` parameter to contain a `ConfFile=<path to our ImagePoolExample.config file>` parameter so that the servlet can load the configuration file. After executing the servlet engine, you should be able to direct your browser to the servlet `ImagePoolExample`. The output on your browser should look similar to Figure 10.2.

Press the **Get Another Pooled Image** button, and you will be shown another pie chart—most likely different from the previous one. Notice that each time you press the button, the text that identifies the image buffer changes at the bottom of the image. This text tells you which buffered image you are using. You may wish to have a friend or two try your servlet at the same time that you are using it to make sure that the image objects are distributed in a round-robin fashion. Also note the increase in speed of image rendering. The image returns almost right away. By using an image pool, we have streamlined the dynamic image-rendering process.

Summary

In this chapter we learned about the fundamentals of dynamic image creation. Dynamic image generation is an important concept, especially in the enterprise. As the Web becomes more competitive, a dynamic Web experience is important, in large part because users expect it. Executives expect to see graphical images of their data in real time when running analysis reports. They expect to be wowed and dazzled. It's clear, then, that images make a powerful impact on our Web experience.

We learned about how the browser and server communicate with each other when images are requested, and how we can fake the browser into believing it is requesting an image file when it is actually requesting a servlet. We saw that Sun includes a powerful JPEG rendering engine with the Java 2 SDK and that in our code, dynamic image creation is a five-step process:

1. Create a `BufferedImage` object as the image memory area.
2. Implement the proper drawing functions on the `BufferedImage` object.
3. Set the image quality.
4. Encode the image in JPEG format.
5. Send the JPEG image to the output stream.

When we work with images, however, we are also potentially working with a large amount of memory. Creation and destruction of the memory can slow down an application and keep the garbage collector busy, thereby making the application inefficient and slow. By implementing a pool of `BufferedImage` objects, we can reuse the memory and recycle the objects, thereby streamlining the application and providing for very rapid dynamic image rendering. Implementing some of the concepts exhibited in this chapter should put you well on your way to delivering robust and media-rich dynamic content in your applications.

CHAPTER 11

Using JSP with Enterprise Servlets

In today's corporate environment we encounter many different methodologies, technologies, and development tactics. The choice of technologies affects not only the languages we use to develop applications but also the subtechnologies within a particular language. A case in point is the debate over JavaServer Pages (JSP) versus servlets. Some corporations that implement Java server-side technologies choose to do Web development in JSP or servlets. Some choose to take a hybrid approach by using both technologies but have a preference or methodology for deciding when to use a JSP and when to use a servlet.

This hot topic is the subject of a great amount of debate in the Java technical arena. Zealots from both sides claim that JSPs or servlets are better. Each side has its own approach and claims its own set of advantages and disadvantages. Whatever the case, both are viable technologies with a common base: Java.

Whether you choose to develop your applications in JSP or servlets is a personal choice, but when you choose the hybrid approach, it is important to understand how to make servlets and JSPs work well together. This chapter will show how to integrate JSPs with the enterprise servlet techniques that have been discussed throughout this book, including how to use the JavaServer Pages tag library to bridge the communication between JSPs and enterprise servlets.

Is There a Preference?

Are servlets a better technology than JSP? Is it easier to code Web pages with JSP than with servlets? This is the basis of one of the most heated controversies in the Java industry. The title of this book would probably lead you think that I prefer servlets over JSP, but that is not entirely true. JSP and servlets have their own advantages, and the choice of when to use one technology over the other is a personal decision. It is reasonable to develop an entire application in JSPs. It is equally reasonable to develop an entire application in servlets with templates. It is also reasonable to write an application using both technologies. Which is easier? Which is better to maintain? These questions are completely up to the developer and the development methodologies implemented.

For example, it is simple to have a project written in JSPs yet riddled with scriptlet code, which makes the JSPs very difficult to maintain. It is just as simple to write a servlet application with embedded `println()` commands to produce HTML, and such an application is just as difficult to maintain. The methodology and implementation of development strategies are what determine if an application is maintainable—whether written in JSP or in servlets. Developing an application so that it can be maintained and understood should be the primary focus.

Although I do not have a preference for one technology over the other, I do have a methodology for integrating these technologies within an application:

- If there is more HTML than Java code in its presentation, write the page as a JSP.
- If there is more Java code than HTML code in its presentation, write the page as a servlet.
- When writing a JSP, use as little scriptlet code as possible to make the page easily maintainable by nonprogrammers. Emphasize the use of JavaBeans, custom tags, and a tag library for any heavy coding.
- When writing a servlet, use templates to make the pages easily maintainable by nonprogrammers.

That's it! That is my methodology. As long as you have a methodology that works for you, integrating JSPs with servlets will yield a powerful and easily maintainable application.

JSPs with Servlets

Because integrating servlets and JSPs in an application is quickly becoming a common method of developing server-side applications (not to mention Enterprise JavaBeans, and so on), understanding how JSPs and servlets interact is critical. Taking a step back, we need to examine on a broader scale how JSP works.

Is JSP a scripting language? *JavaServer Pages* is really an extension of servlet technology. A JSP is a conglomeration of scriptlet code, declarations, directives, actions, and custom tags combined with an HTML layout in the same text document to form a procedural and programmatic way of producing

HTML output. This provides for a scripting perspective with Java for creating dynamic content.

So what really is a JSP? From a very high level, a JSP is simply a text document made up of scriptlets, Java code, and HTML. It is initially compiled on the fly into a servlet by the JSP container, and dynamically loaded into the servlet container. In other words, a JSP is nothing more than a simplistic way of creating a servlet. A JSP really is a servlet, as Listings 11.1 and 11.2 show. Listing 11.1 is a very simple JSP that demonstrates some scriptlet code and produces a "Hello World" HTML output. Listing 11.2 is the corresponding servlet created by a Tomcat implementation of the JSP.

Listing 11.1 A sample JSP page: `hello.jsp`

```
<HTML>
<BODY>
<% int x = 5; %>
<h1>HELLO WORLD!</h1>

The value of x = <%= x%>

</BODY>
</HTML>
```

Listing 11.2 The servlet implementation of `hello.jsp`

```
import javax.servlet.*;
import javax.servlet.http.*;
import javax.servlet.jsp.*;
import javax.servlet.jsp.tagext.*;
import java.io.PrintWriter;
import java.io.IOException;
import java.io.FileInputStream;
import java.io.ObjectInputStream;
import java.util.Vector;
import org.apache.jasper.runtime.*;
import java.beans.*;
import org.apache.jasper.JasperException;

public class _0002fjsp_0002fhello_0002ejsphello_jsp_0 extends
HttpJspBase {

  static {
  }
  public _0002fjsp_0002fhello_0002ejsphello_jsp_0( ) {
  }

  private static boolean _jspx_inited = false;

  public final void _jspx_init() throws JasperException {
  }
```

```
  public void _jspService(HttpServletRequest request,
                          HttpServletResponse  response)
      throws IOException, ServletException {

      JspFactory _jspxFactory = null;
      PageContext pageContext = null;
      HttpSession session = null;
      ServletContext application = null;
      ServletConfig config = null;
      JspWriter out = null;
      Object page = this;
      String  _value = null;
      try {
        if (_jspx_inited == false) {
          _jspx_init();
          _jspx_inited = true;
        }
        _jspxFactory = JspFactory.getDefaultFactory();
        response.setContentType("text/html;charset=8859_1");
        pageContext = _jspxFactory.getPageContext(this,
                request, response,
                "", true, 8192, true);

        application = pageContext.getServletContext();
        config = pageContext.getServletConfig();
        session = pageContext.getSession();
        out = pageContext.getOut();

        out.write("<HTML>\r\n<BODY>\r\n");

        int x = 5;

        out.write("\r\n<h1>HELLO WORLD!</h1>\r\n\r\nThe value of x = ");
        out.print( x);
        out.write("\r\n\r\n</BODY>\r\n</HTML>\r\n");

      } catch (Exception ex) {
        if (out.getBufferSize() != 0)
          out.clearBuffer();
        pageContext.handlePageException(ex);
      } finally {
        out.flush();
        _jspxFactory.releasePageContext(pageContext);
      }
    }
}
```

What does this example tell us? It shows that the JSP technology is an extension of the servlet technology and that a JSP, in its most basic form, is nothing more than a servlet. Every JSP that we create ends up as a servlet. It is parsed, and the source is created by the container and compiled into a servlet the first time the page is accessed. Each additional time that the JSP is called, the request is sent directly to the resulting servlet.

A standard servlet application (one without a single-dispatch-servlet design as presented in this book) may consist of multiple servlets. When JSPs enter the scene, each JSP is just an additional servlet in the application. It fits right into the application, just as if we had added an additional servlet. It shares the session variables, the servlet context, and other application resources like every other servlet. Integrating JSP into a standard servlet application is simple, holding true to the JSP's original design direction: to play very well with servlets.

This discussion will not describe or show how to write JSP because there are many great books on this subject already. However, Table 11.1 lists all of the JSP syntax elements.

Table 11.1 JSP Syntax Reference

Element	Explanation
Directives	
`<%@ include`	Allows for inclusion of a file in a JSP page.
`file="fname" %>`	Identifies the URI of the file to include in the page.
`<%@page`	Allows the developer to set page-specific attributes.
`autoFlush="true" | "false"`	Automatically flushes the page buffer when it's full and this value is set to `true`. If the value is set to `false`, `autoFlush` throws an exception when the page buffer is full. The default value is `true`.
`buffer="#kb" | "none"`	Declares the page buffer size. The value must be a numeric value followed by the *kb* string. For example, `15kb` stands for 15 kilobytes (or 15K). The parameter may also contain the *none* string to signify that no buffering is requested. The default value is `8kb`.
`contentType="MIME content type"`	Describes the MIME content type of the data. Sets the header of the HTTP response to notify the client of the MIME type. The default value is `text/html`.
`errorPage="error.jsp"`	Specifies the error-handling JSP page if error handling is requested. Requires a URI of the error-handling JSP page. There is no default value.
`extends="javaclass"`	Allows the developer to declare a full Java class from which to extend the JSP. Be careful when using this parameter because it may prevent the JSP container from utilizing the proper superclasses to execute the JSP efficiently.

continued

Table 11.1 JSP Syntax Reference (*continued*)

Element	Explanation
`import="package1, package2"`	Allows the developer to import Java packages or classes into the JSP page. Multiple imported items are separated by commas. *Example:* `import="java.util.*, java.text.*"`
`info="Any String"`	Sets an arbitrary string as part of the page. The set string may be retrieved programmatically within the page with `Servlet.getServletInfo()`.
`isErrorPage="true" | "false"`	Designates the current page as a resulting "error" type of JSP. Setting this value to `true` provides the page with the `exception` scripting variable that contains the information from the exception originally thrown. The default value is `false`.
`isThreadSafe="true" | "false"`	Describes the thread capability of the JSP. If set to `true`, the JSP may be accessed from multiple threads simultaneously. If set to `false`, requests are queued and handled in the order received. The default value is `true`.
`language="script language"`	Describes the scripting language used in scriptlets. The default value is `java`.
`session="true" %>`	Designates whether the page will require a session. If set to `true`, the `session` scripting variable (an instance of the `HttpSession` object) is automatically created. The default value is `true`.
`<% taglib`	Indicates that a JSP page will incorporate tags from a tag library.
`prefix=""`	Identifies the prefix that will be used in the names of the tags. This parameter is required.
`uri="">`	Identifies the URI of the tag library descriptor file. This parameter is required.
Declarations	
`<%! declaration %>`	Provides for declaration of a variable or a method inside the JSP. Ultimately becomes a member variable or member method of the resulting compiled servlet, so be careful when declaring these types of variables in a multithreaded environment. *Examples:* `<%! int i = 0; %>` for declaring a variable; `<%! public x(int param){ return param * 5;} %>` for a method

Element	Explanation
Expressions	
`<%= expression %>`	Takes a Java expression such as a variable or returned value from a function or expression and converts the result into a string. *Example:* `<%= "Hello World"; %>` or `<%= 5*I; %>`
Scriptlets	

`<% scriptlet %>`	Code fragment that is executed in its order within the page at runtime. Code fragments may themselves be a complete Java statement; several sequenced fragments together must form a cohesive and complete Java statement.
	Example:
	`<% if (x) { %>`
	`x is true`
	`<% } else { %>`
	`x is false`
	`<% } %>`

Comments	
`<%-- comment --%>`	Provides comments in the JSP. May also be used to comment out scripting in a JSP page.
Standard Actions	
`<jsp:fallback> Text </jsp:fallback>`	Used within the `<jsp:plugin>` tag. Used as text to be presented to the user for browsers that do not support the plug-in.
`<jsp:forward`	Forwards the request to another JSP or servlet for further processing.
`page="uri">`	Identifies the URI of the JSP or servlet to which the request should be forwarded. This parameter is required.
`<jsp:getProperty`	Retrieves the value of a bean property that is converted to a `String` object for output to the HTML page.
`name`	Identifies the name of the bean instance variable declared by the `<jsp:useBean>` tag. This parameter is required.
`Property="property name" >`	Identifies the name of one of the bean's properties. This parameter is required.

continued

Table 11.1 JSP Syntax Reference (*continued*)

Element	Explanation
`<jsp:include`	Includes a page within a JSP. May also be used with `<jsp:param>` to pass parameters to the included page.
`page="uri"`	Identifies the URI of the page to include. This parameter is required.
`flush="true" >`	Indicates whether or not the buffer should be flushed automatically. This parameter is required. For the JSP 1.1 specification, a value of `false` will not be accepted. Only `true` is a valid value.
`<jsp:param`	Provides the ability to pass runtime parameters when used in conjunction with the bodies of the tags `<jsp:forward>` and `<jsp:include>`. May also be used in a `<jsp:params>` body when used with the `<jsp:plugin>` tag.
`name="name of the parameter"`	Identifies the name of the parameter. This parameter is required.
`value="value of the parameter" >`	Identifies the value of the parameter. May also be a request-time expression. This parameter is required.

`<jsp:params>`
`<jsp:param name="abc" value="xyz"/>`
`. . .`
`</jsp:params>`
	Used in the body of a `<jsp:plugin>` tag that is to be used with a set of `<jsp:param>` tags.

`<jsp:plugin`	Generates HTML that provides for `<embed>` or `<object>` elements to aid in the download of a Java plug-in for an applet or bean.
`align="bottom" | "middle" | "top"`	Specifies the alignment of the applet. The value may be `bottom`, `middle`, or `top`.
`archive` `code="class name"`	Identifies the class name for the applet or component. This is a fully qualified name and should include the package name if available. This parameter is required.
`codebase="URI to class file"`	Identifies the relative URI of the class. This parameter is required.
`height="pixel height of component"`	Identifies the height of the applet or component area.
`hspace="horizontal pixel buffer"`	Identifies the number of pixels to buffer on the left and right of the applet.
`iepluginurl="URL to plug-in"`	Identifies the URL for the Internet Explorer Java plug-in.

Element	Explanation
`jreversion="JRE version number"`	Identifies the Java Runtime Environment version required to execute the applet or component. The default is 1.1.
`name="name of applet"`	Identifies the name of the applet.
`nspluginurl="URL to plug-in"`	Identifies the URL for the Netscape Java plug-in.
`title="tool tip title"`	Gives the text to be shown as a tool tip for the applet.
`type="applet" | "bean"`	Identifies the type that represents this object, either `applet` or `bean`. This parameter is required.
`vspace="vertical pixel buffer"`	Identifies the number of pixels to buffer on the top and bottom of the applet.
`width="pixel width of component"`	Identifies the width of the applet or component area.
`<jsp:setProperty`	Sets the value of a bean property or several properties if using the asterisk as a match to request parameters.
`name="bean name"`	Identifies the name of the instantiated bean. This parameter is required.
`property="property name" | "*"`	Identifies the name of the bean's property to set. May also be an asterisk to signify the name of the properties that will match all request parameters. This parameter is required.
`param="request parameter name"`	Maps the name of a request parameter value to the property. This parameter cannot be used if the `value` parameter is declared.
`value="value to assign" >`	Identifies the value to assign to the property. This parameter cannot be used if the `param` parameter is declared.
`<jsp:useBean`	Associates a script variable with an instance of a JavaBean object. The association is attempted by a match of the ID with an already existing instance of the object within the declared scope. If no match is found, creates the instance of the object.
`beanName="name of the bean"`	Identifies the name of the bean. This is the name that is expected as a part of the method `java.beans.Beans.instantiate()`.
`class= "package and class of the bean's type"`	Identifies the full name of the class, including the package name, to declare the type of object to be instantiated. This parameter is required if a type is not being defined.

continued

Table 11.1 JSP Syntax Reference (*continued*)

Element	Explanation
`id="script variable identifier"`	Identifies the script variable name to call this bean. Also identifies the bean within its scope. This parameter is required.
`scope="page" | "request" | "session" | "application"`	Identifies the scope of the bean instance. The value may be `page`, `request`, `session`, or `application`. The default value is `page`.
`type="class, superclass, or interface of the script variable" >`	The type of class, superclass, or interface of the defined scripting variable. Should include the package name. This parameter is required if a class is not being defined.

JSPs and Enterprise Servlets

What does all this mean for a single-dispatch-servlet design as presented in this book? Again, each JSP becomes its own servlet. Therefore when we write an application with many JSPs, we may have many servlets. How does this affect a single-dispatch-servlet design? How do we dispatch a JSP? How do we control access to application resources without the JSP being part of the enterprise servlet structure? These important questions should be the first ones we deal with when we're integrating JSPs with a single-dispatch-servlet design.

Did we do too good a job of isolating a servlet application from other servlets? Remember that one of the primary goals of a single-dispatch-servlet design was to encapsulate and protect its own resources from outside applications. By doing this, however, we prevent JSPs (which become "outside" servlets) from accessing an application's resources. So how can we allow JSPs access to the application's resources, such as security, log objects, pools, sessions, and error handling? From the big picture, this seems like a daunting task—even impossible with the design that we have put together so far. But in reality it can be done very easily, as we will soon see.

As we have learned, the `AppContext` object manages most of the resources of an application, and `BaseEnterpriseServlet` is primarily responsible for protecting this object and allowing access to it. `BaseEnterpriseServlet`'s responsibilities as it pertains to the single-dispatch-servlet design are as follows:

1. To dispatch requests to the proper `HTTPMethod` object or function of the application
2. To provide access to the `AppContext` object for the dispatch methods

3. To provide security authorization if Web-based or form-based authentication is utilized in an application
4. To provide automatic/default error handling for exceptions that may not be caught from an `HTTPMethod` object.
5. To provide a `PoolObjectManager` object for `HTTPMethod` to ensure that all objects are checked in when `HTTPMethod` has completed processing, regardless of an error

How does this relate to a JSP? A JavaServer Page will not be dispatched by `BaseEnterpriseServlet`, nor will it have access to the application's `AppContext`. Because it is not part of `BaseEnterpriseServlet`, a basic JSP will not have access to the pooled objects, the logging, the security, or the error-handling mechanism of `BaseEnterpriseServlet`. However, in order for the JSP to become part of a single-dispatch-servlet application, it will need to have access to the `AppContext` object and provide for responsibilities 2 through 5 listed above. We don't care about the first responsibility because the JSP is already a dispatched call as its own servlet.

To accomplish the required tasks, the JSP must take on some of the functionality that `BaseEnterpriseServlet` implements. It will need to receive a copy of `AppContext`, provide access to the security authorization if it is defined, provide for default error handling and reuse any error templates that may have been defined in an application, and ensure that any pooled objects that are used are checked back in. But this is a lot of code. Do we really have to have the equivalent of `BaseEnterpriseServlet` in each JSP? Yes, we do. Instead of manually adding this code to each JSP, however, we can use the JavaServer Pages tag library to add a custom tag at the beginning of each JSP that handles all of these functions for us. Before we learn how this works, we need to be able to gain access to the `AppContext` object.

Releasing BaseEnterpriseServlet's Grip on AppContext

The key to allowing the JSP to work within the enterprise servlet framework is to have access to `AppContext`. As was stated in Chapter 2, one reason to have `AppContext` is to protect the application's resources from other applications. More important, however, `AppContext` is a central repository for resources that could easily be used between the different classes within an application. So how do we access `AppContext`? We can start by releasing `BaseEnterpriseServlet`'s tight grip to allow access to `AppContext`. A JSP needs to know the following:

- Is the `BaseEnterpriseServlet` class for the particular application available?

- Has BaseEnterpriseServlet completed a successful initialization?
- If BaseEnterpriseServlet has succeeded in initialization, can we access AppContext?

Why does the JSP care about the initialization status? Without a complete initialization, we may not have a valid AppContext and thus may have all types of errors in an application. Therefore, if BaseEnterpriseServlet does not start properly, the JSP needs to notify the user that the servlet did not properly initialize. To accomplish these tasks, BaseEnterpriseServlet must communicate its initialization status and AppContext to the servlet context so that the JSP may retrieve this information.

This would work as follows. BaseEnterpriseServlet can register itself upon initialization with the application's name and set a flag in the servlet context stating that it has not completed initialization. If an error occurs during initialization, BaseEnterpriseServlet will reregister the status with an error condition. If initialization completes successfully, BaseEnterpriseServlet will register both itself and AppContext as having completed initialization successfully.

Most of this occurs in the init() method of BaseEnterpriseServlet. In the destroy() method, BaseEnterpriseServlet should unregister AppContext and update the status by removing these values from ServletContext. We will update BaseEnterpriseServlet with the registration/deregistration code as shown in Listing 11.3.

Listing 11.3 BaseEnterpriseServlet registering with ServletContext

```
public abstract class BaseEnterpriseServlet extends HttpServlet
{

  public static final int    NOT_READY          = 0;
  public static final int    READY              = 1;
  public static final int    ERROR              = -1;
.
.
.
  public final void init(ServletConfig config) throws
  ServletException
  {
    super.init(config);

    String  sConf = config.getInitParameter("ConfFile");

    if (getAppName() == null)
    {
      throw new ServletException(
            "Invalid application name: getAppName() returned null.");
    }
```

```
try
{
  m_appManager.addApp(getAppName());
} catch (Exception e)
{
  sc.setAttribute(getAppName() + ".AppStatus",
                  new Integer(ERROR));
  throw new ServletException(e.getMessage());
}

ServletContext sc = config.getServletContext();
sc.setAttribute(getAppName() +
                ".AppStatus",new Integer(NOT_READY));


if(sConf == null)
{
  sc.setAttribute(getAppName() + ".AppStatus",
                  new Integer(ERROR));
  throw new ServletException(
                  "ERROR - BaseEnterpriseServlet needs a " +
                  "ConfFile param.\n");
}

try
{
  m_ac.parseConfigFile(getAppName(),sConf);

  PoolObjectManager pom =
                   new PoolObjectManager(m_ac.getPoolList());

  try
  {
    initializeApp(m_ac, pom);
  }
  finally
  {
    pom.checkInAll();
  }

  if (m_ac.isLog())
  {
    m_ac.logInfo("****************************************");
    m_ac.logInfo(getAppName() + " Application has started.");
  }
}
catch(Exception e)
{
  sc.setAttribute(getAppName() + ".AppStatus",
                  new Integer(ERROR));
  e.printStackTrace();
  throw new ServletException(e);
}
```

```
        sc.setAttribute(getAppName() + ".AppStatus",new Integer(READY));
        sc.setAttribute(getAppName() + ".AppContext", m_ac);

    }

    public final void destroy()
    {
.
.
.
        ServletContext sc = getServletContext();
        sc.removeAttribute(getAppName() + ".AppStatus");
        sc.removeAttribute(getAppName() + ".AppContext");

    }

}
```

Now that we have released BaseEnterpriseServlet's tight grip on AppContext and have broadcast the status, the JSPs (or other servlets) can check the status of the application before allowing any code HTML to be output and decide how to handle the status that is received, and they can access AppContext. Half of the equation is thus satisfied, but how do we get the JSPs to receive this information in an efficient manner?

Tapping into Enterprise Servlets

There are several different ways to tap into an enterprise servlet:

1. We can write scriptlet code in each JSP that retrieves the status and AppContext.
2. We can write a bean to handle this retrieval.
3. We can create a tag library to handle the function.

Keep in mind that we not only need to retrieve AppContext and the status, but we also need to perform duties similar to those of BaseEnterpriseServlet with respect to pool management, security, and so on. Table 11.2 presents the options in tabular format to make it easier to analyze the advantages and disadvantages of each one.

The comparison in Table 11.2 shows that scriptlet code is not a good choice. So we will narrow the options down to a JavaBean and a tag library. Initially the choice is just a matter of preference. But there is one more very important issue that we need to tackle.

In BaseEnterpriseServlet, we use a try/catch/finally clause to execute the PoolObjectManager checkInAll() method to be sure the pool objects have

Table 11.2 Options for Tapping into Enterprise Servlets

Option	Advantages and Disadvantages
Write scriptlet code	*Advantages:* Quick and easy. *Disadvantages:* May make the JSPs difficult to read or maintain, and needs to be reproduced in each JSP. Requires additional `try/catch/finally` code to manage pools. Could amount to a large amount of replicated code.
Write JavaBean	*Advantages:* Encapsulates more of the code to a single object. *Disadvantages:* May still require a certain amount of scriptlet code. Still requires additional `try/catch/finally` code to manage pools.
Write a tag library	*Advantages:* Simple to use in JSP, and requires very little scriptlet code. Uses the framework's own `try/catch/finally` code to manage pools. Encapsulates all code very neatly. Provides additional maintainability and readability. *Disadvantages:* Setup of the application server takes longer.

been cleaned up properly. Therefore, we need to duplicate this feature in a JSP because this is an integral component of the enterprise servlet architecture. Doing this with a bean is more difficult than it may appear and would require us to override core JSP methods or add a significant amount of code to each JSP. But with a tag library we can tap into the JSP framework so that the process is automatic. With a tag library, however, we will need to do a few extra steps when we configure the application server, which seems a very small price to pay for the convenience of the tag library. In addition, because a tag library is a more readable and elegant implementation of placing logic into a JSP page, using a tag library for the task is probably the best option.

A Quick Look at the Java Tag Library

The following is a brief description of the tag library. Much more detail on the tag library may be found in many of the excellent books available on JSPs. Here just the tag library is covered because it pertains specifically to the solution of our problem. The Java tag library was designed to allow developers to create reusable tag components that can be utilized in a JSP that is very similar to an HTML or XML tag. The main benefit of the tag library is that it follows an XML type of standard that is familiar to page designers, so it is not overwhelming for a designer. For the developer, the tag library is an excellent way to package application logic because it encapsulates and hides the heavy coding that may be associated with application logic.

Each tag library contains a descriptor file, normally referred to as a TLD (tag library definition) file, which describes the different tags available in the library, the different parameters, and which parameters are required or optional. To use a tag library, declare the library in the beginning of the JSP and the location of the TLD file for the library, and associate a prefix name with the library. This action provides access to the library (and its tags for that JSP), which is then referenced by the prefix.

Two types of tags may be developed. One allows the body of the tag—that is, the text between the start tag and the end tag—to be processed, and the other does not. Listing 11.4 shows a hypothetical JSP page that uses a tag library.

Listing 11.4 A JSP page using a hypothetical tag library

```
<%@ taglib uri="/mytaglib.tld" prefix="mylib" %>

<HTML>
<BODY>
This is an example of a tag with a body.
<mylib:select_tag driver="sun.jdbc.odbc.JdbcOdbcDriver"
    dsn="jdbc:odbc:myDB">
  SELECT * FROM EMPLOYEE
</mylib:select_tag>

This is an example of a tag without a body or an end tag.
<mylib:no_body_tag param1="Test"/>

This is an example of a tag without a body, but with an end tag.
<mylib:no_body_tag param1="Test">
  Other HTML and/or JSP goes here
</mylib:no_body_tag>
</BODY>
</HTML>
```

In the first tag (one with a body), the body text is read into the tag and used as dynamic input, and it is processed at runtime. The body is generally not output as HTML, but is instead used to create HTML by the tag itself. The second tag is a tag without a body and is shown without an end tag. We can omit the end flag by ending the tag with />, thus signifying to the JSP container that this is both a start and an end tag. The last tag is also a tag without a body, but it shows the end tag. Listing 11.5 shows a hypothetical TLD file for this particular tag library.

Listing 11.5 The TLD file for a hypothetical tag library

```
<?xml version="1.0"?>

<!DOCTYPE taglib
   PUBLIC "-//Sun Microsystems, Inc.//DTD JSP Tag Library 1.1//EN"
   "http://java.sun.com/j2ee/dtds/web-jsptaglibrary_1_1.dtd">
```

```
<taglib>
  <tlibversion>1.0</tlibversion>
  <jspversion>1.1</jspversion>
  <shortname>MyTagLib</shortname>
  <tag>
    <name>select_tag</name>
    <tagclass>com.mycompany.DBSelect</tagclass>
    <bodycontent>tagdependent</bodycontent>
    <attribute>
      <name>driver</name>
      <required>true</required>
    </attribute>
    <attribute>
      <name>dsn</name>
      <required>true</required>
    </attribute>
  </tag>
  <tag>
    <name>no_body_tag</name>
    <tagclass>com.mycompany.NoBody</tagclass>
    <bodycontent>JSP</bodycontent>
    <attribute>
      <name>param1</name>
      <required>false</required>
    </attribute>
  </tag>
</taglib>
```

The TLD file tells us that we are using version 1.0 of the library and that the short name is *MyTagLib*. The short name is a name that can be used to reference the tag library from the JSP page. Then each tag has its own XML type of description, which includes its name, the class that belongs to the tag, the type of data processed in the body, each of the parameters or attributes, and whether the attributes are required or optional.

The `<bodycontent>` tag has three possible values: `JSP`, `tagdependent`, or `empty`. The `JSP` value, which is the default, tells the JSP container to evaluate the body of the tag as normal JSP and HTML, or that the body may be empty. The `tagdependent` value tells the JSP container that the body will be handled by the tag itself, as we did with the `<select_tag>` tag in the hypothetical example. The `empty` value requires that the body be empty.

What is the point of this TLD file? During the translation phase of the JSP container, or when it is compiling the JSP into a servlet, the container uses the TLD file to check that the syntax of the custom tag is correct and that it is adhering to the rules of its use. Another way to view the TLD file is as a rule book for using the custom tag in the JSP.

Let's concentrate on the simpler tag—the tag that does not process the body—because this is the type of tag we will use to bridge the JSP to

Table 11.3 Methods That Must Be Implemented in All Tag Library Tags

```
int doStartTag()
int doEndTag()
Tag getParent()
void setParent()
void release()
void setPageContext(PageContext pagectx)
```

the enterprise servlet framework. All tags must implement the interface `java.servlet.jsp.tagext.Tag` that is part of the Java 2 Enterprise Edition development kit. This interface requires the tag to implement the methods shown in Table 11.3.

Because these methods are implemented in all tags, Sun provided a helper class called `java.servlet.tagext.TagSupport` that implements a default set of the methods listed in Table 11.3 so that we need only to extend this class and override the methods that we wish to control. The methods that we are most likely to override are `doStartTag()`, `doEndTag()`, and `release()`.

These tags are the most important because they are executed at different intervals and do the hard work of implanting the business logic. The `doStartTag()` and `doEndTag()` methods also allow you to return values that control what happens to the execution of the rest of the JSP found in the body and in the page. The `doStartTag()` method is executed when the custom tag is found on the page. It may return `EVAL_BODY_INCLUDE`, which tells the container to output the body if there is one; `EVAL_BODY_TAG`, which tells the container to let the tag process the body (it may be used only when the tag is a body-processing tag); or `SKIP_BODY`, which tells the container to ignore the body.

The `doEndTag()` method is executed when the end tag is found. It may return `EVAL_PAGE`, which tells the container to continue processing the JSP; or `SKIP_PAGE`, which tells the container not to process any more of the JSP page. The `release()` method is executed as part of a `try/catch/finally` block in the `finally` portion of the compiled servlet, and it is therefore guaranteed to execute, even if an exception is thrown on the page.

Finally, sometimes we want tags to create script variables that we can use in the JSP or as parameters to beans or other tags in the page. Sometimes it's nice to have the tag create a scripting variable for us, as, for example, if we retrieve an object, such as an address, and perhaps display the results to the user. Listing 11.6 shows a JSP that retrieves an address object as part of a query and returns the information to the user.

Listing 11.6 A JSP page using a hypothetical address tag library that creates a script variable

```
<%@ taglib uri="/address.tld" prefix="addr" %>

<HTML>
<BODY>
<addr:getAddr name="myAddr" id="1234">
  Address is:<%= myAddr.getAddress() %><BR>
  City is:<%= myAddr.city() %><BR>
  State is:<%= myAddr.state() %><BR>
  Zip is:<%= myAddr.zip() %><BR>
</addr:getAddr>
</BODY>
</HTML>
```

Notice that we passed in the name *myAddr.* The tag created this parameter as a script variable to make it accessible to the rest of the JSP. In the example in Listing 11.6, we created and used the script variable inside the body of the tag. The scope of the variable can be developed to be within the body of the tag or after the end tag. To implement the creation of script variables in custom tags, we develop an object that uses the `java.servlet.tagext.TagExtraInfo` class for each tag type that wishes to create script variables. We must also update the TLD file to indicate that the tag will be creating script variables and therefore will be using an extended `TagExtraInfo` class. Listing 11.7 shows one possible TLD for the address tag library.

Listing 11.7 A TLD file for the address tag library

```
<?xml version="1.0"?>

<!DOCTYPE taglib
   PUBLIC "-//Sun Microsystems, Inc.//DTD JSP Tag Library 1.1//EN"
   "http://java.sun.com/j2ee/dtds/web-jsptaglibrary_1_1.dtd">

<taglib>
  <tlibversion>1.0</tlibversion>
  <jspversion>1.1</jspversion>
  <shortname>address</shortname>
  <tag>
    <name>getAddr</name>
    <tagclass>com.mycompany.Address</tagclass>
    <teiclass>com.mycompany.AddressTEI</teiclass>
    <bodycontent>JSP</bodycontent>
    <attribute>
      <name>name</name>
      <required>true</required>
    </attribute>
  </tag>
</taglib>
```

Notice the <teiclass> line, which points to the class that contains the TEI (TagExtraInfo) information. The TEI class that we develop has essentially one function: to override the getVariableInfo(TagData data) method, which lets the tag library framework know that it is creating a script variable. The getVariableInfo(TagData data) method allows us to fill in an object javax.servlet.jsp.tagext.VariableInfo with information about the kind of variable that we wish to create. The VariableInfo object takes the following parameters in its constructor:

```
VariableInfo(String varName,
             String className,
             boolean declare,
             int scope)
```

where

- **varName** specifies the name of the scripting variable. This parameter may be obtained from the JavaServer Page by a call to the method data.getAttributeString("name of the parameter") from the TagData object that is passed into the getVariableInfo() method.
- **className** identifies the fully qualified class type that will be created.
- **declare**, if set to true, indicates that this is a new variable.
- **scope** specifies just what the scope of this variable is. If the value is VariableInfo.NESTED, the variable is visible only between the start and end tags. If VariableInfo.AT_BEGIN, the variable is visible after the start tag. If VariableInfo.AT_END, the variable is visible after the end tag.

The getVariableInfo(TagData data) method returns an array of these VariableInfo objects, one for each scripting variable that needs to be created. Therefore, in the address tag library example the AddressTEI class may look like Listing 11.8.

Listing 11.8 The AddressTEI class

```
import javax.servlet.jsp.tagext.*;

public class AddressTEI extends TagExtraInfo
{

  public VariableInfo[] getVariableInfo(TagData data)
  {
    return new VariableInfo[]
    {
      new VariableInfo(
        data.getAttributeString("name"),
```

```
            "com.mycompany.Address",
            true,
            VariableInfo.NESTED
        ),
    };
  }
}
```

In this example the TEI class is looking for the `name` parameter and the class will retrieve the scriptlet name from the JavaServer Pages by calling `data.getAttributeString("name")`. We want the script variable always to be created, so `true` is passed for the `declare` parameter. We also want the script variable to be available only between the start and end tags, so we pass `VariableInfo.NESTED` to the `scope` parameter. If we want to add additional script variables, we simply create a parameter declaration in the TLD file and append another `VariableInfo` object to the array in the TEI class. That's all there is to dynamically creating script variables in JSP custom tags.

Bridging JSPs to Enterprise Servlets

Now that we have seen briefly how a tag library is used and configured, let's see how it will help us bridge a JSP to the enterprise servlet architecture. We'll begin by defining the tag and how we want it to interact with the enterprise servlet application. First and foremost we need an `AppContext` object, so we will need the tag to create an `AppContext` script variable. However, we must remember that `AppContext` may not be available while the application is starting up. Because the dispatch servlet needs to initialize, the JSP may be called while the application is initializing. For this reason we want the application to attempt to retrieve the status of its initialization before displaying an error message to the user. We may wish to have a timeout parameter that gives the application a certain amount of time to register its status with the servlet context.

As noted when we updated `BaseEnterpriseServlet` to register itself with the servlet context, it uses the application name as part of the registration information. Therefore, we will need a parameter that allows us to pass the application name to the tag so that it can obtain the `AppContext` and status. `BaseEnterpriseServlet` delivered a `PoolObjectManager` object to the `HTTPMethod` objects so that they could check out pooled objects. There is no exception here; we need a script variable that returns a `PoolObjectManager` object so that the JSP can use pools as well.

Finally, `BaseEnterpriseServlet` handles authentication when we declare that an `HTTPMethod` object uses security. The JSP may need to use the same security mechanism as the `HTTPMethod` objects in the application, so we will need a parameter that allows us to pass in a proxied `HTTPMethod` object to enable security for the JSP. The security aspect will be described shortly, but for now let's provide a parameter for a security proxy class. Table 11.4 sums up the information we have established thus far.

Let's talk about security for a moment. In Chapter 6 we discussed extending `HTTPMethod` and overriding or implementing the `authorize()` method, thereby creating a customized "secure" abstract `HTTPMethod` object. Normally, in the enterprise servlet framework we would create a new class to extend the "secure" `HTTPMethod` class and then implement the `execute()` method. `BaseEnterpriseServlet` would take care of ensuring that security was properly executed and checked. All of this was possible because the `HTTPMethod` objects were abstract.

Because the JSP has no `HTTPMethod` object and is not dispatched, we cannot instantiate the security `HTTPMethod` object because it is abstract. How do we get around this problem? We create a proxy class that extends the secure `HTTPMethod` version. In the process we create a "dummy" `execute()` method that does nothing, and we pass the new class to the tag. The tag can then instantiate this class and test the authorization for the JSP page. In Chapter 6 we created an abstract security `HTTPMethod` class called `MySecureHTTPMethod` that provided Web-based security for us. If we used this as a security mechanism, we

Table 11.4 Analysis of the Parameters for the New Tag

Parameter	Status	Description
`name`	Required	The name of the `AppContext` script variable. Returns an `AppContext` object in the declared variable name.
`appName`	Required	The name of the application as it would be returned by the `BaseEnterpriseServlet.getAppName()` method.
`poolObjectManager`	Required	The name of the `PoolObjectManager` object script variable. Returns a `PoolObjectManager` object in the declared variable name.
`secureClass`	Optional	The name of a proxy security `HTTPMethod` class that will be instantiated within the tag to implement security. This is optional in that if it is omitted, no security will be implemented for the JSP.
`timeOut`	Optional	The amount of time (in seconds) that the tag will wait for a status to be registered by `BaseEnterpriseServlet`. We will internally set the default to 10 seconds, which is plenty of time for the application to register an initial status. The default will be used if the parameter is omitted from the tag. This parameter may be included if a different timeout value is desired.

would create a proxy HTTPMethod object for this class with the code shown in Listing 11.9.

Listing 11.9 A proxy secure HTTPMethod object for the MySecureHTTPMethod abstract class

```
import enterprise.common.*;
import enterprise.servlet.*;

public class JSPSecureHTTPProxy extends MySecureHTTPMethod
{
  public void execute() throws Exception
  {
  }
}
```

In essence the proxy HTTPMethod object is nothing more than a generic HTTPMethod object used for JSPs. It has an empty execute() method. The JSPSecureHTTPProxy object that we created in Listing 11.9 would thus become the parameter we would use in the tag if we wanted the JSP to have security.

On the basis of what we've learned so far, we can begin by building the TLD file descriptor for the tag library. Because we are bridging the JSP and enterprise servlet framework, let's call the tag ESBridge. We will also call the class ESBridge and the TEI class ESBridgeTEI. We will place the classes in the enterprise.servlet package. The resulting TLD file is shown in Listing 11.10.

Listing 11.10 The esbridge.tld file descriptor

```
<?xml version="1.0"?>

<!DOCTYPE taglib PUBLIC
    "-//Sun Microsystems, Inc.//DTD JSP Tag Library 1.1//EN"
    "http://java.sun.com/j2ee/dtds/web-jsptaglibrary_1_1.dtd">

<taglib>
  <tlibversion>1.0</tlibversion>
  <jspversion>1.1</jspversion>
  <shortname>ESB</shortname>
  <tag>
    <name>ESBridge</name>
    <tagclass>enterprise.servlet.ESBridge</tagclass>
    <teiclass>enterprise.servlet.ESBridgeTEI</teiclass>
    <bodycontent>JSP</bodycontent>
    <attribute>
      <name>name</name>
      <required>true</required>
    </attribute>
    <attribute>
      <name>appName</name>
      <required>true</required>
    </attribute>
```

```
    <attribute>
      <name>poolObjectManager</name>
      <required>true</required>
    </attribute>
    <attribute>
      <name>secureClass</name>
      <required>false</required>
    </attribute>
    <attribute>
      <name>timeOut</name>
      <required>false</required>
    </attribute>
  </tag>
<taglib>
```

Now that we have designed the `<ESBridge>` tag, let's build the library code. As already mentioned, we will build two classes: `ESBridge` and `ESBridgeTEI`. Let's look first at the `ESBridge` class. This class will provide the tag library with functionality similar to that of `BaseEnterpriseServlet`. The brunt of the logic will be placed in the `doStartTag()` method because we want this tag to begin as soon as it is found on the JSP page.

The first thing `doStartTag()` will need to do is retrieve the `ServletContext` object so that we can query for the status. Next we will have it attempt to retrieve the servlet status by looking for the application name that we passed in as a parameter. It will attempt to retrieve the status for `timeOut` number of seconds. Remember that the default value of 10 seconds will be used if no parameter is passed in to the tag; otherwise the passed value will be used. If the status cannot be retrieved within `timeOut` seconds, the user will receive a message that the application has not loaded or could not be locate. If the value `NOT_READY` is returned as the status, the message *Application starting up; please try again in a few minutes.* will be displayed to the user. If `READY` is returned, the `AppContext` object will be pulled from `ServletContext`.

The first order of business is to prepare a `PoolObjectManager` object for the JSP page. We create the `PoolObjectManager` object from the `AppContext` object and then register `AppContext` and `PoolObjectManager` with `pageContext` so that the JSP page will have access to these as script variables. Finally, the `doStartTag()` method will check if security is required. If a `secureClass` value was passed in to the tag, the tag will attempt to instantiate the class and check authorization. It follows the same process as `BaseEnterpriseServlet`: instantiating the proxy class, calling `registerMethod()` with the appropriate parameters, and testing the outcome of the `authorize()` method.

We override the `doEndTag()` method and automatically return the value `EVAL_PAGE`, essentially telling the JSP that if we reached the end tag without error, processing of the JSP should continue. We also override the `release()`

method where we will check in all of the pool objects. We do this here because this method is guaranteed to be executed by the container, since it is executed in a `finally` clause within the JSP's resulting servlet. It doesn't matter if the JSP encounters an error; this code *will be executed,* so we can be assured that the objects will be checked in under all circumstances. The `finally` clause in `BaseEnterpriseServlet` does the same thing.

Finally, we need to include a smattering of setters for the JSP framework to set the values of the parameters passed into the tag. These setters are required for access to the parameter values. Listing 11.11 shows the code for `ESBridge`.

Listing 11.11 The `ESBridge` tag library class

```
package enterprise.servlet;

import javax.servlet.*;
import javax.servlet.http.*;
import javax.servlet.jsp.*;
import javax.servlet.jsp.tagext.*;
import java.io.*;
import enterprise.servlet.*;
import enterprise.common.*;

public class ESBridge extends TagSupport
{
  private String name = null;
  private String appName = null;
  private String pomName = null;
  private String secureClass = null;

  private ServletContext m_sc = null;
  private AppContext m_ac = null;
  private PoolObjectManager m_pom = null;
  private int timeOut = 10;

  public ESBridge()
  {
    super();
  }

  public int doStartTag() throws JspTagException
  {
    // Get ServletContext.
    m_sc = pageContext.getServletContext();

    if (m_sc == null)
    {
        throw new JspTagException("Cannot get ServletContext");
    }
```

```
    // If the main dispatch servlet is not ready, then say so.
    if (!getDispatchServletStatus())
      return SKIP_BODY;

    // Get AppContext.
    m_ac = (AppContext)m_sc.getAttribute(appName + ".AppContext");
    if (m_ac == null)
    {
        throw new JspTagException("Application " + appName +
                          "does not appear to have an AppContext.");
    }

    m_pom = new PoolObjectManager(m_ac.getPoolList());

    // Store the AppContext and PoolObjectManager objects in
    // PageContext for retrieval by the JSP page.
    pageContext.setAttribute(name, m_ac, PageContext.PAGE_SCOPE);
    pageContext.setAttribute(pomName, m_pom,
                             PageContext.PAGE_SCOPE);

    return CheckAuthorization();
  }

  private int CheckAuthorization() throws JspTagException
  {
    if (secureClass != null)
    {
      try
      {
        HttpServletRequest req =
                    (HttpServletRequest)pageContext.getRequest();
        HttpServletResponse res =
                    (HttpServletResponse)pageContext.getResponse();

        Class c = Class.forName(secureClass);
        HTTPMethod j = (HTTPMethod) c.newInstance();
        j.registerMethod(req,res,m_ac,m_pom);
        if (!j.authorize())
        {
          return SKIP_BODY;
        }
      } catch (ClassNotFoundException cnfe)
      {
        throw new JspTagException("Class " + secureClass +
                                  " is not found.");
      } catch (IllegalAccessException iae)
      {
        throw new JspTagException(iae.getMessage());
      } catch (InstantiationException ie)
      {
        throw new JspTagException(ie.getMessage());
      } catch (Exception e)
      {
```

```
        throw new JspTagException(e.getMessage());
      }
    }

    return EVAL_BODY_INCLUDE;
  }

  public int doEndTag() throws JspTagException
  {
    return  EVAL_PAGE;
  }

  public void setName(String name)
  {
    this.name = name;
  }

  public void setSecureClass(String secureClass)
  {
    this.secureClass = secureClass;
  }

  public void setAppName(String appName)
  {
    this.appName = appName;
  }

  public void setPoolObjectManager(String pomName)
  {
    this.pomName = pomName;
  }

  public void setTimeOut(int timeOut)
  {
    this.timeOut = timeOut;
  }

  public AppContext getAppContext()
  {
    return m_ac;
  }

  public void release()
  {
    super.release();

    if (m_pom != null)
    {
      m_pom.checkInAll();
    }
  }
```

```
private boolean getDispatchServletStatus() throws JspTagException
{
  int retry = 0;

  // Attempt to get the servlet's initialization status.
  Integer status = (Integer)m_sc.getAttribute(appName +
                                            ".AppStatus");
  JspWriter jw = pageContext.getOut();

 // If it was null, keep trying for "timeout"
 // seconds to wait for the servlet to at least launch.
  while(status == null)
  {

    // Sleep for a second.
    try
    {
      java.lang.Thread.sleep(1000);
    } catch(InterruptedException ie)
    {
      // Do nothing.
    }

    // Try again.
    try
    {
      status = (Integer)m_sc.getAttribute(appName + ".AppStatus");
    } catch(Exception e)
    {
      // Do nothing.
    }

    // Did we get it?
    if (status != null)
    {
      break;
    } else
    {
      retry++;
      if (retry == timeOut)
      {
        throw new JspTagException("Application " + appName +
          " does not seem to be loaded.  Check the name " +
          "and that it is registered and has loaded.");
      }
    }
  }

  // If we got here, then the servlet has loaded its status.
  // Check the status, and if not ready, say so.
  if ((status.intValue() == BaseEnterpriseServlet.NOT_READY))
  {
```

```
      try
      {
        jw.clearBuffer();
        jw.println("<html><body>Application starting up; please " +
                             "try again in a few minutes.
                             </body></html>");
        jw.flush();
      } catch (IOException ioe)
      {
        ioe.printStackTrace();
      }

      return false;
    }

    // If an error occurred in the servlet's initialization,
    // say this also.
    if (status.intValue() == BaseEnterpriseServlet.ERROR)
    {
      try
      {
        jw.clearBuffer();
        jw.println(
            "<html><body>The application failed initialization "
          + "- Please contact the System Administrator." +
          "</body></html>");
        jw.flush();
      } catch (IOException ioe)
      {
        ioe.printStackTrace();
      }

      return false;
    }

    return true;
  }
}
```

Because we will be creating the AppContext and PoolObjectManager script variables, we will need to define the name and poolObjectManager parameters in the ESBridgeTEI class. Both of these variables will be created when the tag is declared, and we will make them visible only within the start and end tags. Listing 11.12 shows the code for ESBridgeTEI.

Listing 11.12 The ESBridgeTEI tag library class

```
package enterprise.servlet;

import javax.servlet.jsp.tagext.*;
```

```
public class ESBridgeTEI extends TagExtraInfo
{

  public ESBridgeTEI()
  {
    super();
  }

  public VariableInfo[] getVariableInfo(TagData data)
  {
    return new VariableInfo[]
    {
      new VariableInfo(
        data.getAttributeString("name"),
        "enterprise.servlet.AppContext",
        true,
        VariableInfo.NESTED
      ),
      new VariableInfo(
        data.getAttributeString("poolObjectManager"),
        "enterprise.common.PoolObjectManager",
        true,
        VariableInfo.NESTED
      ),
    };
  }
}
```

Using the ESBridge Tag Library

Now that we have created the tag library, let's see how to use it in a JSP. But first we need to establish some rules when using this tag library with JSPs and an enterprise servlet application. It is important to understand that the application must begin initializing before any JSPs are called. The reason is that the JSP will wait for `timeOut` seconds before displaying an error to the user stating that it cannot access the application. Therefore, it is important to configure servlets to automatically launch when the application server is started. Doing this will ensure that the initialization process begins instantly and that the JSPs will be able to access the servlet's status within the `timeOut` period.

How do we do this? Because this chapter relies on the Servlet 2.2 specification, requesting that the servlet automatically launch is as simple as adding a `<load-on-startup>` XML statement and value to the `web.xml` file. Listing 11.13 shows the `web.xml` file for the sample application that we will be building. The boldface lines are needed for the application's autolaunch at startup. It is probably a good idea to have all servlets always autolaunch because doing so takes care of the initialization right away, and then we don't have to wait for a client to call a servlet to get it to initialize.

Listing 11.13 The web.xml servlet configuration file

```
<?xml version="1.0" encoding="ISO-8859-1"?>

<!DOCTYPE web-app
    PUBLIC "-//Sun Microsystems, Inc.//DTD Web Application 2.2//EN"
    "http://java.sun.com/j2ee/dtds/web-app_2.2.dtd">

<web-app>
  <servlet>
    <servlet-name>
        JSPExample
    </servlet-name>
    <servlet-class>
        JSPExample
    </servlet-class>
    <init-param>
        <param-name>ConfFile</param-name>
        <param-value>/WEB-INF/JSPExample.config</param-value>
    </init-param>
    <load-on-startup>
        1
    </load-on-startup>
  </servlet>
</web-app>
```

The numerical value associated with the <load-on-startup> tag represents the order in which we wish to load servlets. Because one servlet may depend on another servlet, we can use different numbers to represent the load order. For example, if we had an accounting application that worked with an administrative application, we would probably want the accounting application to load first. In this scenario we would use the number 1 for the accounting application and any number greater than 1 for the administrative application.

From the web.xml file (Listing 11.13), we can ascertain that the application will be called *JSPExample*. This application will have one dispatched method, which we will call ServletMain. The purpose of ServletMain will be to send out some HTML that states the application is being run from a servlet dispatch. We will reuse the MySecureHTTPMethod class from Chapter 6 and utilize the Web-based security mechanism. We will also use the JSPSecureHTTPProxy class shown in Listing 11.9 for the security proxy class. Let's start with the configuration file, the JSPExample servlet, and the ServletMain class (Listings 11.14, 11.15, and 11.16, respectively).

Listing 11.14 The configuration file for JSPExample

```
# Configuration file
Default.Method=main
Method.main=ServletMain

Application.Base.URL=/servlet/JSPExample
```

Listing 11.15 The `JSPExample` class

```
import javax.servlet.*;

import enterprise.common.*;
import enterprise.servlet.*;

public class JSPExample extends BaseEnterpriseServlet
{

  public String getAppName()
  {
    return "JSPExample";
  }

  public void initializeApp(AppContext appContext,
                            PoolObjectManager pom)  throws Exception
  {
  }

  public void destroyApp(AppContext ac, PoolObjectManager pom)
  {
  }

}
```

Listing 11.16 The `ServletMain` class

```
import enterprise.servlet.*;
import enterprise.common.*;
import enterprise.html.*;

import java.io.*;

public class ServletMain extends MySecureHTTPMethod
{

  public void execute() throws Exception
  {

    PrintWriter out = m_response.getWriter();

    out.println("<html>");
    out.println("<body>");
    out.println("<h1>Welcome to the JSPExample</h1>");
    out.println("<p>If you see this page then you have ");
    out.println("a valid user ID and password!</p>");
    out.println("<p>This is being executed from a ");
    out.println("dispatched servlet method</p>");
    out.println("</body>");
    out.println("</html>");

  }

}
```

Now that we have the application, let's build the JSP. The JSP should begin by declaring the `<%@ taglib %>` tag to tell the container where the tag library definition file can be located. We will place the TLD file in the `WEB-INF` directory, where the `web.xml` file is, so that a client will not be able to accidentally view the file through his/her browser. The `uri` parameter will point to `/WEB-INF/esbridge.tld`, and we will use *esb* as our prefix.

At this point we are ready to use the tag. Many JSPs begin with an `<HTML>` tag. In our case we want to declare the `<ESBridge>` tag as early as possible. We do this for the purposes of handling errors, generating responses resulting from failure of the application, and displaying error information to the user. We want to be sure that the buffers are basically empty. We can do this by having the tag placed as soon as possible in the JSP file.

We declare the `ESBridge` tag by adding the prefix *esb* that we declared in the `<%@ taglib %>` tag with `ESBridge`. We will call the `name` parameter, which will receive the `AppContext` object as `ac` and the `PoolObjectManager` object as `pom`. Because the application name is *JSPExample,* we will set the `appName` parameter to this value. Because we will be using security in this example, we will set the `secureClass` parameter to the proxy and set its value to `JSPSecureHTTPProxy`.

Finally, we will declare a `timeOut` value of 5 seconds because this application should start up relatively quickly. The JSP will use the ac script variable, which contains the `AppContext` object, and show a couple of values that are specific to the servlet application to prove that we do have access to the object. The JSP that we will use, which we will call *espage.jsp,* is shown in Listing 11.17.

Listing 11.17 The `espage.jsp` page

```
<%@ taglib uri="/WEB-INF/estaglib.tld" prefix="esb" %>
<esb:ESBridge
  name="ac"
  poolObjectManager="pom"
  appName="JSPExample"
  secureClass="JSPSecureHTTPProxy"
  timeOut="5">
 <HTML>
 <BODY>
 <h2>Properties for the <%= ac.getAppName()%> application</h2>
 <br>
 <p>This is being executed from a JSP</p>

 <ul>
 <li>The Base URL of this application
         is <%= ac.getAppBaseURL() %></li>
 <br>
```

```
  <% if (ac.isLog()) {%>
     <li>The application is set up for logging.</li>
  <% }else {%>
     <li>The application is NOT set up for logging.</li>
  <% }%>
  </ul>
  </BODY>
  </HTML>
</esb:ESBridge>
```

We are now ready to execute the application and test the results. We will create a subdirectory called *jsp* and place the `espage.jsp` file in it. Although it's not necessary to do so, it's a good idea to place the JSPs in a location that is separate from other content. Having gotten a glimpse of the `web.xml` file, which essentially is the servlet registration, we should be ready to launch the application.

Try going to the JSP first and see what happens. The URL should be in the form *http://<your server>/jsp/espage.jsp*. When you access the page, it should pop up a dialog box requesting your user ID and password. (Remember from Chapter 6 that the user ID is *open* and the password is *sesame*.) If you are successful in entering security, you should see a screen displaying a couple of properties that only JSPExample's `AppContext` could possibly contain.

Try accessing the servlet. You should receive a message saying that you are accessing the servlet page, which means that we successfully tapped into the enterprise servlet application merely by adding a tag to the JSP. How simple! With this single tag, we have unleashed the power of enterprise servlets and extended it to allow JSP pages to join in.

Another thing that you can try with this example is to create a database pool or other pooled object in the `JSPExample` servlet initialization and use the `poolObjectManager` script variable to retrieve an object from the pool. Try checking in the pooled object and "forgetting" to check it back in. You will notice that the JSP seems to automatically check in pooled objects for us when the JSP has completed execution, just as if it were cleaned up by `BaseEnterpriseServlet`.

Accessing the EnterpriseSession Object

We just learned about how simple it is to have a JSP tap into the enterprise servlet framework. But something seems to be missing. We covered a lot of material, but what about the `EnterpriseSession` object? If we were to use the standard session mechanism that the JSP uses, we would not have access to the same session variables as the servlet has because of the enterprise servlet session encapsulation. Although the JSP can now receive the `AppContext` object, implement security, and use the pool-managing mechanism with the `<ESBridge>` tag, it still does not have access to the `EnterpriseSession` object.

Because the `ESBridge` class really duplicated the functionality of the `BaseEnterpriseServlet`, placing session access in this class would not have been appropriate. This leads us to the next question: How do we access the `EnterpriseSession` object? Remember that the `HTTPMethod` object managed the `EnterpriseSession` object with a few method calls that provided for creation and management of the object. Let's do exactly what we did for `ESBridge` with respect to duplicating `BaseEnterpriseServlet` functionality, but this time we can duplicate some of the functionality of `HTTPMethod` instead and create a tag that manages the `EnterpriseSession` object.

First let's analyze what we are trying to accomplish in building this tag. In `HTTPMethod`, when we requested an `EnterpriseSession` object through the `getEnterpriseSession()` function, we cared about two things: the `EnterpriseSession` object and possibly wanting to know if a timeout condition had been met. These two pieces of information are potentially script variables that we would want to retrieve from this new session tag. As Table 11.4 did for `ESBridge`, Table 11.5 gives us a breakdown of the parameters for this new tag.

This seems simple enough. We just need to be able to create a couple of script variables for this session tag. Let's call this new tag *ESSession*. The new tag will be based on an `ESSession` class, and because we will be creating script variables, we will need an `ESSessionTEI` class as well. An analysis of the parameters allows us to update the `esbridge.tld` file to reflect the new tag, as shown in Listing 11.18.

Listing 11.18 The additional tag inserted into the `esbridge.tld` file

```
<tag>
  <name>ESSession</name>
  <tagclass>enterprise.servlet.ESSession</tagclass>
  <teiclass>enterprise.servlet.ESSessionTEI</teiclass>
  <bodycontent>JSP</bodycontent>
  <attribute>
    <name>name</name>
    <required>true</required>
  </attribute>
  <attribute>
    <name>timeOutCondition</name>
    <required>false</required>
  </attribute>
</tag>
```

Now that we have described this new tag, we need to think about the code. The tag will need to have access to the `AppContext` object to retrieve the application name so that it can retrieve the proper session. We could once again

Table 11.5 Analysis of the Parameters for the Session Tag

Parameter	Status	Description
name	Required	The name of the EnterpriseSession script variable. Returns an EnterpriseSession object in the declared variable name.
timeOutCondition	Optional	A returned boolean value that indicates if a timeout condition has occurred. If the value is true, a timeout condition occurred and the EnterpriseSession object is considered new. If false, the EnterpriseSession object has been created before.

retrieve the AppContext object from ServletContext, but why do this when we have already retrieved it with ESBridge? Repeating this retrieval and going through the entire process of checking the servlet status would mean a duplication of code and objects—and not a very elegant solution. Instead we can reuse the AppContext object in ESBridge by creating a dependency for this tag on the page. We can then tap into the ESBridge tag and reuse the AppContext object to retrieve the application name. We will let the <ESBridge> parameter do the dirty work of checking the application status and retrieving the AppContext object.

How can we do this? There is a neat method in the TagSupport class called findAncestorWithClass() that will find an instance of a given class type, thereby allowing us to force dependency from one tag to another and giving us access to the dependent tag. In this case we would have the doStartTag() method begin by executing the following code:

```
ESBridge esb = (ESBridge)findAncestorWithClass(this,
                                    ESBridge.class);
if (esb == null)
{
  throw new JspTagException(
          "ESSession tag without an ESBridge tag first.");
}
```

This code tests for the existence of an ESBridge instance. If one is not found, the ESBridge tag was not declared and we throw an appropriate exception. However, if we do find an instance, we can call the esb.getAppContext() method to retrieve the AppContext object. This code is telling us that it must have a valid and instantiated <ESBridge> tag before we can use the <ESSession> tag. The rest of the tag library code duplicates the functions within the HTTPMethod object with respect to creating an EnterpriseSession object.

Listing 11.19 shows the code for `ESSession`; Listing 11.20, the code for `ESSessionTEI`.

Listing 11.19 The `ESSession` class

```
package enterprise.servlet;

import javax.servlet.*;
import javax.servlet.http.*;
import javax.servlet.jsp.*;
import javax.servlet.jsp.tagext.*;
import java.io.*;
import java.util.*;
import enterprise.servlet.*;
import enterprise.common.*;


public class ESSession extends TagSupport
{
  private String name = null;
  private String timeOutConditionName = null;

  private boolean m_timeOutCondition = null;
  private EnterpriseSession m_es = null;
  private AppContext m_ac = null;
  private boolean timeOutCondition = false;

  public ESSession()
  {
    super();
  }

  public int doStartTag() throws JspTagException
  {

    ESBridge esb = (ESBridge)findAncestorWithClass(this,
                                    ESBridge.class);
    if (esb == null)
    {
      throw new JspTagException(
                "ESSession tag without an ESBridge tag first.");
    }

    m_ac = esb.getAppContext();
    getEnterpriseSession();

    if (m_es == null)
    {
      throw new JspTagException("Cannot create an
                               EnterpriseSession.");
    }
```

```
    pageContext.setAttribute(name, m_es, PageContext.PAGE_SCOPE);
    pageContext.setAttribute(timeOutConditionName,
                             m_timeOutCondition,
                             PageContext.PAGE_SCOPE);

    return EVAL_BODY_INCLUDE;
  }

  public int doEndTag() throws JspTagException
  {
    return  EVAL_PAGE;
  }

  private void getEnterpriseSession()
  {

    HttpSession sess = pageContext.getSession();

    EnterpriseSession eSession =
              new EnterpriseSession(m_ac.getAppName(), sess);

    if (eSession.getAttribute("*ENTERPRISESESSION*") == null)
    {
      eSession.setAttribute("*ENTERPRISESESSION*", new Date());
      m_timeOutCondition = new boolean(true);
    } else
    {
      m_timeOutCondition = new boolean(false);
    }

    m_es = eSession;
  }

  public void setName(String name)
  {
    this.name=name;
  }

  public void setTimeOutCondition(String timeOutConditionName)
  {
    this.timeOutConditionName = timeOutConditionName;
  }
}
```

Listing 11.20 The ESSessionTEI class

```
package enterprise.servlet;

import javax.servlet.jsp.tagext.*;

public class ESSessionTEI extends TagExtraInfo
{
```

```
  public ESSessionTEI()
  {
    super();
  }

  public VariableInfo[] getVariableInfo(TagData data)
  {
    return new VariableInfo[]
    {
      new VariableInfo(
        data.getAttributeString("name"),
        "enterprise.servlet.EnterpriseSession",
        true,
        VariableInfo.NESTED
      ),
      new VariableInfo(
        data.getAttributeString("timeOutCondition"),
        "java.lang.boolean",
        true,
        VariableInfo.NESTED
      ),
    };
  }
}
```

Using the <ESSession> Tag

With the tag library now developed, we are ready to see it in action. Let's create an enterprise servlet application that is basically the same as the last example, but with one main difference: We will remove the security from the dispatched method and from the JSP, and we will change the content in the dispatch servlet to set a couple of `EnterpriseSession` variables, `VAR1` and `VAR2`, and display them to the user. The new `ServletMain` class is shown in Listing 11.21.

Listing 11.21 The `ServletMain` class that sets `EnterpriseSession` variables

```
import enterprise.servlet.*;
import enterprise.common.*;
import enterprise.html.*;

import java.io.*;

public class ServletMain extends HTTPMethod
{

  public void execute() throws Exception
  {
```

```
        PrintWriter out = m_response.getWriter();

        out.println("<html>");
        out.println("<body>");
        out.println("<h1>Welcome to the JSPExample 2</h1>");
        out.println("<p>I have created the following session " +
                    "variables</p>");

        EnterpriseSession es = getEnterpriseSession();
        es.setAttribute("VAR1", "This is set to 1");
        es.setAttribute("VAR2", "This is set to 2");

        out.println("<p>VAR1=" + (String)es.getAttribute("VAR1") +
                   "</p>");
        out.println("<p>VAR2=" + (String)es.getAttribute("VAR2") +
                   "</p>");
        out.println("</body>");
        out.println("</html>");

    }

}
```

The espage.jsp page will be updated to add the <ESSession> tag. By setting the name parameter, espage.jsp will create a script variable named *es* that will receive the EnterpriseSession object, and it will receive the flag timeOutCondition into a script variable named *to*. After creating the script variables, we will access the VAR1 and VAR2 session variables to see their values. We will also check for a timeout condition with some scriptlet code that checks the to variable and sends these results to the HTML output. The new espage.jsp page is shown in Listing 11.22.

Listing 11.22 The espage.jsp page that checks EnterpriseSession variables

```
<%@ taglib uri="/WEB-INF/estaglib.tld" prefix="esb" %>
<esb:ESBridge
  name="ac"
  poolObjectManager="pom"
  appName="JSPExample">
<esb:ESSession
  name="es"
  timeOutCondition="to">

 <HTML>
 <BODY>
 <h2>Information for the <%= ac.getAppName()%> application</h2>
 <br>
 <p>This is being executed from a JSP</p>
 <p>VAR1 = <%= (String)es.getAttribute("VAR1") %></p>
 <p>VAR2 = <%= (String)es.getAttribute("VAR2") %></p>
 <p><% if (to.booleanValue()) %>
 A Timeout condition has occured.
```

```
  <% else %>
  A Timeout condition has NOT occured.

  </BODY>
  </HTML>

</esb:ESSession>
</esb:ESBridge>
```

Now it's time to test the new tag. Launch the servlet container, and the servlet application should automatically load. Use your browser to go to the servlet first so that it will set the `EnterpriseSession` variables. Then use your browser to go to the JSP. You should see the contents of the variables that were set by the servlet. Again we have found a simple way to access the `EnterpriseSession` object: simply adding a tag to the JSP.

Other things to try are to move the `<ESSession>` tag so that it *precedes* the `<ESBridge>` tag. Because of the dependency on the `<ESBridge>` tag, you should receive an error when the program compiles, stating that the `ESSession` tag was declared before an `ESBridge` tag. You can also try doing the opposite, as shown in the example—that is, have the JSP create the session variables and then have the servlet read these variables. Of course you should not be surprised to find that the JSP and the enterprise servlet application are sharing the `EnterpriseSession` object.

Handling Errors

The final subject that we will tackle is error handling. We have all the other functions of the enterprise servlet architecture with respect to the JSP. In `BaseEnterpriseServlet`, the main dispatch servlet allows the dispatched method code to trap and handle its own errors. Any unexpected exceptions that arise will be handled by the `DefaultErrorHandler` object. How do we handle this in JSPs? If we have already defined an error template in an enterprise servlet application, how can we reuse that template in JSPs without having to code a separate JSP to reproduce the error-handling function of `DefaultErrorHandler`?

What's great about JavaServer Pages is that they have a built-in error-handling mechanism. We can trap for any error that we want in the JSP with a `try/catch` block, and allow any errors that we don't trap to "bubble up" to a generic error handler. In the JSP, we can do this by declaring the `<%@ page errorPage="/jsp/error.jsp" %>` tag, where the `errorPage` parameter points to the URL of the error handler JSP, in this case `/jsp/error.jsp`.

What does the `error.jsp` page look like, and can we reuse the functionality of the `DefaultErrorHandler` object so that we can log transaction IDs and display the error template? Remember that just the fact that we are writing a

JSP does not mean that we cannot output a template. A JSP is nothing more than a servlet at heart, so we can easily have a JSP dump a template to the output instead of presenting the HTML that is a part of the page. This `error.jsp` page is primarily just Java code, or one big scriptlet. It retrieves the `AppContext` object of the application and uses it to create a `DefaultErrorHandler` object. If an `AppContext` object cannot be retrieved, a default error message will be displayed and the error will be logged to the common application server log. The code for the `error.jsp` page is shown in Listing 11.23.

Listing 11.23 The `error.jsp` page to handle default errors

```
<%@ page isErrorPage="true" %>
<%@ page import="java.util.*, java.io.*, enterprise.servlet.*" %>

<%
  PrintWriter pw = response.getWriter();

  AppContext ac = null;

  // Change this variable to your application's name as defined in
  // the main dispatch servlet's getAppName() method.
  String appName = "Your application name";

  try
  {
    ServletContext sc = pageContext.getServletContext();
    ac = (AppContext)sc.getAttribute(appName + ".AppContext");
  } catch(Exception e)
  {
    // It's a big problem if we got here because we cannot even get
    // a good ServletContext, so dump both errors to the common
    // application server log.

    pw.println("A System Error has occurred.");
    e.printStackTrace();
    exception.printStackTrace();
  }

  if (ac == null)
  {

    // If we cannot get an AppContext, then produce a default
    // error and dump the error to the application server common
    // log.
    pw.println("A System Error has occurred.");
    exception.printStackTrace();

  } else
  {
```

```
        // Create the DefaultErrorHandler and use it!
        DefaultErrorHandler deh = new DefaultErrorHandler(ac, pw);
        deh.writeError((Exception)exception);
    }

%>
```

The error.jsp page shown in Listing 11.23 can be used for just about any application. However, it is important to change the appName string variable in error.jsp to the name of the application. For example, if we were to use this error handler in the JSPExample application that was developed earlier in the chapter, we would set appName equal to JSPExample in error.jsp. As you can see, implementing a way of handling unexpected errors that is similar to BaseEnterpriseServlet's approach is as simple as using the error.jsp page in your JSP application and setting the <@ page errorPage="/jsp/error.jsp" > tag in the JSPs.

Summary

The debate of JavaServer Pages (JSP) versus servlets has been a hot topic among Java server-side developers. Each camp may claim a preference for one technology over another, along with its own set of advantages and disadvantages. However, both are viable technologies that complement each other. More and more institutions are integrating these technologies to create powerful and easily maintainable applications that enable rapid application development. How a development environment structures its methodologies for writing JSP and servlet code has an impact on the maintainability and readability of the application.

Because a JSP is a servlet at its most basic execution state, integrating JSPs with a single-dispatch-servlet design can present challenges in sharing application resources. By loosening the tight grip that BaseEnterpriseServlet has on the AppContext object, we are able to create a controlled environment for sharing application resources between JSPs and the enterprise servlet architecture. With this in mind, we were able to create the <ESBridge> and <ESSession> custom tags with the Java tag library to create a convenient and elegant solution for sharing an application's resources with JSPs. These tags provide an easy way to integrate pool management, security, session management, and resource sharing with JSPs as though they were part of the single-dispatch-servlet logic.

CHAPTER 12

Taking Enterprise Servlets Further

Throughout this book we have learned about server development techniques that may be applied to just about any server environment, and we built a framework and architecture based on Java servlets. We have covered most facets of servlet development, including sessions, configuration files, templates, security, logging, resource pooling, database connectivity, and LDAP access. Of course, we cannot forget the base-servlet architecture. This enterprise servlet framework makes it very easy to create Java applications in a short period of time, and it is a very powerful framework for Java servlet development. Even if you choose not to use the framework in your development, the techniques and lessons that you have learned should put you way ahead of the game in your software development projects.

This chapter covers some advanced topics on using enterprise servlets and on how to make this library even more robust.

Web Server Startup in a Multiapplication Environment

Chances are that the applications you build will run on a single server, and this server will run several applications. We discussed some of the implications of running multiple applications in Chapters 2 and 3. We learned how `AppContext` separates application variables, and how `EnterpriseSession` keeps session variables from clashing between applications. This covers just about every case in Java servlet development for separating applications. But one other area needs to be mentioned. Applications can affect each other when the servlet engine and Web server are started up.

Most servlet engines have the capability to automatically load the servlets when they boot. Setting up servlets in this way is strongly encouraged because some servlet initializations can take quite a while, especially when we are creating database connection pools. If we don't set these servlets to automatically load on boot-up, they load when the first user accesses the servlet. Then the user must wait for the servlet to start, and if the servlet has a long initialization procedure, the corporate help desk may get a call that the application does not work.

In addition, some applications may be interdependent, either through links on a Web page or through servlet chaining and resource sharing. This is especially true if we wish to use JSPs, which often delegate the hard back-end work to servlets. These JSPs are dependent on the fact that the servlets are up and running. So having the servlets automatically load on startup has many advantages and may very well be a necessity in the enterprise environment.

How do applications affect one another on startup? The issue lies in the fact that most servlet engines that load servlets on startup do this in series, not in parallel. That is, the engine loads each servlet one at a time, waiting for the previous servlet to finish loading before the next one starts. Such serial loading can cause big problems when we are initializing connection pools or other objects that rely on outside servers or resources. If we have ten applications that run on a single server, and the first nine use database pools but the tenth does not, the tenth servlet must wait until all of the first nine have completed their initialization routines before it is launched.

In one such environment in which I operated, it took up to four minutes before the tenth servlet was loaded. And things get really bad when the database is down. Connections can take up to two minutes to time out. The tenth servlet could take an hour or more to load because it is waiting for each servlet's connections in the pools to time out on initialization. In addition, if one of the servlets fails, it may be difficult to distinguish such a failure from a problem with the Web server or servlet engine. When we access the servlet through a browser, all we get is the message *Page not found.* Is it because the servlet has not initialized yet? Is it because the servlet engine has crashed? Is it because the servlet had an error in the initialization and its context was removed from the engine? There's no way to tell.

What is the solution to this problem? We need to make the initialization process parallel instead of in series, and we should internally monitor whether or not the servlet has been initialized. In a nutshell, we must multithread the `init()` routine. We create a nested class called `InitalizeThread` to handle initialization. The `init()` method of `BaseEnterpriseServlet` creates a thread with the `InitializeThread` object and lets it do all the initialization. The `init()` method will return right away. Now there is no wait for the initialization to finish. All servlets will launch at the same time.

And the advantages of multithreading do not stop there. The `InitializeThread` class can monitor whether the initialization process has completed successfully, has thrown an error, or is still running. We can create a member variable in the class that is a flag indicating the status of the initialization. The main `service()` method of `BaseEnterpriseServlet` checks this variable's status. If the application is still initializing, `service()` returns this message to the end user and does not dispatch to the rest of the application. If the initialization has caused an error, `service()` reports that the application initialization has failed and that the user should contact a system administrator; in addition, it does not dispatch to the rest of the application. However, if the initialization process has completed successfully, `service()` dispatches as it normally would.

As just described, there are a lot of advantages to threading the `init()` method of a servlet. Are there any disadvantages? It depends on how you look at it. By multithreading the `init()` method, you are interfering with the specification that the servlet is supposed to remove itself from the servlet engine if an error occurs. This may be important to you, or it may not. In my opinion, the advantages outweigh the disadvantages. Because multithreading completely restructures `BaseEnterpriseServlet`, the entire object is shown in Listing 12.1, with the changes in boldface.

Listing 12.1 Changes to `BaseEnterpriseServlet` for multithreading the `init()` method

```
package enterprise.servlet;

import javax.servlet.*;
import javax.servlet.http.*;
import java.io.*;
import java.net.*;
import java.util.*;
import java.sql.*;

import enterprise.common.*;
import enterprise.db.*;
import enterprise.html.*;

import javax.naming.*;
import javax.naming.ldap.*;
import javax.naming.directory.*;


public abstract class BaseEnterpriseServlet extends HttpServlet
{

  public static final int    NOT_READY          = 0;
  public static final int    READY              = 1;
  public static final int    ERROR              = -1;
```

```
private AppContext          m_ac            = new AppContext();
private int                 m_ready         = NOT_READY;
private ServletException    m_exception     = null;

private static AppManager   m_appManager    = new AppManager();
private static Object       m_lock          = new Object();


public abstract String getAppName();


public abstract void initializeApp(AppContext appContext,
                                   PoolObjectManager pom)
       throws Exception;


public abstract void destroyApp(AppContext appContext,
                                PoolObjectManager pom);


public AppContext getAppContext()
{
  return m_ac;
}


public final void init(ServletConfig config)
       throws ServletException
{

  super.init(config);

  if (getAppName() == null)
  {
    throw new ServletException(
        "Invalid application name: getAppName() returned null.");
  }

  try
  {
    m_appManager.addApp(getAppName());
  } catch (Exception e)
  {
    throw new ServletException(e.getMessage());
  }

  ServletContext sc = config.getServletContext();
  sc.setAttribute(getAppName() +
                  ".AppStatus",new Integer(NOT_READY));
```

```
    InitializeThread it = new InitializeThread(config);
    it.start();
  }

  public final void initServlet(ServletConfig config)
      throws ServletException
  {
    String sConf = config.getInitParameter("ConfFile");
    ServletContext sc = config.getServletContext();

    if(sConf == null)
    {
      sc.setAttribute(getAppName() +
                      ".AppStatus",new Integer(ERROR));
      throw new ServletException(
                    "ERROR - BaseEnterpriseServlet needs a " +
                    "ConfFile param.\n");
    }

    try
    {
      m_ac.parseConfigFile(getAppName(),sConf);

      PoolObjectManager pom =
                        new PoolObjectManager(m_ac.getPoolList());

      try
      {
        initializeApp(m_ac, pom);
      }
      finally
      {
        pom.checkInAll();
      }

      if (m_ac.isLog())
      {
        m_ac.logInfo(
         "*********************************************************");
        m_ac.logInfo(getAppName() + " Application has started.");
      }

    }
    catch(Exception e)
    {
      sc.setAttribute(getAppName() + ".AppStatus",
                      new Integer(ERROR));
      e.printStackTrace();
      throw new ServletException(e);
    }
```

```
    sc.setAttribute(getAppName() + ".AppStatus",new Integer(READY));
    sc.setAttribute(getAppName() + ".AppContext", m_ac);
  }

  public int getStatus() throws ServletException
  {
    synchronized(m_lock)
    {
      if (m_exception != null)
      {
        throw m_exception;
      }

      return m_ready;
    }
  }

  public void service(HttpServletRequest req,
                      HttpServletResponse res)
      throws ServletException, IOException
  {
      PrintWriter   out        = null;

      res.setContentType("text/html");
      res.setHeader("Pragma", "No-cache");
      res.setHeader("Cache-Control", "no-cache");
      res.setDateHeader("Expires", 0);

      // Then write the data of the response.

      PoolObjectManager pom = new
                        PoolObjectManager(m_ac.getPoolList());

      try
      {

        // Check if the app initialized properly.
        try
        {

          // Check if the app is ready.
          if (getStatus() == NOT_READY)
          {
            if (out == null)
              out = res.getWriter();

            // We are not ready, so display this to the user.
            out.print("<html><body>Application starting up; " +
                      "please try " +
                       "again in a few minutes.</body></html>");
            out.flush();
            return;
          }
```

```
    // If a servlet exception occurred during initialization,
    // then it will be caught here.
  } catch (ServletException se)
  {
    if (out == null)
      out = res.getWriter();

      // Let the user know that an error occurred.
      out.print("<html><body>The application failed " +
                "initialization " +
                "- Please contact the System " +
                "Administrator.</body></html>");
      out.flush();

      // Send the error to the server native log.
      se.printStackTrace();
      return;
  }


  String method = req.getParameter("method");

  if (method == null)
  {
    try
    {
      method = m_ac.getDefaultMethod();
    }
    catch (ResourceNotConfiguredException rnce)
    {
      out = getPrintWriter(res);
      HTTPUtils.printErrorMsg(
            "You must specify a method.", out);
      return;
    }
  }

  HTTPMethod methodInstance = null;

  MethodList methods = m_ac.getMethodList();
  Class c = Class.forName( methods.get(method) );

  methodInstance = (HTTPMethod)c.newInstance();

  methodInstance.registerMethod(req, res, m_ac, pom);

  try
  {
    // Check if the method is secure.
    if (!methodInstance.authorize())
      return;
```

```
          methodInstance.execute();
        } catch (Exception e)
        {
          DefaultErrorHandler deh = new DefaultErrorHandler(m_ac,
                                                  getPrintWriter(res));
          deh.writeError(e);
        }

      }
      catch (IllegalArgumentException ex)
      {
        // If we got here, then the method name was
        // not found in the method list.
        out = getPrintWriter(res);
        out.println("<HTML>");
        out.println("Invalid method");
        out.println("</HTML>");
        out.flush();
      }
      catch (Exception ex)
      {
        ex.printStackTrace();
        return;
      }
      finally
      {
        // Close the connections.
        pom.checkInAll();
      }

    }

  private PrintWriter getPrintWriter(HttpServletResponse res)
      throws IOException
  {
    PrintWriter pw = null;

    try
    {
      pw = res.getWriter();
    }
    catch(IllegalStateException ise)
    {
      pw = new PrintWriter(res.getOutputStream());
    }

    return pw;
  }

  public final void destroy()
  {
    if (getAppName() != null)
    {
```

```
      m_appManager.removeApp(getAppName());
    }

    PoolObjectManager pom =
                    new PoolObjectManager(m_ac.getPoolList());

    try
    {
      destroyApp(m_ac, pom);
    }
    finally
    {
      pom.checkInAll();
    }

    ServletContext sc = getServletContext();
    sc.removeAttribute(getAppName() + ".AppStatus");
    sc.removeAttribute(getAppName() + ".AppContext");
  }

  class InitializeThread extends Thread
  {
    ServletConfig m_config;

    public InitializeThread(ServletConfig config)
    {
      m_config = config;
    }

    public void run()
    {
     try
      {
        initServlet(m_config);
        synchronized(m_lock)
        {
          m_ready = READY;
        }
      } catch (ServletException se)
      {
        synchronized(m_lock)
        {
          m_ready = ERROR;
          m_exception = se;
          se.printStackTrace();
          m_appManager.removeApp(getAppName());
        }
      }
    }
  }

}
```

Enhancements for the Reader

The first enhancement—multithreading the `init()` method—was done for you in the preceding section. The rest of this chapter, however, will simply present ideas about how to enhance the enterprise servlet framework yourself. This framework is powerful in its current state, but there are always changes we can make so that it is even more powerful.

In addition, some of the techniques shown can surely be improved upon, or there may be better ways to implement what has been shown. There's always a better mousetrap to be made. The goal of this book was to give you ideas, or a foundation of ideas that you can use as a stepping-stone to build on. If you have learned anything from this book, or it has given you an idea about how to do something better or differently, then I have done my job. Allow me, then, to offer some ideas about how to enhance the enterprise servlet framework.

The Template Engine

The template engine that we developed is very powerful, but it has one very great shortcoming: It needs a restart of the servlet to reload templates in the cache. One enhancement would be to have the template engine store the file date of the template in the cache. Each time the template was requested, the stored template file date could be compared with the actual template date, and if different, the template engine would reload the template in the cache. This enhancement would allow us to make changes to templates on the fly, without having to restart the server. Such capability could be very beneficial on a high-capacity site where downtime costs the company money.

Database and LDAP Pools

Database and LDAP pools are powerful because they reconnect if the connection to the database or LDAP servers was broken. However, this setup works only while the Web server is running, and only if the connections were initialized properly when the Web server started. If the database or LDAP servers are down when the Web server starts up, the initialization code will fail because the pools cannot connect to the database or LDAP server. One enhancement would be to place "empty" connection objects—that is, objects that do not have a valid connection—into the pools if they could not connect on initialization, and then let the ping code catch these empty connections and attempt to reconnect at that point.

Another enhancement would be to make it possible for these pools to implement a sophisticated automatic scaling mechanism so that the pools would change size according to the server's load. The greater the load, the more pooled objects would be created (with a maximum of course). As the load decreased, the pools could shrink to the appropriate size. This would be an extremely efficient way to implement any type of pool. WebLogic connection pools implement this kind of autoscaling, and this feature would be a powerful addition to the enterprise servlet framework.

An Administrative Tool

An internal administrative tool would be a wonderful addition to the enterprise servlet framework. Each application would have an administration page that would allow the developer to view the current load, determine concurrent thread usage, and control various aspects of the servlet. The control could include shutting down the servlet, or creating a time period during which no new users could connect to the servlet. For example, it could send a message to all current users that the servlet was shutting down in a certain number of minutes.

A Pager or E-Mail Monitor

A helpful enhancement would be integration of a mailer or object that paged the system administrator when a problem occurred. This could be integrated into the `EnterpriseLog` class and would be configured in the configuration file. The configuration file would contain parameters for an SMTP gateway, pager, or e-mail address, and other pieces of contact information. Whenever an error occurred, it would send the appropriate page or e-mail to the person specified in the configuration file.

Anything You Want

Integrate whatever you want. You have the source code, so I encourage you to enhance it. This library was made to be enhanced. Change it to your heart's content. My hope is that any knowledge you gain from customizing and enhancing the enterprise servlet framework will prevent you from running into many of the same issues that appear to plague many servlet development efforts, and allow you to build powerful and scalable applications.

Bibliography

Books and Articles

Bergsten, Hans. 2000. *JavaServer Pages.* Beijing, China: O'Reilly.

Callaway, Dustin. 2001. *Inside Servlets: Server-Side Programming for the Java™ Platform, Second Edition.* Boston: Addison-Wesley.

Davis, Thomas E. 1999. Clever Facade makes JDBC look easy [online]. *JavaWorld,* May. (Available at `http://www.javaworld.com/javaworld/jw-05-1999/jw-05-cooltools.html`.)

Hunter, Jason. 2001. *Java Servlet Programming* (2nd ed.). Sebastopol, CA: O'Reilly.

Jannak, Torpum. 1999. Java 2graphics rendering [online]. *Dr Dobb's Journal,* September. (Available at `http://www.ddj.com/articles/1999/9909/9909a/9909a.htm`.)

Pekowsky, Larne. 2000. *JavaServer™ Pages.* Boston: Addison-Wesley.

Web Sources

The Jakarta Project's *Jakarta Project:* `http://jakarta.apache.org`.

The Jakarta Project's *Tomcat:* `http://jakarta.apache.org/tomcat/index.html`.

INDEX

Accounting application
  configuration file for, 82
  session example for, *104*
AccountingForm class, 82, 83, 103, 114
  code for, 84, 106–107
AccountingResult class, 82, 83, 103, 111
  code for, 85–86, 109–111
AccountingServlet, 83, 103, 113
  code for, 105
action parameter, in FORM tag, 75
Active Server Pages, 10, 118, 119
addApp() method, 67
ADD_ATTRIBUTE, 327
addRecord() method, 141
Address tag library, TLD file for, 393
AddressTEI class, 394–395
Administrative tool, internal, 429
Adobe Acrobat (PDF) files, 354
Airius.com, 319
  LDIF file, 317, 344
Airius company directory, *344*
airius.com schema, new entries created in, 326
Alias names, 113
AND operator, 177, 181, 323
Apache, 215
Apache JServ, 79
Apache project, 3
  Tomcat managed by
AppContext, 93, 419
  changes to, to integrate DBPoolParser, 313
  changes to, to provide access to PoolList, 264–265
  changes to, to support BaseURL, 81–82
  DefaultErrorHandler object constructed with, 205
  EnterpriseLog object integrated into, 188, 189–194
  releasing BaseEnterpriseServlet's grip on, 385–388
  TemplateCacheList object retrieved from, 164
AppContext.getValue() method, 304
AppContext object, 42–49, 53, 54, 63, 69, 101, 384
  and accessing Enterprise object, 409–410
  for bridging JSPs to enterprise servlets, 395
  case study, 40–41
  changes to HTTPMethod for supporting, 49
  development of, 43–44
  parseConfFile method within, 46–47
  passing down to HTTPMethod, 55
  and template caching, 157, 158, 159
append() method, 361
Application.Base.URL, 113
  configuration file parameter, 114
Application context, 39–40
Applications. *See also* Case studies; Examples; Servlets
  base servlet implementation of, 35–37
  configuration files for two applications, 56–58
  enforcing uniqueness across differing, 93
  enterprise-level, 1
  forcing uniqueness across:AppManager, 63–69
  integrating JSPs and servlets within, 376
  startup issues with, 419–420
  WAR files for deployment of, 4
AppManager class
  code for, 65–67
  integrating into BaseEnterpriseServlet, 67–69
AppManager object, 93
App1 servlet, 60, 69
  class definition for, 59
  configuration file for, 57
  initialization argument for, 62
  output from, *63*
App2Method class, 61
App2 servlet, 59, 60, 69
  configuration file for, 57
  initialization argument for, 62
  output from, *64*
Architecture
  base-servlet, 37
  single-servlet/multiple-servlet comparison, *15*
ASPs. *See* Active Server Pages
ATL. *See* Address tag library
Attributes
  in LDAP entries, 319–320
  wild-card searches on, 323
Attributes interface, 326
Attributes object, 324, 335
Authenticate Me realm, 219, 223

Note: Italicized page locators indicate tables or figures.

Authentication, 8, 395. *See also* Security
basic, 215, 217, 218–220, 237
digest, 217, 237
form-based, 213, 214, 216, 228–236, 237
interface, 220, 221
and LDAP, 317
and LDAPConnectionPool object, 340
NTLM, 217–218, 237
Web, 213, 214, 216–228, 237
Authorization line, in pluggable security components example, 223, 224
authorize() call, adding to BaseEnterpriseServlet, 221–222
authorize() method, 220, 222, 224, 398
Autocommit flags, 297
autocommit parameter, 306
AWT. *See* Java Abstract Windows Toolkit

B
Backslashes, 133, 134, 160, 305
Bar charts, 351
Base dispatch servlets, 134
BaseEnterpriseServlet, 19, 37, 50–52, 58, 85, 134, 194, 207, 220, 357, 372, 395
AppManager integrated into, 67–69
authorize() call added to, 221–222
changes to, for multithreading init() method, 421–427
creating, 7
DefaultErrorHandler object integrated into, 208
family tree of, *11*
getPrintWriter() method in, 31
init() method of, 27, 420
main service() method of, 421
and PoolList and PoolObjectManager use, 265–269
and pool management, 260
registering with ServletContext, 386–388
releasing grip of, on AppContext, 385–388
restructured, and dispatch mechanism, *50*
restructuring, 49–56
single-dispatch-servlet design and responsibilities of, 384–385
and uniqueness, 65
Base enterprise servlets
basics of, 14, 16–17
configuration file, 16–17
dispatch service, 17
Base pool object, 244–252, 270
Base servlet implementation, 18–37
Class.forName() method, 24–31
ConfFile class, 32–34
HttpMethod class, 31–32
MethodList class, 34–35
sample application, 35–37
Base servlets
advantages with, 8
architecture, 37
creation of, 7
and pool management, 260
BASEURL, 205
BaseURL object, 85
BASEURL parameter, 368
Base URLs, 80, 103, 113, 114, 231
changes to AppContext, in support of, 81–82
in random pie chart example, 368
BasicAttributes object, 326
Basic authentication, 215, 217, 218–220, 237
BEA WebLogic, 79
beforeCheckin() method, 245, 246, 248, 251, 254, 299, 342, 364
beforeCheckout() method, 245, 246, 248, 249, 254, 299, 342
Berners-Lee, Tim, 72
Binary data, for building filters, 177
Binding, 277
bodycontent tag, 391
Browsers, images requested by, 352–354
Budget constraints, 39, 56
BufferedImage objects, 358, 361, 369
conversion of, to JPEG image, 359–360
Pool object for creating pool of, 362–364
buildMethodList() method, 27, 28, 47–48
buildTemplateCache() method, 160, 162

C
C++, Standard Template Library, 117
Cacheable template objects, 118
CachedTemplate application, 163
CachedTemplate class, code for, 164
Cache objects
developing, 155–156
and validation routines, 226
Caches and caching
description of, 144
integrating into enterprise servlets, 157–163
proxy servers, 144
templates, 143–166
CALLABLE cursor, 288
CallableStatement object, 276–277, 287
Callaway, Dustin, 88
Cascading Style Sheets, 352
Case studies. *See also* Applications; Examples
AppContext, 40–41
base URLs, 80
log files, 174–175
pools, 261
reusable image pools, 362
Travel application, 12–13.
Certificates, 214
CGI. *See* Common Gateway Interface
Charts, 351, 352
Checkin method, on pool, 242
checkInPoolObject() method, 251
checkLogSize() method, 182, 183
Checkout method, on pool, 242
checkOutPoolObject() method, 249
checkUser method, 223, 224, 225
Class.forName() method, 23, 24–31, 274
cleanupNamingEnumerations() method, 331
Clear-text buffer, 124
closeLog() method, 181
close() method, 278, 296, 331, 332
cn attribute, 340
Code, 118–119
Colons, 160
Color, in random pie chart, 369
commit() method, 278
Common Gateway Interface, 10
Common Object Request Broker Architecture, 321
CompuServe, 355, 356

com.sun.image.codec.jpeg package, 360
Concurrent Versions System, 11
ConfFile class, 18, 32–34
  members/methods of, *28*
ConfFile object, 27, 28, 46
ConfFile parameter, 37
Configuration files, 21, 35, 37, 41–42, 201, 304, 419, 429
  for Accounting application, 82
  for AccountingServlet, 103, 105
  backslashes in, 305
  for CachedTemplate application, 163
  for DBExample, 300
  for Directory application, 345
  for form-based authentication example, 235–236
  for HR application, 105
  for JSPExample, 405
  for Logger application, 197
  for logging in enterprise servlets, 188
  NestedTemplate, 140
  for pie chart application, 364, 365–366
  for PoolExample, 256
  for templates with enterprise servlets, 134, 135
  for two applications, 56–58
  web.xml servlet, 404, 405
  for WWWSecureExample, 226
Connection management
  building, 284–294
  in server environment, 278–281
  understanding, 281–283
Connection management objects, 315
  database pooling with, 297–304
  graphical view of, *283*
  LDAP, 329–340
  using, 294–296
Connection objects, 275, 277, 282, 284, 295
connection parameter, 306
Connection pools, creating, 340
Constructors
  for EnterpriseLog object, 177–179
  for HTMLCompiledTemplate, 147
  for HTMLTemplate object, 127
Contact pages, 230
Content, avoiding too much code in same file, 118–119
Context management, with base servlet, 8
Control array, 325
Control.CRITICAL parameter, 325
Cookies, 87, 90, 229, 237
  security tracked via, 213
  session, 215
CORBA. *See* Common Object Request Broker Architecture
COUNT placeholder, 137, 141
createHTMLTemplate() method, 152, 157
createObject() method, 247, 248, 254, 299, 341, 363
createPool() method, 247
createSQLCursor() method, 287, 295
CSP. *See* Customer service person
Cursors, running out of, 280, 281, 315
Customer service person, 260
Customized security, 237
Customized Web authentication, 215
Custom values, 58, 60
CVS. *See* Concurrent Versions System

D
Database connection pools, 279, 313–314
Database connectivity, 273–315, 419
  building connection management, 284–294
  database pooling with connection management objects, 297–304
  DBConnectionPool object creation, 304–313
  DBPoolParser used in enterprise servlets, 313–314
  JDBC review, 273–278
  managing connections in server environment, 278–281
  understanding connection management, 281–283
  using connection management objects, 294–296
Database driver, 297
  loading, 274
Database pool enhancement, 428–429
Database pooling
  with base servlet, 8
  with connection management objects, 297–304
Databases, 273
Data encryption, 213
Date/time stamp
  for EnterpriseLog object, 176, 178
  for log files, 172, 175
DBConnection, 283
  cleaning up, 296
DBConnection.AUTOCOMMIT, 296
DBConnection.NO_AUTOCOMMIT, 296
DBConnection object, 282, 304, 315
  code for, 293–294
  pooling of, 297
DBConnectionPool object, 304, 315
  creating, 304–313
  extension of Pool object by, 297–298
  using, 300–304
"DB.ConnectionPool." parameter, 305
DBExample, 304
  configuration file for, 300
DBExample.config file, 313
DBExample dispatch servlet, code for, 301–302
DBExample servlet, new, 314
DBM database, 215
DBPoolParser
  changes to AppContext for integrating, 313
  in enterprise servlets, 313–314
DBPoolParser class, code for, 308–312
DBPoolParser object, 307–313
Debugging, 3, 173, 177
Decryption, 218
Default checks, 30
DefaultErrorHandler class, code for, 205–207
DefaultErrorHandler object, 204–208, 209, 210, 211, 415, 416
defaulterror.html template, 208–209, 210
DEFAULT_PREFIX, 19, 30
Default.Template.Path, 158
destroyApp() method, 52, 53, 54, 58, 267, 367
destroy() method, 54, 68
DHTML. *See* Dynamic HTML
Digest authentication, 217, 237
DirContext, action values of, 327
Directory application, configuration file for, 345
Directory.config file, 349
Directory dispatch servlet class, code for, 346–347
directory.html template, 345–346
DirectoryScreen class, HTTPMethod extended by, 347

Directory services, and LDAP, 317, 320, 321, 349
Dispatch classes, HTTPMethod-derived, 59
Dispatch service, 14, 20, 31
Distinguished names, 320, 325–326, 328, 335
DNS. *See* Domain name service
doEndTag() method, 392, 398
doHTML() method, 132, 152, 153
DOLLAR state, 124, 125, 126
Domain name service, 86, 319, 321
Doorways, 98, 99, 215, 230, 232
doStartTag() method, 392, 398, 410
DrawCircle servlet, 357, 358–359, 361
Dreamweaver, 166
DriverManager.getConnection() method, 274
DriverManager object, 274
driver parameter, 305
Duplicate application names, 64–69
Dynamic dispatch, 77, 78
Dynamic graphics, 351–373
  dynamic images, 355–360
  image requests by browser, 352–354
  image type handling, 354–355
  memory management, 360–364
  random pie chart example, 364–372
Dynamic HTML, 118, 119, 166
Dynamic images, 355–360
  circle, *357*
  presenting, 1
  process behind creation of, 356, 373
DynamicImageServlet, 354
Dynamic pool growth, 243
Dynamic tables, 136–140

E

e-commerce, and security, 214
EJB. *See* Enterprise JavaBeans
e-mail
  free services, 72
  LDAP integrated with, 317
  monitor, 429
Employee information
  and LDAP, 317, 349
  sessions used in systems for, 87
empty value, in bodycontent tag, 391
Encapsulation, 59
Encryption, 213, 214, 215, 236
End users, and error handling, 202
Enterprise
  defined, 1
  form and HTML development in, 79–86
  maintaining state with sessions in, 86–92
enterprise.* class files, 7
enterprise.common package, EnterpriseLog object in, 175
Enterprise.html package, HTMLTemplate object in, 126–127
Enterprise JavaBeans, 2, 119, 120, 321, 376
Enterprise-level applications, 1
EnterpriseLog class, 429
EnterpriseLog object, 210
  development of, 175–188
  integrating into AppContext, 188, 189–194
Enterprise servlet framework enhancement, 428–429
enterprise.servlet package, 7
  classes within, 397
  DefaultErrorHandler object in, 205
Enterprise servlets, 203
  base, 7–11
  bridging JavaServer Pages to, 395–404
  DBPoolParser used in, 313–314
  enhancements for the reader, 428–429
  form-based authentication integrated into, 230–236
  and HTTP forms, 77–79
  and JavaServer Pages, 384–388
  logging in, 188–195
  options for tapping into, 388–389
  and parameters for new tags, *396*
  tapping into, 388–389
  template cache used in, 163–166
  template objects and cache integrated into, 157–163
  templates with, 134–136
  two-application example, 56–63
  Web server startup in multi-application environment, 419–427
  what's needed to run examples, 6
EnterpriseSession, 100–101, 103, 419
Enterprise session, 93–103
ENTERPRISESESSION, 98, 99, 101, 102
enterpriseSession.invalidate() method, 97, 98
EnterpriseSession object, 98, 103, 114, 115
  accessing, 408–417
  building from HttpSession object, 101
  developing, 94
  requirements of, 93
EnterpriseSession variable, ServletMain class and setting of, 413–414
Enumeration object, 96
Environment Hashtable, 321–322
ERROR constant, 177
Error handlers/handling, 169, 201–210, 407
  and base servlet implementation, 25
  centralized, 208, 210, 211
  DefaultErrorHandler object, 204–208
  importance of, 210
  and JSPs with enterprise servlets, 415–417
  Logger application with, 208–210
error.jsp page, for handling default errors, 415, 416–417
Error log lines, 172
Errors, 176. *See also* Error handlers/handling
  bookmarking, 173
  logging, 185, 201
  messages, 202
  and running out of cursors, 280
  and uniqueness, 65
Error screen, with tran ID, *203*
esb.getAppContext() method, 410
ESBridge class, 397, 398, 409
ESBridge tag, 397, 410, 415, 417
ESBridge tag library, 404–408
ESBridge tag library class, code for, 399–403
ESBridgeTEI class, 397, 398
ESBridgeTEI tag library class, code for, 403–404
esbridge.tld file
  additional tag inserted into, 409
  descriptor, 397
espage.jsp page, 407–408
  EnterpriseSession variables checked by, 414–415
ESSession class, 409
  code for, 411–412

ESSession tag, 413–415, 417
ESSessionTEI class, 409
  code for, 412–413
EVAL_BODY_INCLUDE, 392
EVAL_BODY_TAG, 392
EVAL_PAGE, 398
Examples, *See also* Applications; Case studies
  LDAP connection management objects, 343–349
  logging, 195–201
  pluggable security components, 223–228
  PoolList and PoolObject Manager, 269–270
  pool use, 255–259
  random pie chart, 364–372
Exception.printStackTrace() method, 171, 186
Exceptions, 169
Exception stack trace, 171
execute() call, 221
execute() method, 25, 26, 31, 203, 204, 295, 369
executeQuery() method, 283
executeUpdate() method, 275
Executive information systems, and sessions, 87
Extranets, and scalability, 239

F
FAQ pages, 230
Field name buffer, 124
FIELDNAME state, 124, 125, 126
FileOutputStream, 176
File Transfer Protocol requests, 19
FileWriter, 176
FILTER_ALL constant, 177
Filtered searches, 322
Filter masks, 177, 181, 187, 188
Filters, building, 177
finally clause, in BaseEnterpriseServlet, 399
Financial information, and security, 213
Financial Web sites, sessions used in, 87
findAncestorWithClass() method, 410
flush() method, 132
Format, for log files, 172
Form-based authentication, 213, 214, 216, 237
  integrating into enterprise servlets, 230–236
  login screen, 229
Forms
  control types and HTML equivalents, 74
  maintaining state and generation of, 86
  processing, 71
  used with hidden input control, 103, 106, 114
FORM tag, 72–75
Forward slashes, 160
Fragmentation, preventing, 253
FrontPage, 166

G
Garbage collector, 157, 253, 259, 271, 280, 331
  and caching templates, 143, 144
  and dynamic image memory management, 361, 373
  and LDAP considerations in server application, 328, 329
  and pooling, 242
  and String objects/StringBuffer objects, 129
Generation files, 172, 178, 187, 188, 201, 210
Generation log files, 174–175, 176
Generation roll, 175, 183, 201
Generic database-pooling objects, 297
GenericServlet class, 7, 18, 19
getAppBaseURL() method, 85
getAppName() method, 44, 52, 58, 59, 65, 67, 367
getAssistant() method, 335
getAttribute() method, 88, 90, 91, 335
getAttributeNames() method, 95, 97
getCNfromUID() method, 339
getConnection() call, 274
getDefaultJPEGEncodeParam() method, 360
getDNfromAttr(), 335
getEmployees() method, 347
getEnterpriseSession(boolean testTimeOut) method, 99, 100, 102
getEnterpriseSession() method, 99, 101, 102
getEnterpriseSession(true) method, 109
getManager() method, 335
GET method, 114
  packaging query with, 75–76, 77
getOutputStream() call, 358, 360
getOutputStream() method, 55, 56
GET package submissions, 114
getPrintWriter() method, 31
GET requests, 22, 353
GetSessionServlet, 90
getSession(true) method, 101, 102
getStringAttribute() method, 334, 339
getString() method, 276
Getters, 44
  for log filter, 179–180
  for MethodList, 45
  for template caches, 159
getTranId() method, 180
getValue() method, 46
getVariableInfo(TagData data) method, 394
getWriter() method, 55, 56
getXXX(), 283, 287
GIF files, 355
Graphic design/images
  HTML, 118, 119
  impact of, on Web experience, 351, 373
Graphics2D object, 369
Growth issues, and pooling, 239

H
Half template, 195, 198
Hashtable objects, 155, 226, 321
hello.jsp
  sample JSP page, 377
  servlet implementation of, 377–378
hello key, 23
"Hello World" application, 36, 37
Hidden fields, 73
Hidden input controls, 87
  form for enterprise servlets with, 78
  forms used with, 103, 106, 114
Hotmail.com, 72
HR application
  configuration file for, 105
  HRForm class, 108–109
  HRResult class, 111–113
  HRServlet, 106
HRForm class, 114
  code for, 108–109
HRResult class, code for, 111–113
HRServlet, 105, 106, 113

HTML, 3, 4
development of, in enterprise, 79–86
and form-based authentication, 215
log conversion to, 198
pages, 353
with templates, 117–167
typical forms, *73*
HTMLCompiledTemplate, 146, 147
parse file for, 148
objects, 145, 151, 152, 154, 155, 156, 157, 161
HTMLTemplate, 144
HTMLTemplate class, 132, 151
HTMLTemplateItem class, code for, 146
HTMLTemplateItem objects, 145
HTMLTemplate object, 126–134, 151, 152, 166
HTML templates
for dynamic table content, 137, 139
with placeholders, *122–123*
HTTP forms
and enterprise servlets, 77–79
form and HTML development in the enterprise, 79–86
query packaging with GET and POST, 75–77
review of, 72
FORM tag, 72–*75*
HTTP GET example, 75
HTTPMethod
AppContext object passed down to, 55
Authentication interface implemented by, 220, 221
DirectoryScreen extension of, 347
MySecureHTTPMethod extension of, 233
HTTPMethod class, 24, *25*
changes to, to access PoolObjectManager object, 265
changes to, to support AppContext, 49
HttpMethod class, 31–32, 84, 98
HTTPMethod.execute () method, 207
HTTPMethod object, 159, 203, 237
HTTP POST example, 76
HttpServlet, 7, 8
BaseEnterpriseServlet extension, 207
class, 18, 19
methods defined by, 9
HttpServlet.log() method, 170
httpServletRequest.getSession() method, 88, 98
HttpServletRequest object, 2, 24, 25, 84–85
HTTPServletResponse object, 2, 24, 25
HttpServletResponse object, 55, 85, 224
httpServletResponse.setError() method, 224
HttpSession, 2, 94, 115
and EnterpriseSession, 93
methods, *89*
Sun definition of, 87
update of, for managing EnterpriseSession, 100–101
HttpSession object, 72, 94
creation/use of, 90
EnterpriseSession object built from, 101
standard servlets using, 88
Hyperlinks, 72

I
IDE. *See* Integrated development environment
IETF. *See* Internet Engineering Task Force
IIS. *See* Internet Information Services
IIS Web Server, and NTLM authentication, 218
IllegalArgumentException, 251, 252
IllegalStateException, 55, 56
ImageHTML class, 364, 365, 368
imagehtml.html, 364, 366–367
imagehtml parameter, 366
image/jpeg type, 360
Image pool, random pie chart output using, *365*
ImagePoolExample, 364
dispatch servlet, 367
main dispatch servlet, 367
servlet, 372
ImagePool object, 362–364, 369
Image type handling, 354–355
indexPointer variable, 247
INFO constant, 177
Informational logs, 173, 175, 183–184
INFO type, 198
initArgs, 4, 6
Initialization arguments, for App1 and App2, 62
Initialization parameters, passed to/accessed by servlets, 4, 6
initializeApp() method, 51, 52, 53, 58, 157, 267, 269, 367
InitializeThread class, 420, 421
InitializeThread object, 420
init() method, 16, 18, 51, 52, 67, 68, 194
of BaseEnterpriseServlet, 27
changes to BaseEnterpriseServlet for multithreading, 421–427
multithreading, 420–421
Input control tags, 73, 74
Input/output (I/O)
caching templates and slow, 143–145, 157, 167
operations, 143
INPUT tag, 74
Integrated development environment, 3
Internet, 118, 351, 355
and caching proxy server, 144
history behind, 72
Internet Engineering Task Force, 318
Internet Information Services, 3
Intranets
and graphics, 352
and scalability, 239
InvalidSessionException, 99, 101, 102, 109
IOExceptions, 161
iPlanet, 3
Web server, 79
Web site, 318
iPlanet Enterprise Server, 2
4.1, 92
TestServlet registered with servlet, 5
ISAPI SDK, 215
isAuthenticated() method, 225, 234, 235
isLog() method, 189
isUsed flag, 246

J
JAR files, 321
Java, 239, 242
LDAP with, 321–327
SDK, 6, 215
tag library, 389–395, 417
Java Abstract Windows Toolkit (AWT), 244
java.awt.Graphics2D object, 358
JavaBeans. *See* Enterprise JavaBeans
Java Database Connectivity, 273–278
API, 274
closing connection, 278
database driver, 274
JavaDoc for, 274

JDBC statement and ResultSet objects, 275–276
loading driver/connecting to, 274–275
PreparedStatement and CallableStatement objects, 276–277
thin driver, 6
transactions, 277–278
Java Exception class, 48
Java Message Service, 2
Java Naming and Directory Interface. *See* JNDI
Java Properties object, 16
JavaScript, 118, 166, 352
JavaServer Pages, 2, 118, 119, 420
with ATL creating script variable, 393
bridging to enterprise servlets, 395–404
and enterprise servlets, 384–388
with servlets, 376–408
servlets *versus*, 375–376, 417
syntax reference, *379–384*
as template engine, 119–120
using hypothetical tag library, 390
Java servlet container, 2
Java Servlet Development Kit (SDK)
API, 87
value functions in, 96
java.servlet.jsp.tagext.Tag interface, 392
java.servlet.tagext.TagExtraInfo class, 393
java.servlet.tagext.TagSupport, 392
Java tag library, 389–395
Java 2 D package, 355, 358
Java 2 Enterprise Edition, 2, 6, 274, 321, 392
Java Virtual Machine (JVM), 187, 356
javax.naming.directory package, 321
javax.naming.ldap package, 321
javax.naming package, 321
javax.servlet.http library, 18
javax.servlet.jsp.tagext.VariableInfo object, 394
JDBC. *See* Java Database Connectivity
JDBCManager, 282, 283, 287, 293
JDBCManager object, 284, 315
code for, 285–287
JDBC-ODBC bridge driver, 274
JMS. *See* Java Message Service
JNDI, 317, 321, 333
with LDAP connection management objects, 349
LDAP with Java, 317, 321–327
using in Web-based applications, 327–329
JPEGEncodeParam object, 360
JPEG engine, 358
JPEG graphics, 355
JPEG image
BufferedImage object converted to, 359–360
encoding, in random pie chart example, 371
type, 355
JPEGImageEncoder object, 360
JRun, 79
JSP. *See* JavaServer Pages
JSPExample application
configuration file for, 405
JSPExample class, 406
JSPSecureHTTPProxy, 407
JSP value, in bodycontent tag, 391
J2EE. *See* Java 2 Enterprise Edition

L
Layout
HTML, 119
for log files, 172
LDAP, 6, 328, 349
access, 419
advantages/disadvantages of, 320
connectivity, 317–349
description of, 318–320
distinguished names, 320
history of, 318
search filters, 322–323
server enhancement, 428–429
success of, 317. *See also* LDAP with Java: JNDI
LDAP connection management objects
building, 329–340
LDAPConnection object, 329, 337–338, 342
LDAPManager object, 330–337
using, 338–340, 343–349
LDAPConnection object, 329, 337–338, 342
LDAPConnectionPool class, 341
LDAPConnectionPool object, 340–343
LdapContext, 331
LdapContext.modifyAttributes(), 327
LdapContext object, 323, 324, 339
closing, 327
obtaining, 321
pooling, 328
LDAP Data Interchange Format, 317
LDAPManager object, 329, 330–337
LDAP 1.2.2 service provider, 321
LDAP 1.2.3 service provider, 321
LDAP TCP/IP port, 321
LDAPv2, 318, 325
LDAPv3, 318, 325
LDAP with Java: JNDI, 317, 321–327
attributes modified within entries, 327
closing LdapContext object, 327
connecting to LDAP, 321–322
entries added/removed, 325–327
LDAP searched for values, 322–324
sorting results, 325
LDIF. *See* LDAP Data Interchange Format
Lightweight Directory Access Protocol. *See* LDAP
List menus, 73
load() method, in ConfFile object, 28
Local host, 79
logException() method, 184, 198
Log.File.Path, 188, 197
Log files
components of standardized, 172–175
ideal standard, 173–174
Log.Filter, 188, 197
Log.Generation.Count, 188, 197
Logger application
configuration file for, 197
with error handling, 208–210
Logger class, code for, 198
logger.html template, 195–197
Logger servlet, 201
Logging, 169, 366, 419
with base servlet, 8
in enterprise servlets, 188–195
importance of, 210
in random pie chart example, 366, 372
Logging example, 195–201
sample logger application output, *196*
Logging in servlet engine, 169–175
anomalies of servlet engine log file, 171–172
components of standardized log file, 172–175
logInfo() method, 198
login.html template, 231–232
Login pages, 231
Login screens, 72
Login template, 231
Log.Max.Size, 188, 197

logMessage() method, 181
LogMethod, 197, 198
LogMethod class, 209, 210
  code for, 198–201
Logon pages, as doorways, 230
Logs, standardized, 210
logTrace() method, 198

M
Macromedia Dreamweaver, 133
Mainform class, 231
MainForm dispatch method, 227
MainScreen class, 300
  code for, 302–303
Management chaining, and LDAP, 317, 349
MANAGER_ATTRIBUTE, 335
Manual method, of pool size, 243
Maxconnections parameter, 306
MAX_NUMBER_OF_TRIES, 249, 252, 260
m_default, 20, 30
Memory
  buffer pooling, 361–364
  caching I/O into, 144
  management of, with dynamic graphics, 360–364, 373
Method dispatch, with base servlet, 8
MethodList, getters and setters for, 45
MethodList class, 18, 34–35
MethodList object, 28
method parameter, in FORM tag, 75
"Method." prefix, 17, 19, 29, 158
METHOD_PREFIX, 19, 29
m_filterMask member variable, 179
Microsoft Access, 281
Microsoft FrontPage, 133
Microsoft Internet Explorer
  authentication pop-up window, *216*
  NTLM authentication, 217–218
MIME types, 355, 359, 360, 371
m_lock semaphore, 179, 180, 181
m_methodList, 20, 29–30
m_nIncrement member variable, 180
m_object, 24
m_request, 24
m_request object, 85
m_response, 24
m_response object, 85
m_session, 101
ModificationItem object, 327
Multiapplication environment, Web server startup in, 419–427
Multinested tables, 118
Multiple applications, session and form example with, 103–114
Multiple-servlet architecture
  for enterprise dispatch applications, *42*
  single-servlet architecture compared to, *15*
Multiple servlets
  environment for, 14
  multiple applications with, *92*
  single application with, *91*
Multithreading
  advantages of, 420–421
  of init() method, and changes to BaseEnterpriseServlet, 421–427
myplaces.html template, 156, 158
myrecord.html template, 156, 158
MySecureHTTPMethod class, 223–226, 232, 235, 405

N
Name/address requests, 72
name parameter
  in FORM tag, 75
  in INPUT tag, 74
Names and naming
  alias, 113
  distinguished, 320, 325–326, 328, 335
  placeholder, 124, 125, 127, 133
  realms, 217
  unique, 64–65, 69, 93
NameValuePair object, 306–307
NamingEnumeration objects, 324, 325, 329, 330, 331, 342
NamingException, 326
NDS. *See* Netscape Directory Server
NestedTemplate
  output from, *142*
  ShowTemplate class for, 141
NestedTemplate.config file, 140
NestedTemplate main base servlet, code for, 140
NestedTemplate servlet, 163
Nesting templates, 117, 136–143, 166
Netscape, Web site of, 323
Netscape Directory Server, 317, 318, 335
Netscape/iPlanet, 215
  Directory Server, for LDAP server, 6
Network Information System, 321
New Atlanta, 2
newInstance() method, 26
next() method, 276
NIS. *See* Network Information System
Novell Directory Services, 321
NSAPI SDK, 215
NTLM authentication, 217, 237
NT user database, 215

O
Object Database Connectivity, 274
Object pools, 242, 270
Objects
  within LDAP tree, 318, *319*
  reuse of, 239, 242, 243, 271
ODBC. *See* Object Database Connectivity
openLog() method, 181
OperationNotSupportedException, 325
Option buttons, 73
Oracle, 275, 283
  pool, 305
  Web site of, 6, 274
Oracle database, 215, 274
  with scott/tiger schema, 6
Oracle sample DEPT table, query screen of, 300, *301*
Oracle TNSListener, 275
ORA-1000 error, 280
OR operator, 177, 323
oTemplateCaches member variable, 161
OutputStream object, 358, 360

P
Pager, 429
parseConfFile() method, 27, 46–47, 53, 162, 194
parseFile() method, 128
  for HTMLCompiledTemplate, 148
parse() method, 128, 129, 149
Parser
  developing, 128
  pseudocode, 125–126
  template parts identified by, *124*
Password field, for Web authentication, 216
password parameter, 306
Passwords, 93, 213, 215, 408
  with basic authentication, 219, 220
  and database pooling, 297
  in login.html template, 232
  and validation routines, 226
  and Web authentication, 216, 237
Path separators, 160

Personalization, and forms, 71
PieChart class, 365, 368–369
PieChart image renderer, 364
Pie charts, 351, 352
  example of, 364–372
PieChart template, 366–367
ping() call, 342
Pinging, 283, 293, 315
  LDAP connections, 328
ping() method, 293, 299, 304
Ping queries, 281, 282
ping() routine, 338
Ping SQL, 297
pingsql parameter, 306
Placeholders, 118, 135, 166, 276, 345
  adding, 126
  description of, 120–122
  and dynamic tables, 136
  and HTMLTemplateItem objects, 145
  HTML template with, *122*–123
  names for, 124, 125, 127, 133
  question mark, 276, 277
Pluggable security components, 230, 231, 232–236
  example, 223–228
Pool class, 246
Pooled objects check in, 259–260, 261, 270–271
PoolExample application configuration file, 256
PoolExample class, code for new, 269
PoolExample main dispatch servlet, with pool initialization, 256–257
pool.html template, 256, 257, 258
Pooling, 281, 315
  connections, 279
  database, 8
  database, with connection management objects, 297–304
  LDAP connections, 328, 349
  memory buffers, 361–364
  resources, 239, 240, 241–242, 271
  at video store, *241*
PoolInterface class, code for, 245
PoolList, 271, 328
PoolList.add() method, 262
PoolList class, code for, 262–263
PoolList member, in AppContext, 264–265
PoolList object, 282, 305
Pool management, 279, 315, 328, 388, 417
PoolObject, 246
PoolObjectManager, 271, 328, 369, 372
poolObjectManager checkInAll() method, 388
PoolObjectManager class, code for, 263–264
PoolObjectManager object, 279–280, 282, 367, 395
  HTTPMethod class changed to provide access to, 265
  for JSP page, 398
PoolObjectNotAvailableException, 249, 260
PoolObjectNotAvailableException class, code for, 252
Pool objects, 1, 253, 255, 341, 361, 362
PoolPage class
  code for, 257–258
  code for new, 270
Pools, 239–271, 328
  defined, 246
  description of, 240–242
  key requirements for, 244
  pool anomaly, 259–270
  size of, 297
  using: an example, 255–259
  in Web development, 242–259
POST method, packaging query with, 75, 76–77
POST package submissions, 114
POST requests, 22
Pound character (#), 16
PREPARED cursor, 288
PreparedStatement object, 276–277, 287
printStackTrace(), 65
PrintWriter object, 22, 31, 55, 56, 132, 205, 358
Private keys, 218
Process color class, 77–78
processRequest() method, 209, 210
Procurement systems, sessions used in, 87
Properties files, backslashes in, 305
Properties object, 124, 127
Protected setters, 44
Public getters and setters, 44
Pushbuttons, 73

Q
Queries, ping, 281, 282
Question mark placeholder, 276, 277
Qwest Communications, 239

R
Radio buttons, 73
RandomAccessFile, 176
Random pie chart example, 364–372
RDBMS. *See* Relational Database Management System
RDN. *See* Relative distinguished name
Readability, 417
  of log files, 172, 184
  and log types, 177
Reader enhancements, 428–429
Realm field, for Web authentication, 216–217
reconnect parameter, 306
register() method, 398
registerMethod() method, 24, 25
Relational Database Management System, 318
Relative distinguished name, 320
release() method, 392, 398–399
Remote Method Invocation, 2, 321
removeApp() method, 67
REMOVE_ATTRIBUTE, 327
removeAttribute() method, 97
REPLACE_ATTRIBUTE, 327
reset() method, 295, 296, 299, 330, 331, 332
ResourceNotConfiguredException, 189
ResourceNotConfiguredException class, 48
Resources
  pooling, 239–240, 241–242, 271, 419
  sharing, 417, 420
result() method, 83
ResultSet objects, 275–276, 278, 280, 281, 287, 295, 315, 328, 329
Result set processing, 276
Reusability, 7, 13, 143, 144
RMI. *See* Remote Method Invocation
rollback(), 278
Root node, in LDAP tree, 318, 319
Running in-process, 2

S
SBObject, 254
  as StringBuffer object, 253

SBObject class, 255
SBOPool, 269
SBOPool class, 255
 code for, 254
Scalability, 273
 and pooling, 239, 240, 243, 271
 and pooling at video store, 241, 242
Scopes, 323
Script variables
 in custom tags, 393
SC_UNAUTHORIZED constant, 224
SDK. *See* Java Servlet Development Kit
Search base string, 324
SearchControls, 328
SearchControls.getAttributes() method, 324
SearchControls objects, 330
SearchControls parameter, 323
Search engines, 71, 72
Search filters, LDAP, 322–323
SearchResult objects, 324
SECRETARY_ATTRIBUTE, 335
Secure Sockets Layer, 214, 236
Security, 92, 213–237, 388, 417, 419
 critical nature of, 213, 236
 and form-based authentication, 228–236
 and JSPs used with enterprise servlets, 395, 396, 408
 with LDAP, 317, 318
 risks, 3–4, 87
 and stack traces, 202
 types of, 213–216
 and Web authentication, 216–228
 Web server, 215
SECURITY_AUTHENTICATION parameter, 322
Security certificates, LDAP integrated with, 317
SECURITY_CREDENTIALS parameter, 322
SECURITY_PRINCIPAL parameter, 322
Security proxy class parameter, 396
select statement, 275
Semaphore, locking, 184
Server, 325, 355
Server applications, LDAP considerations in, 327–329
Server-Side JavaScript, 10
service() method, 18, 421
 implementing in base servlet, 22
 methodInstance.execute() call in, 207
Servlet containers, 16, 37, 62, 79
 developing, 2–3
 and log files, 171
 servlets registered with, 4–6
ServletContext, BaseEnterpriseServlet registering with, 386–388
ServletContext object, 398
Servlet "dumping ground," 3–4
Servlet engine log file, anomalies of, 171–172
Servlet engines, 279
 logging in, 169–175
 and startup, 419, 420
ServletException, throwing, 67, 68
ServletExec, 12, 79, 113
ServletExec debugger, 2, 3
 sample servlet log, 170
Servlet interface, 7
Servlet log
 sample, 170
 from WebLogic server, 170–171
ServletMain class, 405, 406
 EnterpriseSession variable set by, 413–414
Servlet requests, flow of dispatched, *26*
Servlets. *See also* Applications; Base enterprise servlets; Base servlets; Enterprise servlets
 architecture, 90–92
 chaining, 420
 debugging, 3
 default methods specified in, 30
 developing, 2–3
 dynamic image creation in, 356
 JavaServer Pages *versus*, 375–376, 417
 JavaServer Pages with, 376–408
 LDAP integrated into, 343–349
 methods defined by, *9*
 registering with servlet container, 4–6
 setting up/running, 3–4.
Servlet 2.2–compliant servlet registration, of TestServlet, *5*
Session example, for Accounting application, *104*
Session IDs, 88
Session management, 69, 71, 114, 115, 229, 417
Session objects, unique, 65
Sessions, 419
 detecting creation of, 98–99
 enterprise, 93–103
 and standard servlet architecture, 90–92
Session tokens, passing of (between user and Web server), 90
setAppName(appName) call, 194
setAttribute() method, 88, 90, 91
setAutoCommit() method, 295
setContentType() method, 360
setCursorType() method, 288, 295
setRequestControls() method, 325
setReturningObjFlag() method, 323
SetSessionServlet, 90
setSortAttr() method, 339
setSQL() method, 287, 295
setStatus() method, 224
setTemplateCacheList() call, 161
setTemplateCache() method, 162
Setters, 44, 159, 399
 for log filter, 179
 for MethodList, 45
setXXX(), 283, 287, 295
Shopping carts, 71, 72, 86, 87
ShowTemplate class, 134
 code for, 135–136
 for NestedTemplate, 141
 template cache used by, 164–165
SimpleDateFormat, 176
Single-dispatch-servlet design, 384
Single-servlet approach, 14
Single-servlet architecture, 41
 multiple-servlet architecture compared to, *15*
Single sign-on, 218
Site field, for Web authentication, 216
SKIP_BODY, 392
SLEEP_MILLISECONDS, 249
Sniffing, 215
SortControl object, 325, 333
Sorting, on server, 325
SourceSafe, 11
Speed of image rendering, and image pooling, 362, 372, 373
Splash pages, 30
splitTrace() function, 186
splitTrace() method, 184
SQLCursor, 328, 329
SQLCursor objects, 282, 284, 285, 295, 296, 299, 315
 code for, 288–292

SQL cursors, 282, 283
SQL queries, executing, 295
SQL statements, 274, 275, 276, 277
SSJS. *See* Server-Side JavaScript
SSL. *See* Secure Sockets Layer
Stack traces, 169, 173, 184, 201–202, 210
Startup, in multiapplication environment, 419–427
Statelessness, 71, 87
State maintenance, 71, 72, 86–92
Statement object, 275, 278, 280, 281, 287, 295, 315, 328
Statement types, 282
Static images, 352
Static variables, 40
STemplatePath member variable, 160
StringBuffer objects, 128, 129, 131, 137, 154, 195, 253, 255
StringBuffer value, 126
String objects, 128, 129
  and garbage collector, 143
String value, returning to parsed HTML, 126
Subapplications, deploying under one WAR file, 92
Submit buttons, 74
substitute() method, 124, 127, 133, 153
SUBTREE_SCOPE, 323, 332
Sun, 355, 356, 361
  Java Web site, 6
  JPEG rendering engine included with Java 2SDK, 355, 356, 373
  Web site of, 321
sun.misc package, Base64Decoder object in, 225
super.init() method, 51
super() method, 253
Sybase database, 215
System.err.println() method, 169, 171
System.getProperty ("file.separator") method, 160
System object, 160
System.out.println() method, 169, 171

T

TABLE_CONTENT placeholder, 137, 138
Tables, dynamic, 136–140
tagdependent value, in bodycontent tag, 391
Tag libraries
  Java, 389–395, 417
  methods implemented in tags for, *392*
  TLD file for hypothetical, 390–391
Tag library definition file, 389, 393, 407
  for hypothetical tag library, 390–391
TagSupport class, 410
TEI class, 394, 395
TEI (TagExtraInfo) information, 394
TemplateCacheList class, code for, 156
TemplateCacheList objects, 145, 155, 157, 161, 164
Template caches/caching, 143–166
  advantages/disadvantages with, 166
  building, 146–157
  getters and setters for, 159
  structure, *145*
  using in enterprise servlets, 163–166
Template engines, 166
developing, 120–126
  enhancing, 428
  JSPs as, 119–120
TemplateExample, 134
TemplateExample main base servlet, code for, 134–135
template.html, 133
Template objects
  building, 126–133
  integrating into enterprise servlets, 157–163
Template paths, getters and setters for, 159
"Template." prefix, 158, 161, 163
Template processing, with base servlet, 8
Templates, 419
  directory.html, 345–346
  with enterprise servlets, 134–136
  half, 195, 198
  HTML with, 117–167
  login, 231
  nesting, 136–143, 166
  subcomponents within, 145
  types of, 117
  using, 118–119
TestMethod.class, 20, 23, 24, 26, 27, 36
TestMethod object, 20
TestServlet log, 170
Text boxes, 73
Text fields, 74
TEXT mode, template in, 124
TEXT state, 130
Three-dimensional pie charts, 364, 369, 370
Timeout condition, 98, 99, 101, 102, 109
  detecting, 99, 101, 102, 109, 114, 115
Time-to-market, decrease in, 38
TLD files. *See* Tag library definition file
Tomcat, 2, 3
Tomcat-compliant servlet registration, of TestServlet, 5
toStringBuffer() method, 128, 132, 139, 152, 154
toString() method, 128, 132, 152, 153, 361
TRACE constant, 177
Trace data, 176, 177
Trace information, in standard log files, 173, 175
Trace logs, 169, 183–184
TRACE type, 198
TRANID, 205
Transaction IDs (tran IDs), 173, 175, 211
  for EnterpriseLog object, 180, 181, 184
  error screen with, *203*
  unique, 177
  value of, 202
Transactions, 277–278, 280, 281, 315
Travel application, 12–13
try/catch block
  and error handling, 415
  with pools, 266
try/catch/finally clause, 388
try/finally block, and use of pooled objects, 259, 260
try/finally clause, with pools, 266, 267
type parameter, in INPUT tag, 74

U

uid parameter, 333, 334, 335
Unauthorized response ("401" response), 218, 223, 224
Unified Modeling Language (UML), 283
Uniqueness
  for applications, 63–69
  enforcing across different applications, 93

UNIX/X Windows-based platform, dynamic graphics generated on, 356
URLs, 79
  base, 80, 81–82, 103, 113, 114, 231, 368
  for connecting to LDAP, 321
  rewriting, 90
User authentication, 8, 213
userid parameter, 306
User IDs, 213, 215, 408
  with basic authentication, 219, 220
  common name from, 333
  and database pooling, 297
  and distinguished names, 320
  in login.html template, 232
  and validation routines, 226
  and Web authentication, 216, 237
userid variable, 93
User Name field, for Web authentication, 216
User validation, 225
US West, 239

V
Validation routines, 226, 228
value parameter, in INPUT tag, 74
Values, LDAP searched for, 322–324
VariableInfo object, parameters of, in constructor, 394
Variable placeholders, 122
Variables
  binding, 277
  unique identification of, 93
VBScript, 166
Vector object, 96, 186

W
Web Archive (WAR) files, 4, 92
Web authentication, 213, 214, 216–228, 237
  basic, 215, 217, 218–220, 237
  browser's security authentication pop-up window with, *216*
  customized, 215, 220–228
  description of, 218–220
  types of, 215, 217–218
Web browsers, 3
Web development, pools used in, 242–259
WebLogic, 2, 3, 113, 260, 278, 304
  autoscaling for connection pools, 429
  log files, 172
WebLogic 5.1 servlet registration, TestServlet registered with, *5*
weblogic.properties file, 304
WebLogic server, servlet log from, 170–171
Web pages, 72, 352
  HTML and rich content of, 118–119
Web servers, 2, 215
  pooled object check in and freezing of, 259–260, 270–271
  security layers in, *214*
  separating/managing multiple applications on, 39–41, 49–69
  session tokens passed between user and, 90
  startup in multiapplication environment, 419–427
  and validation routines, 226
Web sites
  graphical images on, 351–352
  sessions use in, 87
web.xml servlet configuration file, 404, 405
WORA concept. *See* write once, run anywhere concept
Work flow management, and LDAP, 317, 349
World Wide Web, 72, 351
World Wide Web Consortium, 72
Wrappers, for getValue() method, 46
writeError() method, 205
write once, run anywhere concept, 7
write once, use anywhere concept, 7
W3C. *See* World Wide Web Consortium
WWWSecureExample
  configuration files for, 226
  dispatch servlet, 227

X
X.500 Directory Access Protocol, 318
XML-based configuration file, 4
Xvfb (X virtual frame buffer), 356

Y
Yahoo! Mail, 72

ava™ Technology from Addison-Wesley

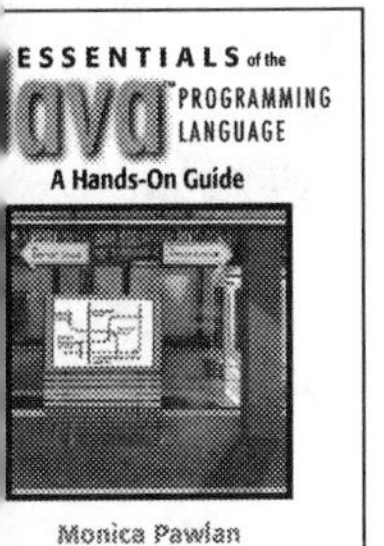

N 0-201-70720-9

JavaServer
PAGES™
Larne Pekowsky

ISBN 0-201-70421-8

ISBN 0-201-70429-3

ISBN 0-201-60446-9

ISBN 0-201-61646-7

N 0-201-72588-6

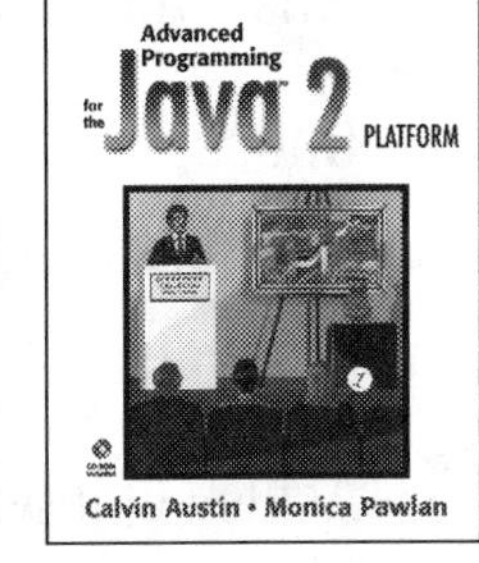

ISBN 0-201-71501-5

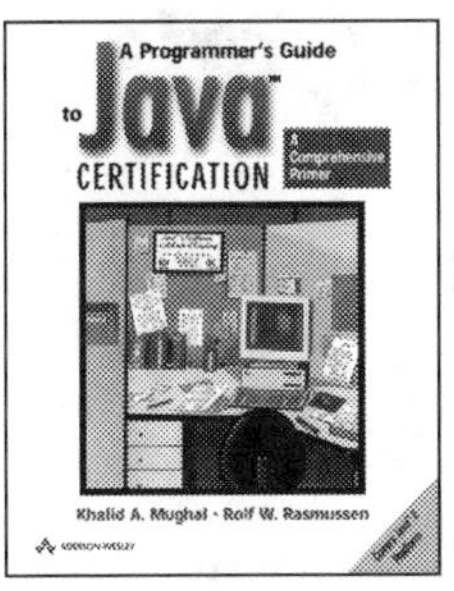

ISBN 0-201-59614-8

PROGRAMMING
for the Java™ VIRTUAL MACHINE
Joshua Engel

ISBN 0-201-30972-6

ISBN 0-201-67491-2

ISBN 0-201-48543-5

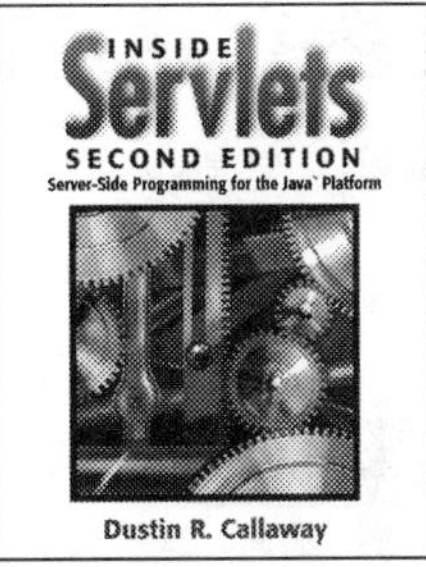

ISBN 0-201-70906-6

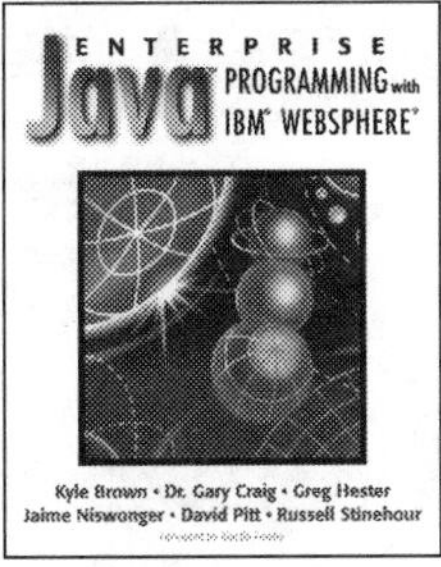

ISBN 0-201-61617-3

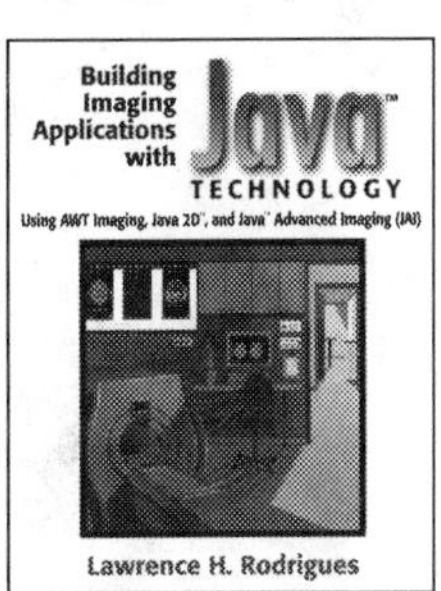

ISBN 0-201-70074-3

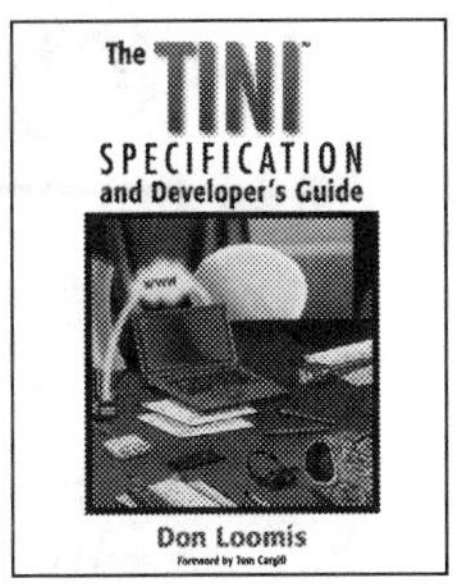

ISBN 0-201-72218-6

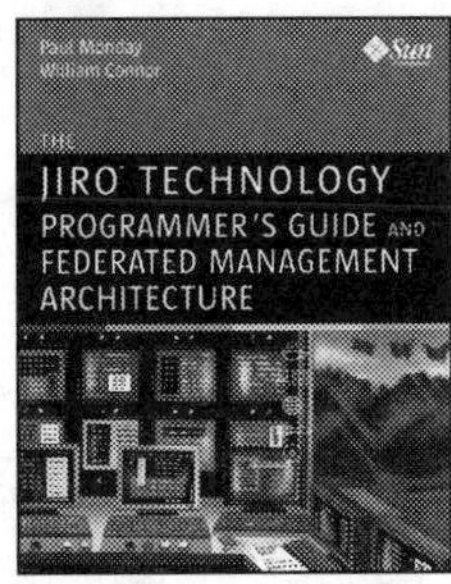

ISBN 0-201-72897-4

ISBN 0-201-70043-3

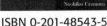

ttp://www.aw.com/cseng

Addison-Wesley

www.**informit**.cor

Articles | Books | Free Library | Expert Q&A | Training | News | Downloa

OPERATING SYSTEMS

WEB DEVELOPMENT

PROGRAMMING

NETWORKING

CERTIFICATION

AND MORE...

Solutions from experts you know and trust.

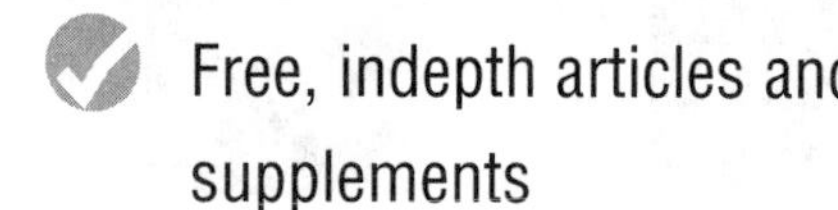

- Free, indepth articles and supplements
- Master the skills you need, when you need them
- Choose from industry leadin books, ebooks, and training products
- Achieve industry certificatio and advance your career
- Get answers when you need them from live experts or InformIT's comprehensive library

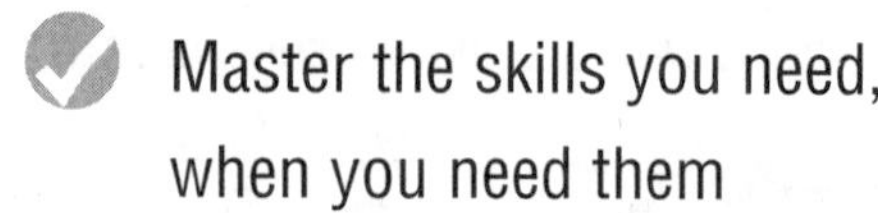

Expert Access. Free Content.

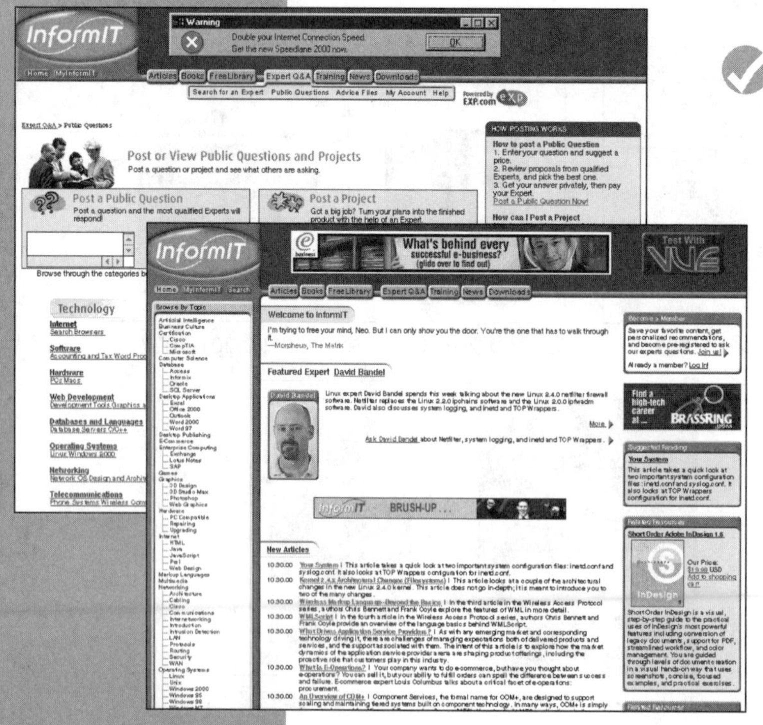

Visit InformIT and get great content from

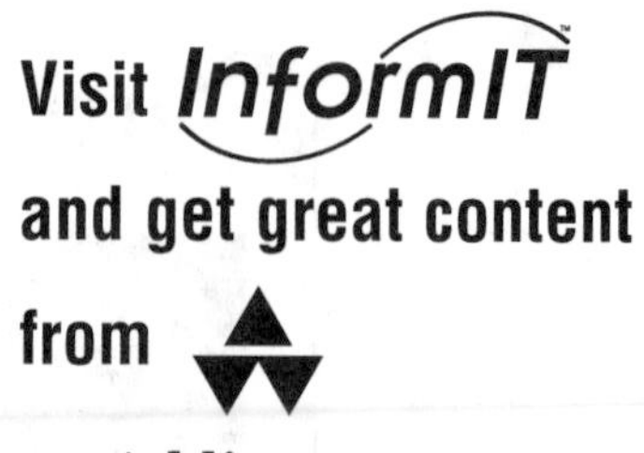

Addison-Wesley and InformIT are trademarks of Pearson plc / Copyright©2000 pearson

www.**informit**.com

Register Your Book

at www.aw.com/cseng/register

You may be eligible to receive:

- Advance notice of forthcoming editions of the book
- Related book recommendations
- Chapter excerpts and supplements of forthcoming titles
- Information about special contests and promotions throughout the year
- Notices and reminders about author appearances, tradeshows, and online chats with special guests

Contact us

If you are interested in writing a book or reviewing manuscripts prior to publication, please write to us at:

Editorial Department
Addison-Wesley Professional
75 Arlington Street, Suite 300
Boston, MA 02116 USA
Email: AWPro@aw.com

Addison-Wesley

Visit us on the Web: http://www.aw.com/cseng

CARROLL COLLEGE LIBRARY
2 5052 00660345 2

CD WARRANTY

Addison-Wesley warrants the enclosed disc to be free of defects in materials and faulty workmanship under normal use for a period of ninety days after purchase. If a defect is discovered in the disc during this warranty period, a replacement disc can be obtained at no charge by sending the defective disc, postage prepaid, with proof of purchase to:

Editorial Department
Addison-Wesley Professional
Pearson Technology Group
75 Arlington Street, Suite 300
Boston, MA 02116
Email: AWPro@awl.com

Addison-Wesley and Jeff M. Genender make no warranty or representation, either expressed or implied, with respect to this software, its quality, performance, merchantability, or fitness for a particular purpose. In no event will Jeff M. Genender or Addison-Wesley, its distributors, or dealers be liable for direct, indirect, special, incidental, or consequential damages arising out of the use or inability to use the software. The exclusion of implied warranties is not permitted in some states. Therefore, the above exclusion may not apply to you. This warranty provides you with specific legal rights. There may be other rights that you may have that vary from state to state. The contents of this CD-ROM are intended for noncommercial use only.

More information and updates are available at:
http://www.awl.com/cseng/titles/0-201-70921-X

JRun™ copyright © 1995–2001, Allaire Corporation. All rights reserved. ALLAIRE PROVIDES NO REMEMDIES OR WARRANTIES, WHETHER EXPRESS OR IMPLIED, FOR ANY OF THE NCDs. NCDs ARE PROVIDED "AS IS." IN NO CASE SHALL ALLAIRE BE LIABLE FOR ANY INDIRECT, INCIDENTAL, SPECIAL, OR CONSEQUENTIAL DAMAGES OR LOSS, INCLUDING, WITHOUT LIMITATION, LOST PROFITS OR THE INABILITY TO USE EQUIPMENT OR ACCESS DATA, WHETHER SUCH DAMAGES ARE BASED UPON A BREACH OF EXPRESS OR IMPLIED WARRANTIES, BREACH OF CONTRACT, NEGLIGENCE, STRICT TORT, OR ANY OTHER LEGAL THEORY.

ServletExec™ is a trademark of New Atlanta Communication, LLC. All rights reserved.

Tomcat 3.1/3.2 copyright © 2001, The Apache Software Foundation (*http://www.apache.org/*). All rights reserved. Portions of this software are based upon public domain software originally written at the National Center for Supercomputing Applications, University of Illinois, Urbana-Champaign. THE SOFTWARE IS PROVIDED "AS IS" AND ANY EXPRESSED OR IMPLIED WARRANTEIS, INCLUDING, BUT NOT LIMITED TO, THE IMPLIED WARRANTIES OF MERCHANTABILITY AND FITNESS FOR A PARTICULAR PURPOSE ARE DISCLAIMED. IN NO EVENT SHALL THE APACHE SOFTWARE FOUNDATION OR ITS CONTRIBUTORS BE LIABLE FOR ANY DIRECT, INDIRECT, INCIDENTAL, SPECIAL, EXEMPLARY, OR CONSEQUENTIAL DAMAGES (INCLUDING, BUT NOT LIMITED TO, PROCUREMENT OF SUBSTITUTE GOODS OR SERVICES; LOSS OF USE, DATA, OR PROFITS; OR BUSINESS INTERRUPTION) HOWEVER CAUSED AND ON ANY THEORY OF LIABILITY, WHETHER IN CONTRACT, STRICT LIABILITY, OR TORT (INCLUDING NEGLIGENCE OR OTHERWISE) ARISING IN ANY WAY OUT OF THE USE OF THIS SOFTWARE, EVEN IF ADVISED OF THE POSSIBILITY OF SUCH DAMAGE.

WITHDRAWN
CARROLL UNIVERSITY LIBRARY